TYR

Myth—Culture—Tradition

TYR

Myth—Culture—Tradition

Edited by
Joshua Buckley
and
Michael Moynihan

2

Arcana Europa

TYR: Myth—Culture—Traditon
Volume 2, 2003–2004
Second Printing: 2008
Arcana Europa Reprint Edition: 2019

Typeset by Joshua Buckley.

Contributors: Peter Bahn, Alain de Benoist, Charles Champetier, Collin Cleary, Julius Evola, Stephen Edred Flowers, Gerhard, Joscelyn Godwin, Jon Graham, Elizabeth Griffin, Annabel Lee, John Matthews, StephenMcNallen, Nigel Pennick, Steve Pollington, Christian Rätsch, Ian Read, Thor Wanzek, Markus Wolff.

Special thanks to John Balance, P. D. Brown, Collin Cleary, Louis Elteto, Eltho, Robert Ferbrache, Stephen Flowers, Joscelyn Godwin, Greg Johnson, Daniel Junker, Annabel Lee, and Stephen O'Malley.

Note: The reader may notice occasional stylistic inconsistencies between articles, as we have retained conventional British spellings and punctuation at the request of some contributors. *The text of this third reprint edition has not been modified from the original, which first appeared fifteen years ago. Therefore, readers are strongly advised to contact the advertisers for updated information regarding products and services.*

©2004, 2008 Ultra Publishing. ©2019 Arcana Europa Media, LLC. All rights reserved. Copyrights for individual articles rest with the respective contributors. No part of this journal may be reproduced, transmitted, or utilized in any form or by any means without the express written permission of the publishers and/or authors, with the exception of brief quotations embodied in literary articles or reviews. To contact the publishers or authors, write to the address below.

ISSN: 1538-9413
ISBN (Æ Reprint Edition): 978-0-9997245-7-6

Arcana Europa, P.O. Box 6115, North Augusta, SC 29861

www.arcanaeuropamedia.com

Email: info@arcanaeuropamedia.com

The editors wish to dedicate this second volume of *TYR* to John Michell, one of a rare breed, indeed: the wise.

In wondrous beauty once again
Shall the golden tables stand amid the grass
Which the gods had owned in the days of old…
—*Völuspá* (Bellows trans.)

Contents

Editorial Preface..7

The Traditional Doctrine of Battle and Victory........................11
by Julius Evola

Summoning the Gods:
The Phenomenology of Divine Presence..................................25
by Collin Cleary

Thoughts on God...65
by Alain de Benoist

On Being a Pagan: Ten Years Later
An Interview with Alain de Benoist..77
by Charles Champetier

Reflections on Disparate Myths of Divine Sacrifice..................111
by Michael Moynihan

Origins of the Germanic Warband..129
by Steve Pollington

Heathen Holy Places in Northern Europe:
A Cultural Overview..139
by Nigel Pennick

There Were Giants in Those Times:
The Guardians of Albion..151
by John Matthews

The Sacred Plants of Our Ancestors......................................165
by Christian Rätsch

The First Northern Renaissance:
The Reawakening of the Germanic Spirit in the Sixteenth and
Seventeenth Centuries in Germany, Sweden, and England....181
by Stephen Edred Flowers

Three Decades of the Ásatrú Revival in America.....................203
by Stephen A. McNallen

Ludwig Fahrenkrog and the Germanic Faith Community:
Wodan Triumphant..221
by Markus Wolff

The Friedrich Hielscher Legend:
The Founding of a Twentieth-Century Panentheistic "Church"
and Its Subsequent Misinterpretations......................................243
by Peter Bahn

Herman Wirth on Folksong...263
by Joscelyn Godwin

Musical Ammunition:
An Interview with Allerseelen's Gerhard..................................285
by Joshua Buckley

Reviews: Books..297

Sagaman and Storyteller:
A Conversation with P. D. Brown..363
by Joshua Buckley

Fermenting Moon Musick:
A Conversation with John Balance of Coil...............................369
by Michael Moynihan and Joshua Buckley

Reviews: Music..377

About the Editors..413

About the Contributors...414

About the Cover Artist..418

Responses to the First Volume..419

Editorial Preface

It has now been over a year since the first issue of *TYR* debuted. It seems fitting, then, to use the space provided here to further clarify our objectives, and to respond, in brief, to various criticisms and confusions that have arisen since beginning this project.

The Two Traditions

We have described ourselves as "radical traditionalists," a designation loosely defined on the back cover of this journal, and in the preface to our first issue. The term originated with the English author and philosopher John Michell, and we felt it represented well our basic orientation. But as might have been expected, many readers have conflated this rather open-ended "traditionalism" with the Traditionalist school of René Guénon, more recently represented by writers like Frithjof Schuon and Huston Smith.

Guénon and his followers assert the reality of a primordial, transcendent "Tradition" (often—but not always—designated with a capital "T"). This Tradition might be understood as a series of abstract but absolute principles, embodied in varying degrees in the individuated spiritual traditions of specific peoples. Obviously, we share many points in common with the Traditionalists, and find much to sympathize with in the Traditionalist critique of modernity (see, for example, Guénon's eerily prescient book, *The Crisis of the Modern World*). However, we do not necessarily believe in Tradition as a metaphysical absolute. One Traditionalist of particular importance to us is Julius Evola, whose work appears in these pages. But here again, we are not strictly "Evolians." Evola's exclusive emphasis on a solar, masculine spirituality (as opposed to the tendency towards dissolution and formlessness he intuits in the "world of the Mothers") is not something we share. There is room in our world for the feminine, the chthonic—and much else besides.

So we are indeed traditionalists, but we are not necessarily Traditionalists.

The Fascist Accusation

There are many who will accuse *TYR* of harboring "fascist tendencies." For some, "fascist" is merely a term-of-convenience, hurled indiscriminately at anyone who still believes in high standards, the primacy of the spiritual, or who dares to question modern assumptions about the benefits of "progress," technology, and an aggressive, egalitarian leveling which would decimate every distinct human culture and tradition. To these critics we can offer little comfort. More justified concerns will no doubt result from the fact that we have examined in detail many of the groups and individuals involved in the *völkisch* subculture in Germany, which some historians have associated with the rise of totalitarianism. In truth, however, most of the people involved in the early-twentieth-century *völkisch* movement (if something so amorphous can really be called a "movement") had far more in common with the Pre-Raphaelites, or William Morris's peculiar brand of folkish socialism, than they did with Hitler's massive state apparatus.

Those traditionalist principles that *were* adopted by the Nazis became bestial through their transformation into an ideology. Much the same phenomenon can be observed in the Muslim world today. In many respects, Nazism could be seen as a quintessentially modern movement, despite its occasional appeals to the heroic past of Siegfried and the *Nibelungenlied*. Watching the impressive spectacle of thousands of black-clad storm troopers marching in lock-step formation, one is reminded of nothing so much as the regimentation of modern, industrial society. The Nazis' overarching emphasis on biological materialism, and the idea that human perfectibility could be achieved through eugenics, is mirrored in the modern obsession (albeit purged of the focus on "racial purity") with cloning, genetic engineering, and mood-controlling pharmaceuticals. That any of these unnatural and frightening panaceas could genuinely reverse the soul-sickness of our age seems highly unlikely.

They will only make things worse.

Ásatrú and Odinism

The contemporary resurgence of interest in reconstructionist Germanic religion began in the United States over three decades ago with the work of writers like Stephen McNallen and Else Christensen, and continues to develop through the efforts of Dr. Stephen Flowers (Edred Thorsson) and others, as well as the ongoing struggles of groups like the Ásatrú Alliance, the Ásatrú

Folk Assembly, the Odinic Rite, and the Ring of Troth. These organizations often quibble over how to best designate their spiritual orientation. Some describe themselves as Odinists or Ásatrúars, while others prefer simply calling themselves "heathens." We use these terms more or less interchangeably in this journal, a fact that will undoubtedly irk partisans of one or another of these slightly divergent, but ultimately very similar, paths.

One limitation of Odinism and Ásatrú is the exclusive focus on the gods, goddesses, and cultic practices (or what little we actually know of those practices) of the medieval Scandinavians. In many respects, this is simply a matter of convenience. Most pre-Christian European religions can be traced back to a common—albeit much more ancient—Indo-European source. Thus, practitioners of these religions worshiped similar gods, conceptualized man's relationship to the divine in a similar way, and realized closely related social and political institutions. Unfortunately, few written records were left behind, and little pagan material culture survived the advancing armies of Christendom. Because of the relative isolation of Scandinavia, and particularly far-flung outposts like Iceland, we know far more about pre-Christian European religion as it was practiced in the North, than we do about pre-Christian religions in most other parts of Europe. But ultimately, we are interested in *all* pre-Christian European (and Indo-European) religions and cultures—not just the Germanic or medieval Scandinavian. We are also interested in how these cultures interacted and cross-fertilized with the non-Indo-European cultures they came into contact with.

One particularly prickly debate within the heathen subculture concerns the "folkish" orientation of many Ásatrúars. Whether or not we consider ourselves "Ásatrúars" in every other respect, we are most certainly folkish. This is because, as traditionalists, we oppose the modern view that each human being is an isolated individual. A true human identity can only be developed within the parameters of certain historical, cultural, and spiritual limitations, which cannot be arbitrarily overcome—at least not without significant peril. One is a member of a "folk" first, and is only an "individual" second. Therefore, we feel it is healthier, and more fitting, to identify with the cultural and religious traditions of one's own people, whoever one's own people happen to be.

Though we share many ideas and opinions with members of the Ásatrú and Odinist "communities," *TYR* was never intended to be an "Ásatrú" or "Odinist" publication. We do not claim to speak for, nor to represent, Ásatrú, Odinism, or any other specific reconstructionist religion.

What *TYR* is, and what *TYR* might become, depends solely on our personal inclinations and inner directives.

Conclusion

For anyone who shares our rather unusual perspective, it is easy to conclude that modern society is irredeemable. Political solutions seem naïve and unworkable. One layer of rot is peeled away to reveal a rot that reaches even deeper—to the roots. It would be silly to think that by simply publishing a journal, one could somehow halt a process of disintegration that had reached its advanced stages long before we were born. We harbor no such illusions about *TYR*. Anyone who wishes to find the germ of some new "movement" or "crusade" between these covers would be better served by looking elsewhere. The same is true for those who would attempt to co-opt our efforts, or harness them to any manner of broken carriage.

We do hope that *TYR* might serve as a touchstone for others, like ourselves, who are earnestly seeking a "return to the origins," and to tradition, if only within their own lives. We have attempted to compile material not only of historical interest, but also to chart the emergence of various cultural phenomena that reflect, to one degree or another, certain traditionalist principles. In no way should the reader expect an absolute consistency between all the groups and individuals represented in these pages. We adhere to no strict "party line"—only to certain general principles—and we expect no more from our contributors and associates. Lastly, we have striven to maintain high editorial and aesthetic standards throughout this journal, as we feel that the ideas expressed herein are deserving of the best presentation possible. In this, at least, we hope we have succeeded.

—The Editors, fall 2003.

The Traditional Doctrine of Battle and Victory[1]

Julius Evola

According to a well-known cultural critic,[2] the decline of the modern Western world is clearly recognizable by two symptoms: first, the pathological development of everything to do with action; and second, the contempt for the values of knowledge *(Erkennen)* and contemplation *(Beschaulichkeit)*.

However, by "knowledge" this critic does not mean rationalism, intellectualism, or the games of the literati—and by "contemplation" he does not mean alienation from the world, renunciation, or misguided monastic seclusion. For him, rather, knowledge and contemplation mean the normal and most suitable forms of human engagement with supernatural, supra-human, and supra-rational reality. However, there is one unacceptable premise to his conception: he takes it for granted that all action is limited to the material realm, and that the higher realm of the spiritual is only accessible through non-active paths.

This assumption obviously stems from a view of life that is essentially alien to the spirit of the Aryan race, but so deeply rooted in the Christianized West that we even find it in Dante's idea of Empire. In contrast, the ancient Aryans saw no opposition between action and contemplation: these were not understood as contraries, but merely as two different paths to an equally spiritual realization. In other words, it was thought that the human being could not only overcome individual limitations and participate in supernatural reality through contemplation, but also through active deeds.

If we assume this, then the decline of Western culture must be judged differently. The active tradition is intrinsically suited to the Aryan and Western races, but has gradually gone astray. The modern Western world has now reached the stage where it recognizes and glorifies only a secularized and materialized action, robbed of any transcendent reference point—a profane action, which inevitably degenerates into fever and mania, into action for the sake of action, or into an action confined merely to a temporal outcome. In the modern world such a degenerated action cannot reflect any ascetic or truly contemplative values, but only a shadow-culture and a pallid, conventional faith. That, at any rate, is how I see it.

If "return to the origins" is today's slogan for every movement of revitalization, then our essential task is to regain consciousness of the ancient Aryan concept of action. This concept should function *transformatively* and summon up vital energies in the new, racially aware human being. So we shall now make a short excursion into the thought-realm of the ancient Aryans, with the aim of bringing to light certain fundamental concepts of our common tradition, with special attention to the meanings of battle, war, and victory.

In general, for the ancient Aryans war was an allegory of an eternal battle between metaphysical forces. On the one side stood the Olympian principle of light, the Uranian and solar reality; on the other side stood raw power, the titanic-telluric, the "barbaric" in the classical sense, the feminine-daimonic. The motif of this metaphysical battle recurs repeatedly in thousands of mythic manifestations in all traditions of Aryan origin. Every material battle was experienced more or less with the consciousness that it signified an episode in this conflict. Since Aryandom saw itself as the militia of the Olympian principle, the ancient Aryans' claim to supremacy, and even to empire, traced its justification and higher consecration to this concept, which highlights the anti-secular character of the latter.

In the Traditional worldview, every reality becomes a symbol. From the subjective and inner perspective, this is also true of war. In this way, war and the divine path could be one.

Everyone knows the characteristic evidence that the Nordic-Germanic traditions offer in this regard, though it must be emphasized that these traditions as passed down to us are fragmentary and corrupted, or else are the remnants of higher primordial Aryan traditions that have become materialized or deteriorated into folk superstitions. Nonetheless, a few prominent motifs can be established. Valhalla, of course, is the home of heavenly immortality, which is primarily reserved for the fallen heroes of the battlefield. The lord of this place, Odin-Wotan, is introduced in the *Ynglingasaga* as he who, with his symbolic sacrifice on the world-tree Yggdrasil, has shown warriors the way to the divine dwelling-place where life springs immortal. In fact, no sacrifice is more appreciated by the highest god, none bears more abundant supernatural fruits, than that offered by those who die fighting on the battlefield. But there is more. Behind the blurred folk notion of the "wild host" lies the idea that the warriors who, in falling, offer a sacrifice to Odin, are swelling the army which this god requires for the last battle against *ragnarökkr*, that is, against the catastrophic "twilight of the gods" which since time immemorial has overshadowed the world. The Aryan motif of the metaphysical battle is clearly expressed here. For in the *Edda* it also states: "As great as are the numbers of heroes who have gathered in Valhalla, there will never be enough when the wolf is unfettered"—the wolf being the symbol of dark and wild forces that have succeeded in binding and subjugating the culture of the Æsir.

Akin to this is the Iranian–Aryan concept of Mithra, the "sleepless warrior" who fights at the head of his faithful Fravartis against the enemies of the Aryan god of light. Shortly we shall examine these Fravartis more closely and see how they correspond to the Nordic tradition of the Valkyries, but first I will clarify the general concept of "holy war" with corroborative evidence.

Not surprisingly, I refer primarily to the Islamic tradition, which takes the place here of the Aryan-Iranian. The idea of "holy war"—at least as it concerns the elements under consideration—came to the Arabian tribes from the Persian intellectual world: thus it implies a renaissance of an ancient Aryan legacy, and in this respect can be used without further ado.

That being the case, in the tradition in question *two* "holy wars" must be differentiated: the "greater" and the "lesser." This distinction stems from a statement of the Prophet who said, upon returning from a military undertaking: "From the lesser holy war, we have returned to the greater holy war." In this context, the greater holy war belongs to the spiritual order, whereas the lesser holy war is the physical battle, the material war waged in the external world. The greater holy war is the battle against the enemies that lie within. More precisely, it is the battle of the supernatural elements within man against everything that is compulsive, determined by passion, chaotic, and enslaved to the powers of nature. This is also the idea expressed in a text of ancient Aryan warrior wisdom—the *Bhagavad Gîtâ:* "Realizing that which is beyond comprehension, strengthen yourself through yourself, and kill the enemy in the form of desire, hard to conquer." (*Bhagavad Gîtâ*, III, 43) The prerequisite for the work of inner liberation is that such an enemy be destroyed.

Within the framework of a heroic tradition, the lesser holy war—the external battle—serves only as a means by which this greater holy war is to be realized. For this reason "holy war" and "divine path" often occur as synonyms. Thus we read in the Koran: "They fight on the path of God who sacrifice earthly life for the life to come; for to him who fights on the path of God, whether he is slain or victorious, we will give a great reward." (Koran, 4, 74) And further: "For those who are slain on the path of God, their realization will not be lost: God will guide them and dispose their souls. He will make them enter into the paradise revealed to them." (47, 5–7) These examples allude to the physical death in war which corresponds exactly to the classical tradition of the so-called *mors triumphalis*—"triumphant death." Yet this same teaching can also be understood in a symbolic sense. He who has come to experience a "greater holy war" within the "lesser" war, has generated the inner strength that makes him capable of conquering the crisis of death. Even without being physically killed, one can also experience death through the discipline of action and combat: one can be internally triumphant and achieve a "survival." Esoterically understood, "paradise," the "heavenly realm," and similar terms are nothing other than symbolic representations, adapted for popular understanding, of transcendent states of consciousness that exist on a higher level than life and death.

These observations allow us to discover the same meanings beneath the Christian cloak which the heroic Nordic-Western tradition was forced to don for outward appearances during the Crusades. Much more than is generally believed, in Crusader ideology the liberation of the Temple and the conquest of the "Holy Land" had points of contact with the Nordic-Aryan tradition, which refers to the mystical Asgard in the distant land of the Æsir and the heroes, where death does not rule and where the inhabitants enjoy immortal life and a supernatural tranquility. The holy war manifested as a thoroughly spiritual war, so that the priests literally compared it to a "purification, the same as the fire of purgatory, only prior to death." Bernard of Clairvaux exhorted the Templars: "What glory for you, to return from battle with no less than a crown of laurel! But how much greater the glory, to win an immortal crown on the battlefield!" The Crusaders were even promised the "supreme glory"—the very same glory which theology attributes to the Lord in the heavenly heights, *in excelsis Deo*. Thus Jerusalem, the goal dreamed of in the "lesser holy war," has

The Doctrine of Battle and Victory

"Slain—you will gain paradise; victorious—you will rule over the earth. Therefore rise resolutely to battle!"

a twofold aspect as an earthly city and a heavenly city, while the Crusade is the prelude to an achievement that truly leads to immortality.

At first the military vicissitudes of the Crusades caused astonishment, confusion, and even shook the faith. However, they had only to purify the effect and the concept of holy war from any residue of materialism. Then the failure of a crusade could be compared to virtue dogged by misfortune, whose value could only be judged and rewarded in terms of a non-earthly existence. With this assessment—beyond victory and defeat—the value-judgment was concentrated on the spiritual side of the action. Accordingly, the holy war was regarded as being independent of its visible results, and as a means by which one could achieve a supra-personal perfection through the active sacrifice of the human element.

In a well-known Indo-Aryan text, the *Bhagavad Gîtâ*, this same teaching appears in a metaphysically heightened style. The compassion and the humanitarian feelings that prevent the warrior Arjuna from entering the battlefield against the enemy are criticized by the god [Krishna] as being "cowardice unworthy of a noble, ignominy, and *distancing from heaven*." (*Bhagavad Gîtâ*, II, 2) He promises: "Slain—you will gain paradise; victorious—you will rule over the earth. Therefore rise resolutely to battle!" (II, 37)

The inner bearing that transmutes the lesser war into the greater holy war is clearly outlined: "Dedicating all actions to me"—says the god—"and with mind fixed on the supreme state of the self, free from the idea of possession, liberated from mental anguish, fight!" (III, 30) In equally clear statements regarding the purity of such an action, it is said that it must be desired for the sake of itself, beyond any passion and beyond any human motivation. "Holding as equal pleasure or pain, gain or loss, victory or defeat, arm yourself for the battle: thus you will remain immaculate." (II, 38)

As a further metaphysical justification, Krishna explains the difference between that which is absolute spirit, and as such indestructible, and that which, as a physical and human element, has only an illusory existence. On the one hand, he makes one aware of the metaphysical unreality of what is lost when one loses, or causes others to lose, the transitory life and the mortal body. On the other hand, Arjuna is led to experience this manifestation of the divine as a power that seizes him absolutely and irresistibly. In comparison to this power, every form of conditioned existence appears as a negation. But when this negation is actively negated, that is, when amid the onslaught all limited existence is torn away or destroyed, this power results in a terrible theophany. The energy required to bring about the heroic transformation of the individual can be precisely described on this basis. Should the warrior be in the position to act unconditionally and with purity, then he will burst his human chains, conjure forth the divine as the metaphysical power of the destruction of the finite, and actively draw this power to himself, finding therein his transfiguration and liberation. The suggestive watchword in this regard, from another text in the same tradition, reads: "Life is like a bow; the soul like an arrow; the target which is to be pierced, the Supreme Spirit. Hold fast to this spirit as the arrow pierces its target." (*Mârkandeya-purâna*, XLII, 7, 8).

If the highest metaphysical justification for combat and heroism can be seen in all this, it is very telling that the *Bhagavad Gîtâ* presents such a teaching as part of a primordial Aryan, solar heritage. It was in fact given by the "Sun" to Manu, the primordial lawgiver of the Aryans, and perpetuated by a dynasty of sacred kings. Over the centuries this teaching was lost, and then later revealed by the deity, not to a priest, but to a representative of the warrior nobility, Arjuna.

What I have described so far also helps us to understand the innermost meaning underlying a further group of classical and Nordic traditions. We start by observing that certain symbolic concepts occur there in a particular combination: the concept of the soul as daimon, doppelgänger, genius, and the like; the concept of Dionysian beings and the goddess of death; and finally, the concept of a goddess of victory, who often also appears in the form of a battle goddess.

To understand these connections, we must start by clarifying what it means when the soul is conceived of as a daimon, genius, or doppelgänger. For classical man, the daimon or doppelgänger symbolized a profound power, the "life of Life," so to speak, for it secretly guided the entire physical and spiritual process. Inaccessible to ordinary consciousness, it nevertheless largely determined the existence and fate of the individual. A close connection was thought to exist between this being and the mystical powers of the race and the bloodline, appearing in many respects the same as the Lares [singular: Lar], the mystical beings of tribe or clan, of which Macrobius says: "They are the gods that keep us alive—they nourish our body and guide our soul." One could say that between the daimon and ordinary consciousness exists a relationship like that between *the individualizing principle and the individualized principle*. According to the teaching of the ancients, the former is a supra-individual power, hence above life and death. The latter, being the individualized consciousness limited by the body and the exterior world, is normally destined to dissolution or a shadowy survival.

In the Nordic tradition, the concept of the Valkyrie has approximately the same significance as the daimon. In many texts the concept of the Valkyrie melds together with that of the *fylgya*—that is, with a spiritual essence operating within the human being, in the power of which lies the latter's fate. And as *kinfylgya*, the Valkyrie—like the ancient Roman Lar—represents the mystical power of blood. The same is true of the Fravarti in the Iranian–Aryan tradition. As a well-known orientalist explains, the Fravarti is "the innermost power of every human being, that which keeps him upright and causes him to be born and to exist." At the same time, the Fravartis, like the Roman Lares, are connected to the primordial powers of a tribe and are, like the Valkyries, terrifying goddesses of war who bestow good fortune and victory.

This is the first connection we must fathom. What can this

enigmatic power, which is the profound soul of the race and the transcendent element in the individual, have in common with the war goddess? In order to be clear on this point, one should keep in mind that Indo-European antiquity had a decidedly aristocratic and exclusive view of immortality. Not everyone, it was believed, is able to escape self-dissolution, that shadowy survival for which Hades and Nifelheim were ancient symbolic images. Immortality is a privilege of the few and, in the Aryan view, above all a heroic privilege. Survival—and certainly not as a shadow, but as a demigod—is only granted to those whom an exceptional spiritual deed has elevated from one nature to the other. Unfortunately I cannot cite here all the evidence that justifies the following assertion: that, technically understood, a spiritual deed of this sort consisted in changing the sense of self from ordinary human consciousness, limited and individualized, into a profound, supra-individual, individualizing power which exists beyond birth and death and which, as I have said, corresponds to the concept of the "daimon."[3]

Indeed, the daimon stands beyond all the finite forms in which it reveals itself, not only because it is the primordial power of an entire tribe, but also on account of its intensity. Because of this, the abrupt transition from ordinary consciousness to the power symbolized by the daimon would cause a destructive crisis, like a lightning-bolt caused by a voltage that overloaded the human constitution. Let us now assume that under truly extraordinary circumstances, the daimon nevertheless breaks through in the individual, so to speak, and is thus able to let its destructive transcendence be felt: then one would have a kind of *active experience of death*. Thereupon the second connection becomes clear: why the figure of the doppelgänger or daimon in the ancient myths could be melded with the deity of death. In the Nordic tradition the warrior sees his Valkyrie precisely at the moment of death or mortal danger.

We can go further. In religious asceticism, mortification, self-renunciation, and the impulse of devotion to God are the preferred methods of provoking and successfully overcoming the crisis I have just mentioned. Everyone knows the expressions which refer to these states, such as the "mystical death" or "dark night of the soul," etc. In contrast to this, within the framework of a heroic tradition, the path to the same goal is the active rapture, the Dionysian unleashing of the active element. At its lower levels, we

HEINRICH GUENTHER, "VALKYRIE."

find phenomena such as the use of *dance* as a sacred technique for achieving an ecstasy of the soul that summons and uses profound energies. While the individual's life is surrendered to Dionysian rhythm, another life sinks into it, as if it were his abyssal roots surfacing. The "wild host," Furies, Erinyes, and suchlike spiritual natures are symbolic picturings of this energy, thus corresponding to a manifestation of the daimon in its terrifying and active transcendence. At a higher level we find sacred war-games; higher still, *war itself*. And this brings us back to the ancient Aryan concept of battle and the warrior ascetic.

At the climax of danger and heroic battle, the possibility for such an extraordinary experience was recognized. The Latin *ludere*, meaning both "to play" and "to fight," seems to contain the idea of release (Bruckmann). This is one of the many allusions to the inherent ability of battle to release deeply-buried powers from individual limitations and let them freely emerge. Hence the third comparison: the daimon, the Lar, the individualizing I, etc., are not only identical with the Furies, Erinyes, and other unleashed Dionysian natures, which themselves have many traits similar to the goddess of death—they are also synonymous with the storm

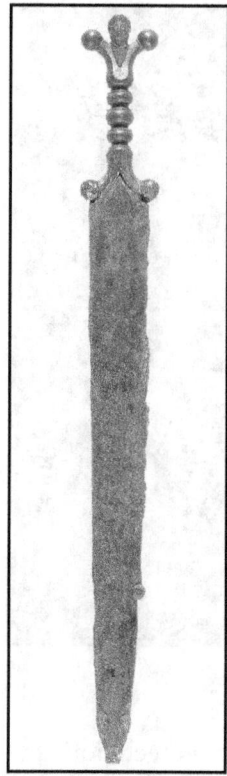

SWORD WITH
HUMAN HEAD,
FIRST CENTURY
B.C.E.

maidens of battle, the Valkyries and Fravartis. In the texts, for example, the Fravartis are called "the terrible, the all-powerful," "those who attack in storm and bestow victory upon those who conjure them," or, more precisely, upon those who conjure them up *in themselves*.

From here to the final comparison is only a short step. In the Aryan tradition the same martial beings eventually take on the form of victory-goddesses, a transformation which denotes the happy completion of the inner experience in question. Just as the daimon or doppelgänger signifies a deep, supra-individual power in its latent condition as compared to ordinary consciousness; just as the Furies and Erinyes reflect a particular manifestation of daimonic rages and eruptions (and the goddesses of death, Valkyries, Fravartis, etc., refer to the same conditions, as long as these are facilitated by battle and heroism)—in the same way the goddess of victory is the expression of the triumph of the I over this power. She signifies the victorious ascent to a state unendangered by ecstasies and sub-personal forms of disintegration, a danger that always lurks behind the frenetic moment of Dionysian and even heroic action. The ascent to a spiritual, truly supra-personal condition that makes one free, immortal, and internally indestructible, when the "Two [elements of human existence] become One," expresses itself in this image of mythical consciousness.

Now we move to the dominant idea of this ancient heroic tradition, namely the mystical conception of victory. The fundamental assumption is that of a true correspondence between the physical and metaphysical, between the visible and invisible, whereby the deeds of the spirit reveal supra-individual traits and express themselves through actions and real events. On this basis, a spiritual realization is presumed to be the hidden soul of certain martial endeavors, which are crowned by the actual victory. Then the material, military victory becomes the correlation to a spiritual event, which has called forth victory in the place where outer and inner connect. The victory appears as a tangible sign for a consecration and mystical rebirth that are fulfilled in the same instant. The Furies and the death which the warrior withstood physically on the battlefield also confront him internally, in his spiritual element, in the form of a dangerous and threatening outburst of the primordial energy of his being. In triumphing over *this*, victory is his.

This connection clarifies why, in the Traditional world, every victory also takes on a sacred meaning. The celebrated commander on the battlefield thus provided the experience of the presence of a mystical, transformative energy. In the same way we can understand the deep meaning of a supra-worldly character that breaks forth in the victor's glory and "divinity," as well as the fact that the ancient Roman triumphal ceremony had far more of a sacred quality than a military one. It sheds a totally different light on those recurring symbols in the ancient Aryan tradition of Victories, Valkyries, and similar beings who lead the souls of warriors into "Heaven," as well as on the myth of a victorious hero such as the Doric Hercules, who receives the crown from Nike, the "victory goddess," enabling him to participate in Olympian immortality. And now it becomes obvious how paralyzing and frivolous that viewpoint is which prefers to see only "poetics," rhetoric, and fairy tales in all of this.

Mystical theology teaches that the sanctifying spiritual vision is fulfilled in *glory*, and Christian iconography encircles the heads of saints and martyrs with the appropriate halo. All this signifies an inheritance, albeit atrophied, from our high heroic tradition. For the Iranian-Aryan tradition already understood glory as a heavenly fire—*hvarenô*—which descended upon kings and leaders, made them immortal, and bore witness to them in victory. Moreover, the radiant crown of ancient royalty symbolized glory as none other than a solar and heavenly fire. Light, solar radiance, glory, victory, and divine kingship are concepts that are found closely connected in the Aryan world, and not in the sense of abstractions or human poetics, but in the sense of entirely real powers and rulerships. In this connection, the mystical doctrine of battle and victory is a radiant summit of our shared tradition of action.

This tradition still speaks audibly to us, so long as we disregard its external and time-determined manifestations. Today, if we want to go beyond a tired, bloodless spirituality formed of abstract speculation or pious feelings, while also overcoming the materialistic degeneration of action, what better support can we find than these ancient Aryan ideals?

But there is more. Material and spiritual tensions have accumulated so much in recent years in the West, that their final release is only possible through combat. With the current war, an epoch is nearing its end; powers are now breaking through that are no longer bound by abstract concepts, universalist principles, or irrationally understood myths—powers which could be transformed into the dynamic of a new culture. Something much more profound and essential is necessary, so that beyond the tumult of a confused and condemned world, a new era might dawn for Europe.

In light of this, much depends on how the individual can shape his experience of battle: whether or not he is able to grasp heroism and sacrifice as an actual catharsis, as a means to freedom and inner awakening. This invisible inner action of our warriors has nothing to do with gestures and grand words, but it holds decisive significance for the formation and meaning of the order that will arise from victory. *In battle itself is the power to arouse and steel us, which will help us over storm, blood, and misery in a new radiance and a mighty calm, to a new creation.*

To this end, on the battlefield one should relearn *pure* action: action not only as masculine ascesis, but also as purification and the pathway to higher life-forms, valid in and of themselves; but this already implies a certain return to the ancient Aryan-Western tradition. From distant times the evocative formula still calls to us: "The life, like a bow; the soul, like an arrow; the target, the Supreme Spirit." Those who experience today's battle in the sense of this creed will be able to remain standing where others collapse—and they will be an unshakable power. This new man will conquer in himself every tragedy, every darkness, every chaos, and make a new beginning in the fertile soil of time. According to ancient Aryan tradition, such heroism on the part of the best men can actually effect an *evocation*, or in other words, bring about the conditions to re-establish the contact that for centuries has been loosened between the world and the supra-world. Then the battle will be neither a horrible bloodbath, nor a merciless fate determined by raw will power, but a testing of a people's right and their divine mission. Peace will then no longer mean sinking back into gray bourgeois mundanity and the relaxation of the spiritual tension that was alive in battle, but rather a consummation of the latter.

For this reason I wish to reiterate once again the creed of the ancients as expressed in the following words: "The blood of the hero is more sacred than the ink of the scholars and the prayer of the pious"—and also the traditional conception at its base, that in the "holy war" it is the original mystic powers of the race, rather than individuals, that are at work. *These primordial powers are what creates empires and leads the people to a "victorious peace."*

(Translated by Annabel Lee)

This essay was originally a lecture presented in the German language on 7 December 1940 at the Palazzo Zuccari in Rome.

Notes:

1. The original title of the lecture from which this essay derives was "The Aryan Doctrine of Battle and Victory." As is evident in the text, Evola does not always use the word "Aryan" in a consistent or specific fashion. Since he draws upon a number of divergent sources for this exploration of the metaphysical and spiritual implications of warfare—ranging from ancient Aryan and Indo-European conceptions to Muslim and Christian beliefs—the present title was deemed not only more accurate, but also more appropriate in light of Evola's Traditionalist outlook. A related discussion of this subject appears in chapter seventeen of Evola's *Revolt Against the Modern World*, "The Greater and Lesser Holy War." (Editor's note)

2. Evola refers here to the German philosopher Oswald Spengler and his magnum opus, *The Decline of the West*. Evola himself was the translator for the first Italian edition of this work. (Editor's note)

3. For a more precise understanding of the general, vital concept which forms the basis for the doctrine described here, the reader is directed to my book *Revolt Against the Modern World* [English edition Rochester, Vermont: Inner Traditions: 1995].

Ride the Tiger
A Survival Manual for the Aristocrats of the Soul
JULIUS EVOLA

Translated by *JOSCELYN GODWIN* and *CONSTANCE FONTAN*

Evola's final major work examines the prototype of the human being who can give absolute meaning to his or her life in a world of dissolution. Presents a powerful criticism of the idols, structures, theories, and illusions of our modern age.
$25.00, hardcover, 248 pgs., 6 x 9, ISBN 0-89281-125-0

Introduction to Magic
Rituals and Practical Techniques for the Magus
JULIUS EVOLA and the *UR Group*

For the first time in English, this classic Italian text collects rites, practices, and the esoteric knowledge of the mysterious UR Group for the use of aspiring mages. Includes instructions for creating an etheric double, speaking words of power, and interacting with entities.
$22.95, paper, 416 pgs., 6 x 9, ISBN 0-89281-624-4

Men Among the Ruins
Post-War Reflections of a Radical Traditionalist
JULIUS EVOLA

Evola viewed the forces of history as comprised by two factions: "history's demolition squad" enslaved by blind faith in the future and those individuals whose watchword is Tradition. These latter stand in this world of ruins at the higher level and are capable of letting go of what needs to be abandoned in order that what is truly essential not be compromised.
$22.00, paper, 328 pgs., 6 x 9, ISBN 0-89281-905-7

The Mystery of the Grail
Initiation and Magic in the Quest for the Spirit
JULIUS EVOLA

One of Europe's greatest esoteric philosophers explores the pre-Christian sources of this powerful symbol and traces its mythology from the Nordic sagas through the Middle Ages.
$14.95, paper, 208 pgs., 6 x 9, ISBN 0-89281-573-6

INNER TRADITIONS
BEAR & COMPANY
One Park St., Rochester, VT 05767   800•246•8648
www.InnerTraditions.com   orders@InnerTraditions.com
Please add $4.50 S/H for one book, $5.50 for two books, FREE SHIPPING for three or more.

Summoning the Gods:
The Phenomenology of Divine Presence

Collin Cleary

1. Introduction

The problem with our modern, Western pagans is that they do not genuinely believe in their gods, they merely believe in believing in them.

My ancestors believed, but I do not know how they believed. I confess that I do not know what it is like to live in a world in which there are gods. Occasionally I will catch some glimpse of what it might be like, but on a day-to-day basis I live in a world that seems thoroughly human, and thoroughly profane. It is no use telling myself that the world seems this way to me because I have been imprinted by modern scientism and materialism. Knowing that this is the case does not automatically open the world up for me in a different way. It is also no use telling myself how much healthier I would be (and the world would be) if we still believed in the gods. This is a purely intellectual, even ideological approach that will simply not do the trick.

So why, it might be asked, am I at all bothered with the "problem" of not believing in the gods? Because I know that it is utterly implausible to think that my ancestors simply sat around and "invented" their gods.[1] The thought nags me that they possessed a different sort of consciousness, or some special sense that has now atrophied in us, which allowed the gods to show up for them. And then there is also my conviction that something very important has been lost to us in the "Post-Pagan" world. I have tried to think my way back into belief in the gods; to convince myself, intellectually, of their existence. I know that this does not work, nor do I think it will work for anyone else. So what are our other options?

In an article in volume one of *TYR* ("Knowing the Gods"), I argued something along the following lines. I rejected the modern approach of trying to "explain" what the gods are by reducing them to something else (e.g., "forces"). I argued that "openness to the gods" involves an openness to Being as such. In saying this I am, of course, drawing on the thought of Heidegger. For

Heidegger, what makes the difference between the ancients and moderns is that the moderns see nature simply as "raw material" to be transformed according to human projects and human ideals. In other words, for the moderns, nature essentially has no Being: it waits on humans to confer identity upon it. According to Heidegger, the attitude of the ancients was quite different. It would probably be a distortion to describe the ancients as facing nature (*phusis*, in Greek) with "reverence." This sounds too much like the attitude of city-dwellers coming upon nature after a long absence from it; it is not the attitude of those who live with nature day-to-day. To use the language of Kant, what may be said is that the ancients regarded natural objects as ends-in-themselves, not merely as means to human ends.

To explain this idea, I will make use of a very simple analogy. It is not uncommon to see marriages in which the husband is the dominant figure—so much so that the wife seems hardly to have a presence at all. He sounds off on some issue, in the company of friends, and shoots a sidelong glance at the wife: "You think so too, don't you dear?" And before she can answer he's off on something else. Even if she were given time to answer, she would never dare oppose him. Such a man is apt to be very surprised when, years down the road, he discovers somehow that his wife is quite dissatisfied with this arrangement. He is in for a shock when he finds out that she has an inner life all her own, and that by forbidding this inner life to ever come to expression, he has made a very unhappy marriage for himself. This situation is exactly analogous to the relationship of modern man to nature. Nature, treated merely as something on which man imposes his will, clams up. She falls silent and ceases to reveal her inner life, her secrets to man. All the while, of course, man thinks that he has plumbed nature's depths, and that she has few secrets left to reveal. But, as Heraclitus said, "nature loves to hide."

Western, Christian man had once believed that the world was an artifact created by an omnipotent God. Modern man has jettisoned God, but retained the idea that the earth is an artifact. Our scientists strive to find out how natural objects are "constructed" or "put together." They break things down into their "parts" or "components." With an artifact one can, of course, tear it down and use its "matter" to build something else—perhaps something better than was originally built. This is how modern man views nature: simply as stuff to be made over into other, better stuff.

"A DARKENING OF THE WORLD IS HAPPENING."
—MARTIN HEIDEGGER

And the stuff we make keeps on getting better and better. Or so we imagine. In the face of a humanity which no longer confronts nature as any thing at all, any being in its own right, the gods, it seems, have left us. As Heidegger has said, "on the earth, all over it, a darkening of the world is happening. The essential happenings in this darkening are: the flight of the gods, the destruction of the earth, the reduction of human beings to a mass, the preeminence of the mediocre."[2]

In closing ourselves to the being of nature, we simultaneously close ourselves to the being of the gods. This is a major part of what I argued in "Knowing the Gods." The gods and what we call nature belong to the same realm: the realm of the "of itself so." In Chinese, "Nature" is *tzu-jan*. It is written using two pictographs, one of which can be translated as "of itself," and the other "so." What does this mean? The "of itself so" is that which is, or has happened, independently of conscious, human action or intervention.[3] It has approximately the same meaning as the Greek *phusis*.

I was once at a conference, and had occasion to speak to an academic about "nature." She demanded to know what I meant by this word. I expressed surprise that she did not know, whereupon she informed me that nature is a "social construct." We were seated at a table and I asked if she would extend her arm and bare her wrist. I took her wrist in my hand, and when I had found her pulse I instructed her to put her other hand there and feel it. "There," I said. "That's nature. Society didn't construct that. Nor has it come about of your own choice or design. It just happens, whether you like it or not." This is the "of itself so."

Human beings have the choice of opening to the "of itself so" or closing to it. Modern man has chosen to close. But although the "of itself so" is translated "nature," it is a much broader category. In closing to the "of itself so," man has closed to otherness as such: to what we call nature, and to anything else that is in its own right, apart from humanity—including whatever might be "super-natural."

The purpose of this essay, which I think of as a sequel to "Knowing the Gods," is to ask specifically how we can restore openness to the "of itself so." This was the question that the other essay left largely unanswered. In case it is not clear, let me state again what I take openness to the "of itself so" to entail. I take it to mean an awareness and acceptance of that which has being in its own right. I take "nature" to be part of this "of itself so," along with that which has been designated the "supernatural": the gods, as well as god-knows-what.

First of all, it must be understood that what is "of itself so," is also a part of us. The pulse that beats in our wrists is an example of this. So is the hunger that one feels when a meal is a long time in coming, or the sexual desire that wells up, quite without the intellect's permission. When I say that modern man has closed himself to otherness, I do not mean that he has closed himself to all that is outside his skin. Modern man has identified himself with his conscious intellect alone. He treats his body in the way that he treats every other natural object: as something that "belongs" to him, and that must be mastered, and even, as we often say today, "made over." We do not have to go "outside ourselves" to encounter nature or the "of itself so," provided we have a conception of self that encompasses more than conscious intellect.

Openness must therefore involve rejecting the idea that the mind is all there is to one's identity. It must involve the recognition that much of one's "self" is not consciously chosen or controlled. Openness then becomes not so much the opening of a space that then gets filled, but rather a kind of communing with an other that is now, in a way, no longer so other.

In an essay on, of all people, Benjamin Franklin, D. H. Lawrence offers his own "creed," in opposition to the "sensible," Enlightenment creed of Franklin. He writes that he believes

> 'That I am I.'
> 'That my soul is a dark forest.'
> 'That my known self will never be more than a little clearing in the forest.'

'That gods, strange gods, come forth from the forest into the clearing of my known self, and then go back.'
'That I must have the courage to let them come and go.'
'That I will never let mankind put anything over me, but that I will try always to recognize and submit to the gods in me and the gods in other men and women.'[4]

The soul is indeed a dark forest. As Heraclitus said, "You would not discover the limits of the soul although you traveled every road: it has so deep a logos."[5] But modern man has identified himself with the little clearing of the known self. Outside that clearing is a great dark forest, and beyond lies the greater wilderness that is the world itself. Man shines his flashlight into it and imagines that outside the corona of his beam there is only void. And "lumber" is the clever word he uses to describe the tiny bit he illuminates.

2. How to Summon the Gods

Let's stop and examine when it is—on what occasions—we experience a sense of the reality of otherness. The best examples are when things break down or somehow frustrate our expectations. This is how Heidegger approaches the issue. We get in the car to set off on a busy day of doing business and running errands—and find that it won't start. My experience in such situations is that there is at first almost a feeling of "unreality." We want to say (and often do), "I can't believe this is happening." And suddenly the being of this two-ton concatenation of metal and plastic confronts us in all its frustrating facticity. A still worse situation is when the body becomes ill, when it suddenly does not work as we expect it to. The body then seems to us to be a brute other. Both these situations, and all others like them, are occasions when something that has been taken for granted, suddenly seems to assert itself. What had been regarded merely as a tool, as an extension of human will, becomes a being in its own right. The result is frustration, amazement, fury, and something like awe.

But, in religious terms, what we want is not to be put in awe of this or that, but somehow to come to find the world itself aweful in its otherness. Must the world "break down," like a car, for us to experience this? Of course, the answer is that it cannot. What very often happens instead is that we break down and the world confronts us as something that may be lost to us forever. I have in mind situations where human beings have a brush with death or insanity, or come face to face with their own mortality or fragility. And I've often thought that some men deliberately take risks—deliberately precipitate a brush with death—just so that they may feel a renewed sense of awe or wonder in the face of existence. Such men very often develop a "sense" not only of the world's strange otherness, but also a "mystical" intuition of something like divine providence working behind the scenes.[6]

Fortunately, we need not jump out of airplanes or climb mountains in order to achieve openness of the kind I am concerned with. We need only ask and ponder a single question: why are there beings at all, rather than nothing? Here, again, I am borrowing from Heidegger, but in order to take things in a direction Heidegger did not really explore.[7]

In India, there is a very simple meditation exercise often performed by seekers of wisdom. It consists in taking any object, no matter how mundane—it could be a rock, or a cigarette butt—placing it on the earth, and drawing a ring around it in the dirt. The effect is to take an object that normally is taken for granted, that figures in life merely as a tool or as something barely noticed, and to make us aware of its being. Say that it is a cigarette butt. When we place a ring around it, it becomes a suitable object of meditation. What we meditate on is not its gross cigarette-butt-nature, but the fact of its being—the very fact that it has being at all. It is a way of becoming attuned to the wonder of being.

To ask the question why are there beings at all, rather than nothing? is to put a ring around that which is, as such. It is a way in which, in the twinkling of an eye, the entire world in which we find ourselves can become an object of meditation—and of awe and wonder.

When we confront being-as-such as a miracle it is natural (and inevitable) that we should ask where it comes from. The childish version of this question is "who made it?" The more sophisticated version asks not about the physical coming-into-being of the universe considered as a totality, but about the source of the abundance that confronts us in the universe. We wonder at the inexhaustible richness of the universe, at the infinite multiplicity of types of things, and variations on these types, and at the infinite complexity of each thing, no matter how mundane. We wonder at the continual replenishment of beings—the continual parade of types giving rise to others like themselves, and the resilience of beings in regenerating and healing themselves. It is natural to wonder at the source of all of this. It is the "source of being" that this fundamental question, why are there beings at all, rather than nothing?, makes thematic.

Think for a moment of the source of a spring. Where does the spring end and the source begin (or vice versa)? At its source, the spring disappears into the ground. Is the source the hole in the ground? Obviously not. Is the source a body of water distinct from the spring? Again, obviously not. The spring and its source blend together. The origin of the stream is invisible. But we understand that the spring flows out from this invisible source. This is exactly how the Greeks conceived *phusis*, as surging forth continually out of an ultimate source—*archē*, in Greek. This realization is the meaning of such ancient symbols as the horn or cauldron of plenty, and the Holy Grail. The *archē* is the groundless ground of all abundance.

The root problem with human beings is that they want to, in effect, make themselves the *archē*, the source of all things. All of our attempts to understand something involve coming to see how the being of the thing flows from certain principles we have discovered. We strive, in effect, to cut away an object's grounding and to make ourselves the ground by coming to see how the object's being flows from our ideas. When the scientist, for example, understands phenomena, he insists that the phenomena flow from principles he legislates.[8] But when we turn our minds to the ultimate *archē*—from which we ourselves flow—being, in spite of all our claims to have conquered nature, shows up as a mysterious, miraculous given. The *archē* is the ground against which the figure of being-as-such shows up.

However, as the example of the ring around the cigarette butt indicates, one can find wonder in a single being, as well as in being-as-such. And when we turn, with this attitude of wonder, toward the individual phenomena within existence, another fundamental question arises. We may ask of anything, why should this particular thing be, and be the way that it is? Take the phenomenon of sex. When the mind attempts to think dispassionately about sex it comes off seeming like a rather absurd and grotesque activity. Why should this be so fascinating? Why should this absorb so much of our time and be so important to us? And yet there it is. And the more one tries to think about it this way the more one worries one might wind up ruining the whole thing! The result is that, awed by the sheer, inexplicable reality of

"WHEN THE MIND ATTEMPTS TO THINK DISPASSIONATELY ABOUT SEX IT COMES OFF SEEMING LIKE A RATHER ABSURD AND GROTESQUE ACTIVITY. WHY SHOULD THIS BE SO FASCINATING?"
AGOSTINO CARACCI, "MARS AND VENUS."

sex, we continue to wonder at it and pursue it as before. In fact, this may be the only area, in the lives of many, in which wonder still happens.[9]

But everything else may be approached with this attitude of wonder. A beautiful animal is to be wondered at. Why should this particular thing be, and be the way that it is? The fact of the wind and the rain, the sun and the stars, all may occasion wonder, and the asking of this question. And it need not be a physical or perceptible entity: it might be the fact of birth, or of death, or of natural cycles, etc.

Now, when we do ask this question, it may sound like we are asking for some sort of official, scientific explanation, but we are not. No lecture on natural selection will have the effect of removing my wonder at the being of my cat—my wonder that such a thing is, and is the way it is. I do not have any quarrel with scientific explanation. But scientific explanation cannot remove this ultimate, metaphysical wonder at the sheer existence of things. I am perfectly willing to accept the scientist's explanation of how cats came into being—but I still look at my cat and say, "Isn't it incredible that we live in a world where such marvelous things would come about?"

My thesis is this: our wonder at the being of particular things is an intuition of a god, or divine being.

Am I saying that when I look at my cat and experience this sense of wonder I am intuiting that my cat is a god? Yes and no. The wonder I experience is that things such as this exist at all. I can just as well have this experience when contemplating the sun, the wind, the rain, the ocean, the mountains, etc. My wonder at the being of these things just is an experience of their divinity. Thus, there are gods of the sun, the wind, the rain, the ocean, the mountains, and, yes, of cats (the Egyptians saw this quite well). In truth, all things shine with divinity; all things are God. And there is no contradiction between this statement and the statement that there are gods. These are just two different ways of looking at the same thing. Insofar as the divinity of cats shines through my cat, it is the god of cats.

There is a further aspect to this experience. When we confront things in their being, and wonder that such things are at all, our perception of time and space changes. When a thing is regarded with wonder, in the sense I have described, we simultaneously experience its being as stretched beyond the temporal present. The object is there before us, in the present, but simultaneously we intuit an aspect of eternity in the thing. When I wonder that such things as my cat exist at all, what I am wondering at is, in a sense, the "fact of catness" in the world. As Alan Watts would probably have put it, we wonder at the fact that there is catting, and dogging and peopling and flowering, and fruiting in this world. This is the aspect of divinity that shines through the thing, regarded in a certain way.

We might think of the gods as "regions" within being. There are as many gods as there are regions of being.[10] Our awareness of regions of being does not come through philosophical analysis or speculative system-building. It comes through experience and intuition. There are as many regions as there are experiences of wonder at the fact that "things such as X" exist at all. And there are regions within regions. It was thus with supreme good sense that the Indians left things very vague with respect to the number of their gods. Hindu accounts differ. Some say that there are 330,000,000 gods. Such a huge number is not meant to be an exact figure. It is meant to suggest, in fact, the infinity of gods, an infinity grounded in the fact that there are infinite possible experiences of wonder at things. In just the same way, ancient Chinese authors speak of "the ten thousand things," not to give an exact figure, but to suggest the incomprehensible vastness of existence.

3. Objections and Replies

The position outlined above is simple, but likely to produce a great deal of skepticism. And the skeptics will come from almost every established "camp": rationalists, empiricists, theologians, and even pagans. In order to try and answer some of their complaints in advance, I present the following set of objections and replies.

Objection One: I have said that the question why are there beings at all, rather than nothing? allows us to "set off" all of existence and to regard it with wonder. I said, further, that the question why should this particular thing exist, and be the way that it is? allows us to experience objects within the world with wonder, and that this wonder at the sheer being of things is an experience of the divine. But are we to believe that our ancestors gamboled about the forest (or elsewhere) looking at things and thinking, in whatever language was theirs, "why should this particular thing exist, and be the way that it is?"?

Reply: Of course not. In fact, one of my claims is that our ancestors had a natural and spontaneous capacity for wonder, a childlike capacity that we moderns (even modern children) have mostly lost. The questions I present here are attempts to formulate in words the tacit mental attitude necessary to make divinity come to presence. Nevertheless, they are not merely descriptive, but prescriptive also. For those of us who have lost the capacity for spontaneous wonder, the conscious asking of these questions may be a way back into the mentality of our ancestors.

Objection Two: A related objection might go as follows: the mental attitude of regarding things with wonder is a kind of "second order" achievement of consciousness. Most of us go through the day with a purely "worldly" focus: i.e., we are involved with things themselves, not with the wonder of their "sheer being." From this, two problems follow. First, it stands to reason that the farther we go back in time, the more "worldly" the focus of our ancestors had to have been, given the harshness of the conditions under which they lived. They would have had little occasion for "reflection." And from this problem flows a second one: if I am merely describing the "tacit mental attitude necessary to make divinity come to presence," and the turn to wonder is not conscious or deliberate, then it must be occasioned by certain events. In other words, something had to "happen" in order for man to turn from a "worldly" focus, to an attitude of wonder. What was it?

Reply: As to the first problem, it may be that the capacity to turn from a worldly focus to an attitude of wonder is what makes human beings unique in the animal kingdom. At some point in our evolution, it became possible to "switch attitudes" toward the world in this fashion. As to what occasioned this extraordinary leap in mental capacities, I have no theories of my own to offer. Obviously, it has nothing to do with the establishment of agriculture, or technology, or cities, or an increase in leisure time, since we find experiences of the divine in both planting and hunting cultures, in those with technology and in those without, in those located in villages and in those located in cities. But a word about leisure: modern people tend to exaggerate the degree to which "hardship" made the lives of ancient men chaotic and perilous, with little time for rest, let alone religion. The fact of the matter is that ancient men, particularly in hunter-gatherer cultures, had a tremendous amount of time for reflection, since hunting mainly involves sitting quietly and waiting. (I tend to think, also, that far from freeing us and providing us with more leisure, technology has made life more complicated, busy, and burdensome.) So, if we assume that the capacity to experience wonder came into being at a certain point, it is safe to assume that there was ample "free time" in which to actualize it.

As to the second objection—what occasioned the experience of wonder?—I immediately think of Vico, who claimed in *The New Science* (1730/1744) that awareness of divinity began at the first clap of thunder, when our primitive ancestors scattered back to their caves with cries of "Jove!" (the first God name). There is something to this theory, in spite of its naïveté. As I discussed earlier, what moves us from worldly involvement with things to reflection on their Being must be some kind of arresting experience. Things have to surprise us, frustrate us, overcome us, in some fashion. (And it need not be a "negative" sense of "overcoming" or "surprise.") In my own experience, I sometimes have a spontaneous sense of wonder at things, and very often I can't put my finger on what occasioned it.

Objection Three: Let's return for a moment to the cigarette butt mentioned earlier. I said that one could draw a ring (literal or figurative) around any object and come to wonder at its being, including a rock or a cigarette butt. Is there then a god of cigarette butts? Are there gods of trash bags, coffee cups, toy trucks, and TV sets? This, certainly, seems absurd. And if my position compels us to declare, for consistency's sake, that there are such gods, then that surely qualifies as a *reductio* of it.

Reply: Fortunately, my position does not require this. First of all, what I said earlier still stands: it is perfectly possible to wonder at the sheer existence of cigarette butts and TV sets. These are artifacts: objects created by human beings. When one wonders at natural objects, the root of the wonder, the sense of mystery which cannot be eradicated, lies in the mysteriousness of the ultimate source of their being. In the case of artifacts, there is no mystery at all about their source: human beings created them.[11] Thus, when we wonder at the facticity of an artifact, what we are actually wondering at is the being of man himself, the *archē* (or architect) of the artifact. Is man himself a god? Of course. But there are no gods of his creations, no god of the machine.[12] This is why the very idea of a god of cigarette butts is immediately absurd to us, whereas it does not seem absurd at all to wonder at the being of the animal capable of creating such things and, especially, much grander things like supersonic jets, symphonies, computers, epic poems, suspension bridges, space shuttles, and cathedrals. One may argue that some of these things—perhaps even man himself—are a cancer on the planet, but one must still be awestruck by what man can do, by the fact that there is a being who wields such remarkable powers.

But if man is a god, he is only one god among infinitely many. If people today seem to behave as if they think man is the only god, this is perfectly explicable. We live in a world in which it is artifacts, not natural objects, which are most ready-to-hand. We live in immediate contact with cigarette butts, trash bags, coffee cups, TV sets, supersonic jets, computers, suspension bridges, and space shuttles. For most of us, our contact with such things as the wind, the rain, the ocean, the mountains, and "nature" in general is mediated through artifacts. Our houses and buildings shield us from the sun, the wind, and the rain. Most of us, remarkably enough, have seen the entire world: but only through photography books and over our TV sets. Our climate control systems shield us even from the seasons: we are pleasingly warm in winter and pleasingly cool in summer. Some people live by the ocean, but very few live by means of it. And their dwellings shield them from its violence (most of the time).

If artifacts are what we come into contact with on a regular basis, and if through and by means of artifacts the only god we intuit is ourselves, is it any wonder that such "isms" as "humanism," "scientism," and "atheism" reign? Is it any wonder that modern people live their lives on the assumption that they are the highest beings of all, and masters of all? Cut off from direct contact with nature, they are cut off from the experience of its wonder, which is the experience of the infinity of gods. This is the "flight of the gods." The gods have not, to be exact, flown. We have merely blinded ourselves to them, by erecting a fabricated world that has obstructed the real world.

Objection Four: Now, it might be charged that the above attempt to account for the experience of the divine constitutes an abuse of language. I have said that our wonder at the being of things is an intuition of divinity. Thus, wonder that there is such a thing as the wind just is the experience of the "god of wind." But, the critic may charge, this is not what we have in mind by what a god is. I have merely substituted an entirely different understanding of divinity, one that has little to do with the traditional understanding (or so the objection would go). The god of wind is a personality. In India, he is Vâyu. He is depicted as white, riding a deer, and carrying a bow and arrows. The myths involve the feelings, thoughts, speeches, and actions of such gods. The gods, in short, are supposed to be conscious beings who run around and do things.

Reply: The trouble with this way of understanding things is that it confuses symbols with their referents. The god of wind is a personality because human beings have consciously and deliberately personified him. And separating the personified symbol from its referent is very difficult. Note that I said that "human beings have consciously and deliberately personified him." I should, perhaps, have said "it." But that somehow doesn't sound right. We personify because we have a drive to personify in order to hold the god in mind. Really, what this means is that we personify in order to hold in mind the wind, taken not as a "natural phenomenon" (as a scientist would take it) but as a *noumenon*, as a being awakening wonder. The drive to personify is natural, and it may be the case that some of the concrete ways in which we personify are also "built into" our consciousness. The researches of C. G. Jung and his students seem to confirm this. But it is hard to know where to draw the line. That Ganesha is depicted as having the head of an elephant is obviously attributable entirely to the historical accident that his symbolism was developed in India.

The symbolism of a god, the god's sex (male or female), the god's attributes, and associated myths, all serve to tell us something about the nature of some phenomenon taken in its numinous aspect. There is no better symbolism with which to illustrate this than that of Hinduism. Hindu iconography is extremely complex, and each element is symbolic of some power or aspect of a god.

Within any religion there are levels of understanding. There are undoubtedly Hindus whose piety consists in a lifelong confusion of symbol and referent. In other words, there are undoubtedly Hindus who think that truly believing in Vâyu means believing that there actually is an all-white being who rides a deer and carries a bow and arrows. We tend to assume that such "low level," or literal-minded understanding is a characteristic of the "common people," but that the higher-ups (the priests, the Brahmins) understand better. Assuming this is a dangerous business, however. In the West, for example, particularly in America, confusing the symbol with the referent is by no means confined to simple folk. It is a feature of the belief of most Christians, regardless of their level of education. Western atheists also confuse the symbol with the referent, and on that basis declare that religion is manifestly absurd. Seminarians understand that a symbol is a symbol, but find it very difficult to believe in that which it is a symbol of. Hence, they declare that we can keep religion, if we understand that it is really all about the "religious community," or about moral instruction, or social activism.

Some time ago I watched a British documentary about Hinduism, which included footage of a week-long festival in honor of a goddess (I think it was Sarasvati). The celebration involved the molding and painting of an elaborate clay figure of the goddess. A new one was created each year, and at the conclusion of the festival it was joyously dumped into the river. The British host asked a Brahmin if the people were worshipping the statue. The Brahmin smiled and said that he very much doubted that any of the celebrants, no matter how simpleminded, thought that the clay statue actually was Sarasvati. After all, they had to notice that each year it was a new statue! In truth, it was the Western journalist here who was simpleminded. Indeed, the typical way we Westerners understand polytheism (or so-called "primitive" religion) is, to put it mildly, psychologically naïve.

Objection Five: Referring back to my earlier essay, "Knowing the Gods," I can imagine someone objecting to the present essay by saying, "Look, in the other piece you begin by rejecting any attempt to explain what the gods are, or to explain the experience of the gods. To take such a reflective standpoint, you said, is to immediately distance ourselves from the phenomenon; to cut ourselves off from it even more decisively. But in this piece you do precisely what you say shouldn't be done: you've offered an explanation of the gods by claiming that 'the gods' are what show up when we are struck by the mysterious being of a being."

Reply: In fact, I have not explained the gods, or the experience of the gods, at all. To explain a phenomenon is to take it as an effect of some cause, and then to ferret out the cause (e.g., the explanation of why the water boiled is that it was heated to the temperature of 212 degrees Fahrenheit). But this is not what I have done. What I have given is not an explanation, but a phenomenological description. In other words, I have merely described how the divine "shows up" or "appears" to us. I have described the circumstances in which the divine shows up, the attitude of mind necessary for man to "notice" the divine, and how he responds to the divine once it shows up. This may seem like an oversimplification of what I have done in the preceding, rather lengthy text, but it is not. It is just that in this case, with a matter as mysterious as this one, phenomenological description is a bit more difficult than, say, the phenomenological description of how a mailbox shows up for us. If the reader will go back and think over what has been said, he will find that the theory I have given of how the divine shows up is actually fairly simple. Unfortunately, we have been conditioned to think of the divine in such a wrongheaded way, that getting to the right description involves a great deal of explanation, examples, definition of terms, etymology (as we shall see), and, in general, unlearning.

Finally, *Objection Six:* This is perhaps the most serious objection of all. Doesn't my account completely "subjectivize" the gods? Aren't I saying that the gods are somehow functions of the way we regard things, and that without us, there would be no divine? The whole phenomenological, neo-Kantian approach described above seems to suggest this very clearly.

Reply: I can certainly see why someone might react this way—especially given my appeal to phenomenology, but, in fact, the objection represents a misunderstanding of my position (as well as a misunderstanding of phenomenology and of Kantianism, but I can't go into those points here). I have not said anything even approaching the idea that "the divine" is a subjective, mental category and that without human perceivers there would be no gods. I would certainly contend that without a certain cognitive "structure" (whatever it might be) we could not be aware of the gods, but this does not commit me to subjectivism. We need ears in order to notice sound waves, but nobody thinks that this means that ears "create" sound waves.[13] To repeat, I have given a phenomenological description of, to quote my earlier formulation, "the attitude of mind necessary for man to 'notice' the divine." I did not say "create" the divine, I said notice it. I have spoken of the divine coming to presence, not of being invented or "posited" by humans.

However, someone might say at this point, "all right, but apart from the appearance of the gods to us, are there really any gods out there?" Put in Kantian language, this says: aside from the phenomenal appearance of gods, do gods exist in themselves? The best I can do to answer this is to paraphrase Kant himself: even though we can never perceive things as they are in themselves (i.e., apart from our perceptions of them) we must at least be able to think of the same objects as things in themselves, lest we be landed in the absurd consequence of supposing that there can be appearance without anything that appears.[14]

4. Precedents: Usener and Cassirer

The foregoing theory shares some features in common with the views of Hermann Usener, as expounded and developed by Ernst Cassirer. In Cassirer's *Language and Myth*, he explains how Usener believed that the oldest (and, I would say, purest) stage of religious experience, was marked by the "production" of what he called momentary deities.[15] Cassirer writes:

> These beings do not personify any force of nature, nor do they represent some special aspect of human life; no recurrent trait or value is retained in them and transformed into a mythico-religious image; it is something purely instantaneous, a fleeting, emerging and vanishing mental content, whose objectification and outward discharge produces the image of the "momentary deity." Every impression that man receives, every wish that stirs in him, every hope that lures him, every danger that threatens him can affect him thus religiously. Just let spontaneous feeling invest the object before him, or his own personal condition, or some display of power that surprises him, with an air of holiness, and the momentary god has been experienced and created.[16]

Now, as I said, this theory shares some features in common with my own. What is vague in the Usener-Cassirer account is what it means to have "spontaneous feeling" invest an object. And what is "an air of holiness"? My own theory attempts to account for specifically how some object (or state of affairs) could be taken in so unusual a way as to produce in us an intuition of a god. In other words, I attempt to describe specifically what it means to take something as holy.

Furthermore, I maintain that while the experience of the "momentary deity" is not immediately that of a personified god, it can develop into that later (on this point, I doubt Usener-Cassirer would disagree). Cassirer continues, "Usener has shown through examples of Greek literature how real this primitive religious feeling was even in the Greeks of the classical period, and how it activated them again and again."[17] And then he quotes Usener:

> By reason of this vivacity and responsiveness of their religious sentiment, any idea or object which commands, for the moment, their undivided interest, may be exalted to divine status: Reason and Understanding, Wealth, Chance, Climax, Wine, Feasting, or the body of the Beloved ... Whatever comes to us suddenly like a sending from heaven, whatever rejoices or grieves or oppresses us, seems to the religious consciousness like a divine being. As far back as we can trace the Greeks, they subsume such experiences under the generic name of daimon.[18]

According to Usener, after the stage of "momentary gods" comes the stage of "special gods." Although what Usener seems to have in mind here, narrowly, is deities associated with human activities (see my endnote 12). Nevertheless, as reported by Cassirer, Usener's ideas are thought provoking, and intersect with my own:

> Every department of human activity gives rise to a particular deity that represents it. These deities too, which Usener calls "special gods" *(Sondergötter)*, have as yet no general function and significance; they do not permeate existence in its whole depth and scope, but are limited to a mere section of it, a narrowly circumscribed department. But within their respective spheres they have attained to permanence and definite character, and therewith to a certain generality. The patron god of harrowing, for instance, the god Occator, rules not only this year's harrowing, or the cultivation of a particular field, but is the god of harrowing in general, who is annually invoked by the whole community as its helper and protector upon the recurrence of this agricultural practice. So he represents a special and perhaps humble rustic activity, but he represents it in its generality.[19]

Building upon the work of Usener, Cassirer goes on to argue in *Language and Myth* that language originated essentially as a means to fix in mind these momentary deities (recall that he characterizes them as a "fleeting, emerging and vanishing mental content"). Thus are born words used to communicate and retain these experiences. (On this point, there is an interesting parallel between Cassirer's link between "deities" and words, and my link, described later, between deities and Platonic Forms; see section 6 below). "Special gods" are deities invested with special names. Eventually, these names become disengaged from the divinity and stand alone as "terms" denoting the activity governed by the original divinity (so, if in some language Word X means "harrowing," X may originally have been the proper name for the god of that activity).

Usener gives a multitude of examples of "special" and "functional" gods, a great many of which are drawn from ancient Roman religion. The highest religious achievement, according to Usener, is the development of "personal gods." Cassirer writes: "The many divine names which originally denoted a corresponding number of sharply distinguished special gods now fuse in one personality, which has thus emerged; they become the several appellations of this Being, expressing various aspects of his nature, power, and range."[20] It is not very hard to discern a Judeo-Christian bias in such a theory, which construes monotheism not only as the telos of all religious development, but also as its apex.

In truth, it is possible, as I suggested earlier, to be both monotheist and polytheist. We can certainly look at the world as an expression of a multiplicity of individual gods. If we see these divinities as, in a sense, "regions of being," we can also see them as different manifestations or expressions of an underlying unity. These are simply two ways of looking at the same thing. There is no contradiction in saying that the true God is Brahman, and in saying simultaneously that there are 330,000,000 gods. Most religions have totalized one or the other of these approaches, and the historical trend, it seems, is from polytheism to monotheism, and not the other way around. Why this should be the case is not a question I can address here.[21]

5. The Language of the Divine

If we look at the etymology of the words we use to speak and think about the divine, we will find further support for my position. This is important, for it is deeply engrained in us that we take the word "god" simply to mean a personal super-being. (In fact, I think this is what the earlier objection—that I am not talking about what people have meant by "gods" at all—really is based upon.)

The reconstructed Proto-Indo-European term for divinity is *deiwos*, and here are some of its forms:

Old Irish: *dîa*
Old Welsh: *duiu-tit*
Latin: *deus*
Old Norse: *Týr* (pl. *tívar*, "gods")
Old English: *Tīw*
Old High German: *Zîo*
Lithuanian: *diẽvas*
Latvian: *dìevs*
Avestan: *daéva*
Old Indic: *devá*

One source says of **deiwos*, "In origin a thematic derivative of [**dyeu-*] 'sky, day, sun (god)' meaning '± luminous one, god (in general).'"[22]

Now, if **deiwos* or God means something like "luminous one," there are at least a couple of very different ways to take this. Since the word is derived from **dyeu-*, "sky, day, sun," it is generally assumed that the original Indo-European gods (or, at least, the upper echelon of gods, e.g., the Norse Æsir) are gods of the heavens. Nor is this phenomenon of looking to heaven for divinity confined to the Indo-Europeans, as we all know from Sunday school. But I wonder if there is not, perhaps, a deeper meaning to the idea of God as "the luminous one." As I have discussed above, when we come to awareness of the wonderful being of individual things, it is as if they are suddenly "lit up." And I do not mean this in an exclusively figurative way. Very often the experience literally seems to be one in which things shine with a new light. Descriptions of mystical experiences abound with such language. We speak of ourselves, and things, as being "illuminated." To go back to an earlier example, when I experience the wonder that such things as my cat exist at all, my cat is "lit up" for me in a new way, and the light that shines through my cat is the divinity, the luminous one.

It was only natural that our ancestors should have associated the physical experience of the awesome brightness of the sun, with the psychical experience of the awesome brightness of Being shining through beings. Thus, *deiwos* as "luminous one" is, in effect, an abstraction derived from all that is *dyeu-*, or all that "shines," with "sky," "day," and "sun" being exemplars of shining.

Looking outside the Indo-European tradition, among the Chinese we find what seems to be a similar conception. The oldest Chinese terms for divinity date back to the Shang Dynasty (ca. 1751–1028 B.C.E.). The supreme god is conceived as celestial. Oddly enough, he is called Ti (which simply means Lord) or Shang Ti (Lord on High).[23] According to Mircea Eliade, "Ti commands the cosmic rhythms and natural phenomena (rain, wind, drought, etc.); he grants the king victory and insures the abundance of crops or, on the contrary, brings on disasters and sends sicknesses and death."[24] There are other gods (and the Chinese worshipped their ancestors as well), but these are subordinated to Ti. As with Tyr in the Germanic tradition, however, Ti remains somewhat remote from the lives of ordinary believers, and eventually became, in effect, a *deus otiosus*. It would be fascinating to trace out the etymology of "Ti," but I do not know Chinese at all, and I can find few sources in English which deal with this topic.

Returning to the Indo-Europeans, let us consider some other terms for the divine. In an article originally published in *Rûna*, Edred Thorsson analyzes the Germanic terms for "the holy."[25] In Proto-Germanic, these are *wîhaz* and *hailagaz*, in Old English *wîh* and *hâlig*, in Old High German *wîh* and *heilig*, in Gothic *weihs* and *hailigs*, in Old Norse *vé* and *heilagr*. Modern German preserves both terms, in *weihen* (to consecrate), and *heilig*. Modern English preserves only the second, as "holy."

As Thorsson points out, *wîhaz* derives from the Proto-Indo-European root *vîk*, which means "to separate." The sense of separation involves a religious or ritual context. From *vîk* comes Latin *victima*, "sacrificial animal."[26] Thus, what derives from *vîk* has the sense of being something "separate in some way from the every-day."[27] The *wîhaz* is what has been "drawn out," as it were, from that which is ready-to-hand, and invested with significance of a very special sort.

What Thorsson does not mention, however, is that *vîk* (sometimes given as *wîk*) can also mean "appear," as well as separate (or "consecrate"). We thus have Old English *wîg~wîh~wêoh*, "image, idol." Lithuanian *į-vỹkti*, meaning "happen, occur; come true, be fulfilled" originally seems to have meant "come into sight."[28] Greek *eikōn*, meaning "image, likeness," is derived from this same root. Plato opposes the *eikōn* to the *eidos*, the Form (see section 6 below). But how can the same linguistic form convey "to separate," "to consecrate," and to "appear," simultaneously? The answer is that something appears in its own right only when it is separated. All appearance involves an opposition of "figure" to "ground." To appear, an object must be somehow "marked off" from its background. "Sacred" objects are objects that have been marked off from profane space (set apart from mundane activities and objects) and profane time (linked to what is eternal).

Thorsson gives the following meanings for the basic Germanic **wîh-*:

1. "a site for cultic activity, sacred ground"
2. "a grave mound"
3. "a site where court is held"
4. "an idol, or divine image"
5. "a standard or flag"[29]

What all of these have in common is that they are, ordinarily, "mundane": a patch of ground, a mound of dirt, a clearing, a carved piece of wood, a piece of cloth. But all of these are capable of being regarded in a special way and invested, by association, with significance (with something like that which anthropologists call "mana").[30] When the mundanity of things is negated in this fashion, they are made "sacred," and then a split in the world comes into being between that which is sacred and that which is profane.[31] As Thorsson discusses, there is even a verb in Old Norse which designates the action of drawing objects out of the realm of the profane and making them sacred: *wîhian*. From that which is **wîh-* comes one of the most significant Norse names for divinity: Vé, who is one of the three divine brothers described in the Norse cosmogony: Óðinn, Vili, and Vé. The term *vear*, from Vé, also is used to mean the plural "gods" in general.[32]

As to the Proto-Germanic root **hail-*, an analysis of the words derived from it in the various Germanic tongues indicates the following set of meanings:

1. "holy"
2. "whole, healthy" (e.g., English "hale and hearty")
3. "health, happiness" (e.g., English "health")

4. "luck, omen"
5. "to heal" (e.g., English "heal")
6. "to greet" (e.g., English "hail!" and German "heil!")
7. "to observe signs and omens"
8. "to invoke spirits, enchant"[33]

Thorsson writes that *hail- "is that which takes part in the numinous quality which is blessed and whole, and which evokes the feeling of 'wholeness' or 'oneness' in the religious subject."[34]

Essentially, *hail- involves the participation of the human subject in the divine, whereas *wîh- refers to the divine presence itself. The man who is "whole, healthy" is the man who is permeated by a state of rightness or harmony which is thought of as connected with divine being. This is very close to the original Greek sense of *eudaimonia* (poorly rendered, in translations of Aristotle, as "happiness"), which literally means something like "well-demoned *(daimoned)*."[35] "Luck" is divine favor dwelling within a man. "To heal" means to restore that divine-oriented "rightness" to the body or mind. Today, it's pretty uncommon to hear someone greeted with "hail!" and unheard of (post–World War II) to hear a "heil!" When people said that to one another, were they greeting or recognizing the divine within the other person? Was "hail!" in short, similar to the Indian greeting (still in use today) *namaste?*[36] The observation of signs and omens means being watchful for the manifestation of the divine within daily life. Finally, to "enchant" means to place someone under the influence of some kind of divine power.

Finally, turning to classical Greek, it might be mentioned that the Greek word for piety or religion, *eusebeia*, comes from the verb *sebein*, meaning "to step back from something in awe."

6. Plato: *eidos* vs. *theos*

The foregoing analysis of the experience of the divine sheds special light on Greek philosophy, in particular on the relation of Plato's "doctrine of Forms" to traditional Indo-European religion. Looking at this connection also seems to lend further support to the plausibility of my theory of the experience of the divine (which is the primary reason I have included this section). Indeed, readers may have noticed something vaguely "Platonic" in my description of the human experience of divinity. I will argue, in fact, that Plato's philosophy constituted a transformation of Greek religious experience. If I am right, then we may be able to learn a good deal about the nature of that experience from Plato.

I'm sure my readers have some acquaintance with Plato's Forms. Plato believed that the world of experience is, in a sense, unreal, and that what is truly real (or, one could say, what truly is) are the "Forms" or "natures" things exhibit. These forms are non-physical and, unlike the individuals that exemplify them, they last. The Greek word translated "Form" is *eidos* (plural: *eidē*), which is why, somewhat less often, the term is translated "idea."[37] But the literal meaning of *eidos* is "look" in the sense of "appearance." The *eidos* is the "look" of a thing. In German, the same concept is rendered by *Schein*, which is related, of course, to our "shine."

At first glance, there seems to have been a complete transformation in the sense of the Greek *eidos*. What originally meant the "look" of a thing comes to mean, in Plato, its intelligible nature, which presents itself not to the eyes but to the mind. But on closer examination, a subtle connection between the two reveals itself. Let us consider first how Plato describes the way in which we come to be aware of Forms. A classic example is to be found in the *Symposium* (210e). In a "flashback," Socrates recalls how he was instructed in the nature of the beautiful by the wisewoman Diotima. She describes a "ladder of beauty," and tells Socrates that he will come to awareness of Beauty itself (the Form of Beauty) by examining different things said to be "beautiful":

> You see, the man who has been thus far guided in matters of Love, who has beheld beautiful things in the right order and correctly, is coming now to the goal of Loving: all of a sudden he will catch sight of something wonderfully beautiful in its nature [the "Beautiful itself"]; that, Socrates, is the reason for all his earlier labors.[38]

A second, less familiar example occurs in the late dialogue the *Parmenides*. Here, Socrates, depicted as a young man, is conversing with another of his early gurus, the philosopher Parmenides. At 132a, the older man puts Socrates's theory of Forms (then in its earliest and crudest form) to the test:

> I suppose you think each form is one on the following

ground: whenever some number of things seems to you to be large, perhaps there seems to be some one character, the same as you look at them all, and from that you conclude that the large is one.[39]

These two phenomenological descriptions of how Forms show up for us depict them as appearing to the thinker as he contemplates sensible objects. To be sure, it is not as if the Form pops out of things and presents itself as a separate, sensible object. One could say that it appears to "intellect," but this oversimplifies things. What seems to happen in our coming-to-awareness of Forms is that sense and intellect cooperate in some peculiar, ineffable manner. There seems to be a literal transformation of the sensible experience when the Form "appears." We are still seeing the same sensible thing, but we are now seeing a new dimension of it. What I am saying is that if I come to awareness of "Catness" looking at my cat, it seems right to say that the literal "appearance" of the cat doesn't change—but, in another sense, the appearance does change. I am now seeing the atemporal aspect of the cat (its nature, its Catness) through it, and the sensible experience does feel as if it has been transformed. It is important to note that the verb *eidenai* (to know), which is related to *eidos*, originally meant "to see" or to "catch a glimpse of."

I think this is why Parmenides seems to be forcing Socrates, in the latter part of the dialogue, to go beyond a conception of Forms as things "separate" from sensibles, and toward the idea that the sensible *just is* the Form considered in its unchanging aspect.[40] In earlier dialogues, sensibles are treated as "images" or "likenesses" of the Forms. This is metaphorical, and not meant to be taken literally. Seeing a painting of someone I have seen in person is very different from seeing a painting of someone I have never laid eyes on. In the former case, there is an additional dimension to the experience. I see the real person in, or through the painting. In the same way, for Plato, we see the true nature of something (e.g., Catness) shining through individual things (e.g., cats).

Now, the same idea seems to be conveyed, in a more sophisticated form, in the latter part of the *Parmenides*, in the peculiar series of "deductions" presented there. Sensibles are said to be "appearances" of Forms. The Greek translated as "appearances" is *phainomena*, which does not have the sense of "mere semblance"

"THE 'DIVINITY' OF THE CAT ... IS SOMETHING
THAT TRANSCENDS THIS PARTICULAR CAT."
JAN TOOROP, "THE SPHINX."

or "seeming" that our word "appearance" usually has. In *Being and Time*, Heidegger attempts to recover the originary Greek sense of *phainomenon* which survives in our language, of course, as "phenomenon." Heidegger writes that *phainomenon* means "that which shows itself, the manifest ... [T]hat which shows itself in itself, the manifest. Accordingly, the *phainomena* or 'phenomena' are the totality of what lies in the light of day or can be brought to the light—what the Greeks sometimes identified simply with *ta onta* (beings)."[41] Heidegger goes on to distinguish "phenomenon" from "semblance." By semblance he means something like "image." A semblance could be an illusion, a hallucination, or a representation, such as a painting. None of these are phenomena, in the original Greek sense. A phenomenon is not an image of something (least of all a misleading "semblance"), it is the something showing itself. Even our word "appearance" can mean this.

If someone tells me that the Queen "made an appearance" in Scotland, I don't take that to mean that somebody saw a picture of her there. I take it to mean that she showed up there herself.[42]

Now, I think it can readily be seen that there is a parallel between how I have described the experience of the gods, and how Plato describes the experience of the Forms. Both the gods and Forms are phenomena: they themselves shine forth from the things in our experience. When Catness shines forth from the cat, in a way it is as if something else shines forth from the cat, and in a way it is not. Clearly, in seeing the Catness of the cat we have, in a certain sense, "seen beyond" this particular cat, but in another way we have seen what is fundamental about this cat.[43] Both are correct, and they illustrate the dual aspect of Forms as simultaneously transcendent and immanent. Seeing the divinity in the cat, as I have described the experience, is practically identical to this. In an attitude of wonder, struck by the fact that beings such as cats exist at all, a hitherto concealed aspect of the cat shows up for us: the miraculous being of the cat. And simultaneously, we have the sense of this wonder as having emerged from an equally miraculous source, what I have called the *archē*. The "divinity" of the cat, as I said earlier, both is the cat itself, and is something that transcends this particular cat.

In the *Republic*'s famous "allegory of the cave," the ascent from ignorance to wisdom is likened to the ascent out of a cave and into the sunlight, in which we find the true natures of things "illuminated" (cf. 516a–b). In the *Parmenides*, the young Socrates uses a simile to explain the relation of sensibles to their Form. The Form, he says, is "like one and the same day. That is in many places at the same time and is none the less not separate from itself. If it's like that, each of the forms might be, at the same time, one and the same in all" (131b).[44]

Despite the similarities, there is, in fact, a huge difference between awareness of divinity and awareness of Plato's Forms. What has been banished from Plato's account is wonder. What has been banished is mystery. The divinity of the cat that shines in it is no longer divinity, it is merely the "intelligible nature" of the thing. The sense in which awareness of the *eidos*, the "look" of the thing straddles the sensible and the intellectual, the sense in which awareness of the *eidos* transforms the actual sensuous experience of the thing, has been, for the most part, lost. To be sure, this *eidos* is still "supernatural," it is "above" nature, and outside space and time. But it is treated as a pattern or *paradeigma* (see *Parmenides*, 132d) and it is mathematicized. Under the influence of Pythagoreanism, Plato developed a complex secret teaching which is only hinted at in the dialogues, involving a mathematical conception of reality, flowing from two ultimate "principles," the "One" and the "Indefinite Dyad."[45] It was the ongoing project of Plato and his students to understand the Forms in terms of this mathematical system. The Forms may be "mysterious" in being quite unlike mundane, sensible objects, but they stand in relation to those things as a blueprint stands in relation to a house, and there is nothing inherently mysterious (let alone religious) about that.[46]

My thesis is that Plato is taking up the experience of the divine, and the concept of divinity, and recasting them in a philosophical, even "scientific" form. Religious or mystical experience becomes philosophical or scientific "insight," and the gods become "Forms" or patterns in nature. Plato develops this approach using the mathematical philosophy of the Pythagoreans, while retaining certain "mystical" aspects of Pythagoreanism (especially the doctrine of reincarnation; see the *Phaedo*). Plato makes it possible for a man to be religious, and to take great care with his soul, while disbelieving in "gods."[47] Christianity, as Nietzsche said, may have been Platonism for the people, but Platonism itself was polytheism for atheists. And even Plato's doctrine of reincarnation in the *Phaedo* is defended on pragmatic grounds (see *Phaedo*, 114d–e). Platonism is mysticism without mystery.[48]

Plato is open to metaphorical descriptions of the Being of things, but anything like the sort of religious iconography discussed earlier is rejected entirely. Such imagery, as I have said, helps one to fix in mind and contemplate the mystery and wonder of beings. But Plato's purpose is understanding: i.e., the analysis of beings. Thus, in spite of his recognition of the supernatural status of the Being of beings, his Forms are "mundanizations" of being. With Aristotle, the mundanization is pushed even further. Aristotle declares that all philosophy "begins in wonder," but that philosophy has as its task the removal or cancellation of wonder through scientific explanation. He takes over the doctrine of Forms but alters it, and opposes Form to "matter" (an opposition Plato does not really employ). All reality is conceived by Aristotle on the model of human artifacts: a combination of some stuff, and a plan or pattern.

Now, it might be objected that I have been unfair to Plato in claiming that he wants to take the supernatural that shines through things and denude it of wonder and mystery. After all, doesn't Plato very clearly suggest (most famously in the *Republic*) that we can never know the Forms as they are in themselves, that they always transcend our powers to grasp them?[49] This is true, but this doctrine is not presented as an occasion for wonder, or as bringing us back around to religion, but as a regulative ideal à la Kant's Ideas of Reason. While total or pure knowledge of the forms is impossible, the goal of total knowledge is one which we approach asymptotically. Knowing the Forms thus becomes an infinite task, and motivates our (scientific) inquiries into the nature of things.

7. Conclusion

A significant problem remains. How exactly do we recapture the ability to make the divine manifest, to invoke the gods? To go back to the beginning, it seems like our ancestors did this effortlessly, but that in us the power has atrophied. Why this is the case is the main focus of "Knowing the Gods." But what can we do about our situation?

In "Knowing the Gods," I made some concrete suggestions, which essentially amounted to saying "get back to nature, get rid of all your gadgets, and don't trust modern science." Some readers found this unsatisfying—and so, I might add, did the author. It's not much, but it seemed to me to be, unquestionably, a good way to start. (One reader accused me of hypocrisy, since I live in an apartment and write articles on a computer! To this, I plead *nolo contendere*). I stand by these suggestions, and eventually I do intend to follow them myself. However, I think I can now offer more.

The reader may have noticed that the experience of the divine described herein attributes to ancient man something very much like a child's capacity for wonder. This is nothing new, but in the past the "childlike wonder" of ancient man was held to be a mark of his "primitive" nature. It is impossible, however, to recover the capacity to respond to the divinity of the world without reawakening this capacity for wonder.

In discussing this subject, I am reminded of three texts. I will surprise my readers first by quoting the New Testament (Matthew 18:3): "Verily, I say unto you, if you should not turn and become as little children, you may not enter the kingdom of heaven." The second text could well be regarded by some as the antithesis of the first: it comes from Nietzsche's *Thus Spake Zarathustra*. In "On the Three Metamorphoses," Zarathustra tells us "how the spirit becomes a camel; and the camel, a lion; and the lion, finally, a child."[50] As camel, the spirit is a beast of burden, loaded down with "thou shalts." "In the loneliest desert" (a place of spiritual transformation, as Moses, Jesus, and Mohammed knew) the spirit throws off the "thou shalts" and becomes a lion. But the lion is purely reactive: he smashes the thou shalts and lives a life in rebellion against them. He cannot create new values. This must be left to the third metamorphosis, the child. "The child is innocence and forgetting, a new beginning, a game, a self-propelled wheel, a first movement, a sacred 'Yes.'"[51]

The third text is seldom, if ever, quoted. It comes from a marvelous letter D. H. Lawrence wrote to Bertrand Russell from Cornwall on 19 February 1916. Lawrence writes:

> One must be an outlaw these days, not a teacher or preacher. One must retire out of the herd & then fire bombs into it … Do cut it—cut your will and leave your old self behind. Even your mathematics are only dead truth: and no matter how fine you grind the dead meat, you'll not bring it to life again. Do stop working & writing altogether and become a creature instead of a mechanical instrument. Do clear out of the whole social ship. Do for your very pride's sake become a mere nothing, a mole, a creature that feels its way & doesn't think. Do for heavens sake be a baby, & not a savant any more. Don't do anything any more—but for heavens sake begin to be—start at the very beginning and be a perfect baby: in the name of courage.[52]

Someone might say that it's easy for a child to experience wonder, since the world is all new to him. But once one gets used to the world, it's natural for wonder to cease, and even for cynicism and weariness to set in. We must reject this. The child's wonder ceases not just because things become familiar to him, but because the adults around him gleefully trample on his wonder, "explaining" everything reductively in the form of "Oh, X? Why, you silly boy, that's only Y" (see my earlier comments on science and pornography).

The recovery of wonder involves a change in the subject. No change in the object is required. There are essentially two "paths" one may follow in seeking change, and these correspond to the old Taoist distinction between "internal" and "external" alchemy (or *neidan* and *waidan*, respectively—I hasten to add that the two paths are not mutually exclusive and can, and should, blend).

"ONE MUST BE AN OUTLAW THESE DAYS."
–D. H. LAWRENCE

External alchemy, for the Taoists, involved the use of specially prepared elixirs designed to produce some transformation in the subject (e.g., making him immortal). What we need is an elixir that would alter our awareness of the world and make everything, including what had seemed thoroughly mundane, new and wonderful. Such an elixir would make the profane sacred. I am referring, of course, to psychedelic drugs, which are a useful adjunct to spiritual reawakening, if used wisely and with the utmost seriousness. I use the phrase "spiritual reawakening" because what must always be kept in mind is that we are not attempting to acquire some new ability, but to reawaken an ability that has been slumbering.

The following is an interesting analogy, which may help us to understand our situation better, and what is required of us. In the 1880s and 1890s the railroad was being laid from coast to coast, across the great plains of America. Two obstacles stood in the way: the buffalo, and the Indians who hunted them. By dispatching men to slaughter the buffalo, the government and industry were killing two birds with one stone. With the buffalo depleted, the plains Indians were deprived of their major food source, and pressured into submitting to life on government reservations. But the loss of the buffalo meant much more to the Indians than the loss of their food source. The buffalo was the central figure in their religion. Their mythology was based upon the relation of men to the buffalo, who (it was believed) willingly gave themselves to be hunted and eaten. The devastating result of the mass buffalo slaughter, therefore, was the destruction of the religion of the plains Indians within a few short years. The response to this disaster, however, quickly came in the form of small, edible buttons which made their way up from Mexico and into the hands of the Indians. The plains Indians began taking peyote. With great solemnity and ritual, they would gather in lodges and take the peyote, looking within themselves for new myths to fill the void left by the White man's destruction of the buffalo cult. Ironically, this is much the same situation the White man finds himself in today.[53] And taking peyote buttons (or some such) may be part of the answer for us as well.

Psychedelic drugs awaken wonder immediately and dramatically. They do not produce "hallucinations"; they open a channel through which we may view the world in an entirely new way. But to approach such drug experiences casually is a sacrilege and may backfire on the user. Approached properly, the drugs themselves may produce immediate and lasting personal transformation (as in the cases of alcoholics who were spontaneously, and completely cured, after one dose of LSD). However, I think that they are largely valueless unless one can retain what one has learned on the "trip," and translate that into a new way of looking at things and, in general, being in everyday life.

As to that everyday life—by which I essentially mean the long gaps between psychedelic experiences—this is when "internal alchemy" takes place. Internal alchemy embraces all activities the self engages in (without the benefit of elixirs) which have as their end the transformation of consciousness. Reading this article is an act of internal alchemy for you, just as writing it was for me. Self-study, where enlightenment is the goal, is internal alchemy. Yoga, with, again, the transformation of consciousness in mind, is internal alchemy. Initiatic paths, such as that offered by the Rune-Gild and other organizations, are a form of internal alchemy. Sitting *za-zen* is internal alchemy.

The problem here is selecting a particular form of internal alchemy, since one cannot do everything. A first step is to actually ask the questions I gave earlier, as attempts to articulate the pre-reflective attitude of our ancestors: why are there beings at all, rather than nothing? and, why should this particular thing be, and be the way that it is? In other words, the first step is to begin to experience wonder in life.

But let me say something briefly about meditation and yogic practices. The description I have given of religious experience bears a great deal in common with descriptions of the Zen experience of *satori*. *Satori* is commonly described as an experience of "awakening," or "enlightenment." Describing it is tricky, as no description can actually convey what it is like to experience *satori*, but it seems to involve at least two components. The first is an intuition that what is is right. When one experiences *satori*, one feels that everything, just as it is now, is fundamentally right, and that it must be the way it is. Second, time and space seem to be annulled. The experience happens in what is felt to be a kind of "eternal now." And the sense of separation between oneself and the object is also removed. This is not because (as is often stated) one feels that the self and the object are the same. Rather, it is because in the experience of *satori*, the ego drops out, and one is completely overtaken by the experience of the other. But, again, it is a very special experience of what is "other." It is the other experienced in a timeless mode, in which we acquiesce to it, surrender ourselves to it, and affirm it unconditionally.

Given the close relationship between *satori* and my account of the experience of the gods, it stands to reason that the entire Eastern tradition of practices dedicated to effecting *satori*, nirvana, or what have you, ought to be of great interest to us. This does not exactly narrow things down, however, for the East provides us with as many ways to Enlightenment as there are types of individual persons. To each, there is his own yoga. What all these methods have in common, however, is that they are ways to overcome a profane attitude toward things. The best of them teach us to recognize the sacred in the profane, and thus to transform the world before our eyes.

Notes:

1. I am assuming that the readers of *TYR* do not need me to convince them of the naïveté of the nineteenth-century view that myths are primitive attempts at scientific explanation. Lawrence J. Hatab handles this quite well: "Explanation answers the question why or how something is by discovering a prior cause, tracing the cause of a thing back to (another) profane thing. Myths, on the other hand, should be seen to disclose *that* something is, the first meaningful form a world takes, the background of which is hidden. Myth is therefore not explanation but presentation of the arrival/withdrawal of existential meaning. The shift from mythical disclosure to rational and scientific thinking cannot be seen as a correction of myth because it was a shift to a new intention—the reduction of beings to the explanatory capacities of the human mind or verifiable natural causes. To see myth as an error (a wrong explanation) is an anachronistic misunderstanding of the function of myth." See Lawrence J. Hatab, *Myth and Philosophy: A Contest of Truths* (La Salle, Ill.: Open Court, 1990), p. 23. See also (especially) p. 26. Later in the same work, Hatab writes of Hesiod's *Theogony*, noting that it is not, properly speaking, a story of "creation." The first gods "simply appear; we are not told from where" (p. 64).

2. Martin Heidegger, *Introduction to Metaphysics*, trans. Gregory Fried and Richard Polt (New Haven: Yale, 2000), p. 47.

3. See Alan W. Watts, *Nature, Man and Woman* (New York: Vintage, 1970), p. 10.

4. D. H. Lawrence, *Studies in Classic American Literature* (New York: Penguin, 1991), p. 22. Italics in original.

5. Trans. Richard D. McKirahan, in *A Presocratics Reader*, ed. Patricia Curd (Indianapolis: Hackett, 1996), p. 40; fragment 104.

6. Which is essentially why the way of the warrior is also a path to wisdom.

7. I should point out that although I owe a great deal to Heidegger, I am not a Heideggerean, nor is this an essay in Heideggerean philosophy. In particular, I must warn the reader that my use of the terms "being," "beings," and "existence" does not strictly accord with Heidegger's use.

8. Hatab says the following: "The path of philosophy turns away from the sacred imagery of myth toward empirical and conceptual models of thought. This entails a turn from the existential

lived world toward abstract representations of the world. Now the world is measured according to principles of unity, universality, and constancy, and the mind aims for empirical and conceptual foundations which permit a kind of certainty. Thus disclosure of the world moves from a process of unconcealment toward a kind of foundationalism, where thought is reduced to a knowable, fixed form and structure." Hatab, p. 13.

9. Most of what qualifies as "pornography" constitutes a concerted effort to demystify sex and to deny or destroy its wonder. The pervasive irony and irreverence of pornography and its packaging (which is not in the least "sexy") are an attempt to, in effect, "laugh off" the awesome mystery that is sex, and make it nonthreatening to modern men, whose goal is the destruction of mystery, and the achievement of complete control and knowledge of reality. What is perceived by feminists as the "misogyny" of porn also has its root in this: woman, as the source of the mystery, is brutalized and mocked precisely in order to deny her mystery. Much of what counts as "science," qualifies as pornography. A scientist who tells young people "It's silly to think there's anything mysterious about lightning: it's just atmospheric electrical discharge," is no less a pornographer than a Larry Flynt, who tells the same young people "It's silly to think there's anything mysterious about the vagina: it's just a cunt."

10. I have borrowed the term "region" from the phenomenology of Husserl, but my idea of a region has little in common with Husserl's. Actually, the term Husserl uses is "regional essences." These represent fundamental divisions in reality itself. Their fundamentality is demonstrated by the fact that the differences between them are qualitative, as opposed to quantitative (i.e., they differ in kind, rather than in degree). Two vegetables—a lettuce and a cucumber, let us say—do not differ in kind, and thus they belong to the same "region." But a dog and a cucumber are not just very different, they are fundamentally different in kind. As are a cucumber and a quartz crystal. Thus, we can easily identify three regions corresponding to a traditional, commonsensical division: animal, vegetable, and mineral. My regions are also "divisions" within reality, but my concept of a region is more open-ended, as will shortly become apparent.

11. Of course, the materials we create artifacts out of are, ultimately, natural. But when we contemplate an artifact as artifact, this is not the dimension of their being that is given to us.

12. However, it is the case that, traditionally, there are gods of human activities, e.g., of human crafts. One need only think of the various divinities associated with the smith and with metalworking, such as the Irish Goibniu, Welsh Gofann, Latin Vulcan, and Greek Hephaistos. In Indian mythology we encounter Tvástr and Visvakaram (the "all accomplishing"). Very often such divinities not only play a role in creation, but are the teachers of skill to mankind. Probably the best example of such a figure would be the Greek Hermes. The "source" of these deities seems thus to be, at least in part, intuition of the marvelous character of the crafts by which we transform nature. They are thought to require a transhuman origin in order to be explicable.

13. However, as I suggested earlier, in mentioning Jung, there may be certain innate structures that determine, to some degree, the manner in which we personify or depict the gods. N.B.: In actual fact we can "notice" sound waves without hearing them. Their vibrations can be felt indistinctly by the tactile sense. If there is something like a "sense" through which we become aware of the divine, might the presence of the divine also be registered by other senses, though indistinctly? I think this is a possibility and, again, the tactile sense seems to be involved. I am thinking of such phenomena as feeling one's flesh "crawl," or feeling the hair stand up on the back of the head. Such things happen when individuals have a brush with the "uncanny," and they often happen even in the absence of any cognitive awareness of supernatural presence.

14. Cf. Immanuel Kant, *Critique of Pure Reason*, trans. Werner S. Pluhar (Indianapolis: Hackett, 1996), p. 28 (Bxxvi–Bxxvii). My appeal to Kant is not intended to imply that he would have been sympathetic to my phenomenology of the gods. He would most certainly not have been. Kant divides human knowing into sensibility (perception) and understanding (thought), and claims that "phenomena" are objects as perceived by the five senses. However, the experience of the divine described here seems to belong neither to sensibility nor to the understanding, but, in a way, to straddle the two. Thus, my "phenomenal appearances" of the gods should not be understood in the Kantian sense of sensory perceptions (what Kant calls *Anschauungen*).

15. The work by Usener that Cassirer is principally relying on is *Götternamen: Versuch einer Lehre von der religiösen Begriffsbildung* (Bonn, 1896).

16. Ernst Cassirer, *Language and Myth*, trans. Susanne K. Langer (New York: Dover Books, 1953), pp. 17–18.

17. Ibid., p. 18.

18. Usener, p. 290f. Quoted in Cassirer, p. 18. The translation is presumably Langer's. Note the very problematic language here: "Whatever comes to us suddenly like a sending from heaven ... seems to the religious consciousness like a *divine being*" (my italics). My contention is that whatever came to man in this way was, for him, a divine being, a sending from heaven. Usener is speaking as if he thinks man operates with a determinate idea of divine being, and regards certain objects as divine because they resemble it.

19. Cassirer, p. 19.

20. Cassirer, p. 21.

21. It was addressed, to some extent, in "Knowing the Gods" in *TYR*, vol. 1.

22. *Encyclopedia of Indo-European Culture*, ed. J. P. Mallory and D. Q. Adams (London and Chicago: Fitzroy-Dearborn, 1997), p. 230.

23. A further oddity is that the Aztec word for god was Teo. These linguistic similarities are treated by most reputable scholars as pure coincidence, since Aztec and Chinese belong to language groups which developed quite independently of Indo-European. Nevertheless, the coincidence is striking.

24. Mircea Eliade, *A History of Religious Ideas*, vol. II, trans. Willard R. Trask, (Chicago: University of Chicago Press, 1982), p. 7.

25. Edred Thorsson, "The Holy," *Rûna*, vol. I, no. 2, Yule, 1982. Reprinted in *Green Rûna* (Smithville, Texas: Rûna-Raven, 1996), pp. 41–45. All references are to the anthologized text.

26. Also, Old Norse *vîgja*, "to consecrate," and Old English *wicca*, "witch."

27. Thorsson, 41. Thorsson goes on to say that this means it is "completely other," and draws on Rudolf Otto's discussion of the *mysterium tremendum* as that which is totally other from mundane or everyday human existence. I'm not sure I can go along with this identification, however, if I have adequately understood Thorsson's point. Otto's analysis of religious experience tends to be heavily prejudiced in favor of Judeo-Christian experience, in which the divine is indeed something "wholly other" in the sense of absolutely transcendent of the world.

28. *Encyclopedia of Indo-European Culture*, p. 25. This one should be especially exciting to Heideggereans.

29. Thorsson, p. 42.

30. How objects associated with divinities take on this mana-like property is not something I have dealt with here. My analysis has been concerned solely with how the divine is "noticed" in the world to begin with. I hesitate to use the term "mana" because of its association with thoroughly secular and reductive anthropological theory, but I know of no better term.

31. The Latin *profanum* means literally "before the sanctuary." It designated the ordinary ground outside the enclosure of a sacred place. Hatab writes, "To the mythical mind ... the profane is that which is meaningless, the sacred is that which is meaningful." Hatab, p. 23.

32. Thorsson, p. 42.

33. Ibid., p. 43.

34. Ibid.

35. From the Proto-Indo-European root **sakros* (e.g., "sacred") comes Tocharian A *sākär* meaning "blissful, happy, auspicious." Tocharian B *sākre* means "blissful, happy, blessed, auspicious."

36. And, I might add, does today's rather trite "hi!" derive from hail/heil?

37. The reason *eidos* is translated Form rather than the more natural "Idea" is simple. "Idea" suggests something subjective, whereas Plato's Forms are objective entities existing in a separate, non-spatio-temporal dimension.

38. Plato, *Symposium*, trans. Alexander Nehemas and Paul Woodruff, in *Plato: Complete Works*, ed. John M. Cooper (Indianapolis: Hackett, 1997), p. 493.

39. Plato, *Parmenides*, trans. Mary Louise Gill and Paul Ryan, in Ibid., p. 366.

40. See Mitchell H. Miller's *Plato's Parmenides: The Conversion of the Soul* (Penn: Pennsylvania University, 1991) in which this thesis is developed masterfully.

41. Martin Heidegger, *Being and Time*, trans. John Macquarrie and Edward Robinson (New York: Harper and Row, 1961), p. 51.

42. The very recent usage of "phenomenon" to mean "big deal" (as in "the hula hoop phenomenon") obviously has little to do with the meaning I am discussing here.

43. There are basically four ways in which Plato describes the

relation of Forms and sensibles: (a) *mimēsis* or imitation (sensibles are "imitations" of Forms), (b) *methexis* or "participation" (sensibles "partake of" Forms), (c) *koinōnia* or community, and (d) *parousia* or presence. A and B represent rather naïve, literal-minded construals of the relation which prove inadequate on analysis (the *Parmenides* is devoted, in part, to demonstrating this). But *koinōnia* and *parousia* are far more interesting, and defensible. *Koinōnia* means that the sensible "communes with" or is "in communion with" the Form. *Parousia* indicates that we encounter the Form as "present in" the sensible; or, in phenomenological jargon, the Form "presences itself" in the sensible if the sensible is regarded in a certain way.

44. Plato, *Parmenides*, p. 365.

45. The primary testimonies to this come from Aristotle. See *Physics* (209b13-6) and *Metaphysics* (I.6). There are also a number of recent books by Plato scholars dealing with this topic. See Hans Joachim Kramer, *Plato and the Foundations of Metaphysics*, trans. John R. Catan (Albany: State University of New York, 1990); and Giovanni Reale, *Toward a New Interpretation of Plato*, trans. John R. Catan (Washington, D.C.: Catholic University of America, 1997).

46. The "divine figure" of the Demiurge in the *Timaeus*, who creates the world according to the eternal Forms, was recognized even by the members of Plato's Academy as merely a poetic device.

47. While also, it must be added, seeming religious enough to avoid the fate of Socrates. Socrates was charged with two crimes: corrupting the youth, and not worshipping the gods of the city.

48. Nevertheless, it is not without myth, as any student of the dialogues knows. Plato very often interrupts the discussion in a dialogue to have Socrates, or some other character, present a mythos. But Plato's myths all fit the nineteenth-century conception of what a myth was: i.e., they are all "likely accounts" which serve an explanatory function. They are essentially substitutes for scientific explanation. This is not to say that they do not very often convey profound truths, but Plato employs myth when no "rational" answer is available.

49. Actually, Socrates in the *Republic* explicitly states that Forms are knowable. But this is an example of Socratic irony. At 516b he has his escapee from the cave stare directly at the Sun, but this is impossible for any length of time without blindness result-

ing. The implication is that the Form of the Good (symbolized by the Sun), is also not knowable directly or fully. Presumably, this applies to other Forms, as is suggested by some of the other dialogues.

50. Friedrich Nietzsche, *Thus Spake Zarathustra*, trans. Walter Kaufmann (New York: Penguin, 1978), p. 25.

51. Ibid., p. 27.

52. *The Selected Letters of D. H. Lawrence*, ed. Diana Trilling (New York: Farrar, Straus and Cudahy, 1958), p. 129.

53. I owe this analogy to Joseph Campbell, who presented it in a public lecture in the early 1970s. To my knowledge, the lecture has only been released as an audiocassette: "Confrontation of East and West in Religion" (Joseph Campbell Foundation, 1996).

Thoughts on God

Alain de Benoist

1.

"*Dieu*" (God) is a word. In French this word is composed of four letters—three vowels and a consonant: d-i-e-u. It has a feminine form *(déesse)* and a plural *(dieux)*. In the Indo-European language system this word designates superior beings worshiped by man. The most common designation, which is also the oldest, both in form and content, is **deiwos* which means "he of the diurnal sky" and, by extension, "the luminous, shining being." This name goes back to the "cosmic religion" stage of the Indo-Europeans. It can be found in the Sanskrit *dyâus*, the Hittite *sius*, the Greek adjective *díos*, the Lithuanian *dievas*, and the names of Zeus and Jupiter (Iuppiter), among others. Other names are more recent, like the Slavic **bogu*, the result of a borrowing from the Iranian, or the Germanic **guda* (cf. German *Gott*, English "God," Danish *Gud*). This last term, whose neutral gender is incompatible with personal deities, is an adjective that is probably derived from the verb **gheu* "to pour," with a possible meaning of "libation." The Greek *theos* is another indirect designation, possibly similar to "destiny."

The gods in the Indo-European universe are simultaneously forces, powers, and exemplary figures. None of them is individually meaningful; their meaning comes from the relations they share with each other. It is not a question of believing in their existence but of awakening to their presence. They do not dispense truths but conviction. They test others but are not themselves subject to being tested for proof. They are not radically different from men, but this does not make men gods. They attest to the solidarity of all that exists on every level and in every dimension of reality, but they do not combine with the world either. They are not the "supreme value" but provide the basis for the concept of value to have meaning.

The Bible totally disregards the existence of a "god." It recognizes a supreme being, El, to whom three names are attributed: Eloha or Elohim ('LHYM), Adonai, and IHVH (Jehovah) sometimes abbreviated as Jah, or Jahwa. The meaning of El, which belongs to the common vocabulary of the Semitic peoples, remains a hotly debated subject. Elohim, a plural, is the form most often used in the Torah. Most often it names the Supreme Being in his manifestations and characterizes him as the creator of the world. Adonai is the plural of Adon meaning "master." The Septuagint translated it with the word Kyrios meaning "Lord." IHVH is a sacred expression, the unpronounceable Tetragrammaton that corresponds to the Elohim of the ancestors of Israel (Exodus 3; 13–15). It contains all the active modal forms of the verb "to be" (HYH).[1] Reverential substitutes such as Yahweh or Jehovah represent attempts at modern reconstructions.

The supreme being mentioned in the Bible is eminently different from the gods of the Indo-European universe. He is a moral "God," a creator "God," a God who reveals his presence historically and thus his relationship to the world implies a definite beginning and end to this world. Christian theology conventionally defines him as an individual being of infinite perfection, who has created everything that exists out of nothing (without becoming one with his creation) and who calls on man "to realize his salvation" through obeying his "commandments"—all characteristics that are perfectly foreign to the gods of paganism.

In paganism, gods are not confused with Being. They are not the cause of all states of being. In the same spirit, Heidegger said in 1951:

> Being and God are not identical, and I would never try to conceive the essence of God by the means of Being [...] I believe that Being can never ever be conceptualized as the root and essence of God, but that experience of God and his manifest state, such that men can perceive it, flashes within the dimension of Being, which in no way means that Being may take on the sense of a possible predicate for God.[2]

Heidegger implies by this that it is through Being that the god may arrive, but he does not come as Being's last word. Christian theology, to the contrary, identifies Being with the Creator God, making him the primary and unconditional foundation, the absolute and infinite cause of every state of being.[3] In doing so, Christianity has condemned itself to be incapable of extending out over the ontological horizon summoned by the mystery of Being.

Strictly speaking, Indo-European languages do not have any

real term for designating the supreme being of biblical monotheism. The attribution to the latter of the word "God," embellished with a capital letter, and more importantly stripped of its feminine and plural aspects, is a perfectly arbitrary convention. Instances where it has become customary to read "Jehovah your God" (Deut; 18, 15) should really read, in accordance with the Hebrew text, "Jehovah, Adonai, your Elohim." Such a translation empties the word "god" *(dieu)* of its original meaning in order to bestow another meaning upon it. It creates the illusion that all religions have a "God," and only differ in the name they give him, concealing with the same stroke the fact that entirely different realities are being designated under the same name. Anyone who wishes to speak of "God" is unable to do away with this ambiguity.

2.

Just as I do not for an instant believe that "God" is a term whose equivalent is to be found in every religion, I do not believe that every belief system is a "religion," and even less that any "transcendental unity" connects them all together, allowing them to be viewed as mutually compatible, around one essentially common core, whose identification will provide a unifying, intelligible structure for all beliefs. However, there is a particularly widespread tendency today to consider "religions" as systems that are restricted to approaching the same fundamental reality by different paths. Every "encyclopedia of religion" available on the market today is more or less based on this error of perspective, which consists of setting up an artificial universal category ("religion"), then listing and describing a certain number of beliefs, rules, and examples of group behavior as so many illustrations of this category.

The division of "religions" into polytheism, monotheism, animism, fetishism, and so forth, is no less conventional. The essential feature of Christianity is not monotheism, but the ideology of the schism (between Being and the world, between the world and man, between immanence and transcendence, the soul and the body, the temporal and the spiritual, being and becoming, etc.), and the fact that the existence of God is contrived as inseparable from a universal problematic of salvation. Another categorization could furthermore consist of distinguishing between "native" religions (like paganism) and universalistic religions (like Christianity or Islam), as irreducible to each other. This would permit an explanation for the birth of Christianity within Judaism, from a starting point of Pauline preaching or the Baptist milieu.

Christianity has accustomed us to thinking that there is no religion without its savior God, and that morality can find no true foundation except in the belief in this God. (Dostoevsky has Karamazov say: "If God does not exist, then everything is permitted.") Both these assertions are equally erroneous. Buddhism is largely concerned with liberation from the suffering engendered by desires and passions ("illusion"), but is fundamentally indifferent to the question of God. The law of karma has nothing in common with the judgment of a deity who keeps watch over moral behavior. The gods *(kami)* of Shintoism are akin to spirits or forces whose favor is worth gaining, but who do not play any role in creation or salvation at all. The faithful of Confucius consider respect for ancestors as sacred, without feeling any need to speculate on a divine world. The pillars of their belief are only the love of others *(ren)* and virtue *(de)*. Similarly, Jainism recognizes no deity who would have created the universe or who plays any role in the salvation of men. Taoism posits the Tao as an eternal regulating principle of the universe, which does not bear the slightest resemblance to the Christian God.

Even in the Abrahamic religions, it is to my mind a mistake to believe that the Jews, Christians, and Muslims are professing three different concepts of the same "God." The truth is that they did not honor the same God at all. Historically speaking, Christianity is a religion of governance, Islam a religion of conquest, and Judaism a religion of survival. Christianity additionally provides the distinction of basing itself on the postulate of the existence of a man (Jesus) about whom we know nothing. (The historical value of the canonical Gospels is non-existent; their literary value even more so, while their spiritual value is mediocre.) With respect to Protestantism, which is a religion of conscience, Catholicism replaces the scriptural experience with the sacramental. It thereby implies the institution, and thus exteriority—in this sense it is fundamentally Mediterranean. As for Judaism, where universalism expands and extends the distinctive element, and not the reverse, it is certainly not a religion in the sense that Christians give this word.[4] Disregarding the orthodoxy that is so important in Christianity, Judaism is primarily an orthopraxy, based on the remembrance and observation of *mitsvoth*, directed towards separation and selection, and by that towards survival. To be Jewish is to be an integral part of the "holy people" (*goy quadoch*) and the "kingdom of priests" (*mamlé'het kohanim*). Membership counts more than belief here. In Christianity one can be a believer without practicing, while in Judaism one can practice the faith without being a "believer." Judaism refuses, moreover, to use emotion (still too closely connected to nature) as its foundation, but looks primarily to reason. It attaches the highest price to life and challenges any connection between worship and death, which is why it rejects martyrdom or the idea that the purpose of belief is to learn how to die, and does not accept in any fashion that the "kingdom of heaven" will only arise when humanity has been extinguished. It does not place salvation in the other world, but seeks to "repair" this one (*tikkun olam*). Given these assumptions, the "Judeo-Christian dialogue" is doomed to never lead anywhere.

If the different beliefs are not substantially branches growing out of the same trunk, the very word "religion" becomes problematic. Etymological explanations can only shed light on a word's meaning with respect to a given language system. They tell us nothing of the exact meaning of the terms with which we think we can translate this word into other systems. One may certainly still define "religion" through reference to "transcendence," the "supernatural," "ultimate concerns," the distinction between the "sacred" and the "profane," and so forth, but these expressions in no way allow any comprehension of what someone really understands "religion" to mean. To declare that all religions imply belief in a transcendent reality as opposed to empirical daily life, teaches us nothing more about this reality. External observation may allow us to define religious forms but certainly not to understand what this "religion" is to the individual who does not exactly consider it as a belief, but as that which gives direction to his life.

The difficulty is amplified by our ignorance with regard to precise knowledge of the origin of the "religious act." Nineteenth-century researchers (Müller, Tylor, Frazer, Spencer, Durkheim, etc.) tried to do so without great success. The theories claiming to explain the "purpose" of a belief system or how the religious act "operates" are only shoving the problem aside. The predisposition to believe in a reality that exceeds the human condition or that transcends immediate existence, a predisposition still open to debate, would seem to make man, henceforth defined as *homo religiosus*, a "naturally religious" being. The fact is that no one knows of a period in history when man did not express himself "religiously"—even if there have always been, if not unbelievers, at least skeptics and the indifferent. This does not mean that "religion" is a meaningful category in itself, but that the predisposition to believe may also possess a bio-anthropological dimension.

Belief systems may well cover similar forms, which reflect what the human species has in common anthropologically. They influence each other mutually, give birth to new systems or diverse syncretisms. But their content nonetheless remains irremediably different. Christianity appropriated numerous pagan practices, which did alter its outside appearance to some extent, but its kerygmatic core remains nevertheless irreducible to paganism. A current error is the belief that a belief system can be isolated from its anthropo-social suppositions. Removed from its cultural matrix, "religion" becomes an abstract set of symbols and myths, teachings, and rituals that no longer have any connection with what it means to those who live it in their concrete existence. It is the very principle of conversion. The underlying idea is that one can adhere (or force others to adhere) to any belief without having to inhabit it within its own compost. In reality, "religion" is inseparable from a general way of living and way of looking at the world, specific to each of these cultures. The diversity of "religions" echoes the diversity of peoples.

3.

Atheism is an even greater absurdity than theism: where the former seeks to demonstrate an absolute existence, the latter intends to prove an absolute non-existence, whereas, strictly speaking, atheists can only say why the alleged proofs for God's existence are not convincing. Fichte has already shown that one cannot use existential propositions to speak of God. To the contrary, Christian theology conceives God in terms of a substance of which certain predicates can be affirmed (his bounty, his omnipotence, his mercy, etc.). Thus God inevitably becomes a finite object, in contradiction to his definition. The Christian God is *Something Completely Different*, about which, because he is *Something Completely Different*, nothing can be said. To claim to speak of God while presenting him as radically different from all his creatures is a necessarily futile endeavor. John Scotus Eriugena had a more correct view when he went so far as to apply the word

"Nothing" to God. From this point of view, the unknown (and unknowable) God of apophatic theology at least has the merit of consistency. A "demonstrable" God, meaning one dependent upon human reason, would in fact no longer be in any way divine. Now, as there is nothing to be said about God, because he is beyond all words, it is equally absurd to deny or assert his existence. To be an atheist is to remain a prisoner of the Christian idea that "God" is in the order of things that can be shown to be true or false. It is one means of denying God, who still remains in the revealed belief.

But atheism is already present in the Christian means of conceiving of God. "The hardest strike against God," writes Heidegger, "is not that God is regarded as unknowable, that God's existence has been shown to be indemonstrable, but that a God held as real would be erected as the supreme value."[5] Postulating that God incorporated into Being as the "supreme value," in fact implies that there is no longer any truth to Being. Being becomes an object of man's will to power, as a determinative of what holds value. Being supreme, it becomes at the same stroke the cause of all other states of being, while truth is subjugated and reduced to the absolute "good" it allegedly represents. Truth, in other words, has been transformed into a value. Now what has been established as a value is thereby torn from Being. Any possibility of making one's way toward an experience of Being vanishes at the same time.

Atheism, in the full sense of the word, is finally a pure product of modernity. A post-Christian phenomenon, it presupposes Christianity in the sense that only in the latter can it find its proper conditions of feasibility. Contrary to paganism, Christianity posits the world as profane and God as sacred, establishing a distinction between them that is infinitely qualitative. It can thus be inferred that only when God has been radically conceptualized as the Christian God, can he be radically denied. It is only when the radical transcendence of God is taken seriously that it is possible for the radical immanence of an autonomous world to be posited as the "simple world." This world is stripped of all inherent sacred dimensions and exists as the pure object of a human will to appropriate and to transform it by way of a technique aiming to "inspect" it, by which I mean subject it to the principle of reason. This is why, inversely, in paganism there is no atheism properly speaking, but only a potential indifference to worship.

The relationship of modern atheism to Christianity is a relationship of critical kinship. Before degenerating into simple practical materialism, modern atheism began by turning Christianity's own weapons against it, starting with the primacy of reason. It took the process of the "disenchantment of the world" set off by the Christian desacralization of the cosmos to its natural conclusion. It brought fundamental Christian aspirations (replacing happiness with salvation and the future with the beyond), back down to earth, meaning it now opposed it with its own now secularized values, while still claiming it no longer needed the keystone to this arch: God. As René Girard said, modernity rejected the Christian tradition "in the name of the ideals it accuses Christianity of ignoring and that it believes to better embody." Paradoxically, modernity has opposed Christianity with the claim of being more Christian, and being so more rationally, more completely, and more immediately.

4.

The "history of God" in the Western world can be summarized quite easily. The gods were first replaced by God, at the end of a long struggle for influence from which Christianity emerged as the official victor. The Christian God then gradually lost credibility and his hold weakened. The God, whose "death" Nietzsche proclaimed in 1886, was only this moral God, the God of Western metaphysics. But his death in the collective consciousness made that consciousness unhappy. The "dead" God continued to manifest itself as a gap, which was perceived as something missing. To fill this gap, modernity invented a series of profane substitutions (People, Nation, Country, Class, Race, Progress, the Revolution, etc.), all of which, without exception, showed themselves incapable of serving as alternative absolutes. The hopes invested in political action (which people entered "religiously") only engendered disillusionment, discouragement, and sometimes horror. The death of the revolutionary hope for an earthly salvation constitutes the spiritual event of the end of the twentieth century. Contemporary nihilism signals the failure of these substitute approaches, not that their defeat has made the return of ancient belief possible.

Secularization has marked the end of religion's structuring role within society. Henceforth endowed with the status of "opinion" (one among many), religion increasingly retreated back into private life. In parallel fashion, political systems also reorganized on the basis of a secularization of religious concepts ("political theology"). Under the influence of the liberal ideology, we have witnessed the separation of civil society and the state.

Supporting themselves with an (apocryphal) citation of Malraux, there are those today who think that they see the advent of a "return of the religious." I do not believe it for an instant. It is not a return of the religious that we are witnessing but—to the contrary—the increasingly accelerated dissolution of every form of religious hold upon society. This is particularly true in Europe, where the trigger for the restoration of a social order organized along religious principles is not detectable anywhere. But even elsewhere—for example, the Islamic Arab countries—what has been interpreted as a return in strength of religion smacks mostly of its transformation into an instrument of politics. The noisy activity of "God's fanatics" (the ultra-orthodox and the fundamentalists) is itself, paradoxically, the fruit of their growing isolation. For its part, the rapid increase of sects merely betrays a sense of uneasiness and dissatisfaction. In a more general fashion, the recourse to affiliation with a religious group is merely one manifestation among many of a vast, subjectively formed movement that is primarily the expression of a quest for identity. As noted by Marcel Gauchet in his most recent book, this tendency derives much more "from adaptation of belief to the modern conditions of social and individual life than it does to a return to the religious structuring of the human institution."[6] The error here would be the confusion of the "religious" with simple belief, which is ever present and has the potential to be reactivated, but whose status has changed profoundly. This has been taken to such lengths that public life is now immanent. Where there is no longer any "politics of God" possible, belief is now nothing more than an opinion. It no longer makes collective sense and it no longer plays any part in the organization of society. It is no longer anything but an individual supposition.

What is new, on the other hand, is the appearance of public individualism, in other words an individualism that will no longer settle for being billeted in private life, but seeks to make private rights public custom. That is to say, it seeks to obtain political and institutional recognition of what was once solely the sphere of the civil or personal concerns of the individual. Hence the vogue for claims seeking to acquire public acknowledgement of sexual, cultural, ethnic, and linguistic identities, and so on. This phenomenon is indicative of a redeployment of the problematical aspect of identity, not a "return to the religious."

"Religion" can only have a meaning to the extent that it "informs" the overall society, which requires that its principles be shared by all or the majority. Those circumstances have not been experienced for a long time. The Church was its first victim, but is also the first to bear responsibility: the separation between the secular and the spiritual that it imposed brought about its downfall. The authority of the secular "clergy" then collapsed in turn. Politics no longer offered an answer to everything, starting with an answer to the question of the meaning of life. Public authority was thereby "neutralized" at the very moment when, by virtue of private life being made public principle, it found itself confronted more than ever before by a demand for meaning. The State no longer provides orientation for anything. It is only allegedly supposed to guarantee the cohesion of everything within a society that has been definitively blown apart. This is something it finds increasingly difficult to achieve, as it tends to operate on the model of the marketplace, meaning under the illusory horizon of instinctive regulation.

Atheism diminishes to the extent that God becomes nothing more than a personal choice. Secularism no longer has any worthy opponents, and postmodern Christianity no longer provokes the virulent criticisms that the Church of yesterday had to confront. Nobody opposes the Pope today as many once did, as long as he does not impose moral regulations on anybody. A paradoxical situation: on the one side the churches decline, on the other the associations of free thinkers no longer have any reason to exist. Antagonisms are vanishing everywhere. Indifference and neutralization have replaced taking any kind of firm stand. *Anything goes.* [In English in the original.—*Translator's note*]

5.

Does God give meaning to the world? It is incontestable that he does give it one meaning, but it is not His meaning. A "world without God," by which I mean this God, would not be stripped of meaning, but would be in the process of rediscovering its own meaning. I have not personally had any experience of the divine (I am the opposite of a mystic). I have, on the other hand, felt the sacred in a certain number of privileged locations, from Delphi to Machu Picchu. For me the sacred is inseparable from a place. I have no connection to any religion nor do I feel the need to connect to one. As I have a theological mentality, the interest I bring to belief systems is of a purely intellectual order, that is to say, it is connected to my desire for knowledge.

I have more esteem for believers than I do for non-believers, but what they believe in rarely seems worthy of faith, in my opinion. I am hostile to all metaphysics because, in contrast to ontology, metaphysics does not conceive of any difference between Being and beings, and only grants reality the status of an inferior form of existence. I do not believe for a minute that "religion" has anything to do with morality. The sympathy I feel for certain currents of thought or Eastern spirituality does not manage to transform my position as an outsider to them. In the world of paganism I am not a believer but a guest. I find pleasure and comfort there, not revelation. I believe that the world is eternal and infinite. And I also like this phrase of Nietzsche's: "What is now decisive against Christianity is our taste, no longer our reasons."[7]

In a famous passage, Heidegger writes: "It is only by beginning from the truth of Being that the essence of the sacred lets itself be thought. It is only by beginning from the essence of the sacred that the essence of divinity is to be thought. And it is only in the light of the essence of divinity that whatever the word 'God' names can be thought."[8] In *Off the Beaten Track*, he also writes: "Distress as distress reveals the trace of salvation. Salvation evokes the sacred. The sacred links the divine. The divine approaches the god." And again, in *The Hymns of Hölderlin:* "The fact that the gods have fled does not mean that the divine has vanished from the *Dasein* of man, it means it rightly reigns but under an incomplete form, a twilight, dark, and yet potent form." This prompting to rediscover the god—the "last god," he who is both the newest and the oldest—out of the distress caused by his absence appears to me more relevant than ever. "We have arrived too late for the gods and too soon for Being," says Heidegger again. That is precisely what it is. The question is not to know whether "God" exists or not, but whether the divine is approaching or stealing away. "God" for me is, in the strict sense: nothing. The gods: the possibility of a presence.
(Translated by Jon Graham)

Notes:

1. Contrary to the Indo-European designation of the verb "to be," the Hebrew verb *hâyâh*, "to be," denotes unachieved time. Most often it designates an existence that manifests itself through an activity.

2. Martin Heidegger, "Zurich Seminar," in *Poésie 13*, 1980, p. 16.

3. This idea has several Greek precedents (cf. Plutarch, *De E apud Delphos*). However, with the Greeks it was to Being that all characteristics of the divine were attributed, whereas in Christian metaphysics, it is the Creator God who is himself considered as the Being.

4. "Judaism is not a 'religion.' Any comparison between Judaism and what other cults consider as forming the essence of their belief is inadmissible." (*Kountrass*, January–February 1999, p. 68.)

5. Martin Heidegger, *Chemins qui ne menent nulle part* (Paris: Gallimard, 1958), p. 313.

6. Marcel Gauchet, *La religion dans la démocratie: Parcours de la laïcité* (Paris: Gallimard, 1998), p. 247.

7. Friedrich Nietzsche, *The Gay Science*, aphorism 132, Walter Kaufmann trans. (New York: Vintage, 1974), p. 186.

8. Martin Heidegger, "Lettre sur humanisme," *Questions III* (Paris: Gallimard, 1966), pp. 133–34.

On Being a Pagan:
Ten Years Later
An Interview with Alain de Benoist

Charles Champetier

The French New Right first appeared in the 1970s. Also known by the acronym GRECE (groupement de recherché et d'études de la civilisation européenne), it was a movement that shared many of the same concerns as the New Left: the inherent dangers of mass society, the subordination of politics to economics, and the emergence of Marcuse's "one-dimensional man" as the archetypal modern European. Although GRECE drew heavily on the revolutionary conservative heritage of thinkers like Oswald Spengler and Carl Schmitt, it also distinguished itself from nineteenth- and early-twentieth-century right-wing movements by rejecting narrow nationalism in favor of a pan-European perspective. But more profoundly, Alain de Benoist, the most important New Right visionary, has consistently argued for the preservation of *all* distinct peoples and cultures. This has involved a trenchant reevaluation of any monolithic ideology that would force these peoples into the same egalitarian mold. In this respect, de Benoist's critique of American-style liberalism has been even more damning than his earlier encounters with Soviet communism. So long as the latter enforced its political will with the Gulag and the truncheon, it could be opposed on its own terms. But the "soft totalitarianism" of American consumer culture is a far more insidious threat to real human diversity. Like Huxley's Brave New World—with its soma and celluloid diversions—a mass society based on the American model is an "air-conditioned Hell," but a Hell nonetheless. The Catholic philosopher Thomas Molnar has written of de Benoist's position: "there is no question of conquering the planet but rather to promote an *oikumena* of the peoples and civilizations that have rediscovered their origins. Thus, the assumption goes that the domination of stateless ideologies, notably the ideology of American liberalism and Soviet socialism, would come to an end."[1]

Like Nietzsche before him, de Benoist traces the origins of these monolithic, "stateless ideologies"—a description which encompasses virtually every modern school of thought—back to Christianity. Whether of the Left or of the Right, these ideologies share with Christianity the universalist impulse for "conversion," the Manichean tendency to divide people up in terms of absolute good and absolute evil, and the progressive notion that history is moving ever closer to a secularized, utopian "Kingdom of God." Thus, paganism emerges as a viable alternative. As Stephen Edred Flowers has pointed out in his essay on integral culture,[2] pagan societies were structured such that culture, religion, and ethnic identity were woven together in a holistic, seamless tapestry. This being the case, they are intrinsically resistant to the economically driven, homogenizing tendency that is the chief characteristic of modern, market-driven politics. The return to folkish paganism, then, represents the first, and perhaps the most significant, step towards the "rediscovery of origins."

The interview that follows first appeared in the French magazine *Éléments*. Conducted roughly a decade after the publication of de Benoist's important book *On Being a Pagan*,[3] it contains both an overview of de Benoist's thoughts on the subject, and his assessment of the various groups and individuals who have assumed the "pagan" mantle. Often, this assessment is negative. In many instances, de Benoist's criticisms could be applied to the groups and individuals represented elsewhere in the pages of *TYR*. But whether or not you agree with everything he has to say, de Benoist's ideas carry behind them the weight of a tremendous erudition, and a lifetime spent thinking through his ideas meticulously and methodically. Contrast this with many neo-pagans, whose "religious transformation" is often based on little more than the adolescent fantasies of nerdy role-playing gamers and historical reenactors (or the romantic delusions of lonely, sex-starved women), and it becomes clear that de Benoist's paganism is at least worthy of consideration.

(Introduction by Joshua Buckley)

Neo-paganism burst onto the French intellectual scene with the appearance of *On Being a Pagan* fifteen years ago. Looking back now, what do you think of this manifesto? And basically, why go that way?

You have to begin with simple things. For several millennia, the peoples of Europe practiced religions that are usually called "pagan," an old name which was pejorative from the start. These religions formed a system of representations, values, and specific figures. They were the spiritual support and framework for a great many cultures and large civilizations to which we are directly or indirectly, but not exclusively, the heirs. The pagan religions were then challenged by Christianity, which had another system of representation and conceptualized the religious event in an entirely different way. Comparative study of these two systems allows us to understand why they clashed, but at the same time, encourages us to define ourselves in relation to them. Taking a stand for paganism means trying, not to perceive, but rather to *see* the world using the guidelines of the system of representation inherent to it.

There are many paths to paganism. You could approach it by way of aesthetic sentiment or instinctive rejection of the Christian worldview. It could be the desire to connect with a tradition or with sources intimately associated with it. It could also be, and this would be the case for me, through the conviction that the pathologies of the modern world are the illegitimate but obvious offspring of Christian theology. It would be an entirely natural move, then, to glance with tacit complicity at this other religion, paganism, which put up such a resistance to Christianization for as long as it did. Of course, ultimately, there is never an absolutely pressing reason for belonging to one system over another. If there were one, it would justify this system being offered to or imposed on the entire world, something I would not allow myself to do. At most, we can observe that one of these systems corresponds better to our sensibilities, that in the past it had produced effects we considered to be better, that it is the proper extension of a tradition to which we want to belong, really that it simply corresponds more than another to what we believe to be the truth.

Paganism is an all-encompassing system. It was this system I tried to describe in *On Being A Pagan* by systematically shedding light on those areas where it seems to stand in implacable opposition to the Christian concept of man and the world. Some considered this approach too "intellectual." It is, in fact, but I don't see any other way of doing it. Studying paganism offers not only the pleasure of knowing that you are getting something out of it, but also an alternative which is both intellectual and spiritual. It allows us to see how our most distant ancestors perceived the relationship between man and the world and the relationship of

ALAIN DE BENOIST, 1990.
(PHOTO COURTESY OF ALAIN DE BENOIST)

human beings to one another, what ethical attitudes they favored, what place they accorded the social bond, their idea of temporality, what their concept of the sacred was. The learning we derive from this exercise will be valid for all time, but first and foremost for our own time, setting us guidelines for conduct and assisting us in the work of thinking. When the myth tells us that in marrying Themis, goddess of order and justice, Zeus begets the Seasons and the Fates, for example, we learn something that far exceeds the account itself. Likewise, the myth of Gullveig warns us against "gold lust." The fate reserved for Prometheus teaches us about technical cunning and the consequences of allowing it to run unbridled. And the Delphic precept "nothing in excess" helps us understand the perverse nature of the modern principle of "more, more, more."

Neo-paganism currently assumes a number of identifiable forms. I can see three main groupings, myself: community or "sectarian" neo-paganism, based on imitation of ancient rites or revival of regional popular traditions; literary neo-paganism (see, for example, the interview with Christian Laborde recently published in *Éléments*), based mainly on intuition and poetic inspiration; and finally, intellectual neo-paganism, wherein myth, the imagination, the archetype, or the "polytheism of values" are the elements actively used to interpret and comprehend the world. Do you think there is a unity between them or are the groupings more disparate?

The pagan tradition (or in a more general sense, reference to Antiquity) has always inspired writers and artists to varying degrees. Most of the German Romantics, beginning with Schelling, Göres, or Novalis, pitted against what they considered to be a soulless modern world the memory of an ancient world where, as Schiller said, "everything was the vestige of a god." In the nineteenth century, ancient times were also a major source of inspiration both for the neoclassicists and for the Symbolists or Parnassians. But in fact, there are entire sections of contemporary literature we would have to cite if we wanted to make a complete inventory of this "paganism." Just to mention a few, there are: Leconte de Lisle, José Maria de Hérédia, Théodore de Banville, Louis Ménard, Jean Moréas, Pierre Louÿs, Edouard Schuré, Hugues Rebell, Edouard Dujardin, Gabriele D'Annunzio, D. H. Lawrence, Jean Giono, Knut Hamsun, Henry de Montherlant,

Marguerite Yourcenar, John Steinbeck, Henry Miller, not to forget Fernando Pessoa, who wrote in *The Return of the Gods:* "The gods are not dead; only our perception of the gods is dead. They have not left: we have only stopped seeing them ... but they are still there, and live as they have always existed, in the same perfection and the same serenity."

Of course, the "pagan" inspiration in the authors I have just cited takes different forms. In some, this reference might be a formal one, using only the aesthetics of the images and the words. In others, it could be a nostalgic reaction against the disenchantment caused by the ideology of progress. Others more clearly sought to establish, through paganism, another type of relationship to the world. But in all cases, these ongoing attempts to reach back, this spontaneous desire to link to a perceived past, more or less consciously, as a remedy for the ills of the present, should be considered a symptom.

Community or "sectarian" neo-paganism is obviously something different entirely, and I would have more reservations on this point. I already wrote in *On Being a Pagan* that "what seems especially dreadful to us today is not so much the disappearance of paganism, but rather its resurgence in primitive and puerile forms, resembling the second religiosity which Spengler justly identified as one of the characteristic traits of cultures in decline." The flowering of neo-pagan groups which we have witnessed for fifteen years now has only reinforced my opinion on this. The very fact of the extreme diversity of these groups is enough to give pause. For some, "paganism" is essentially reduced to happy get-togethers, pleasant evenings where people celebrate with a few appropriate rituals their community life and the pleasures of existence. Others gather in actual "churches" or religious communities, the ceremonies of which are internalized in more of a protestant or neo-Pietist way. Still others drag "paganism" in the direction of pure transgression, ranging from "sexual magic" to the black mass. The entire thing is invariably accompanied by complicated rituals, grandiloquent invocations, pompous titles. This means that "pagan ceremonies" can resemble boozy community festivals or austere meditation, and they can have the trappings of fringe masonry, a sexual orgy, or a costume ball. By all evidence, a great many of these movements do not actually have anything to do with paganism, despite their use of the word. As for groups with a more strictly religious vocation, their modus operandi often makes them more like sects. While condemning the anti-cult hysteria we are witnessing today, a hysteria that only adds to the confusion due to the fact that all of these groups are lumped in together, I should say that I myself feel pretty foreign to all of that. I see a lot of pastiche in it, a lot of parody, but very little paganism!

The confusion reaches its peak with the neo-pagan groups, mostly Anglos who are part of the New Age movement. More or less the result of the hippie movement and the Californian protests of the 1960s, the main characteristic of this sphere of influence is its syncretic and composite nature: "anything goes." Its main themes are eco-feminism, Aquarian millenarianism, an irresistible attraction to any form of occultism and the paranormal, and an aspiration toward personal transformation allowing the individual to vibrate in unison with the "world soul." Its touchstones are eclectic: the "Northern Path" and "runic astrology" mix gaily with Sufism, the Kabbalah, Eastern spirituality, spiritualism (now called channeling), theosophy, or "astral travel." The central idea is that we are entering the Age of Aquarius, characterized by fluidity in human relations and the emergence of a planetary consciousness. The many neo-pagan groups developing in this milieu rarely escape this syncretism, which is in fact a patchwork of beliefs and themes of all sorts, where the Tarot rubs shoulders with karmic "charms," interpretation of dreams and invocations to the Great Goddess, the Egyptian Hermetic traditions and the *Upanishads*, Castaneda and King Arthur, Frithjof Schuon and Jungian psychology, Thor's hammer and the I-Ching, "Thelemic magic" and yoga, the Tree of Life and "shamanic trances," and so on.

Obviously we shouldn't reject everything from out of this jumble, starting with themes such as eco-feminism, the holistic view of things, non-dualism, etc. But these subjects are routinely thrown into the indiscriminate hodgepodge, based on the implicit postulation of compatibility, or even convertibility, of all beliefs, all wisdom, and all practices. Added to this is a profusion of well-meaning sentiments, which often turn into the naïve optimism so typical of Americans, especially this naïve belief that individual experience is the only criterion by which the inner path can be judged, and that one can pull ready-made spirituality down from the shelf as if it were one of any number of recipes for happiness and "bliss." Ultimately, with all of its successive trends and infatuations (Hildegard von Bingen, runic divination, "guardian angels"), the New Age is a subculture which can't seem to help but draw on the composite types of belief which cropped up in Rome in the latter part of ancient times, at the fringes of the official rites, and which haphazardly combined Egyptian or Chaldean speculations, fragments of Oriental cults, astral theories, superstitious practices, "gnoses" of Iranian or Babylonian origin, oracles from any and everywhere.

Of course, not all the current neo-pagan groups fall within this sphere of influence, but rarely is the boundary that separates them an impermeable one. One trait they all have in common, for example, is their propensity for esoteric or "magical" speculation. I will not take a position here on esotericism in general, but it only too evidently serves as a support for all their delusions. And in fact, a number of the neo-pagan groups make up for their lack of knowledge, or more particularly the fact that they have no criteria allowing them to assess the value of what they know, with an overactive imagination: personal interpretations flung up as authoritative arguments, groundless assertions, whimsical extrapolations, and so on.

You are judging them rather harshly. Don't these neo-pagan groups, sprouting up in almost all the Western countries, even in Eastern Europe, at least have the merit of returning a long-forgotten subject to good standing?

It was just a general assessment. If we examined each of these groups separately, which would be difficult to do here, I would be the first person to make corrections and add nuances. Obviously certain neo-pagan communities have more substance and are more serious-minded than others. Among their leaders, whose sincerity and good intentions are not being called into question, there are those who have a genuine knowledge of ancient pagan religions and who are always working diligently to learn more. Their publications are sometimes well done, and I would not make the mistake of believing that these groups appeal only to gentle dreamers or monomaniacs, or even to individuals who have a sense of failure and who hope to relieve their frustrations and personal problems by joining groups where they hope to find a place that real life has refused them. Nevertheless, it remains that, taken as a whole, this sphere of influence is very much a part of the current "spirituality supermarket" where anyone, based on a

On Being a Pagan: Ten Years Later

"A NUMBER OF NEO-DRUIDIC OR 'DRUIDIST' GROUPS CLAIM TO BE DEVELOPING A 'DRUIDIC EDUCATION.'"
PRINCESS ELIZABETH'S INITIATION INTO THE MYSTIC CIRCLE OF THE BARDS.

sort of spiritual do-it-yourself-ism, can come as he pleases to shop from among different possible religions and "wisdoms." This "market," where a number of fringe spiritualities vacillate between the attempt at fusion represented by the sects and a desire to "heal the soul" using à la carte recipes, is one of the most obvious symptoms of the spiritual crisis of our age.

The entire question is in fact whether one can or cannot breathe life back into ancient cults without straying into sectarianism or sham, that is, without ultimately falling back into this nihilism which any true paganism would, to the contrary, have to be doing all it could to surmount. I do think that the attempts made in this area seem to be running up against serious obstacles.

First there is the problem of filiation. There is, of course, no continuity between ancient paganism and modern neo-pagan groups, regardless of what they might say. This does not, however, prevent them from asserting that they are transmitting an inherited knowledge which came from the depths of the ages, in spite of the fact that this knowledge is often just the product of their imaginations or a compilation of speculations advanced by others before them. The truth is that, although we know a lot of things about the ancient European religions, there is still a lot more to know. I will take a simple example. A number of neo-Druidic or "Druidist" groups claim to be developing a "Druidic education." But, although it is quite certain that the ancient Druids did teach *something* (a fact to which witnesses from that era attest), we do not actually know anything about what exactly this teaching was. The classical texts, whether Greek or Latin, say nothing on this point. The medieval texts, essentially accounts from medieval Ireland, are compilations of pre-Christian oral accounts, often well preserved, but lacking any commentary that is Druidic per se. The rituals adopted by most of the modern Druidist groups were actually fabricated out of whole cloth in the eighteenth century by the Welsh scholar Iolo Morgannwg (Edward Williams). Add to this borrowings from Scottish freemasonry, and from certain Welsh tales such as the *Mabinogi*. All this is very interesting, but it tells us nothing at all about the "Druidic tradition." Since no Druidic filiation has survived Christianity, any Druidic resurgence can only be parody or folklore. The same goes for "runic astrology" or "Nordic magic." We know that the runes were used in the past for divination, and that there is a good chance that they had a "religious" or "cosmic" origin. We also know that more or less all the ancient cultures made use of magic. Finally, we know that certain popular traditions, preserved mainly in rural areas, carried on longer with their ancient beliefs. But we know nothing more than that. Everything written on the subject is therefore, again, just contemporary speculation or a compilation of previous speculations.

Of course, we cannot exclude the fact that intuition, combined with an in-depth knowledge of what we know for certain about pagan religions, can come to restore part of our lost knowledge. An approach such as this one is still arbitrary, however, and to a large extent subjective.

Some of these groups, moreover, seem to fall back on Christianity. We know about these circles where the *Edda* texts have replaced the Bible, but also where they have retained the same system of patronage and apparently continue to expect out of paganism the same thing that Christians expect out of Christianity: moral norms and recipes for health. These groups seem to me to have taken back on board two traits which Walter F. Otto describes, not without reason, as being specifically

Christian: the "virus of interiority," that is, the idea "that religion is inseparable from a personal relationship with God, that the only commerce with the divinity is established through the individual person," and the idea "that religious feeling is born of a need for health which goes hand in hand with transcendence." But in paganism, not only is there no health angle, but God does not arise from within the individual's heart of hearts; rather, the individual encounters God through earthly things.

More generally, it should be said that the current "neo-pagan" literature often points to a rather impoverished level of thought. The "holistic" approach frequently serves as a pretext for a sort of cosmic egalitarianism in which whatever is specific to man disappears completely. In-depth reflection is replaced by an agreed-upon rhetoric based on references to the "awakening," "cosmic energy," "identifying with the one world" or with the "great all." The very notion of paganism as an apologia for "life," by way of example, can usually be traced back to a popular Nietzscheanism (the God of the Bible being the expression of a resentment of life) or a mixed-up vitalism (health, robustness, vitality, fighting spirit) going hand in hand with a vaguely biological "super-humanism" which is itself also naïve. To do this is to forget that almost all religions assign a positive value to life. Although none of them, perhaps, give it anywhere near the value that Judaism does, which goes so far as to challenge martyrdom and make survival a value in and of itself. Christianity, for its part, also considers that every human life has an absolute value, while paganism does not profess this idea, and moreover, pagans have always considered that there are things worse than death, that is, things for which it would be justifiable to give one's life, or without which one would choose to die.

The definition of paganism as a "nature religion," a recurring theme in neo-pagan literature, is no less problematic. We forget that this originated with the Christians, who saw an intrinsic limitation in "nature" compared with "super-nature." This sentiment was so strong that in spite of Saint Augustine's eulogy to creation in his *City of God*, we had to wait for the early thirteenth century to watch it fade. But after the work of Eliade and Dumézil, ancient pagan religions could no longer be reduced to simple nature cults. Paganism has never been pure naturalism even though "natural" and cosmic elements do play a central role in it. Nor has it ever been pantheism, as Giordano Bruno or Spinoza would have asserted, even though pantheistic elements can be found in almost all religious cultures. Among some neo-pagans, pantheism is moreover nothing but a pretext to replace God with man, in the best modern tradition! Speaking of "nature," finally, we cannot pretend that this word is not one of those most loaded with ambiguity in the history of Western thought. Nor can we pretend that Christian theology has never existed, that is, not without taking a stand on the problems it has raised. What can we say, exactly, when we speak of "returning to harmony with nature" or "reviving natural law"? Doesn't the very fact that a "natural law" could be violated throw doubt on its "naturalness"? Philosophy has brought nature into association (or opposition) with culture, artifice, history, or liberty. Christian theology has complicated matters even further by bringing nature into association with grace (human nature is the prerequisite to grace, that is, a man capable of finding God) which goes back to defining nature, according to the philosophers, in terms of its correspondence to anti-nature, that is, to freedom. We also know that translating the Greek concept *physis* into Latin *natura* resulted in the term actually being "denatured." So it is from the idea of *physis* that we should rethink the idea of "nature." If we consider the nature of things on the basis of their origin proper, of *physis* specifically, and not *ktisis* (or *creatura*), we understand that paganism could not render God as a flat-out synonym for nature, but rather would make Being the dimension which allows all beings to exist, without, however, being the cause for their coming into existence.

But there is yet another problem, a more fundamental one, perhaps. In paganism, there is no sense to our being in this world except for paganism to be the general atmosphere in which we dwell. If, in paganism, the city is defined above all as a "religious association," to borrow the words of Fustel de Coulanges, religion is defined conversely as the soul of the city or of the collectivity. By setting himself apart as self-sufficient, the modern individual brings to earth for his own benefit the idea of one God sufficient unto himself. But in paganism, the gods themselves formed a sort of society: even if you could "be like them," it would never be to find yourself alone again. Society is personhood extended: personhood, society condensed. The question arises, then, whether paganism could perhaps be, per the example of so many current beliefs, an opinion expressed in private by a few people. Some would even have it that there could be a "paganism of the catacombs" similar to what used to be the "Christianity of the catacombs." But this does not at all appear to be the case, because Christianity rests on the bedrock of individualism, which does not exist in paganism, the former being less strictly dependent on external circumstances. Living as a pagan in a non-pagan world is therefore not anywhere near as straightforward. Of course, a person can individually attempt to tap into myth, or seek to awaken meditative thought. But it has to be remembered that this sort of approach implies mentally withdrawing from the world, that is, doing exactly the contrary of what paganism extols: active participation in, and unreserved belonging to, the world. Of course, there is nothing in common between today's world and the world of Antiquity. Today's world is a world that has been changed, remodeled, by those who first found things in it to denigrate. And that is exactly where the problem lies. Because, and I will say it again, we cannot pretend we have not had two millennia of non-pagan history behind us: these years are not just a drop in the bucket. One cannot pretend this history has not happened in an attempt to revive, without further ado, an interrupted tradition. This history shapes us profoundly in spite of ourselves. It informs our way of looking at the world, even when we disagree with it. It renders us incapable of seeing in paganism what the ancients saw in it, that is, the very reflection of all that was real, a founding "discourse" organizing all of our perceptions. In other times, paganism was life itself. Today it can only be one conviction among others, professed in private by a handful of people. So, then, is paganism still a contender? This is the reason I doubt sincerely that our modern neo-pagans belong to their gods in the same way that their distant ancestors could have done. Not that they could even if they wanted to: today's world prevents them from doing so by its very existence. We can go commune with Delphi and take a lesson from the myth of Apollo, but Apollo cannot be to us what he once was for the Greek who went to consult Pythia. And just as faith cannot be decreed, the risk is great that we will fall, yet again, into sham or commemoration.

Outside of the groups that officially declare themselves neo-pagan, is there a milieu today that one could consider more receptive than others to pagan themes? I am thinking of course, straight off, of ecologists.

WITCHES RAISING A STORM.
(WOODCUT BY OLAUS MAGNUS)

Ecology is obviously very close to paganism, due to its global approach to environmental problems, the importance it assigns to the relationship between man and the world, and surely also due to its critique of the devastation of the earth under the effect of the productivist obsession, the ideology of progress, and the technical yardstick we use to assess value. This proximity is especially dramatic in radical ecology, sometimes called "deep ecology," even if, in my opinion, the latter commits the error, symmetrically opposite to that of Cartesian humanism, of destroying in a reductionist fashion the idea that humans are unique in the living world. Adversaries of deep ecology have also notoriously accused it of reviving old pagan cults.

But ecology is where it's at. Certain neo-feminist circles, mainly in the United States, but also elsewhere, are becoming singularly receptive to pagan ideas. That this receptivity often falls within the framework of a New Age–type ideology does not prevent it from being just another symptom. In *Noa Noa*, Gauguin says: "The gods of old kept themselves a sanctuary in women's memory." I, too, believe that there is a fundamentally feminine element in paganism. For one thing, because the witches were sometimes considered wise women who would have had to preserve ancient beliefs (the truth is that we do not know a great deal about that). For another, the paganism we have inherited is also the pre-Indo-European paganism that, as we know, accorded an essential place to feminine divinities: behind the Christian cult of Mary we can easily find the Mother Goddess of the pre-Indo-European neolithic civilizations. And finally, too, because the pagan traditions carried down in their purest form are those which fell under the third function, in Dumézil's sense of the term, and that this function, given greatest priority in rural areas where these traditions were preserved, corresponds in particular to the area of production and reproduction. (The survival of paganism owes much more to the common people, the peasants, and women, than to the elites, city dwellers, and men. And it is within the third function that most of the beliefs rooted in a pre-Indo-European foundation were incorporated.) But also, very simply, because paganism, like any cosmic and traditional religion, has numerous characteristics that symbolically link it to nature and the feminine universe.

That Indo-European society was essentially patriarchal, and that its pantheon was most often organized around a Father God, that its universe assigned an important place to masculine and warrior values, must not create confusion here. Comparison with the biblical universe, itself a masculine one, is revealing. In fact, the primacy of law (over mores), hearing (over seeing), *logos* (over *physis*), concept (over image), abstract (over concrete), history (over myth) is typically masculine. Also masculine is the linear concept of history, a rectilinear concept as opposed to the cyclic or spherical outlook, which perceives the universe to be a large organism subject for all eternity to the law of cycles. Conversely, feminine thought, in terms of what is specific to it, is directly linked to pagan thought to the extent that both are characterized by a more global (holistic) approach to things, a more concrete approach (but at the same time giving more space to the imaginary) than one which is strictly analytic or conceptual, a greater proximity to things of the body, corporeal realities, to nature conceived as a whole and perceived through the visible, etc. This aspect, which I believe to be a fundamental one, has often been lost to view.

One sometimes has the impression that God is absent from neo-paganism. We speak willingly of myth or the sacred, but only rarely of the divine. Our critiques of Christian inspiration also voluntarily suggest that paganism equates with

atheism. Isn't this absence of God (or gods) simply the result of a change in terminology, with the sacred being in fact equivalent to the divine? Or does this on the other hand mean that paganism does not recognize transcendence? Finally, to summarize this question, does paganism presuppose a faith or a belief?

First, a quick comment: the word "god" (Indo-European *deiwos*) is a strictly pagan word, which originates in the Indo-European designation of the "diurnal sky" (*dyeu-*). The Bible never mentions "God." It speaks of Yahweh, Adonaï, Elohim, the Eternal, Father, Christ, the Messiah—when it does mention "God" it is referring to a term of pagan origin!

I've explained many times that what Christianity and other biblically derived religions set out is not monotheism at all (and anyway this was originally only *monolatry*), but rather its dualist ontology, which means that a distinction is made between the created being and the uncreated being. The entire Christian faith implicitly contains not the first words of the creed: *"credo in unum Deum"* but rather those which follow it: *"patrem omnipotentem, factorem caeli et terrae."* This distinctive trait radically separates the Abrahamic religions, which are "historic" religions, from all the other religions of the world, which are "cosmic" religions. The Christian dualism is expressed to perfection in this formula from the fourth Lateran Council: "because no similitude can be asserted between the creator and the created without implying an even greater dissimilitude." In presenting the world as the result of a chance creation that, by definition, adds nothing to the perfection of its creator, this dualism affects the world of a lesser being, and thus devalues it. "Love not the world, neither the things that are in the world," reads the first epistle of John (2:15). In Christianity, this imperative forms the negative foundation of the love of God and love of others, standing in opposition to any solidarity with an "inferior Nature." Being desacralized, profaned in the true sense of the word, that is, shoved over to the profane side, the world then finds itself transformed into an object. As authors as different as Etienne Gilson, Alexandre Koyré, or Martin Heidegger have shown, it is at that point no longer a part of the cosmos, forming a harmonious whole where men and the gods coexist in the visible and invisible, but rather just an object that can rightfully become the prey of the technical assessors. And thus the path is opened to secularization and therefore atheism.

The accusation of atheism that Christians launch against paganism is therefore completely stripped of meaning. Because both atheism and Christianity turn out to have this very same form of *inherent* denial. The new status that Christianity confers upon man is also one that disallows man from opposing it. Atheism therefore still puts God in opposition to the world. It no longer explains one by the other, but brings them into competition with one another, awarding to the second all those things it methodically undertakes to remove from the first. It tries to show that God does not exist, in exactly the same way as Christians strive to prove that he does, but the entire idea of God is not one that can be expressed in terms of proof. Atheism is well and truly a modern phenomenon that implicates Christian theism as its antithesis, without which it could not exist. In paganism, though, it is different. The pagan peoples did not know atheism, at least in the sense that we mean it. I believe therefore that paganism is incompatible with atheism, if we define the latter as the radical denial of any form of the divine or the absolute that cannot be boiled down to man. And I would add that paganism is not "Promethean": On the contrary, it implies a rejection of this Titan's hubris which led him to rob the gods of their duties in the vain hope of taking them on himself.

That said, to believe that pagans venerated their gods as Christians adore theirs would be a mistake. Simultaneously immanent and transcendent, the god of the Christians exists only self-referentially, in absolute self-sufficiency, a reality with no conditions placed on it, a perfect freedom. In paganism, there is no revelation, just *monstration*, unveiling, epiphany. And the world is transparent to the divine in its totality: while in Christianity the relationship between man and god is primarily hierarchical (I must obey God), in paganism the relationship of man to the gods is primarily on the order of gift and counter-gift: the gods give to me, I give to the gods. Sacrifice is not evidence of obeisance but rather a way of maintaining and contributing to the order of the cosmos.

The gods, one could say, are not the last word in paganism, precisely because paganism exempts the gods from being judged by the criterion of Being. Remember the wise words of Heraclitus: "This world was created not by god or men, but it existed, exists and will exist forever like an eternal and living flame that burns in a specific way and in the same way, burns out" (fragment 30). It allows us to understand why myths place Fate above the gods. And also why paganism places so much importance on reasoning by analogy, which Plato saw as the most beautiful of all associations, because it is based on the idea of cosmos.

As far as whether paganism could be considered a faith or a religion, we have to begin by asking ourselves: isn't it semantically facile to indiscriminately use the word "religion" today to designate any form of belief attested to in the world? It has, above all, the advantage of allowing our contemporaries to expound on the assumed convergence of these religions, whether in an ecumenical perspective or in an imaginary "primordial Tradition." In northern Europe, in any case, the word "religion" is an imported, foreign term. I would be tempted, for my part, to say that a pagan does not *believe* but rather that he *belongs*. And that this membership, which cannot be dissociated from a collective belonging, also involves *pietas*, which is a clear awareness that finality is assumed as a common reality.

For some time now, we've been seeing a rather frenzied offensive aimed at linking paganism with morbid practices such as grave desecration or Satanism professed in certain "hard" music circles mostly associated with the extreme right. What do you think of this parallel? More generally, is paganism necessarily anti-Christian? And conversely, has Christianity always been anti-pagan?

There's no doubt that Satanism is just the flipside of Christianity. To endorse Satan is to worship the fallen angel, that is, the double-negative of the biblical god. The contradiction of any Satanic path is that it cannot escape the god it tries to oppose, because if this god did not exist, the transgressions would make no sense. What good does it do to blaspheme against God if you are convinced that he does not exist? What sense does profaning a host make if it's just a disc of unleavened bread? It could be asserted that from this point of view Satanism contributes—from the dark side—to perpetuating Christianity, while at the same time feeding yellow journalists with sensational copy well in keeping with the spirit of the times.

As far as the circles to which you are referring, there's not much to say. You find mostly adolescents there who are into

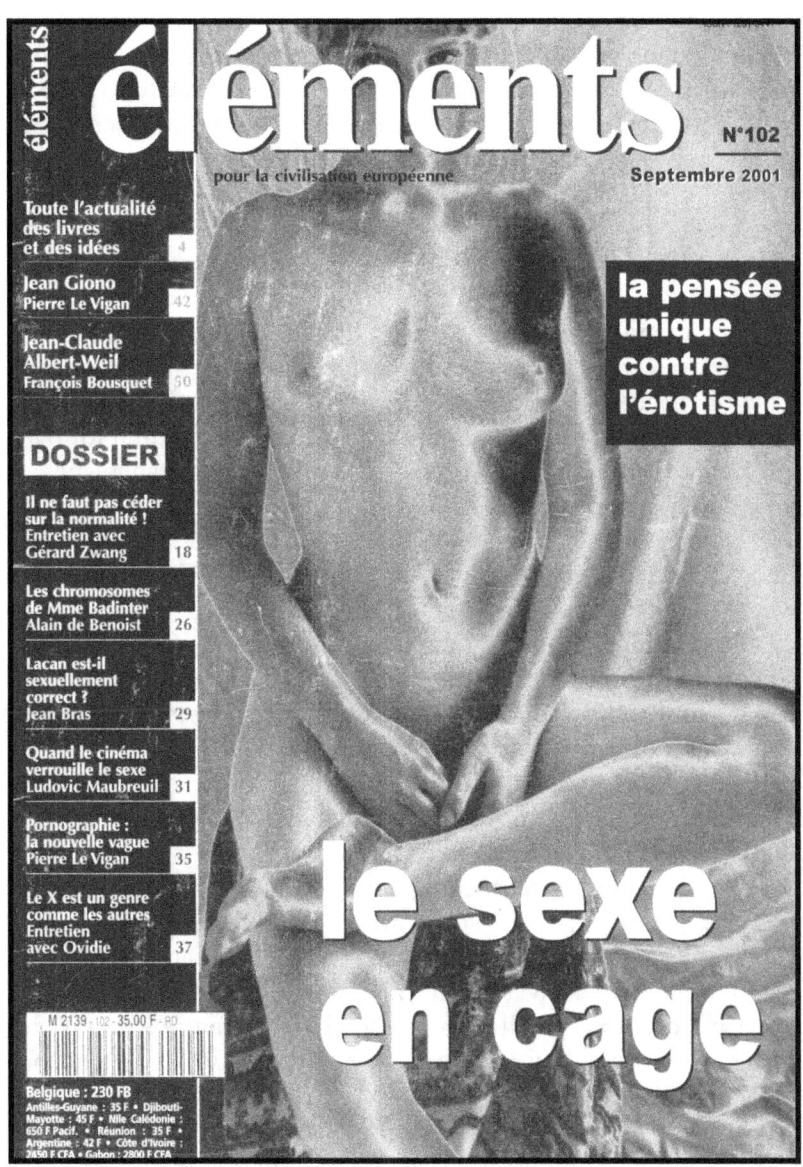

"ÉLÉMENTS," ONE OF SEVERAL PUBLICATIONS
OF THE FRENCH NEW RIGHT.

upstaging one another through provocation, and who navigate between ephemeral fanzines and aggressive musical creations of the heavy metal style or the gothic style. Some of these are just plain psychopaths, inexorably attracted to brutality, cemeteries, black masses, or even necrophilia. Most of them luckily have been influenced by nothing worse than comic books and science-fiction! Their "paganism" consists mainly in dreaming about heroes with huge biceps and jawbones of concrete or espousing the very antithesis of paganism: pure violence and chaos. You would have to call it *Conan the Barbarian*–style or *Dungeons and Dragons*–style paganism.

The relations between Christianity and paganism are a more complex question, and the truth requires that we state that they have often been bloody. While in the Roman Empire Christians were only ever bothered for political reasons, the Church for over 1,000 years persecuted pagans for religious reasons. Paganism was prohibited in the Roman Empire in the year 392, and finally in 435 was made punishable by death. The era of the morally justified—even recommended—massacre began historically with the wholesale slaughters ordered by Yahweh (Deuteronomy 7:16; 20:16). The epoch of religious wars, and heresies (a term which simply has no meaning in paganism) began with Christianity. In late Antiquity and the early Middle Ages, evangelization led to the eradication of paganism by any means. Beginning in the eleventh and twelfth century, as Robert Moore demonstrated effectively, Western society became, under the impetus of princes and Christian prelates, a structurally persecutory society. A part of this society thought to incarnate "evil"—whether it was pagans, heretics, Jews, "lepers," "sodomites," or "witches,"—had to be cast out and sometimes even eradicated. Christian intolerance, based on the imperative of conversion and on belief in an absolute good and evil, thus resulted in segregation. Its transposition in the secular world resulted in all the standard practices of exclusion, relegation and the shutting-away of "non-conformists" studied by Michel Foucault. This would tend to shed doubt on the opinion of René Girard, who asserts that Christianity is the only religion not to resort to the practice of scapegoating, that is, the only one not to make persecution and the use of legal infamy one of the means of social cohesion.

The Christians first denounced paganism as a cult given over to "idolatry" or demon-worship. Then, failing in their attempt to root out popular beliefs, they appropriated everything they could "recoup" from the pagan tradition without detrimentally affecting the essential foundations of their own faith. Western Christianity thus became a mixed phenomenon, which finally, as P. Festugière said, turned out to be the "consummation of what many pagans had already thought." In reality, it should be understood that this sort of heritage was accepted only after having been rendered inoffensive. In the Middle Ages, the author of the life of St. Aloysius *(Vita Eligii)* railed against pagan letters with a revelatory invective inspired by St. Jerome: "What do Pythagoras, Socrates, and Aristotle advise us to do, in their philosophy? What benefit do we derive from reading these criminal poets called Homer, Virgil, and Menander? Of what use to Christian society are Sallust, Herodotus, Livy, recounters of pagan history? How can the speeches of Lysias, Gracchus, Demosthenes, and Cicero, exclusively occupied with the art of oration as they are, compare with the pure and beautiful doctrines of Christ?"

When discussing relations between paganism and Christianity, then, we have to take two fundamental givens into account. On the one hand, in terms of doctrine, there is no possible conciliation between Christian theology and pagan ontology. On the other hand, from the historical and sociological perspectives, it is obvious that Christianity is a hybrid phenomenon, which led it, for example, to develop a sort of unacknowledged polytheism through the cult of Mary and the cult of the saints. Fernando Pessoa, there again, seems to me to have his finger on it when he writes: "What the pagan accepts most willingly in Christianity is the popular devotion to the saints, the rites, the processions ... the pagan willingly accepts a procession, but turns his back on St. Theresa and the child Jesus. The Christian interpretation of the world takes his heart from him, but a church festival with its lights, its flowers, its chants ... he accepts all those things as good things, even if they come from a bad thing, because these are truly human things and they are the pagan manifestation of Christianity." It should be mentioned in passing that it is to this "pagan manifestation of Christianity" that traditionalist Christians are often most attached, while the more modern variety on the other hand would rather see it eliminated.

In the biography that he dedicated to Heidegger, Rüdiger Safranski relates an anecdote that runs along the same lines. Whenever he entered a chapel or a church, Heidegger always dipped his hand in the holy water basin and genuflected. This surprised Max Müller, who according to Safranski, "remarked to him one day that his attitude was somewhat inconsistent, since he had rejected the dogma of the church," and Heidegger responded, "We have to think historically. And in a place where so many have prayed, the divine is close in a very special way." What a nice answer.

All this is to say that if paganism is defined only by its opposition to Christian dogma, it would condemn itself by that very fact in that it would have no identity other than one which referred back to this dogma. It would just be Christianity all over again (in the sense that Joseph de Maistre had in mind when he made a distinction between a counterrevolution and a "revolution in the opposite direction"). This is the reason why, while obviously being critical of Christianity, I personally define myself not as anti-Christian, but rather as *a-Christian*.

And since paganism wishes to be hospitable about differences, it considers the idea of a "war between the religions" as simply nonsensical. So it does not find the existence of Christianity bothersome any more than it does the existence of Judaism or Islam. It is even ready to go to bat for them if their religious freedom is threatened. The problem begins where the proselytizing starts. From the pagan point of view, any wish to *convert* others—that is, ultimately, to *change* them—is in fact an aberration. Judaism, in this regard, poses no problem, because it is first and foremost the religion of a single people. Islam is more problematic, because its mission is to grow beyond the civilization that gave birth to it. But it is Christianity most of all which, with its universalism, condemns itself to an inability to accommodate paganism, which will always in its eyes be an insult to the true faith and an obstacle to the kingdom of Christ. I believe that there is a powerful link between this Christian desire to convert the world, which is above all the desire to produce and reproduce others through its own discourse, and the Christian concept of "love." Philippe Forget shed some light on it in an article on the "Catholic virtues," which appeared in the magazine *Panoramiques*. "The Catholic aspires to love," he writes, "but he always encounters others through a feeling of incompleteness. He wants completion. Thus he never welcomes anyone in his singular otherness, his fundamental 'strangeness.' He tries to put meaning into others, his own meaning. So he is not actually acknowledging the other person's reality, and cannot let that person grow and excel in his own unique identity. The other person is always lacking in some way. He has to be shown the truth ... Thomas Aquinas defined love as covetousness: Catholic love is an incessant hermeneutic covetousness, which aims to immerse the sense of others. Here, Catholicism, exposed in its originality, shows itself to be the matrix of the West, wherein lies an insatiable will, which—by defining and standardizing the existence of others—incarnates in a planet of homogeneity. The Other as oneself: that is the purpose *(telos)* of this will which has its origins in Catholicity, this will of which the Greek, radical enemy of excess (hubris), the Jew, or Hindu is ignorant."

In the past, religions have always been normative. They were not just grand morality tales, but also imposed a certain number of rules that were to be obeyed. This holds true of course for Christianity, but also for pre-Christian religions. After all, the apostles of "pagan tolerance" should not forget that Socrates was sentenced to drink hemlock for the crime of atheism, or that the refusal to recognize the divine nature of imperial Roman power was sometimes severely punished! Does neo-paganism aspire to be normative? Could the sacred that it so single-mindedly ferrets out and exposes in turn define prohibitions and therefore laws? In other words, is neo-paganism neutral or does it structure values? Does it have an imperative discourse on good and evil?

The question is ill-phrased, to my way of thinking. By putting it like that, you are presupposing that religion is necessarily the source of morality, which is not an assumption you can automatically make. Christianity is surely a moral religion, since its raison d'être is offering the possibility of "health." The absence of morality is therefore confused with sin, that is, failure to obey the commandments of God. Conversely, "if God does not exist, anything is permitted." But this is not the equation in paganism. The gods of paganism do not exist to sanction lapses in compliance with mores and still less to devote themselves to making lists of naughty or nice actions. Their own actions can even seem "immoral" to us. Does this mean that pagans are released from the obligation to respect any ethical norms? Obviously not. All it means is that for them religion is not the foundation of morality, which nevertheless still does not prevent it from being normative in another sense (any rite is normative, without for all that being moral). When Titus, Pythagoras, or Publius Syrus earnestly recommend that we practice charity, when Seneca or Marcus Aurelius preach goodwill and generosity, they have no need to base their exhortations on a decree of the gods. Plato asserts of course that there can be no morality without belief in retribution in the afterlife. However, Aristotle wrote *The Nicomachean Ethics* while explicitly denying the personal immortality of the soul. It is that pagan morality is not a morality of retribution: morally, man does not need to be "saved," but rather helped to build himself.

Humanity had developed moral concerns long before Christianity came along. Societies that could not distinguish between the morally good and morally bad, could not even actually exist. You have to laugh, from this point of view, when you read in certain neo-pagan publications that good and evil do not exist for a pagan (or even that "pagan morality" can be summarized by the liberal hedonistic viewpoint: "do what you will, but harm none!"). However, Kantian idealism is itself quite capable of defining the foundation for moral exigency (that is, according to Kant, the source of aspiration to a pure and formally autonomous will). Aristotle sees it even more clearly when he says that morality is an "inherited virtue" (*Politics*, 4.9). The fundamental source of morality is in fact human flexibility. Man is not entirely determined by his instincts, and his instincts are not entirely programmed in their object. The result of this is that he is always in a position to build himself or lose himself, to shrink himself or grow himself, and that the realization of his desires could just as easily lead to his destruction. Not being integrally influenced by his nature, being—as Heraclitus says—just as capable of the best as he is of the worst, he can only build himself from presuppositions of his nature if he avails himself of a moral code which lends sense to these words: the best and the worst. It is in this sense that one could say that morality, even before it is inculcated and learned, is first and foremost based on a disposition (*hexeis*), in the Aristotelian sense of the word.

Speaking of morality, I also believe that there are three different levels. First there are elementary moral rules which are indispensable to any life in a society. These rules are more or less universal, which would tend to suggest that they have been acquired over the course of the evolution of the species. They are transformed into laws which define behavior in such a way that the latter will comply with moral requirements even if it is not actually inspired by a sense of morality (for example, by fear of sanction). Then there are ethical values (or value systems) which are crystallized within different cultures, and which may vary considerably from one culture to another. These values also have a social content, but the law does not always sanction the transgression of these values. In paganism, the dominant value system is the honor system, which places the strongest accent on gifts, generosity, and pride, giving one's word. Jean-Pierre Vernant, according to Dodd and many others, very rightly described the Greece of antiquity as a culture of shame and honor, as contrasted with cultures of fault and duty. "When a Greek has behaved poorly," he writes, "he does not have the feeling that he is guilty of a sin, which would be like an internal ailment, but would feel unworthy of what he himself and others expect out of him, of having lost face. When he behaves well, it is not because he has conformed to an obligation which is imposed on him, a rule of duty decreed by God or the categorical imperative of universal reason. It is because he has succumbed to the attraction of values, both aesthetic and moral, the Good and the Beautiful. Ethics are not about complying with a constraint, they are about the individual's intimate agreement with the order and beauty of the world" (between myth and politics).

Finally, the third level corresponds to the ethic of virtues, that is, the personal efforts we force ourselves to make in order to attain a private excellence through the practice of virtues. The term is obviously to be understood in its original sense of "good natural quality." This ethic of virtues has a more obvious personal dimension, but this dimension is no less independent of the system of values in which it operates. The word "ethic" goes back to the Greek *ethos*, "custom or habit," just as the word "moral" goes back to the Latin *mores*. Aristotle says that virtues do not arise within humans by nature or against nature but that we are by nature capable of acquiring them and attaining to excellence of virtue by habit, that is to say by an ongoing desire to build the self.

The difference between pagans and Christians is therefore not at all a "moral" difference, in the sense that one group behaves morally better than the other. It has more to do with the foundation and motivations underlying the moral act, and the values to which they respectively choose to give preference. Vladimir

Soloviev, for example, maintained that only pity can serve as an internal foundation for a moral relationship with others. This idea is foreign to paganism, in which there are ways of recognizing the value of others that do not involve demonstrating pity for them. Likewise, the question is not whether morality is necessary or superfluous, because it is obviously necessary, but rather whether the very sense of our presence in the world—and this world itself—needs to be morally judged at all. I myself obviously believe it doesn't. Paganism does not morally judge the world. There is only one Being for a pagan, and no good greater than this Being.

As for Socrates's trial, which is an exceptional case, one can only understand it by putting it back in its political context. I will note only that the disciples of Socrates were never persecuted and that the most famous among them, Plato, was able to teach without hindrance in his academy. But I should also bring up the fact that Socrates's trial at least was important in that it showed, contrary to what some have rather too hastily stated, that the ancients believed in their myths. Had they not, they would have found a better way of getting rid of Socrates than to accuse him of "atheism"! André Newton writes, "The absolute faith of the larger pagan masses for several millennia is unquestionable." Had this not been the case, it would not have been necessary to persecute pagans for centuries in order to make them renounce a faith they had already lost.

The tone of *On Being A Pagan* was rather Nietzschean. But since then, your writings on the sacred—I'm thinking of *Eclipse of the Sacred* and also *The Empire Within*—appear to be inspired more by Heidegger. How has the Master of Freiburg influenced your thinking? Do you think the major Heideggerian themes define a pagan ontology?

I think actually that by resolving the antinomy of Being and Becoming, and by radically separating metaphysics and ontology, Heidegger fully restores what is deepest in pagan concepts of Being. Being comes into being. Being is not the world, but it cannot "be" without it. Heidegger's essential criticism of Western metaphysics is that it has prospered at the expense of Being, and has created the conditions for this neglect to continue to worsen. Western metaphysics does not consider Being as the necessary reason but simply as the first cause of a being. This approach finally resulted in modern subjectivity, which is none other than realized metaphysics. For Heidegger, the beginning of any work of thought does not consist in speculating on the raison d'être of a being, but rather in focusing on the fact that there is something, and not nothing. So I think that paganism finds its own source in a sense of wonder, in the wondering gaze cast upon the world and pondering the fundamental question: how is it that there is something, instead of nothing?

Heidegger believes that the "dawning" moment of thought occurred in ancient Greece. But unlike those before him, he does not want to limit himself to reading Aristotle or Plato, because he believes that Greek philosophy of the classical era already had an unsuitable foundation vis-à-vis the essence of truth. The true origin of thought for him lies with the pre-Socratics. They are the ones who represent the absolute original origin. For Heidegger, Greek origin points at a "not yet," in the sense that it contains even more than what to date has been able to be determined of the origin, that is, a "disposition" allowing Being to be grasped in terms of history as a spiritual destiny, in such a way as to create the conditions by which the beginning can be begun again in a more authentic and original way. That is where the dialogue with the Greek thinkers of origin "has not yet begun."

Here, the "origin" does not go back to a "primitive" event, nor even to a certain place. It means rather that which is when a thing begins to be what it is, that is, the provenance of its essence. In paganism, that is the only place you can go towards or come from, to the first giving, where Being blends with the inaugural gift wherein Man is brought into harmony with the entire world, without diminishing anything inherent to him. This attachment to the foundation does not exclude any other influence. He does not seek to emancipate an element that is "purer" than the others, but rather limits himself to recognizing the determining role of what he is based on. The "past" orders the spiritual experience, very simply because memory is a major place in which the sacred takes root. Any spiritual consciousness is the consciousness of a foundation that is linked to the origin without for all that being antagonistic to history. History is open to the most diverse influences. Consciousness of the origin puts them in perspective by stimulating the faculty of memory. Recourse to memory is now running into direct confrontation with a dominant ideology that belongs only in the instantaneous (the perpetual present) and in the operative. It constitutes a vital counterweight to the omnipotence of processes aimed at dominating the real that operate only in the ledger of immediacy and efficacy.

Certain critics of neo-paganism, experts in the practice of *"reductio ad Hitlerum"* once denounced by Leo Strauss, freely assert that Nazism can be interpreted as a large pagan movement of the twentieth century (thereby making neo-pagans by the same stroke neo-Nazis!) What exactly was the relationship between Nazism and religion?

The fable of "Nazi paganism" has been kept perpetually alive by certain people, for obvious propaganda purposes. The exaltation of the "ancient Germanics" during the Third Reich appears to be what they are basing their assertions on, in spite of the fact that it had a purely nationalistic character with no more pagan significance than the exaltation of Vercingétorix in the Vichy régime. Add to this the frenzied speculations about "Nazi magic" or "Nazi occultism" which have been attracting the attention of weaker souls since the era of *The Morning of the Magicians*.

Nazism is first off a pure product of modernity. In historical terms, as Denis de Rougement wisely remarked, the National Socialist revolution of 1933 is the equivalent of the French Revolution of 1789 and the Russian Revolution of 1917. All three, despite their indisputable doctrinal differences, were characterized by the institution of a single party, the rule of public health, centralization, mobilization of the masses, deliberate use of terror, the conviction that a "new era" was being born, producing a "new humanity," and so forth. In practice, Nazism was brown Jacobinism, just as bolshevism was red Jacobinism. Its motto (*"Ein Volk, ein Reich, ein Führer"*) with the insistence on *one*, is clearly political "monotheism." Born in Bavaria, Catholic turf par excellence, the Nazi party, although less monolithic than one might think (the *Führerstaat* was in many regards a polycracy), also secularized the Catholic concept of the institution. It comes off as a church led by an infallible pope (the Führer) with its clergy (the party officials), its elite group of Jesuits (the SS), its dogmatic truths, its excommunications, and its persecution of "heretics."

The twenty-fourth item on the official program of the

NSDAP, adopted in Munich on 24 February 1920, stipulates "the Party as such stands for Positive Christianity, but does not bind itself in the matter of creed to any particular denomination." By "positive Christianity" *(positives Christentum)*, they meant, ideologically speaking, a Christianity that was as de-judaized as possible, and in particular, politically speaking, a Christianity that abstained from any opposition to the regime. In January 1933, moreover, it was with the support of the Catholic party, the Zentrum—at that time directed by Franz von Papen—that Hitler came to power. It was also with Zentrum votes that the law of 23 March 1933 *(Ermächtigungsgesetz)* was instituted by the Reich and the Vatican, thanks to the efforts of Franz von Papen and Monsignor Ludwig Kaas. It required the bishops to take an oath of loyalty to the Reich. This signature removed immediate opposition in the anti-Christian circles. Von Papen was later appointed the Reich's ambassador to Turkey, before being raised to the title of Chamberlain to the Pope after the war by Pius XII.

In *Mein Kampf*, Hitler asserted his express willingness not to become involved in religious disputes, writing: "For God's will gave men their form, their essence, and their abilities. Anyone who destroys His work is declaring war on the Lord's creation, the divine will. Thus everyone must act—of course, within his Church—and everyone must consider that the first and most sacred of duties is to take a stand against any man who, by his conduct, words or acts, leaves the terrain of his own faith to seek dispute with another." He added, "I have no hesitation in saying that in those men who seek today to embroil the patriotic movement in religious quarrels I see worse enemies of my country than the international communists ... It will be always one of the first duties of those who are directing the National Socialist Movement to oppose unconditionally any attempt to place the National Socialist Movement at the service of such a conflict. And anybody who conducts propaganda with that end in view must be expelled forthwith from its ranks."

Hitler was actually thinking in terms of what was politically expedient. He knew that his supporters were Catholic or Protestant in their majority, and greatly mistrusted the *völkisch* or neo-pagan groups which appeared at the beginning of the century, and which were intending to openly fight Christianity. "These obscurantist professors who propagate their Nordic religions are just spoiling everything," he said. At the same time, like any dictator, he disagreed with the churches' right "to get involved in earthly affairs," that is, to interfere with his policies. His official objective was "the de-confessionalization of public life." Religious life was therefore pushed back to the private sphere, in the best tradition of laicism. After 1928, he had Artur Dinter thrown out of the party, accusing him of wanting to found a Christian church where Catholics would have been placed in a subordinate position. As for Hitler himself, moreover, to his death he continued to pay his dues to the Catholic Church. Convinced that "the state should remain the absolute master," what he really wanted was a national church entirely detached from Rome. "I have nothing to say against a church which identifies itself with the state, as is the case in England," he stated on 1 December 1941. This is the reason why he encouraged the movement of "German Christians" (*Deutsche Christen*) organized in 1925 within the Deutschchristliche Arbeitsgemeinschaft, which, under the Third Reich, defined itself as the "intra-ecclesiastical branch of the National Socialist movement."

Paganism was tolerated in the Third Reich only to the extent that it remained cantoned in the private domain and did not conflict with official policy. The pagan groups were in fact gradually brought to heel over time, as were the churches, in particular after the publication of the *Mit brennender Sorge* encyclical in 1937. Erich and Mathilde Ludendorff's Tannenbergbund was banned in 1933, and the Bund für deutsche Götterkenntnis (League for the Recognition of the Germanic Gods), which succeeded it in 1937, was also placed under surveillance. In March 1936, Indologist and Sanskrit scholar Jakob Wilhelm Hauer had to step down as president of the Deutsche Glaubensbewegung (German Faith Movement). "German Faith and the Jews are pulling the same strings!" proclaimed the anti-semitic journal *Der Stürmer* in 1938! Friedrich Bernhard Marby, who founded the Bund der Runenforscher (League of Runic Researchers) and published the Marby-Runen-Bücherei, had all of his publishing activity prohibited after 1935. Arrested in March 1937 and sentenced to life in prison, he spent close to nine years in concentration camps, in particular Dachau and Flossenburg, before being freed in April 1945 by the Allied troops. H. A. Weis-haar (Kurt Paehlke), founder of the Bund der Goten (League of the Goths) in 1918, was himself also interned until the end of the war in the Bergen-Belsen camp. The *völkisch* writer and dramatist Ernst Wachler,

THE ARMANEN RUNEMASTER SIEGFRIED ADOLF KUMMER (B. 1899) WAS OPENLY ATTACKED BY THE NATIONAL SOCIALISTS. HIS FATE UNDER THE REGIME REMAINS UNKNOWN, ALTHOUGH ONE REPORT HAS HIM FLEEING TO SOUTH AMERICA. (PHOTO BY ERICH MENZEL)

founder in 1903 of the Harz Bergtheater near Thale, was persecuted for "racial" reasons and died in September 1944 in the Theresienstadt camp. Wilhelm Kusserow, founder in 1935 of the Nordische Glaubensgemeinschaft (Nordic Faith Community), was denounced as a British agent. By 1941, almost all the pagan groups had been banned.

Far from being a form of "paganism," Nazism was a secularized theology with a number of Christian features (ecclesiastic organization of power, obsession with being unique, rejection of diversity) and modern features (scientism, rationalism, progressivism). Most of the neo-pagan groups were moreover shoved aside, even prohibited or persecuted.

In private, Hitler revealed himself to be much more radical towards the churches. But the critique that he launched at them had nothing "pagan" about it. It had much more to do with straight-out rationalism and scientism. The edition of *Hitler's*

Table Talk that Flammarion published in 1952 was illuminating in this regard. As for the Catholic Church, whose skill in combining spiritual and earthly power he nevertheless admired, Hitler criticized it mainly due to its "exploiting human stupidity." For him, religion was just "obscurantism" and "superstition," against which, as opposing lights, stood the "scientific spirit" and prerogatives of "reason." "But there will never be any possibility of National Socialism's setting out to ape religion by establishing a form of worship. Its one ambition must be scientifically to construct a doctrine that is nothing more than an homage to reason." And on 14 October 1941, in the presence of Himmler: "Man, burdened by a superstitious past, fears things which he cannot or cannot yet explain, that is, the unknown. If someone were to prove that there were needs of a metaphysical nature, I could not satisfy them with the Party's program. Time will move on, until that moment when science can answer all questions ... the myths are crumbling to pieces bit by bit. All that remains to be done is to prove in nature that there is no boundary separating the organic from the inorganic. When knowledge of nature is widespread ... then Christian doctrine will show itself to be absurd ... Science has already permeated humanity. Thus, the longer Christianity clings to dogma, the faster its decline ... Nothing would be more foolish in my eyes than to resurrect the cult of Odin. Our old mythology has lost all value since Christianity took root in Germany ... A movement like ours mustn't let itself be drawn into metaphysical digressions ... it must stick to the spirit of exact science!"

As many who have seriously studied Nazi ideology have concluded, National Socialism, when all is said and done, appears to be a millenarian religion of health. A secular religion, of course, but nevertheless perfectly recognizable, aspiring with its spellbinding mass liturgy spectacularly staging the hopes and fears of every man, but also through a cult of the leader presented as a heaven-sent savior, to fulfill a promise of collective health based on a total transformation of life, absolute domination of the earth and the establishment of a thousand-year reign.

As in all secular religions of this type, the agents of evil and corruption had to be eliminated in order to usher in the new age, and this was the function assigned to Hitlerian anti-Semitism, which—while based on a social Darwinist philosophy ("the ends justify the means")—also reinterprets history in terms of absolute Good (Aryan) and absolute Evil (Jew): one has to disappear so that the other one can survive. "The Jew," writes Hitler in *Mein Kampf,* "advances on his fatal road until another force arises to oppose him, and in a mighty struggle hurls the heaven-stormer back to Lucifer"! The "master race" being by all evidence only a caricature of the idea of the Elect, it would not be exaggerating to speak of mimetic Messianism. Jean-Joseph Goux, in his book on *The Iconoclasts,* said it very well: the "practical theology" of Nazism was controlled in its entirety by a Judeo-phobic obsession which pushed Hitler to fashion the German people into a "Chosen people" to rival the Jews, that is, to try to move his own people in the direction of the "religious hallucination of the Covenant." He also stated to Hermann Rauschning: "There cannot be two chosen peoples. *We* are God's chosen people. These few words determine everything." A delusion like this is obviously entirely foreign to paganism, a delusion that, in my opinion, would allow men and women to be persecuted merely for belonging to a people. "As with the jealous gods of Christian and Muslim monotheism, the racist delusion was a totalitarian one," wrote François Perrin, "Paganism was not." *(Franc-parler).* That was also what Christopher Gérard said recently in *Antaios:* "The ultimate blame lies in what the Greeks, our masters, called hubris, overbearing presumption ... The most terrible examples of contemporary hubris are those instances of modern totalitarianism which have attempted to 'change Man'—only to ultimately debase him."

(Translated by Elizabeth Griffin)

Notes:

1. Quoted in Tomislav Sunic, *Against Democracy and Equality* (New York: Peter Lang, 1990), p. 70.
2. See Stephen Edred Flowers, "The Idea of Integral Culture" *TYR,* vol. 1, (2002), pp. 11–21.
3. Alain de Benoist, *Comment peut-on être Païen?* (Paris: Albin Michel, 1981). An English edition of *On Being a Pagan* will be published by Ultra in 2004.

Dominion Press Is Proud to
Announce the Publication of

The Golden Thread:
The Timeless Wisdom of the Western Mystery Traditions

by Joscelyn Godwin

Foreword by Richard Smoley

The Western Esoteric Tradition—which includes magic, Hermeticism, Gnosticism, alchemy, and theosophy—can be viewed as a continuous thread running beneath the surface of Western history. Those within the walls of traditional faith, and even more so those outside it, have all drawn upon its perennial wisdom throughout the ages.

The Golden Thread traces the interconnectedness of esoteric wisdom in the Western world, from classical antiquity to contemporary Europe and America. Every chapter makes reference to some aspect of contemporary life and issues of immediate concern. Educated readers who are curious about the esoteric and mystery traditions and interested in finding surprising new approaches that veer away from the trends of current thought will be particularly drawn to *The Golden Thread*.

NOW AVAILABLE AS A LIMITED CLOTHBOUND EDITION

A beautiful clothbound edition of this important book by a masterful modern scholar of esotericism is now exclusively available from Dominion Press. The edition is strictly limited to 200 copies, signed and numbered by the author and will never be available again in this form. Each book features sewn signatures, dark maroon cloth with gold stamping of a calligraphic design by Joscelyn Godwin, and a special translucent protective dust-wrapper.

5¾" x 9", 200 + xii pages. ISBN-13: 978-0-9712044-5-4

A trade paperback edition of *The Golden Thread* is published by Quest Books.

"Thoughtful and thought provoking, this is a delightful and erudite collection of gently subversive essays—a book to savor."
—Arthur Versluis, author of *Song of the Cosmos: An Introduction to Traditional Cosmology*

Price: $40.00 postpaid in the U.S.A., or $60.00 airmail postpaid to the rest of the world. Please send check or money order payable to:

Dominion
P.O. Box 129
Waterbury Center, VT
05677

Inquiries and Paypal payments may be directed to our email address:
dominionpress@comcast.net

Reflections on Disparate Myths of Divine Sacrifice

Michael Moynihan

One of the Norse god Odin's most intriguing deeds is the self-hanging episode described in strophes 139–42 of the "Havamal" section of the *Poetic Edda*.[1] Odin serves as "Allfather" among the Æsir pantheon, and certain powerful indicators of his sovereignty (magical knowledge and the runes) were gained through this act of self-sacrifice. Given both Odin's position as a high god and the particularly dramatic nature of his sacrifice, it is not surprising that comparisons are often made between this mythological episode and that of the crucifixion of Jesus Christ at Golgotha.[2] Jesus functions essentially as a "highest god" in Christian iconography, for he is the focal point of the New Testament and the intermediary to the world of men, whereas the technically mightier "Father God" has evolved into more of a shadowy figure from his former predominance in the Old Testament. Thus, one of the most important tasks of the early Christian missionaries in the Germanic territories of Europe was to convince the heathen peoples that they should accept Christ as their Lord, put him in the place of Odin, and abandon the latter along with the rest of his divine counterparts. It is certainly possible that this process may have been eased somewhat due to the superficial similarities between Odin's act of self-hanging and the motif of Christ's crucifixion.[3] As Kevin Crossley-Holland has remarked:

> The parallels between Odin's death and Christ's crucifixion are striking: both die voluntarily; Odin is pierced with a spear and so is Christ; Odin alludes to the lack of a reviving drink and Christ is given vinegar; Odin screeches or shrieks before he dies, and Christ cries out 'in a loud voice.'[4]

Given these similarities, it comes as no surprise that over the years scholars have have often debated whether this possibly indicates a deliberate Christian overlay—or even a partial source—for the "Havamal" episode, as might also be the case with certain other passages in the *Poetic Edda*. What is much less frequently discussed is the nature of these sacrificial acts as rituals or deeds in and of themselves, and the resulting implications for those who would align their spiritual outlook with one or the other of these deities. Examined from this perspective, the surrounding details of Odin's and Christ's sacrificial "deaths" can be recognized in many respects as nearly diametrically opposed. And if one looks carefully at the raisons d'être of these two religious sacrifices, it becomes likewise evident that on a metaphysical level they have very little in common.

The Sacrifice as Ritual

In the case of Odin's hanging on the world-tree Yggdrasil, the fact that the account is given in the first person voice is of primary importance. He begins:

> I ween that I hung on the windy tree
> Hung there for nights full nine
> With the spear I was wounded, and offered I was
> To Othin, myself to myself,
> On the tree that none may ever know
> What root beneath it runs.
> None made me happy with loaf or horn
> And there below I looked;
> I took up the runes, shrieking I took them
> And forthwith I fell back.[5]

It is immediately apparent that Odin's hanging is a voluntary one, done "to himself, for himself." While it undoubtedly sounds like an unpleasant affair to the average person, it must be recognized that this was not merely an act of masochism. Such a deed has many precedents in various cultures around the world, and can be viewed as a shamanistic or initiatory rite—but in either case, one which fulfills a significant function. Other aspects of Odin's persona confirm such a tendency, as Mircea Eliade notes in his *History of Religious Ideas*:

> We certainly have here an initiatory rite that is parashamanic in structure. Óðinn remains hanging from the cosmic tree; Yggdrasil means "the horse *(drasil)* of Ygg," one of Óðinn's names. The gallows is called the

hanged man's "horse," and we know that victims sacrificed to Óðinn were hung on trees. By wounding himself with his spear, by abstaining from water and food, the god undergoes ritual death and acquires secret wisdom of the initiatory type. Óðinn's shamanic aspect is confirmed by his horse with eight legs, Sleipnir, and by the two ravens that tell him everything that goes on in the world. Like the shamans, Óðinn can change his shape and send out his spirit in the form of an animal; he searches among the dead for secret knowledge and obtains it; he declares in Havamal (strophe 158) that he knows a charm that can make a hanged man come down from the gallows and talk with him; he is skilled in the art of *seiðr*, an occult technique of shamanistic type.[6]

One key element in shamanism, which differentiates it from other occult activities like "astral travel" or "supernatural" voyaging, is the imperative that the shaman return from his journeys to other dimensions of reality with something positive—not just for himself, but also for his fellow tribesmen. Generally it takes the form of healing powers or knowledge that will aid in combating specific demons or entities which cause psychological or physiological illness. In the case of Odin this paradigm is evident in his acquisition of the runes, which serve many magical functions, but specifically the very first rune he obtains *"is called help, and help it can bring thee/In sorrow and pain and sickness."*[7]

The nature of Odin's self-hanging can be viewed as a reaching, faring forth, or "descent" to another realm (since he describes gazing "below," this is presumably a reference to Hel, the repository of the dead, where he is able to acquire specialized knowledge and wisdom from its denizens). In another sense, to borrow a term from Nietzsche, it is an exercise in "self-overcoming" whereby Odin subjects himself to extremes of binding (tied to or hung from a tree), pain (wounded by a spear point), and starvation/fasting (denying himself food or drink). Each of these acts alone might lead to an altered state of consciousness, and in Odin's case they are combined and thereby amplified into a frightening ritual that takes him to the brink of death, allowing him a penetrating gaze into the mysteries of the realm where the dead reside. While the means employed are self-abnegating, his ultimate goal is self-enhancing. By enduring and overcoming this trial, Odin returns

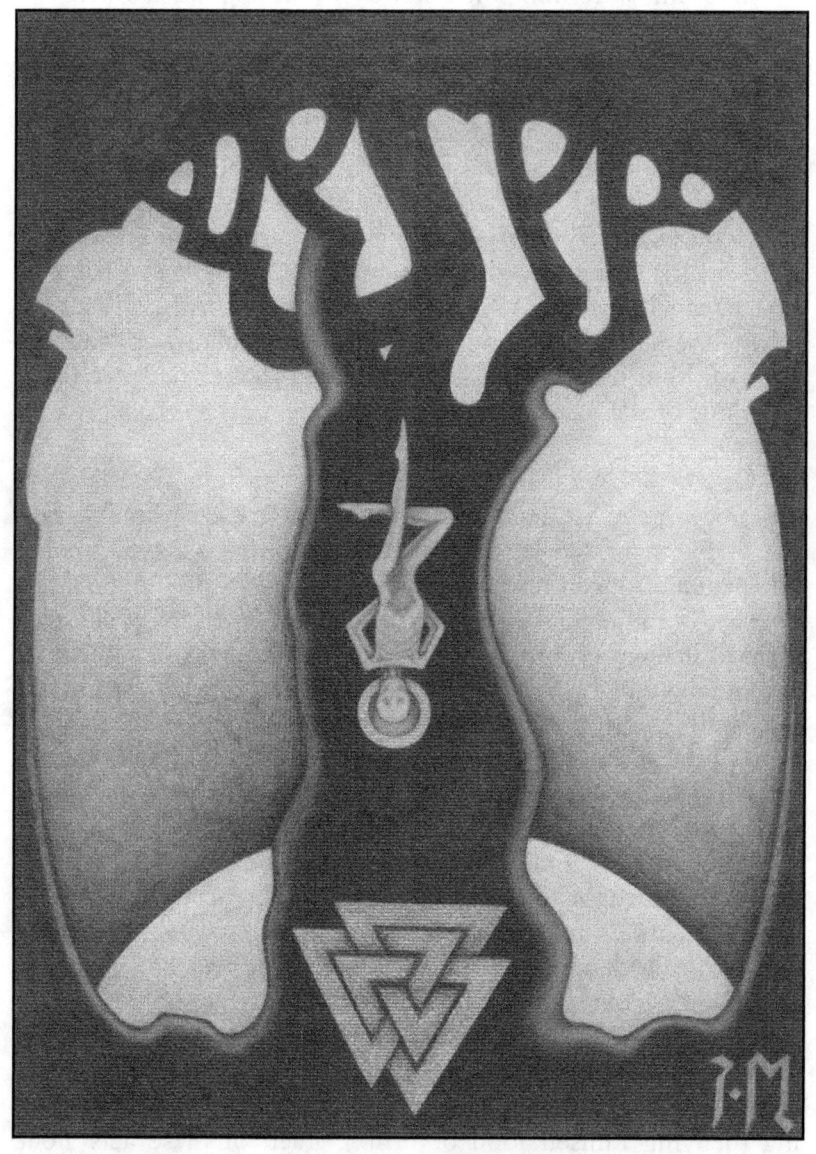

HAROLD A. MCNEILL, "ODIN HANGING ON THE WORLD TREE."
(COLLECTION OF THE AUTHOR)

to the more familiar worlds of gods and men as a superior being with newfound illumination and powers. His rite is successful, and ultimately confirms his position as the supreme entity among the gods of the Æsir.

Odin's deed is most commonly viewed as a sort of a shamanistic exercise, but there are a number of other possible explanations, all of them of a ritualistic nature. One of the most elaborate was put forth by Jere Fleck in his 1971 essay "Oðinn's Self-Sacrifice—A New Interpretation," which uses comparative Indo-European mythological material to arrive at a more detailed explanation of the operation and function of the sacrifice.[8] One of the most valuable conclusions for which Fleck provides strong evidence is the idea that Odin must have hung from the tree in an *inverted* position. This inverted alignment also offers the only reasonable explanation for how Odin could reach down and pick up the runes from below (presuming the latter were tangible objects, which is how the description reads), an action that would be physically impossible if he were hanging upright. Fleck also addresses the resulting parallel between the inverted Odin and the Major Arcana Tarot image of the "hanged man," which opens up another realm of related symbolism.

Whatever its exact form or motivation, the ritual of self-hanging is unlikely to be an anomaly grafted onto Odin's history by a later Christian scribe, for the grim nature of the rite is fully in keeping with the god's character. Students of the mythological and historical literature of the pre-Christian North will find mention of cultic practices that clearly reflect key aspects of Odin's self-sacrifice.[9] In addition, I would simply point out that a more allegorical analysis shows the ritual to be a perfect reflection of Odin's primary characteristics. He is a stirrer of battle and strife, in this case within his own being; he is a daring wanderer/traveler, who journeys to other realms simply to "test" himself and his abilities; and throughout everything he is a gatherer of wisdom, who in another central myth pledges one of his own eyes in return for the knowledge contained in Mimir's Well. Regarding the location where Odin's self-sacrifice takes place, this does not appear to be an allusion to the Christian cross. The Germanic peoples envisioned the world-tree Yggdrasil as a form of cosmic axis, a vertical and interconnective pole at the center of the nine worlds, and it is therefore entirely fitting that the High One would choose this same tree as the site of his most personal rite. By doing so he was able to gain insight into the mysterious workings of the greater universe itself.

The crucifixion of Jesus is a wholly different type of event; the circumstances surrounding it are so starkly at odds with those just discussed that any significant connection between them is highly doubtful.[10] Viewed in its historical context, the crucifixion of Christ is a thoroughly mundane act. Crucifixion was simply an extreme form of execution. It was, of course, deliberately painful and thus reserved for certain types of criminals, but its ultimate purpose was to kill someone. Therefore, leaving aside any spiritual beliefs concerning the mechanism of death itself, there is nothing inherently metaphysical about crucifixion. In contrast to Odin, the highest of the Germanic gods, who hangs himself from Yggdrasil, the most important of trees, Jesus was considered by society-at-large in Judea to be a lowly figure, a blasphemous heretic, and was nailed up in the most demeaning manner. Crossley-Holland asserts that Christ's death is "voluntary" like Odin's, but this is questionable. True, it may be voluntary in the sense that Jesus brings it upon himself through his activities and sermons, which are perceived as a threat to the existing Jewish religious establishment. He also willingly accepts his sentence and does not resist the Roman soldiers who carry it out, becoming the first—and at the same time the ultimate—martyr for Christianity. However, this form of "voluntary" death is submissive at root: it is not chosen by Christ, nor is it the outcome of any specific, active deed on his part, bur rather the work of external forces. Odin's sacrifice is, in contrast, both voluntary and chosen; furthermore, it is self-initiated and self-achieved.

Christ's death sentence comes about by his betrayal at the hands of Judas, after which he is found guilty of blasphemy by the local Jewish court, the Sanhedrin. But in order to crucify him a decree from the Romans is needed, for they are the ruling powers entitled to mete out capital punishment. Jesus is brought before the Roman authorities, and is twice exonerated. While he believes himself to be the "son of God," the reality of the matter is that the Imperial Roman government, the most powerful in the world, took no notice of him or his teachings. They do not even want to expend the effort to kill him, and it is only at the insistence of the Sanhedrin and segments of the local populace that they finally relent.

When examined in detail, the subsequent execution bears very little in common with Odin's sacrifice. Jesus is subject to scourging before being nailed to the cross, which was a standard procedure. He is never offered food or water, but rather a bitter analgesic drink before the nailing begins, and some accounts state that after he is on the cross a cloth soaked in vinegar is raised to his mouth as a petty humiliation. Jesus does cry out a number of times, most famously to shout "Father, why hast thou forsaken me?" His screams are of agony and frustration, unlike Odin's cry (of victory?) which is uttered right at the moment of "overcoming" when the acquisition of the runic mysteries occurs. Jesus' death on the cross is simply the unpleasant route by which he reaches the "afterworld" or "heaven," where he remains "at the right hand of the Father."[11]

The Meaning of Sacrifice

The word sacrifice comes from the Latin noun *sacrificium*, which has its roots in the adjective *sacer*, "sacred, holy, consecrated," and the verb *sacrare*, "to make sacred/holy." Sacrifice is a religious ritual that has been interpreted in various ways by anthropologists, historians, psychologists, and others, and there are various explanations as to its function in different religious systems. Sacrifice can be seen as a form of communication between the worlds of the profane and the sacred. Therefore, when a living thing is offered as a sacrifice it must be killed; communication takes place when the object of sacrifice (the "messenger") travels over to the other, non-material realm.[12] Sacrifice often functions to initiate an exchange of gifts between men and gods, whereby an offering is given with the hopes that it will be accepted. In return, a god or gods will fulfill a request or bestow a positive reward upon the one who performed the rite or, by extension, upon his fellow men. In a cynical sense, certain forms of sacrifice can also be considered a form of religious "bribe," through which a god is appeased: the one who sacrifices must present an offering in order to continue to receive the benevolence of the deity, who holds the power to make life miserable for the human.[13] A related form of sacrifice is that of purification or expiation—in other words, a means for man (whether an individual or a larger, collective group), having previously transgressed some divine ordinance, to make amends with the god and rectify the situation. In these latter scenarios the innate distance between god and man is emphasized, and man lives in fear of what might occur if he does not sacrifice in accordance with custom.

The death of Christ can only be understood as a religious sacrifice if one accepts its significance according to Christian theological doctrine. Christ is "sacrificed" by others, and it is never implied that he needed this to happen for any personal, otherworldly gain on his part. If the act of crucifying him served any expedient benefit on the material plane, it was that of having removed a troublesome element from society. The death itself is rather banal: as far as crucifixions go, he died rather quickly and without much ado, with only minor "supernatural" phenomena accompanying the event—the biblical accounts make claims of the "skies darkening" and so on, but this sounds more like a later poetic embellishment. The importance of the crucifixion comes then not from the deed so much as it does from the notion of exactly to *whom* it was done. He is the "son of God," a "perfected" being, yet ironically he suffers a particularly demeaning demise at the hands of those who are oblivious to his stature.

There is, however, a fundamental sacrificial exchange which occurs here according to Christian doctrine. Jesus does not die for his own sins—for, in Christian terms, can he be said to have had any?—but rather *for those of mankind*. It is an example of a peculiar expiatory act, as E. O. James comments: "However the account of what took place is interpreted, the fact remains that the Passion and death of Christ introduced into the Jewish Messiah tradition the ancient conception of the divine Saviour King suffering and dying for the salvation of mankind."[14] He has been sacrificed in order to "take upon himself the sins of the world." According to Christian belief, this state of sinfulness exists within every human being and is called "original sin," with its roots tracing back to Adam's disobedience in the Garden of Eden. A paradox is thus created, for if by suffering his crucifixion Jesus really did take upon his shoulders the sins of mankind, one might logically assume that henceforth man no longer had any. Subsequent world history and its legacies of bloodshed—a fair portion of it done in the name of Christ—amply demonstrate the falsehood of any claim to man's having sloughed off his tendency toward so-called sins, so clearly this "taking away of sin" was a symbolic rather than literal act. By keeping the concept of "original sin" intact while simultaneously proffering the immoderate metaphysical assertion about the implications of Christ's crucifixion, a formula of spiritual extortion was erected by Christian doctrine. Consequently, this demands another sacrifice: in order to receive "salvation" one must pledge faith in Jesus and accept him as "Lord"—after all, *he did magnanimously suffer torture and even death on your behalf.* If you don't pledge all your faith, you will be rewarded with nothing after you die. Added to this is the threat of punishment in hell for those who do not adopt the faith, which raises the degree of compulsion even higher. The death of Jesus can be seen as integral to all this as well, for it was necessary that he reascend to heaven in order to eventually sit in Judgment over each man following the Apocalypse.

Odin's sacrifice does not lend itself to any expiatory parallel, for his act is entirely self-contained: he is its recipient. In order to fit Odin's rite into such an equation, the only metaphysical solution might be to say that his "lower" or "unevolved self"—that is, his initial state of being—has been sacrificed and immolated in order to reconfigure itself in, or "receive," a "higher self." By doing so the lower self is destroyed and left behind, so there can be no ongoing demand of "bribery" from the higher self. The sacrifice achieves its desired end and is thus complete. Clearly the better explanatory paradigm would be that of a sacrificial exchange. Odin pledges an offering (his body, sanity, and soul) in order to receive a higher—or, one could also say, deeper—level of illumination. It is a formula of self-transcendence, and Odin goes on to explain its consequences a few strophes later in his account:

> Then began I to thrive, and wisdom to get,
> I grew and well I was;
> Each word led me on to another word,
> Each deed to another deed.[15]

Here the self-aware Odin recognizes how he functions in his newly achieved state, taking in wisdom and employing words (i.e., the art of communication—not surprising, considering that he has now acquired the runes, written symbols for the original Germanic phonemes). His knowledge and words lead to deeds, which in turn beget further, presumably greater, deeds. The esotericist philosopher Julius Evola explains the dynamics of the act in these terms:

The same notion of a primordial power that reacts against itself, frees itself, and ascends to a higher plane of being that defines its peculiar divine aspect (the *Upanishad's* "highest and most perfect form of itself") ... is expressed through Odin's sacrifice to the cosmic tree Yggdrasil, through which Odin draws out of the abyss the transcendent wisdom contained in the runes and puts it to good use; also, in one specific version of this myth Odin, who is viewed as a king, through his sacrifice points the way that leads to Valhalla, namely to the type of action that allows a person to partake of the heroic, aristocratic, and Uranian immortality.[16]

An accelerated cycle of evolution has been initiated which is not simply mundane, but rather "magical" in its very essence. It is not only an exercise of noumenal mind and numinous spirit, but also translates into actions in the phenomenal world(s). Odin's exchange has been that of a trial in return for the reward of magical insight, which he then puts to tangible use on both material and spiritual planes.

The Implications of a Sacrificed God

Christianity requires absolute faith or it becomes meaningless. If faith in Jesus as the messiah is not present, his life and death bear little relevance to anyone. If one wishes to find eloquent pacifists throughout history, there are certainly finer examples than Jesus—his teachings become unique or imperative only if the Christian doctrine is, in fact, true. If, on the other hand, one attempts to simply view Christ as a historical or mythical role model, he would be difficult to emulate, and many of his actions appear downright absurd. His "reality" is far removed from our indigenous European one, and is in many respects incomprehensible. An astute analysis of this conundrum has been given by Lawrence Brown in his Spenglerian history of Europe, *The Might of the West*, and it is worth quoting at length:

How can anyone respect, let alone worship, a character who is so dull-witted he does not know that people cannot live as the birds and plants live, who cannot protect himself against a stupid traitor about whom he knows already, who cannot find an intelligent answer to a deadly but unprovable charge, who does not realize when the whole ground of the case is shifted in a different jurisdiction? ... Instead of being willing to realize that his physics were not our physics, that reality to him was not what reality is to us, we want to have him motivated by calculations and principles that would motivate us. And so his motives instead of being different become inane, and a mighty would-be conqueror who had the courage to force both heaven and earth to his will becomes a pusillanimous victim of petty mistakes, petty intrigues, petty men. Perhaps his sense of reality was wrong and ours is right—or at least so it seems today. But within his own world, within the Levantine concept that cannot ever entirely separate this world from the next, he is the epic hero beyond comparison. He alone dared to stop the clock of the world. True, it did not stop, and we Westerners do not believe it is a clock that can be stopped. But we cannot have Jesus both ways. If we insist on judging him under our sense of the real, he becomes familiar but empty. If we judge him within his own, he becomes one of the mightiest men of history and one of the most tragic—but a total stranger.[17]

If we are to look at the sacrificial deaths of Odin and Jesus as mythic episodes rather than theological "truths," the differences rather than the similarities are yet again apparent. What if we take these sacrifices as allegorical instructions for our own behavior? Allegedly Jesus' torture and torment is a path to salvation, and it indeed follows that his teachings urged those desiring to reach "heaven" to be meek, humble, pacifistic, "turn the other cheek," and so on. The fact that Christians throughout history have often misinterpreted these teachings, or committed violence in spite of them, is beside the point. In the case of Odin we have a wholly different archetype. It is characterized by a striving toward self-knowledge; a certain bold type of egoism; a desire for independent evolution; pride in one's accomplishments (including his remarks about no one giving him bread or drink during his hanging, which could be seen as boasts of his endurance); fearless journeying to unknown places and states of consciousness; and a desire to turn ideas and words into actions. Odin's hanging is a symbolic paradigm of self-initiation, self-development, and self-becoming; it is in many ways the antithesis of the symbol of the tortured Christ, who is frequently depicted in Christian iconography as submissively nailed to the cross. This implies a complete negation of the physical realm, that is, the earth and the world of deeds. A permanent sacrifice such as Christ's can ultimately only be symbolic of a mystical utopia (i.e., "salvation" and heaven), in other words, one fully divorced from earthly reality.[18]

The realization of the incompatibility of these allegories is, of course, nothing new. The gap between the two spiritual orientations, the "world-accepting" folk-religious outlook versus the "world-rejecting" universalist one, became readily apparent in a practical sense when efforts were undertaken to Christianize the Germanic tribes of northern Europe throughout the first millennium of the Common Era.[19] The fact that Christ had been sacrificed in a manner vaguely similar to Odin may have helped the process of acceptance of an alien worldview, but such a similarity was far from sufficient to convince the heathens to adopt the new faith. An intriguing indication of this is to be found in the *Heliand*, an early version of the Christian Gospels written in Old Saxon vernacular. Conceived by an anonymous missionary poet of the ninth century C.E., the *Heliand* recasts the story of Christ's life in a completely new setting. Jesus is no longer a renegade Jewish prophet in the dusty world of Roman-controlled Judea, but a forest-dwelling Germanic chieftain with a *comitatus* of dedicated warriors surrounding him in place of the apostles. The pacifistic nature of his teachings is deftly rephrased so as to sound fairly innocuous to a Germanic heathen audience, and the culminating crucifixion scene is altered from its original form. Here the poet has depicted the final earthly hours of Jesus as a noble battle between Christ the *Drohtin* (chieftain) and his warband versus the Roman soldiers. After he is killed, the Savior ascends to heaven where he will sit for eternity on his throne "and from there he sees all things, the ruling Christ sees whatever is happening in the world."[20] This final image is distinctly Odinic,[21] and only one of many such allusions throughout the *Heliand*. Combined with this clever "reimaging" of a Christ figure who would be palatable to a Germanic heathen are countless exhortations that one must have "no doubt" after receiving the new doctrine. For if one questions or remains doubtful of its fundamental article of faith, the entire basis of the Christian doctrine crumbles. It is a radical contrast to the figure of Odin, whose inquisitive and questioning nature leads

HIBERNO-GERMANIC CRUCIFIXION SCENE IN WHICH CHRIST APPEARS AS AN ODIN-LIKE FIGURE WITH TWO ANGELS (RAVENS?) PERCHED ATOP HIS SHOULDERS. THE SOLDIER WHO GAVE CHRIST A SPONGE DIPPED IN VINEGAR SEEMS TO BE DEPICTED HERE AS OFFERING HIM AN ALE HORN INSTEAD. VIKING-ERA BRONZE ORNAMENT, ORIGINALLY INTENDED TO DECORATE THE FRONT OF A GOSPEL LITURGY BOOK. (IRELAND, TENTH CENTURY)

him to "attack" even himself, if only for his own ultimate development and benefit. Jesus would demand you bank everything on a promise of reward in the afterworld, thus playing upon man's innate fear of death, while Odin's example provides a questing paradigm for self-overcoming and evolution in the world of the here-and-now, by which one may achieve his own glory and be remembered for his deeds in the minds of his tribe and progeny. Emulating Jesus you should remain faithful and even suffer in hope of receiving divine "salvation" from above; whereas following the example set by Odin—enduring one's own sacrifices and initiations on the enchanted trees of knowledge, insight, and danger—the awe-inspiring demigod you are likely to encounter will arise mightily from within.

My thanks to Ronald Murphy, S.J., who kindly provided additional background information on the bronze crucifixion scene reproduced in this essay. This same image appears on the cover of Fr. Murphy's fascinating study The Saxon Savior: The Transformation of the Gospel in the Ninth-Century Heliand *(New York: Oxford, 1989).*

An earlier version of this essay originally appeared in Rûna *4 (1999).*

Notes:

1. The strophes that follow (143–65) should also be kept in mind, as they elaborate on the details of Odin's runic magic which he learned via his rite of self-sacrifice.
2. A succinct example is found on pp. 42–43 of E. O. G. Turville-Petre, *Myth and Religion of the North* (New York: Holt, Reinhart and Winston, 1964).
3. The case of Odin is not the only heathen god "sacrifice" which bears similarities with aspects of Christianity. Various authors have contended that the biblical scribes for both Old and New Testaments based much of their theology on pagan/heathen sources, grafted together to create a "new" religion. Examples of popularizing works in the genre include Kersey Graves, *The World's Sixteen Crucified Saviors* (New York: Truth Seeker, 1875; numerous reprints); J. M. Robertson, *Pagan Christs* (London: Watts, 1903; abridged edition New York: Dorset, 1996), and Lloyd Graham, *Deceptions and Myths of the Bible* (New York: Bell, 1979). Such books—as well as certain statements made in this essay—will probably not sit well with some Christian readers. My intention here is not, however, to attack any person's adherence to a particular set of religious beliefs. These are the concern of the individual, just as it is the individual's prerogative to reflect upon—and ultimately accept or reject—the deeper meanings of

the belief-systems they have been exposed to.

4. Kevin Crossley-Holland, *The Norse Myths* (New York: Pantheon, 1980), p. 187. Turville-Petre discusses these similarities in even more detail (see note 9), and remarks (p. 43): "If the myth of the hanging Óðinn did not derive from the legend of the dying Christ, the two scenes resembled each other so closely that they came to be confused in popular tradition."

5. I have taken this version from the eloquent translation of *The Poetic Edda* by Henry Adams Bellows (New York: American-Scandinavian Foundation, 1923), where it appears on pp. 60–67.

6. Mircea Eliade, *A History of Religious Ideas*, vol. 2 (Chicago: University of Chicago, 1982), p. 160.

7. "Havamal," strophe 147. Bellows, *The Poetic Edda*, p. 63.

8. Published in *Scandinavian Studies*, vol. 43, pp. 119–42 and 385–413. I am indebted to Stephen Flowers for bringing this article to my attention.

9. This issue is specifically addressed, for example, on pp. 42–50 of Turville-Petre, *Myth and Religion of the North*. Further relevant material in this regard can be found in my article in *TYR* vol. 1, pp. 89–91.

10. I have based my comments on the details of the crucifixion on two sources: first, the detailed 340-page analysis of the entire event in Haim Cohn, *The Trial and Death of Jesus* (New York: Harper & Row, 1971); second, the "scientific" analysis from an article entitled "On the Physical Death of Jesus Christ" by William D. Edwards, M.D., Wesley J. Gabel, M.Div., and Floyd Hosmer, M.S., AMI, which originally appeared in a 1986 issue of the *Journal of the American Medical Association* and was later reprinted in an abridged form as an appendix to *Tortures and Torments of the Christian Martyrs* by Rev. Antonio Gallonio (Los Angeles: Feral House, 1989).

11. As Joscelyn Godwin pointed out to me, an apocryphal story known as the "Harrowing of Hell" tells that in the time between his crucifixion and resurrection, Christ descended to hell or Hades to bring salvation to the souls in captivity there. This story, a fourth-century addition to the Gospel of Nicodemus, sounds like a syncretistic concession or a convenient embellishment to make the Christian teachings more palatable to non-believers. Such a story could help convince a reluctant convert that their own ancestors (who could never have heard the Gospels) might also reach heaven through some mystery of

Christ's grace. But apparently some missionaries didn't realize the utility of this. Such was the case with Wulfram, who was sent to convert the Frisians in the late seventh and early eighth centuries. According to the *Vita Wulframi*, the last heathen king, Radbod, was about to go through baptismal conversion when he asked Wulfram whether his ancestors were in heaven or in hell. The missionary replied that they were in hell, with all the other unbelievers. Radbod broke off the ceremony, stating that he would rather be damned to live in hell with his honorable ancestors than ascend to heaven with a "parcel of beggars."

12. For a socio-linguistic investigation of the implications of these terms and their cultural origins in ancient Indo-European religious practices, see Emile Benveniste, *Indo-European Language and Society* (Coral Gables: University of Miami, 1973), pp. 452–56. The etymological origins of the word "victim" are also interesting to consider in this light. The fact that Odin seems to travel to the realm of the dead during his rite of self-hanging resonates strongly with this Indo-European notion of sacrifice.

13. The various definitions of sacrifice, as well as its function as a religious "bribe" are discussed on pp. 13–35 of E. O. James, *Sacrifice and Sacrament* (London: Thames and Hudson, 1962).

14. James, *Sacrifice and Sacrament*, p. 73.

15. "Havamal," strophe 142. Bellows, *The Poetic Edda*, p. 61.

16. Julius Evola, *Revolt Against the Modern World*, trans. Guido Stucco (Rochester, Vermont: Inner Traditions, 1995), pp. 30–31.

17. Lawrence Brown, *The Might of the West* (Washington, D.C. and New York: Joseph Binns, 1963), pp. 224–25.

18. A necessary clarification: it is not my intention to portray Odin here as some sort of deified "self-help" guru for mankind, and his overall symbolic character bears with it many problematic aspects due to his multifarious nature. In ancient times only a relative few probably considered him their patron deity, and these were generally from the highest level of the aristocracy. The demands made on those who would dedicate themselves to him were often extreme, and could spell death for the devotee. He is also well known for his deceptive and morally ambiguous nature, which, if actively emulated by a large segment of the populace, would likely spell disaster for any society.

19. For a detailed discussion of these matters in the context of the continental Germanic conversions, see James C. Russell, *The Germanization of Early Medieval Christianity* (New York: Oxford,

1994). Chapters three ("Sociohistorical Aspects of Religious Transformation") and four ("Sociopsychological Aspects of Religious Transformation") are particularly relevant.

20. G. Ronald Murphy, S.J., *The Saxon Savior* (New York: Oxford, 1989), p. 115.

21. In the commentary to his translation of *The Heliand*, Murphy notes: "In Scripture Christ is seated at the right hand of the Father, but there is no comment on His gazing down on the world. In Germanic mythology it is an ultimate characteristic of Woden that, after suffering on the tree, he always looks down on this world from his throne and is aware of all that happens." (*The Heliand: The Saxon Gospel*, trans. G. Ronald Murphy [New York: Oxford, 1992], p. 198, note 319.) More specifically, Odin's ravens Hugin and Munin serve as his "eyes and ears" as they fly forth and report back to him all that transpires in Midgard.

Dominion Press Is Proud to
Announce the Publication of

Confessions of a Radical Traditionalist
by John Michell

Confessions of a Radical Traditionalist is a wide-ranging collection of colourful essays by English author and philosopher John Michell. For those readers only familiar with his better-known writings on Earth Mysteries, unusual phenomena, and eccentric figures, much of the material here will be a pleasant surprise.

Since its inception, Michell has regularly contributed to the monthly magazine *The Oldie*, one of Britain's best-kept publishing secrets. Michell's column, "An Orthodox Voice," is a perpetual font of erudite insights, charming commentaries, wittily scathing pronouncements, and divine revelations. Writing in clear, exquisite language, he deftly applies traditional wisdom to various aspects of the modern conundrum. In author Patrick Harpur's words, "If Socrates had ever written a column, this would be it."

Divided into nine sections, *Confessions of a Radical Traditionalist* presents Michell's thoughts on a wealth of heretical topics, from ancient echoes of a Golden Age to the madness of modernity and the unfolding apocalypse. Undergirding these ruminations is the rarely heard perspective of an enlightened, idealistic Platonist. Even when slaying sacred cows or lancing contemporary buffoons, he never forgets that the elusive "paradise of the philosophers" is within reach for those with the strength of vision to see it. In our inverted modern world, these disarming orthodox writings have the delicious flavor of forbidden fruit.

The 108 essays in this volume have been carefully selected and introduced by Joscelyn Godwin, a long-time admirer of John Michell's work and himself an acknowledged authority in matters esoteric and metaphysical.

The book itself is beautifully typeset and produced, making use of traditional design and sacred measurements. The cover features a stunning tempera portrait of John Michell painted in 1972 by Maxwell Armfield (1881–1972), as well as artwork by Michell himself.

John Michell was born in London in 1933 and educated at Eton and Trinity College, Cambridge. His early books *The Flying Saucer Vision* (1967) and *The View Over Atlantis* (1969) exposed new generations to the lost wisdom and sacred sciences of the ancient world. His voluminous subsequent writings have chronicled forgotten eccentrics and illuminated the mysterious worlds of crop circles, ley lines, simulacra in nature, Stonehenge, and sacred geometry. Some of his recent works include *At the Center of the World* (1994), *The Temple at Jerusalem: A Revelation* (2000), and *The Measure of Albion* (with Robin Heath, 2004). An exhibit of his geometrical and other watercolour paintings was held in London in 2003 at the Christopher Gibbs Gallery. He lives in Notting Hill, London.

"Refreshingly original, yet genuinely grounded in tradition. John Michell is wise, amusing and mischievous. He has expanded the frontiers of British sanity, and enriches the lives of those who know him and his works."
—*Rupert Sheldrake*

"A delightful read. Maybe there's some hope for the world after all!"
—*Thomas H. Naylor*, The Vermont Review of Books

As a special offer for readers of *TYR*, *Confessions of a Radical Traditionalist* is available for $25 postpaid in the U.S.A. and $60 airmail postpaid to the rest of the world. Please send check or money order payable to:

Dominion
P.O. Box 129
Waterbury Center, VT
05677

Inquiries and Paypal payments may be directed to our email address:
dominionpress@comcast.net

Clothbound, with full-color dustjacket, 5¾" x 9¼",
352 + xxi pages, Dominion, 2005, ISBN 0-9712044-4-6

Origins of the Germanic Warband

Steve Pollington

In the first volume of *TYR*, I looked at some aspects of the role of Woden in the Germanic pantheon. In the present article I wish to consider not so much who Woden is, but rather how he came to be.[1]

It is a truism that the nature of a divinity is a reflection of the hopes and fears of its worshippers. Societies with an uncertain food supply accentuate abundance in their cults; those who live near the sea emphasise the sustaining and destructive qualities of that phenomenon. Communities living in areas prone to infestation or plague reflect those aspects in their religious life. God is created in man's image.

With this in mind, it is worthwhile to consider what the cult of Woden can tell us about the early history of its practitioners. Likewise, where archaeology or linguistics can throw some light on early history, this may help to explain details of cult practice.

We must begin by looking to Tacitus, who says of the tribes of first–century C.E. Germania that kings were chosen for their nobility, while war-leaders were chosen for their ability: "They lead because of being admired if they are brash, if they are conspicuous, if they fight at the forefront."[2] Tacitus found it remarkable that when they went to war, they brought with them their mothers, wives, and children, in order to win fame before their kinsfolk in battle. The women bound and tended their wounds, and offered them food and encouragement. The tide of battle, he states, was sometimes turned by these women reminding their men of the horrors that might befall them if victory was not secured.

The military formations presented in Tacitus's account are the "national" armies of whole tribes, not the small, single-leader warbands of later historical times. The accuracy of his depiction is partly confirmed by the account of the Germanic leader—and later, rebel prince—Julius Civilis, who had the war songs of his men mingled with the shrieks of their mothers, sisters, wives, and children. In the context of Germanic tribal society, it was the females of the group who praised the upright and shamed shirkers and cowards. This duty to apportion praise and blame gave women the right to speak in the hall-assembly, to offer their advice, and to give their opinions.

The Iron Age Germanic warband was not a male-only grouping, but a complex structure based on interaction between leader, wife, household officers, and followers. For example, when King Masyos of the Semnones journeyed to Rome in 92–91 C.E., his party included one Ganna, a seeress who customarily advised the ruler. Scholars have been divided over the meaning of the passage in question. Some have seen it as a literary embellishment, intended to emphasize the differences between barbarous Germania and Roman civilisation. Others have treated it as a statement of common opinion, and this latter approach seems to be supported by the fact that Germanic women were sometimes regarded as sibyls, acted in the political sphere, and had some influence (if not control) over the warrior bands.

Michael Enright suggests that the Bructeri maiden Veleda, whose clairvoyant powers were legendary in Tacitus's day, was manipulated by the rebel leader Julius Civilis, and that the prophecies she delivered were based on his military and political strategies.[3] Access to the maiden was granted exclusively through a kinsman of hers, a situation that clearly offers grounds for suspicion that the messages handed down by her could have been influenced by this intermediary. Germanic sacral kings were customarily deemed to be in charge of interpreting omens, as with the snorting of sacred horses,[4] so the notion of restricted access to such information was not itself new.

The Germanic name for the "warband," or group of armed followers, is reconstructed as *druhtiz*, giving OE *dryht* or *driht*, with reflexes in most of the older Germanic languages. These words are all based on the verb *dreugan*, which appears in OE as *dreogan*, "suffer, undergo an experience," while its Gothic reflex *driugan* means "to perform military service." The earliest attestation of *druht* in the West is in the Frankish *Lex Salica* (ca. 500 C.E.) where it apparently refers to the wedding procession and, specifically, the passage of the bride among a group of youngsters from her paternal home to the home of her groom. From this it has been argued that the original meaning of *dreug-* concerned the "armed escort for the bride" and that, from this meaning, two sense developments took place. First, *druht* came to refer to an armed group of young men (without the notion of a festive occasion). Second, a series of derivatives such as OE *dream*, "pleasure, entertainment, enjoyment," retained the festive aspect of the meaning, but excluded the military dimension.

A derivative of *dryht* in OE is *indrihtu* which normally means "honour, glory" but may originally have denoted "growth magic" based on the notion of the *dryht* as a cult group associated with fertility. Associated OE derivatives of **druhtiz* include *dryhtealdor* which glosses *paranymphus*, "one who brings the bride to her groom"—yet the vast majority of these words have a greater emphasis on military features; e.g., *dryhtguma* can mean "best man at a wedding," but generally means "warrior in a warband." The likely ritual origins of this office are suggested by the association between the warband and the marriage procession.

It is worth recalling that the Germanic tribal army was composed of kindreds or "clans," groups of men who fought alongside their relatives, who were in many cases also their neighbours.[5] Leaders of these groups were known in Gothic as *kindins* and in OE as *cyning*, both derivatives of **kuni*, "kin, family group." The remarkable thing about the *gedriht* or "warband" was that it cut across family structures. It is possible that when the *gedriht* transformed itself from a mainly ritual to a mainly military association, it retained the only native name for an armed group drawn from many kindreds, that of the "wedding procession."

The rise of the "leader" and his "warband" (the *dux* and his *comitatus*) was due to contact with the Mediterranean world. The small-scale warfare of Bronze Age northern Europe was transformed by the military ruthlessness of the Romans and others, whose purpose was to capture able-bodied slaves for their home markets. Defending themselves against these foes meant that the traditional styles of fighting were transformed, and successful war-leaders could earn great respect, wealth, and prestige. No doubt, in time the armed groups who had gathered to protect their folks from the Mediterranean states were able to turn their adopted techniques and technologies to new purposes, and take part in settling old scores. As the *dux* grew in importance, the role of the traditional king (the *rex* of Tacitus) was narrowed, and eventually became largely symbolic.

Similarly, with the rise of new power structures a new divinity comes to the fore: the god whose name *Woðenaz gives rise to OE Woden and ON Óðinn. The root of this name is *woð, which denotes "anger," "madness," and also "poetry" and "song." In Old Irish, the same root gives rise to the word *faith*, "poet," and Latin *vates*, "seer," is also cognate. The essential idea is madness as "ecstatic possession" by a god, giving rise to battle fury, as well as to soothsaying and clairvoyance.

In the context of both wedding and warband, there is a parallel structure: "lord"/"groom" as the leading male, "lady"/"bride" as the leading female, and "warband"/"wedding party" as the gathering. The context also evokes ideas of transference from one kindred to another, and of a conjoining of several groups into a temporary or fictive relationship of kinship. The ceremony celebrated and marked the transference of one party (the bride and her followers) into the kindred and social group of her husband; it was a rite of passage. The entry into the new household was marked by some ceremony—often involving the husband's weapons and the taking of a communal drink of ale.

In a further set of wedding/warband parallels, the rites attending the entry of a bride into her new, adoptive household are mirrored in those performed for a warrior entering into the household of his lord, his *dryht* and hall. The entrant was "adopted" as the lord's fictive kinsman, entered his *sibbegedriht*, "band of relatives," and thenceforth stood in the same relationship to the lord as son would to father in a normal, kin-based household. Logically, his comrades were then his brothers-in-arms and they formed a kind of substitute family. The bond was enacted when the leader handed weapons to the newcomer. This rite mirrored the normal rite of passage, whereby a youth became a full man and received his weapons from his father or a close kinsman. In a rite of closure, the members of the group drank a communal horn of strong drink together, in an act of affirmation of their new relationship.

The strong and close association of free women with both drinking and binding agreements is found in English, German, and Scandinavian literature from the earliest times into the Middle Ages. Typically, when a solemn or important announcement was to be made, it was rendered more potent (or sacred) by being accompanied with a drink served formally by a female. There are grounds for believing that the handfasting ceremony itself may have involved the bride pouring a cup of strong drink and offering it to the groom: his acceptance and drinking of the stoup signified his acceptance of the bride as his wife. The cup-offering then seems to denote the completion of an agreement, whether between lord and follower or maiden and man. Furthermore, the admission of a member to the warband was parallel to the marriage ceremony in detail, because in both cases the head of the household took in a new fictive family member—the bride as fictive daughter and the warrior as fictive son. The leader's position as head of the household gave legitimacy to his authority over others: the authority of the bestower of goods over that of those who receive them.

Despite the theoretical "flat" structure of the *comitatus*, the warband must always have been highly stratified in reality. While group members called each other *wine*, "friend," this extended also to the leader (e.g., *goldwine*, "gold-friend," etc.) and suggests that the ranking was very carefully delineated. Tacitus specifically says of the first-century C.E. Germanic *comitatus* that it contained an array of ranks that were determined according to the leader's wishes. The combination of strong drink and armed warriors doubtless led to fighting, bloodshed, and deaths. It seems likely that warriors vied with each other for a position close to the lord, and that the whole occasion was heavily charged, even politicised.

Looking further afield than the historical Germanic warband, Kris Kershaw has proposed an alternative possibility for the origins of the leader-based structure of the *druht* and the patron god, *Woðanaz. Beginning with the close association of Norse Óðinn with the destructive military force called in OE *here* and in ON *herr*, he notes the Odinic byname *herjan*, which appears to mean "lord of the *herr*." This suggests the question: what was the *herr*?

The Germanic original of OE *here* and OHG *herr* is **harjaz* (from PIE **koryos*), a word meaning "a group of young warriors," which occurs in some Celtic tribal names (Tricorii, Petrucorii, with three and four such groups, respectively). In Norse mythology, the special champions of Óðinn are known as the Einherjar "select/singled-out warriors," also based on the same root as *herr*. They traditionally ride with the god through the night sky in the Wild Hunt, a cavalcade of spectral warriors and huntsmen seen across northern Europe from France and England to Scandinavia. Details vary from place to place and time to time, but the original Ghostly Rider was the god *Woðanaz.

It has long been recognised that these stories reflect memories of actual cult processions which once took place, connected with the worship of the god. Furthermore, the leader of the procession was a figure known as the *Herlaking* (which eventually became the Harlequin of early modern theatre). One explanation for the name links it to **harja-kuning* "king of the **harjaz*" and sees the

LUDWIG FAHRENKROG, "THE WILD HUNT."

harjaz as a cult grouping rather than a specifically military arrangement.

An early English reference to such a procession is found in the *Anglo-Saxon Chronicle* under the year 1127:

> Let no man think it strange which we truly tell, since it was well known through all the land that as soon as he [Abbot Henry] came there—that was the Sunday when one sings Exurge quare O. D.—then soon thereafter many men saw and heard many hunters hunting. The hunters were black and large and ugly, and their hounds all black and big-eyed and ugly, and they rode on black horses and on black goats. This was seen in the deer-fold itself in the estate at Peterborough and in all the woods which extended from that same estate to Stamford, and the monks heard the horns blowing which they blew at night. Truthful men who kept watch at night said this: that it seemed to them that there might well be around twenty or thirty hornblowers.[6]

Tacitus refers to a Germanic people called the Harii (evidently the plural of *harjaz*) who were noted for destructiveness, blackening their bodies, and fighting at night. This may have been a misunderstanding on his part regarding the nature of the group. Elsewhere he notes the custom of allowing certain very fierce, dedicated warriors of the Chatti tribe a privileged lifestyle among the farming settlements. These men owned no property except weapons and a neck-ring that marked their status. They grew their hair long as a badge of distinction, whereas normally youngsters would cut their hair after their first successful military encounter. These men were outside the normal rules of society, and fought in an ecstatic trance, rushing wildly at the foe—much as untrained youths might do, with great enthusiasm but little caution or restraint.

Furthermore, Kershaw sees the *harjaz* as identical to the foot soldiers whom Tacitus[7] describes as fighting in a wedge formation, while the mounted troops form up in the rear. Apart from the tactical value of a solid, determined infantry unit, it may be that they fought on foot because—being young and still landless—they did not have the means to buy or keep a horse. The wealthier, mounted troops were the *þjoðo*, a word which denotes the people as a whole, the body of freemen.

It may be that the *harjaz*—or rather its predecessor, the *koryos*—was a cult group in historical times, but originally its purpose was quite different: an "age-set," a gathering of pubescent males from a single community having reached the stage of physical maturity at which they must graduate to adulthood. This process involved a period of separation from friends, family, and community; a time of rough living in the woods or wilderness, accepting hospitality where it was offered, or taking supplies (especially food and strong drink) by force if necessary. Under the tutelage of an elder, they learnt to survive by hunting and foraging, and also by stealth. They adopted animal personas, wore skins, and developed hunting strategies based on animal behaviour. At times, they ate the hearts and drank the blood of the beasts they wished to emulate.

In this liminal state between boyhood and manhood, the members of the *koryos* were technically (and legally) outside the family and its obligations. They lived and behaved as free individuals not subject to the traditional strictures of life within the community. In this state of being associated with their kin groups but not structurally part of them (being neither boys nor men), they took a ritual status akin to that of "ancestors." They painted or blackened or masked themselves and dressed in pelts to disguise their individual appearances, and so took on a ritual or symbolic role of the "ancestors returned among the living."[8] In this role, they were accorded great honour and hospitality at religious festivals and processions involving weapon-dances and singing. The return of the ancestors brought with it blessings and prosperity for the community.

Prolonged dancing was also a means of inducing the ecstatic trance state. Tacitus[9] describes Germanic youths undertaking spear-dances, and seventh–century C.E. helmet-plate formers from Torslunda, Sweden, depict dancing men with spears, while the Sutton Hoo helmet also features plates showing sword- and spear-bearers in a contorted pose suggestive of dancing. Sword-dances are relatively well attested throughout northern Europe, and may reflect a vague memory of the tradition. Often, the weapon is replaced by a harmless wooden wand which is used to link the dancers in an endless, undulating chain.[10]

Kershaw also sees the dedicated warrior as a "sacred person" *(ver sacrum)* whose function it is to lead his *koryos* band away in exile from the tribal lands and found a new settlement. As a founder, the *ver sacrum* is able to constitute a new society for his group. This is alleged to explain the many lupine, ursine, equine, and canine references in the Germanic onomastic tradition—the spirit of the animal guardian is held to be responsible for the new group, and is commemorated through their group name.

Where does Woden fit into all this? The youth group was tutored by an elder whose function it was to lead and protect the boys, but also to expose them to various forms of danger in a structured and progressive manner. Óðinn with his Einherjar is the last, misunderstood vestige of the tribal elder and his youths, the **koryos*.

Notes:

1. This article is based on research undertaken for my book *The Mead-Hall: Feasting in Anglo-Saxon England* (Norfolk: Anglo-Saxon Books, 2003).

2. Tacitus, *Germania*, trans. James B. Rives (Oxford: OUP, 1999), ch. 7.

3. Michael J. Enright, *Lady With A Mead Cup: Ritual, Prophecy and Lordship in the European Warband from La Tène to the Viking Age* (Dublin: Four Courts Press, 1996), pp. 61–68. Enright sees the prophecying as a useful device for keeping headstrong tribesmen under control, by telling them that the omens were against a military engagement. In tribes where neither kings nor military leaders had an absolute right to command, other ways had to be found to achieve long-term aims without provoking internal challenges. The propaganda value of a prophetess was great, and her usefulness was enhanced if her prophecies could be influenced to order. There is also the morale aspect to allegedly supernatural endorsement, which is easily downplayed but must have been an important factor in early times when wars were fought hand to hand.

4. *Germania*, ch. 10.

5. *Germania*, ch. 7.

6. From the Laud manuscript, text "E," in Charles Plummer, *Two of the Saxon Chronicles Parallel* (Oxford: OUP, 1952).

7. Ibid., ch. 6.

8. The warriors of the Chatti mentioned above were remarkable not for entering this phase, but for refusing to emerge from

it. They retained the trappings of teenage excess into their adult years, and paid with their lives for their refusal to adopt full manly status within the community. Kershaw suggests that other tribes knew the same phenomenon, and that this is demonstrated by the relatively common iconography of weapon-dancers in Germanic art. The *berserkar* and other consecrated warrior groups are a historical residue of this.

9. *Germania*, ch. 24.

10. Dances of this kind form part of the English Morris tradition; some still blacken their faces, a further link with the **koryos*, rationalised as a depiction of a Moor.

Sources not Specifically Cited in the Notes:

Green, D. H. *Language and History in the Early Germanic World* (Cambridge: CUP, 1998).
Haymes, Alan. "Anglo-Saxon Kinship" in *Wiðowinde* 116 (1998), pp. 15–27.
Hedeager, Lotte. *Iron-Age Societies: From Tribe to State in Northern Europe, 500 B.C. to A.D. 700* (Oxford: Blackwell, 1992).
Kershaw, Kris. *The One-Eyed God: Odin and the (Indo-)Germanic Männerbünde*, JIES monograph no. 36 (Washington, D.C.: Institute for the Study of Man, 2000).

Abbreviations:

OE: Old English
OHG: Old High German
ON: Old Norse
PIE: Proto-Indo-European

Heathen Holy Places in Northern Europe: A Cultural Overview

Nigel Pennick

During the 1950s when I was a child, I made regular visits to my grandmother in Guildford, to the south-west of London, where I lived. She was an English countrywoman from the labouring class, born in 1884, living on the edge of poverty and feeding herself with vegetables grown in her garden according to the traditional way of "Old West Surrey."[1] I remember helping her to dig the garden on one occasion, when I was admonished not to touch the vegetation of a triangular corner, which looked like weeds to me. She told me that it should not be dug because "the fairies live there."

Later I learnt that this custom of fencing off pieces of non-ecclesiastical holy ground was not just a personal custom of my grandmother, but a folk tradition with venerable roots. It is well known in Scotland where pieces of fenced ground called the Halyman's Rig, the Gudeman's Croft, the Black Faulie, or Cloutie's Croft are places which neither spade nor plough is permitted to touch. Typically, they are the triangular corner of a field, fenced and dedicated by the farmer with a promise never to till the earth there.[2]

The Halyman's Rig and the *Stafgarðr*, Scandinavian "fenced enclosures,"[3] are instances of land deliberately set aside from everyday usage. Inside the boundary, the pristine condition of the earth prior to its tilling by man is preserved. There, the land wights still have a place to be, and the former "wilderness" is remembered. In England and Cornwall, uncultivated triangles of grass at the junction of roads are frequently called No Man's Land, perhaps a memory of their non-human ownership. Some of them still have stone crosses that may denote the Christianization of a holy place of the elder faith. There is one, over a thousand years old, on the triangular place called No Man's Land at the top of my ancestral hill, Penknight (Pen-knegh) at Lostwithiel, Cornwall.

Early Christian legislation against heathen practices in England, Norway, and Sweden forbade people from worshipping at groves, stones, in sanctuaries and at places designated *Stafgarðr*.

EASTER VÉBOND OF EGGS AROUND A SPRING IN
A VILLAGE NORTH OF NUREMBERG, GERMANY.
(PHOTO BY NIGEL PENNICK)

The *Chronicle of Helmold* (1156) records that the holy grove of the god Prove at Stargard (Szczecinski) in Pomerania, was enclosed by a fence.[4] In the Polish countryside to this day, one can see crosses by the roadside and at "no man's land" triangles, with fences around them.

The Norse heathen sacred enclosure called the *Vé* is part of this tradition. It was characteristically a triangular enclosure, fenced off from the everyday world by a row of *bautasteinar* (uninscribed stones) or a fence called the *Vébond*. The Danish royal sanctuary at Jelling was such a *Vé*.[5]

Related to the *Vé* is the enclosure created for *Holmganga* (single combat) in heathen Iceland. Judicial combats (duels) were conducted formally in places separate from the everyday world: either on an island (the meaning of the word); in a special enclosure such as a circle of stones (*Egils Saga*) or a hide held down by *tjosnur*, ritual pegs with heads (*Kormacs Saga*, X). Single combat was banned in Iceland in the year 1004. In Anglo-Saxon tradition, temporary enclosures for judicial single combat and even full-scale battles were delineated from the everyday world by a fence of hazel *(Corylus avellana)* posts, erected by the heralds in charge of the proceedings. The decisive Battle of Brunanburgh (937 C.E.), in which English forces under King Aethelstan defeated the much larger confederation army composed of Scottish, Welsh, Irish, Danish, and Norwegian units, was on such an "enhazelled" field.[6]

As safe storage of food is a matter of life and death, customarily storehouses are the focus of particular rites and ceremonies. Across the North, from the British Isles to western Siberia, traditional granaries and storehouses for provisions are small wooden buildings raised above the ground on posts, stones, or pillars.

Some wayside shrines in the North may have developed out of storehouses. In Estonia it is customary to keep images of the gods Tönn, Metsik, and Peko in storehouses that stand on stones.[7] Until the latter part of the nineteenth century, the Ob-Ugrian (Ostyak or Khanty) people in Siberia built "spirit-sheds" to contain their sacred objects. These are wooden structures raised off the ground by six vermin-repellent wooden pillars clearly derived from storehouses.[8] They were accompanied by groves of elder *(Sambucus nigra)* trees, revered in folk tradition from Siberia to Ireland, whose veneration was specifically banned as a "heathendom" by the English King Edgar (who reigned 959–975).

Inside the Ob-Ugrian shrines were boxes containing sacred objects and clothing, possibly votive offerings. In the granaries of Estonia, the images of Tönn were kept in special oval boxes, resembling the traditional oval birch-bark bread boxes made to this day in Russia. Related forms include the traditional winnowing and grain-sowing baskets of western Britain and Ireland such as the *wecht* or *dallan*. It is also the form of the shamanic drums of the Saami and the ceremonial *bodhrán* of Ireland.

In Estonia there was sometimes no image in the granary, but only Tönn's box, in which offerings were placed. Typically, they included pieces of each batch of bread, and something from each animal slaughtered. If problems needed addressing, or an accident occurred, copper coins were put in the box. The last known reverence of Tönn was in Vändra parish in the early years of the twentieth century.

In Scandinavia, the traditional storehouse of the Saami is a log building on poles, accessed by ladder.[9] Food-storage structures must be raised off the ground to prevent animals from entering and eating the contents. Similar granaries existed in traditional villages in the Balkans. In England and Wales, mushroom-shaped *staddle stones* which supported long-vanished granaries[10] are sometimes used as garden ornaments. I have been told on a number of occasions that they have a magical function to ward off bad luck.

Even in times when the established Christian religion was dominant, parallel spiritualities recognized this connexion. In seventeenth- and early-eighteenth-century Wales, nonconformists held their services in barns, because they were persecuted by the established church and could have no chapels of their own. These barns were known by devotees as "the Granaries of God." The Capel Pen-rhiw, reconstructed at the Welsh Folk Museum at St. Fagans near Cardiff, is a Unitarian chapel of 1777 built in this barn form. According to the local lore of the Fens to the east of Cambridge (England), there is an East Anglian magical text called *The Secret Granary*, used by cunning men and Toadswomen in their practise of "the Nameless Art."

At least some of the larger north European temples had earth floors, which places their origin in houses for habitation rather than storehouses. The development of Norse temples (and perhaps Anglo-Saxon and Frisian ones) from noblemen's halls or farmhouses in which sacred rites took place is understood. The famed northern *hof* was just another, sanctified, part of the farmhouse of the local *goði*. In Christian times, the religious parallel was the chapel that was an integral part of the castle or manor house.

But there were also purpose-built, separate temples in the heathen North. The first Norwegian settlers of Iceland (in the period 870–930 C.E.) transported holy buildings there. *Erbyggja Saga* 4 tells how, after making a divination, the *goði* Thorolf Mostur-skeggi dismantled his temple in Norway and shipped it, with the earth beneath it, to Iceland. The earth floor was recipient of the libations and offerings made in the temple, and so it had to be taken along with the timber building. The site of the new temple was chosen geomantically. When his ship approached the Icelandic coast, Thorolf Mostur-skeggi cast overboard the high seat pillars, on one of which was carved an image of the god Thor. Where they came ashore, there he erected the temple.

The temple that Thorolf Mostur-skeggi "let be raised" at the designated place was described as a great house, with the entrance in one of the side-walls by the far end. Before the door, inside were the high-seat pillars that had divined the temple location.

Heathen Holy Places

OLAUS MAGNUS'S FANCIFUL DEPICTION OF THE UPPSALA TEMPLE, BASED ON ADAM OF BREMEN'S DESCRIPTION. ON THE RIGHT, A SACRIFICIAL VICTIM IS BEING DROWNED.

They had "god-nails" driven into them. The images of the gods stood on a pedestal at the centre of the building.[11] *Eyrbyggja Saga* is not contemporary with the construction of the heathen temple, but Hilda Ellis Davidson deems it likely to preserve local tradition reliably though it appears to have been written at the monastery of Helgafell in the late twelfth or early thirteenth century.[12]

Heathen temples certainly existed on the sites of the present medieval churches at Uppsala in Sweden, Maere in Norway, and Jelling in Denmark. Excavations have shown that earlier, timber buildings existed beneath the present churches. At Jelling, Ejnar Dyggve found the recognizable remains of a timber stave church beneath the stone church, and a clay floor beneath that with the remains of post holes he believed to be those of a temple. But from such meagre remains it is not possible to reconstruct the form of the buildings, or even to tell whether they were earlier churches or temples.

The temple at Uppsala in Sweden is recognized as the greatest heathen sanctuary in Scandinavia. The eleventh-century commentator Adam of Bremen (circa 1070), who lived when the temple was in existence, described it as "completely adorned with gold." To his manuscript a scholiast later added a note (*scholium* 139) telling of a golden chain running round the temple.[13]

This chain appears in a famous woodcut of 1554 from the works of Olaus Magnus, made 450 years after the temple was destroyed. It is the earliest of a succession of fantastic pictures purporting to represent the temple. Thus, Erik Dahlberg's seventeenth-century "reconstruction" shows the temple as an ornate stave church. In *Hørg, Hof og Kirke* Olsen lists eight different conjectural reconstructions of the temple at Uppsala drawn up by archaeologists between 1923 and 1950 alone. Like the earlier attempts, they are all considerably different from one another.

As traditional northern European buildings, including the existing Norwegian stave churches, are made completely of timber with no metal fittings except door hinges and perhaps shingle-nails, it seems an unlikely description.[14] If it has any meaning at all, it might refer to gilded or painted carvings on the *takfot*, the beam at the top of the wall that supports the tie-beam rafters known as *bindbjalke* or *stickbjalke*. Carvings of the *takfot* exist from remaining medieval longhouses and churches in Scandinavia, including the churches at Hagbyhöga, Kumlaby, and Väversunda in Sweden, which have dragons, beasts, and interlace patterns on the *takfot*.[15] The form of hogbacks, stone monuments of the Viking Age in northern England and southern Scotland, mostly in churchyards, recall shingle-roofed buildings with the richly carved *takfot* beneath.[16] The heathen themes of the figurative carvings on hogbacks, Scandinavian stone stelae and some crosses in Cumbria and the Isle of Man give a flavour of what the temple carvings may have looked like.

Temples of the West Slavonic gods in what is now Germany and Poland were also significant timber buildings developed in the early medieval period from house- and fortress-building traditions. Many of them were in towns on islands, strongly defended with ramparts of earth and timber. They existed into a period from which contemporary accounts survive, as there are references to the temples in the works of Thietmar, Einhard, Bruno von Querfurt, Adam of Bremen, Helmold, Saxo Grammaticus, Ebbo, Herbord, the monks of Priesling, the *Knytlingasaga*, and the *Chronicle of Richard*.

The West Slavonic name for a temple was *continen*, the modern Polish *konczyna*, meaning an "end" or "gable," for according to Herbord, the Pomeranian temples were buildings with gables.[17] At Gozgaugia, the building was described as "a temple of wonderful size and beauty,"[18] whilst the main *continen* at Sczeczin (Stettin), enshrining the three-headed image of the god Triglaus

SEVENTEENTH-CENTURY WROUGHT-IRON VÉBOND
AROUND A FOUNTAIN IN STUTTGART, GERMANY.
(PHOTO BY NIGEL PENNICK)

or Triglav was "rich in ornament and art," having painted sculptures on the wall. These images of people, birds, and animals were "so natural that one could take them for living and breathing beings."[19] By this temple stood an oak tree and a holy well.

Temples were famed for certain holy objects associated with

specific deities. At Wolgast, the temple held the shield of the god Gerovit. One of the Sczeczin temples contained gilded aurochs horns bedecked with jewels. That town boasted a religious complex with four separate temples and halls where the nobles gathered for sacred feasts served on dishes of silver and gold.[20]

Rügen was a holy island with two major temple complexes, at Karentia and Arkona. The temple at Arkona had an earth floor, into which the legs of the four-headed image of Svantovit were set. The temple had a single entrance, and, according to Saxo, the roof was supported by four columns. In the early twentieth century, the Russian spiritual artist Ivan Bilibin (Ivan of the Iron Hand) drew a fine-spirited reconstruction of the interior of this temple. A squared stone pillar of the heathen period, found in 1857 in the River Zbruch at Husjiatyn, Galicia, is topped by four faces, like the description of Svantovit's image. This four-faced image was also found in the seventh-century Anglian burial at Sutton Hoo (Suffolk, England) in the form of a royal whetstone. These images are related in form to the posts surrounding the *Stafgarðr* and similar sacred enclosures of the North.

A good idea of the form of construction of some of the Slavonic temples has been gained from archaeology. The excavated buildings appear to have been made from vertical timbers, roofed with shingles. An idea of what their walling was like can be seen in the remaining parts of the oldest timber church in existence, at Greensted-Juxta-Ongar in Essex, England, dendrochronologically dated to 845 C.E.[21]

This Saxon church is composed of oak trees cleft in half. They are grooved on each side and set vertically, being joined by narrow wooden strips set in the grooves. Structurally, the Greensted church must have been very close to the contemporary heathen temples further east. Comparable oaken staves carved with human faces at the top were excavated from the ninth-century remains of the Wendish temple of Ralswieck-Scharstorf on the isle of Rügen.[22] Similar humanoid knobs also existed at the top of the vertical planks that formed the walls of the Slavonic temple at Gross-Raden in eastern Germany.[23]

The Slavonic heathen shrines and temples were destroyed by German and Danish expansion during the eleventh and twelfth centuries and the Nordic temples through the conversion to Christianity of the indigenous ruling elites. Retra was destroyed in 1068, and Uppsala around 1100. The Pomeranian temples succumbed to the evangelical incursions of Bishop Otto of Bamberg between 1124 and 1128. The temples at Brandenburg were demolished in 1136. The Rügen temples, which had been defended by 300 dedicated men-at-arms, fell in 1168–69 after the death of their patron, Duke Nyklot, to a Danish-German crusade.

Clearly, many of the incidental practices of piety were retained once the holy places became churches or had crosses planted upon them. The images of the old deities, or at least their memory, remain in obscure carvings in some churches erected on the sites of temples. The name of the Gertraudenkapelle in the church of St. Peter in Wolgast, Pomerania (Poland) may recall the worship of Gerovit at that place. A granite slab built into the wall of the church at Altenkirchen on Rügen has a carving of a man holding a horn. The man is known locally as Svantovit.[24]

The veneration of the triangular corner is maintained in central Europe in the shape of the *Herrgottswinkel* or *Heilige Hinterecke*, ("Lord God's Corner" or "Holy Back Corner") a house-shrine in the corner of the main room overlooking the family table. Largely maintained by Catholic families, its corner position relates it to the Halyman's Rig and the dwelling-place of the house spirits in Heathen times.[25] In the countryside of northern Europe, the hidden heritage of fenced enclosures, "no man's land," and the Halyman's Rig attest to an unbroken continuity of venerable age that has not yet been completely suppressed.

Notes:

1. The expression "Old West Surrey" was coined by Gertrude Jekyll. It describes a traditional culture and way of life now totally destroyed by modernity in the form of commuter suburbia. Cf. Gertrude Jekyll, *Old West Surrey* (London: Longmans Green, 1904).

2. F. Marian McNeill, *The Silver Bough* (Glasgow: William MacLellan, 1957–1968), 4 vols., I, p. 62.

3. O. Olsen, *Hørg, Hof og Kirke* (Copenhagen: Aarbøger for Nordisk Oldkyndighed og Historie, 1966), p. 280.

4. A reconstruction appears in Zdenek Vána, *Mythologie und Götterwelt der slawischen Völker* (Stuttgart: Urachhaus, 1992), p. 178, fig. 44.

5. Ejnar Dyggve, "Gorm's Temple and Harald's Stone Church

at Jelling," *Acta Archaeologica*, vol. XXV (1954), p. 221ff.

6. Nigel Pennick, *The Power Within: The Way of the Warrior and the Martial Arts in the European Tradition* (Chieveley: Capall Bann, 2002), pp. 125–133.

7. Information from the Eesti Rahva Museum, Tallinn; H. Moora & A. Viires, *Abriss der estnischen Volkskunde* (Tallinn: Estonian State Publishers, 1964), p. 253.

8. J. Kodolányi, Jr., "Khanty (Ostyak) Sheds for Sacrificial Objects," in V. Diószegi, ed., *Popular Beliefs in Siberia* (Bloomington: Indiana University Press, 1968), pp. 103–106.

9. Leif Pareli, "Sørsamenes Byggeskikk," *Forenigen Til Norske Fortidsminnes-Merkers Bevaring Årbok* (1984), p. 116.

10. Jeremy Lake, *Historic Farm Buildings* (London: Blandford, 1989), p. 25.

11. *Eyrbyggja Saga*, 4; *Kjalnesinga Saga*, 2.

12. Hilda Ellis Davidson, *The Lost Beliefs of Northern Europe* (London: Routledge, 1993), pp. 102–103.

13. Ibid., pp. 87–88.

14. For an overview of traditional building in timber in northern Europe, see Nigel Pennick, *Masterworks: Arts and Crafts of Traditional Buildings in Northern Europe* (Wymeswold: Heart of Albion Press, 2002).

15. Peter Sjömar, "Romansk och gotisk—takkonstruktioner i svenska medeltidskyrkor," *Hikuin* 22 (1995), pp. 219, 222.

16. See, e.g., James Lang, "The Govan Hogbacks: A Reappraisal," in Anna Ritchie, ed., *Govan and its Early Medieval Sculpture* (Stroud: Alan Sutton, 1994), pp. 123–131, figs. 56, 58–60.

17. Herbordus Bambergensis [Herbord], *Leben des Bischofs Otto von Bamberg* (Leipzig: Dyk, 1894), II, p. 31.

18. Ibid., III, p. 7.

19. Ibid., II, p. 32.

20. C. Schuchhart, *Arcona, Rethra, Vineta* (Berlin, 1926), *passim*.

21. Philip Clucas, *Churches and Cathedrals of England* (London: Tiger, 1987), p. 29.

22. Vána, *Mythologie und Götterwelt der slawischen Völker*, p. 171, fig. 39.

23. Ewald Schuldt, *Der altslawische Tempel von Gross-Raden* (Schwerin; 1976), reconstruction in Vána, p. 169, fig. 37.

24. C. Albrecht, "Slawische Bildwerke," *Mainzer Zeitschrift*,

vol. XXIII, pp. 46–53.

25. M. Pokropek, "Interior," in *Folk Art in Poland* (Warsaw: Arkady, 1988), p. 46; Linda J. Ivanits, *Russian Folk Belief* (Armonk: M. E. Sharpe, 1989), p. 54.

This essay is part of a longer "work in progress" on holy and sacred places in northern Europe, their continuity and renewal.
—N.C.P., 9 October 2002.

TESCO-ORGANISATION
Label + Mailorder + Distribution +++ http://www.tesco-germany.com

More items? Order the catalogue!

DEATH IN JUNE
"Nada!" CD
BADVCCD 13

BOYD RICE AND FRIENDS
"Music, Martinis and Misanthropy" CD/pic.LP
BADVC 1996

CHANGES
"Fire of Life" CD/LP
HAURUCK 22

BLOOD AXIS
"The Gospel of Inhumanitiy" CD
STORM 05

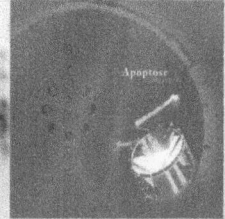

APOPTOSE
"Blutopfer" CD
TESCO 052

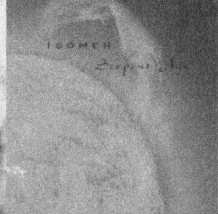

ISOMER
"Serpent Age" CD
TESCO 054

FIRE+ICE
"Birdking" CD
FREMD 2000

DERNIÉRE VOLONTÉ
"Les Blessures de l'ombre" CD
HAURUCK 49

COTA
"Marches and Meditations" CD
SORCERY 02

TESCO ORGANISATION GERMANY
P.O BOX 410118 - D-68275 MANNHEIM - GERMANY
FAX: +49(0)621/8280742 - E-MAIL: Tesco-Org.-MA@t-online.de

FOR CUSTOMERS FROM THE U.S.A: http://www.tesco-distro.com
E-MAIL: tescousa@tesco-distro.com

There Were Giants in Those Times: The Guardians of Albion

John Matthews

> "There are giants in the sky..."
> —Steven Sondheim, *Into the Woods*

One of the earliest names for the island of Britain is derived from a giant—that same giant Albion written about by William Blake and earlier by that redoubtable historian of ancient Britain, Geoffrey of Monmouth. Once one starts looking at these (literally) huge figures, one begins to see all sorts of deeper meanings to them. To our medieval ancestors, giants were the residues of a primordial race believed to have first inhabited this island thousands of years ago. Similar stories have been told in most parts of the world at one time or another. From this we might conclude that they are in fact a kind of ancestral memory of an ancient race of ordinary-sized people, who have grown larger with the passing of time; or maybe they are the distant memory of a pantheon of aboriginal gods, who may actually have been huge, or at least perceived as such by their worshippers.

We do tend to see the distant past through a distorting lens—making the older inhabitants of the land either bigger or smaller. The aboriginal inhabitants of Britain itself—we can call them the Picts, though there may have been others—having been forced to retreat into caves and holes in the distant North, became known as "the little dark people" and were quickly subsumed into the notion of the faery folk, who have also been seen as little, at least since the Middle Ages.

Where even more ancient races are concerned there may well be a tradition that made them gigantic. We may infer here the Welsh story of "Rhonawby's Dream," found among the great myth lore of the *Mabinogion*, in which the dreaming hero (who dates from c. 1300) encounters Arthur, who seems gigantic and comments on how the world is full of "little men" not like the great heroes of his time.

What we are actually looking at in the stories of these gigantic figures is almost certainly a series of foundation myths—stories linked with the primordial shaping of the land, with its first gods and its earliest heroes, and with a series of guardian figures who still remain.

So, with these thoughts in mind, let us briefly examine some of the traditions regarding giants in the ancient, myth-haunted land of Britain. Geoffrey of Monmouth is as good a place to begin as any. His knowledge of ancient folkloric sources was considerable, and while his *History of the Kings of Britain* is unreliable as history, his eye for obscure detail is excellent. Here is what he has to say about the giants of Albion:

> Nought gave him [Corinius] greater pleasure than to wrestle with the giants, of whom was greater plenty there [Cornwall] than in any of the provinces that had been shared amongst his comrades. Among others was a certain hateful one by name Goemagog, twelve cubits in height, who was of such lustihood that when he had once uprooted it, he would wield an oak tree as lightly as it were a wand of hazel. On a certain day when Brute was holding high festival to the gods in the port whereat he had first landed, this one, along with a score of other giants, fell upon him and did passing cruel slaughter on the British. Howbeit, at the last, the Britons collecting together from all quarters prevailed against them and slew them all, save Goemagog only. Him Brute had commanded to be kept alive, as he was minded to see a wrestling bout betwixt him and Corineus, who was beyond measure keen to match himself against such monsters. So Corineus, overjoyed at the prospect, girt himself for the encounter, and flinging away his arms, challenged him to a bout at wrestling. At the start, on the one side stands Corineus, on the other the giant, each hugging the other tight in the shackles of his arms, both making the very air quake with their breathless gasping. It was not long before Goemagog, grasping Corineus with all his force, brake him three of his ribs, two on the right side and one on the left. Roused thereby to fury, Corineus gathered up all his strength, heaved him up on his shoulders and ran with his burden as fast as he could for the weight to the seashore nighest at hand. Mounting up to the top of a high cliff, and disengaging himself, he hurled the deadly monster he had carried on his shoulder into the sea, where, falling on the sharp rocks, he was mangled all to pieces and dyed the

waves with his blood, so that ever thereafter that place from the flinging down of the giant hath been known as "Goemagog's Leap," and is called by that name unto this present day. (*Historia Regum Britanniae*, bk. 1, ch. 16, trans. Sebastian Evans)

This gives us the name of another giant, Goemagog, to whom we shall return in a moment. For further information about Albion we have to look to the romantic Elizabethan chronicler Raphael Holinshead—the source of so many of Shakespeare's plays—who gives us a more or less complete picture.

According to Holinshead, the story of Albion takes us firmly into the realm of classical mythology—to the story of Hercules, in fact. The Greek hero's tenth labour took him to Spain to recover a unique herd of cattle. On the way he passes through Gaul, where he and his companions are attacked by the Ligurians, who live near the mouth of the Rhône. The Ligurians are either giants themselves, or they are helped by giants—specifically, two sons of the god Poseidon. Albion himself, we learn, was also sired by the same god. And, hearing word of this battle, Albion goes off to join his brothers. Hercules is hard-pressed, and prays to his father Zeus for help. Zeus sends a shower of meteorites. The heroes use these as missiles and slay all the giants—including Albion. After this, the race of giants lives on for another 600 years in the island named after Albion (i.e., Britain)—but in the end they dwindle until there are only a few left in outlying places such as Wales and Cornwall.

The great poet Edmund Spenser sums it up vividly in his vast, mythic poem *The Faerie Queene:*

> But far in land a savage nation dwelt;
> Of hideous giants, and half beastly men
> That never tasted grace, nor goodness felt
> ....
> They held this land, and with their filthiness
> Polluted this same gentle soil long time:
> ....
> Until that Brutus anciently derived
> ....
> Driven by fatal error, here arrived,
> And them of their unjust possession deprived.

THE CERNE ABBAS GIANT, AS SEEN FROM ABOVE.

....
He fought great battles with his savage foe;
In which he them defeated evermore,
And many giants left on groaning floor
That well can witness yet unto this day
The western Hough besprinkled with the gore
Of mighty Goemagot, whom in stout fray
Corineus conquered, and cruelly did slay.
And eke that ample pit, yet far renowned,
....
[And] those three monstrous stones do most excell
Which that huge son of hideous Albion,
Whose father Hercules in France did quell,
Great Godmar threw, in fierce contention,
At bold Canutus . . .

(Bk. II, canto X, vs. 7–11)

There Were Giants In Those Times

This story has several interesting aspects. First there is the connection with Hercules. Folklorists have long recognised that stories of the Greek hero were known in Britain and may have influenced our own native mythology. There is a possibility that the giant chalk figure carved onto the hillside at Cerne Abbas in Dorset may represent Hercules—complete with club and lion skin (archaeologists found vestiges of a cloak once carried over one arm when the site was investigated a few years back). Some authorities have even pointed out that the Greek name Ialebion or Alebion might be the original of Albion, though this is not perfectly provable. In the writings of the classical author Lucian there is also an interesting account which describes how the Celts saw Hercules as a god of wisdom, rather than as a hero:

> We Celts do not agree with you Greeks in thinking that Hermes is Eloquence: we identify Heracles with it, because he is far more powerful than Hermes. And don't be surprised that he is represented as an old man, for eloquence . . . is wont to show its full vigour in old age . . . This being so, if old Heracles . . . drags men after him who are tethered by the ears to his tongue, don't be surprised at that either: you know the kinship between ears and tongue. ("Heracles," in Lucian, *Works*, vol. 1, trans. A. Harmon)

Two shadowy figures—or perhaps one—thread our history. In Geoffrey of Monmouth we heard about Corneas, the captain of Trojan Brutus's men, wrestling with the giant Goemagot. Long after this, two figures are said to have been carved out of the chalk on the cliffs above Plymouth—these are called Gog and Magog. They were still to be seen as late as 1671, after which they vanished forever beneath the foundations of a new building.

Gog and Magog are the names of the kings of the biblical land of Mesech, alluded to in Chronicles and Ezekiel. But how did their names get applied to the giants of Plymouth? The first editor of the Welsh version of Geoffrey of Monmouth's book—the *Brut Tysilio*—suggested that Gogmagog or Gomagot is a corruption of Cawr-Madog or "The Giant Madog," an ancient and now virtually forgotten Celtic hero. But there is another suggestion, which, if it is right, puts a whole different complexion on the matter of the giants.

This idea centres around the figure of Ogma—also called

Ogmios in Gaul, where he was worshipped as a god of light and learning. It was this character whom Lucian identified with Hercules in that passage referred to above. So, if Ogma is to be identified with Hercules, and in Ireland the so-called "inventor" of the old secret alphabet called Ogham is also found in Gaul, we have at least two links between the giants of Albion and the classical giants—remember that we have Hercules fighting Albion and his brothers in Gaul, where Ogma is Ogmios, and that the Celts apparently saw Hercules as a god of wisdom, just as Ogmios was seen.

This is further born out by the land itself—in particular, the Gogmagog Hills in Cambridgeshire, where the archaeologist T. C. Lethbridge uncovered a somewhat controversial figure in the 1950s. This figure or figures seemed to show a primitive warrior in a chariot, carrying a club and with a cloak over his arm, another possible image of this merging of the hero Hercules with an older, Celtic figure, possibly Ogmios.

In London around 1522, two huge figures guarded the gate to the city. To some they were "Colebrand" and "Brandegore" (significant names, as we shall see), but they were popularly known as "Hercules" and "Sampson." These huge statues were paraded through the streets of the city on civic occasions, until they were destroyed in the Great Fire of London in 1622.

After that two new statues, smaller than the originals, were lovingly carved out of wood and installed in the Guildhall. These were called "Gog" and "Magog," and survived until the Blitz during World War II, when they were destroyed. The name changes cannot be without significance. My belief is that these two giant guardians were seen as British versions of Hercules and Sampson, even if no one really remembered why any longer, and that these ancient figures, once Cole and Bran, had become associated with the giants of Plymouth.

Later, when William Blake wrote his great series of prophetic poems, he made Albion in some sense represent an ideal version of humanity—the fall and salvation of Albion was also, symbolically, the fall and salvation of man. But in "The Ancient Britons" Blake also wrote that "The giant Albion ... is the Atlas of the Greeks, one of those ... called Titans. The stories of Arthur are the acts of Albion, applied to a Prince of the fifth century..." For Blake, Albion indeed represented a vast principle of human destiny, of whom Arthur was the merest offshoot, an earthly representative of the divine energy of God.

But what about those other names for the giants of London, Colebrand and Brandegore? Both these names have survived, in more ancient forms, as Cole (the same Old King Cole of nursery fame) and Bran—a very different figure, and one who is central to an understanding of the purpose of the giants in Albion.

Colebrand is almost certainly a distant memory of Coel Hen (the Old), a probable historic figure who predates Arthur and is described in several texts as a King of Britain. In one account he marries Helena (later Saint Helena) and their son is Constantine the Great, Emperor of Rome. Coel is also the supposed founder of Colchester—but none of this makes him a giant. Perhaps he was remembered as a great leader and warrior and, as we have seen happen so often in our own history, time makes him seem larger than life—literally larger!

"GOGMAGOG" FIGURE IN LONDON'S GUILDHALL.

But Bran is something else altogether. He is none less than the Celtic god Benegied Vran (Bran the Blessed), who is the prototype of the Wounded King of Arthurian Grail traditions. His story tells us a good deal.

Bran the Blessed is King of Britain and a giant. He arranges for his sister Branwen to marry Matholwch, the King of Ireland. At the wedding feast one of his brothers, Evnissien, takes slight at the Irish king and mutilates his horses. Strife seems immanent, but Bran offers Matholwch the Cauldron of Rebirth, into which dead warriors are placed and come forth alive again. Matholwch already knows of the Cauldron, which came originally from Ireland and was owned by a giant and his wife, Llassar Llaes Gyfnewid and Cymedei Cymeinfoll, who gives birth to a fully armed warrior every six weeks. They had been driven out of Ireland and had taken refuge with Bran.

Branwen now went to Ireland, where she bore Matholwch a son, but was so unpopular with the people that she was forbidden his bed and put to work in the kitchens. There she trained a starling to carry a message to her brother, who, once he heard of her ill treatment, came with all his warriors across the sea. Matholwch retreats and sues for peace, which is granted on condition that he abdicates in favour of Gwern, his son by Branwen.

At the feast which ensues, Evnissien again brings disaster by thrusting the child into the fire. Fighting breaks out and the Irish are winning because they put their fallen warriors into the Cauldron. Evnissien then crawls inside and, stretching out, breaks both the vessel and his own heart. Bran is wounded in the foot by a poisoned spear and instructs his surviving followers, who number only seven, to cut off his head and bear it with them.

They journey to an island named Gwales, where they are entertained by the head of Bran and the singing of the Birds of Rhiannon for eighty-five years, during which time they know no fears or hardship and forget all that they have suffered. Then one of their number opens a forbidden door, and at once the enchantment ceases and they remember everything. Bran's head tells them to carry it to London and bury it beneath the White Mount with its face towards France, whence it guards the land of Britain from invasion until the time of Arthur, who orders it disinterred and reburied.

The most important thing here is Bran's guardian aspect. He is not alone in this however. A number of such figures—the technical term for them is "paladians"—are recorded. For instance, Vortimer, the son of the fifth-century tyrant Vortigern, became such a well-loved hero that at his death he requested that he should be interred at the port where the Saxons normally landed, facing towards the enemy.

Another interesting point about the majority of the giants listed here is that they are nearly all associated with rivers, estuaries, or coastal areas! What if, like Bran, Vortimer, and his kind, these giants had originally been guardians of the coastline? The more I investigated the matter, the more certain I became.

Let us look, for a moment, at one or two of these characters. There is Treyryn, a Cornish giant—one of many such found in this area—who has a castle held up by a magical key. There is actually a rock, which may be seen to this day, called "The Giant's Lock." This rock has a hole in it with a round stone called "the key." It is said that if the stone is ever removed, the whole promontory will sink into the sea.

Then there are two giants at St. Michael's Mount—Cormoran

and his wife Cormelian. They are said to have raised the mount single-handedly and, it is also said, could demolish it just as easily!

Other guardian giants (in Cornwall alone) are:

Holiburn at Cairn Galva
Trebegan at Land's End
Bolster at St. Agnes Beach
Bolster at Portreath
Ordulph at Tavistock (on the River Tavy)

Gog and Magog (or Cole and Bran), as we have seen, guarded London.

There is also Leon Gawr, who is said to have founded Chester (another river town)—he is almost certainly the same as Brandegore or Bran of Gower, mentioned in several Welsh annals, and who is probably not only the same figure as Bran the Blessed, but reappears throughout the Arthurian cycle under various guises as Brandelis, Brendegoris, Brangore, Strangore, and so on.

There are a number of references to giants in the Arthurian legends—and though this is not the place to discuss all of these, one might just mention Ogryvan Gawr, who is said to be the father of Arthur's Queen Guinevere (he becomes Leodegran in the later stories). But the interesting thing about this name is that the Welsh word *ogryvans* was applied to a bardic verse form which particularly applied to gnomic or wisdom poetry—suggesting that Ogryvan may well, like Bran, have been associated with the preservation of knowledge or ancestral memory.

This same idea is probably carried over into references to two other Welsh giants, Idris (or Arthur) who lived at the top of Cader Idris in Snowdonia, and Trichnug, from Plylummon. It is said that anyone who spends the night in Idris's chair—a natural rock outcrop—will waken in the morning either mad or a poet. Trichnug has both a chair and a bed. The chair has the same effect as Idris's, while the bed shapes itself to the height of anyone who lies on it.

In Wales we might glance, too, at a giant variously called Rion, Rhiance, Ritho, or Ron, who gives Arthur a lot of trouble at the beginning of his reign. He has a cloak trimmed with the beards of other kinglets he has defeated and killed. Accordingly he comes demanding Arthur's beard, and there is an inevitable battle, which of course Arthur wins. There is a variant to this story where Arthur goes to the help of Ogryvan (Leodegran) who is being attacked by Ritho—so here Arthur is helping one giant against another.

By far the worst giant in Welsh tradition is Yspaddaden Penkawr, one of the chief giants of Albion according to the story of "Culhwch and Olwen" from the *Mabinogion*. The story is too long and rich to tell here, but briefly it concerns the quest of young Culhwch—Arthur's nephew—for Olwen, who is both the giant's normal-sized daughter, and a very clear memory of the goddess of spring. It is said of her that wherever she walks, she leaves a track of white flowers on the earth behind her—for which she is called Olwen White Track. The description of the first encounter with her father is so vivid that it is worth quoting here:

> "The greeting of Heaven and of man be unto thee, Yspaddaden Penkawr," said they.
> "And you, wherefore come you?"
> "We come to ask thy daughter Olwen, for Kilhwch the son of Kilydd, the son of Prince Kelyddon."
> "Where are my pages and my servants? Raise up the forks beneath my two eyebrows which have fallen over my eyes, that I may see the fashion of my son-in-law." And they did so.
> "Come hither tomorrow, and you shall have an answer."
> They rose to go forth, and Yspaddaden Penkawr seized one of the three poisoned darts that lay beside him, and threw it after them. And Bedwyr caught it, and flung it, and pierced Yspaddaden Penkawr grievously with it through the knee. Then he said, "A cursed ungentle son-in-law, truly. I shall ever walk the worse for his rudeness, and shall ever be without a cure. This poisoned iron pains me like the bite of a gadfly. Cursed be the smith who forged it, and the anvil whereon it was wrought! So sharp is it!" (*Mabinogion*, trans. Lady Charlotte Guest)

There are several references in this story which suggest it was once part of a seasonal myth—Culhwch's mother is called Goleuddydd, which means "light of day" and Culhwch himself is the youngest of twenty-four sons, a probable reference to the twenty-four hours in the day. One derivation of Yspaddaden's name is "Hawthorn," which prompted one commentator to suggest that he too was once a god associated with the springtime.

In fact there are enough references in these stories of the giants to suggest that they may be the memory of an almost forgotten pantheon of primal gods—a notion born out by such figures as the Scottish Cailleach Bheur, or Blue Hag, one of the few female giants of Albion. She really belongs to the "formative" type of giant—those who are involved in the "terraforming" of the land. As she walks she lets fall giant boulders from her apron and in Scotland she is known as "The Daughter of the Little Sun"— the sun of winter. She is in fact a kind of personification of winter—though she has other aspects as well, as a goddess of agriculture and deer—described as having a blue-black face, and hair like frosty twigs. As she walks across the wintry landscape, she is accompanied by deer, sheep, and wolves. Storm clouds are said to be "the Cailleach with her company of hags." When storms approach, local people still say "the Cailleach is going to trample the blankets tonight."

A whole myth has built up around the Cailleach. In her lair below Ben Nevis she holds the nymph of summer prisoner, imposing heavy tasks upon her. But one of the Cailleach's sons falls in love with the prisoner and they elope together in March/April. As they run off, the Cailleach sends wild weather to punish them, but her son responds by driving her ever deeper into the North, and when he finally overtakes her puts out her single eye. She is said to have two sons, one white with a single black spot on him, the other black with a single white spot—symbolising the interaction and cyclicity of winter and summer.

There are a number of other giants who have only one eye— Balor, one of the major giants of Ireland, has an eye which (like Yspaddaden's) shoots out fire and is so toxic that it kills anyone who looks at it (the word "baleful" is said to derive from his name, and though that is etymologically inaccurate, it shows how he was seen.) The fact that Balor is eventually defeated by the sun god Lugh, bears out his original status as a god of winter.

Interestingly, the giants of Scotland seem to be far more associated with foundation myths and the shaping of the land than those in Britain—perhaps simply because it is the gentle, more low-lying areas in the South that need guarding, while the highlands to the North were seen as a natural home of giant builders.

From all of this we can see that the Giants of Albion perform

"IF WE LOOK AT THE SACRED LANDSCAPE OF
BRITAIN AND IRELAND, WHAT DO WE SEE? STONES."
"STONEHENGE," AS IMAGINED BY CHARLES HAMILTON SMITH IN 1815.

the role of guardians, wisdom-keepers, and foundation gods. They are also intimately connected to the landscape, which they helped to form. If we look at the sacred landscape of Britain and Ireland, what do we see? Stones. Stone circles. Megaliths. Standing stones. Henges. And what do these look like? Giants. In fact, there are literally dozens of stories that describe these ancient megalithic stones as giants—from Stonehenge, which is called "The Giant's Dance" to the Whispering Knights or the Rollright Stones—all of which are said to be giants frozen in stone. This suggests that it could well be memories of these ancient monoliths—themselves not infrequently set up as guardian stones, or as altars to ancient gods, as well as for tapping the energies of the earth—that gave rise to the stories of giants in the land. And I can't help thinking as well of something C. S. Lewis wrote in one of his letters to someone who asked about the giants in his Narnia books:

> I have seen landscapes which, under a particular light, made me feel that at any moment a giant might raise its head over the next ridge. Nature has that in her which compels us to invent giants: and only giants will do.

This makes more than perfect sense. Only giants will do. Only they are large enough to represent the huge forces of the earth involved in creation. They are literally emanations of the land; vast, semi-human forms that emerge from the earth and are its eternal guardians.

The Mead Hall: Feasting in Anglo-Saxon England
Stephen Pollington

Communal meals were an important part of Anglo-Saxon and Northern European life. Some of the feasts were informal communal gatherings *(gebeorscipe)* while others were formal ritual gatherings *(symbel)*. Using the evidence of texts such as *Beowulf* and the *Anglo-Saxon Chronicles*, Stephen Pollington shows that the idea of feasting remained central to Anglo-Saxon social traditions long after the physical reality had declined in importance. The words of the poets and saga-writers are supported by a wealth of information about halls, settlement layouts, feasting gear, and the structure and origins of the warband. 24 illustrations, 288 pages, £14.95.

Other Titles By Stephen Pollington

Leechcraft – Early English Charms, Plantlore and Healing, £25.00.
The bulk of the book contains the three healing texts—*Bald's Third Leechbook; Lacnunga; Old English Herbarium*. There is also information about charms; amulets; Anglo-Saxon witchcraft; tree lore; gods; elves and dwarves.

First Steps In Old English: Learn Old English—A Complete Course, £16.95.
Wordcraft: A Concise English to Old English Dictionary & Thesaurus, £9.95.
An Introduction to the Old English Language & Its Literature, £4.95.
Rudiments of Runelore, £4.95.
The English Warrior From Earliest Times Till 1066, £14-95.

Payment may be made by Visa / Mastercard or by a cheque drawn on a UK bank in sterling. UK deliveries add 10% up to a maximum of £2-50. Europe, including Republic of Ireland, add 10% plus £1—all orders are sent airmail. North America add 10% surface delivery, 30% airmail. Elsewhere add 10% surface delivery, 40% airmail. Overseas surface delivery 6–10 weeks; airmail 6–14 days.

**Anglo-Saxon Books, Frithgarth, Thetford Forest Park,
Hockwold, Norfolk IP26 4NQ, England.
tel: 44 (0)1842 828430, fax: 44 (0)1842 828332,
enq@asbooks.co.uk, www.asbooks.co.uk**

The Sacred Plants of our Ancestors

Christian Rätsch

> Golden Apples grow in her garden;
> she alone knows how to tend the apples!
> By eating the fruit, her kindred are endowed
> with eternal, never-aging youth;
> yet sick and pale their blossom falls,
> old and weak they dwindle away,
> and must do without Freia.
> —Richard Wagner, *Rheingold* [1]

The religious experiences of our Germanic-Celtic ancestors were significantly influenced by the considered and responsible use of consciousness-expanding plants. Because these plants made contact with the goddesses, gods, and divinatory beings possible, and revealed the secrets of the universe, they were held in esteem and worshiped as sacred objects. The plants bestowed the people who ingested them with visions of a joyful world in which everything was right. The brutal Christianization of Europe robbed Europeans of their sacred knowledge of how to use these plants in meaningful ways. The plants were demonized by the Church and mystical experience was forbidden (Cf. Müller-Ebeling 1991). Today, European culture still suffers from the gaping wound that was ripped open by Christianization. Modern man is uprooted, culturally divided, and lost in a demystified universe that seems meaningless. He has forgotten the beneficial use of sacred plants and suffers from the uncontrolled abuse of alcohol, tobacco, barbiturates, and other substances. Perhaps the time has come to honor our ancestors and to once more place our trust in the protection of sacred plants.

The Way the Plants are Used Determines Their Effect

The earth provides humans with everything they need. It offers them plants that nourish, heal, stimulate, or intoxicate. Certain plants can be used raw, others must be prepared. Often the preparation of a plant is complicated and demands knowledge, experience, and technology. Many plants are suited only as food when they are prepared by cooking or juicing. Some commonly eaten plants can be fatally toxic if prepared in the wrong manner. Someone who eats raw potatoes, for example, will be ingesting a very dangerous poison. But those who know how to prepare potatoes will not poison themselves.

This holds even truer with medicinal plants than with plants used for food. In the hands of an inexperienced person, foxglove *(Digitalis purpurea)* is a terrible, deadly poison, but in the hands of experienced doctors and herbalists, digitalis preparations have already saved the lives of thousands of people suffering from heart problems. Nearly every medicinal plant can be medicinal or poisonous—sometimes fatally so—depending on the dosage. To be able to use medicinal plants in a wise and truly healing way demands superior expertise concerning application, dosage, and the spectrum of effects. If medicinal plants are used incorrectly, they can do more harm than good (Storl 1986). The same is true for intoxicating or psychedelic plants that expand consciousness. To use these naturally intoxicating plants in a wise and beneficial manner demands the most precise knowledge of preparation and dosage, as well as thorough experience so that the desired effect occurs at the right place and at the right time (Zinberg 1984).

Evidence for the wise use of intoxicating and psychedelic plants has been established as early as the Neolithic period. The disastrous abuse of plant drugs is a manifestation of recent centuries. The sacred or ritual use of such plant drugs has existed in nearly all cultures throughout the history of the human race (McKenna 1992). Their inherent powers, which expanded consciousness and triggered mystical experiences, caused them to be seen as "plants of the gods," "plant teachers," and "magical plants" (Rätsch 1988; Schultes and Hofmann 1979).

In the *Rig Veda*, the most ancient written source of the religion of the Aryans and Indo-European tribes who settled in the Indus Valley, hundreds of songs are sung about the mystical and wondrous effects of the sacrificial drink soma. The soma ritual was quite simple, but all the more potent as a result. It was said that under the guidance of the divine soma drink the creation of the universe could be relived in a mystical way and one could understand oneself as a part of the whole. For this the people gathered together in a circle, lit an altar fire, and sacrificed soma to the gods by ingesting the drink. The body was considered to be the Vedic temple, which was filled and illuminated by the gods incarnated in the draught. In addition to grain and milk, the beer-like drink contained the juice of the soma plants (which still have not yet been definitively botanically identified). In post-Vedic times, the soma drink was brewed with hashish or other *Cannabis* products. It was considered a drink of inspiration. The intoxicated artists referred to in the Vedic hymns attest to the mystical experience of cosmic consciousness (Wasson 1968).

The soma drink of the Aryans corresponds to many intoxicating sacrificial drinks of the Indo-European peoples (Huber 1929; Wohlberg 1990). The Zoroastrian Persians (the ancient Parsi) knew the drink *haoma*, which was brewed with ephedra (*Ephedra* sp.), rue *(Peganum harmala)*, and pomegranate *(Punicum grantum)* (Flattery and Schwartz 1989). The ancient Greeks drank ambrosia, nectar, and *kykeon*—the initiation drink of the Eleusinian mysteries (Wasson et al. 1984). The Thracians became intoxicated on oat beer and wine in which mushrooms had been soaked. The Celts worshiped a magical cauldron that contained the mead of poetry (Maurizio 1933). All of these heathen sacrificial drinks were brewed with the addition of plant drugs (hemp, mushrooms, opium, nightshade plants, etc.), the uses of which are currently subject to laws and regulations. Why were the intoxicating plants of our Indo-European ancestors sacred, and why are they demonized and illegal today? Apparently people back then knew better than they do now how to handle—that is, how to beneficially make use of—consciousness-expanding drugs.

Like many archaic peoples and tribal cultures, our Celtic-Germanic ancestors recognized, cultivated, and integrated the basic human need for intoxication and mystical experience into their lives in a meaningful way (Siegel 1989; Weil 1986). They knew about the divine origins of intoxicating plants and drinks: "Mead itself, which dropped down like heavenly dew from the world tree, was, for the Germanic peoples, the symbol of the drink of the gods" (Delorez 1963: 23).

Our ancestors recognized the cosmic significance of this means of intoxication. It was to open the human being to the fairy world, to raise the rainbow bridge to Valhalla, the fortress of the gods, and offer them sanctuary in a clear, magical, and mystical universe. For this reason the secrets of the sacred plants were guarded by wise women, seeresses, prophets, magicians, priests, and Druids. Sacred drinks were not drunk like the nightly beer in front of the television, but rather as part of communal rituals on special occasions in an extraordinary environment, in order to

IN THE FOLKLORE OF NORTHERN GERMANY, THE BELIEF AROSE THAT WITCHES DRANK BEER AT THEIR GATHERINGS. ("WITCHES' SUPPER," WOODCUT BY ULRICH MOLITORIS, 1489)

glimpse into the beyond—to see the gods (Rätsch 1990).

During the libational ceremonies of the Germanic peoples, the sacred beverage (mead or beer) that had been brewed specifically for the festival was passed around to the circle of participants in large drinking horns decorated with mythical motifs. The priest or chieftain took the horn and drank to the gods, offered some of the liquid to the earth, and sprinkled a few drops to the heavens. He thanked Wotan [Odin], the god of ecstasy and the lord of magical drinks. He called to the ancestors and the heroes who founded the culture of the humans, and wished his tribe peace, well being, and health. Then he passed the horn along. The next round he toasted again to the gods, to friends, or to special ancestors, and passed the horn again, further and further around the circle, until it was empty. As soon as it was, a refilled horn was brought, passed around the circle, and drained—until all the participants in the circle were communally and concurrently intoxicated and the gods descended among the humans (Gaeßner 1941).

Sacred plants were not only used to flavor the sacrificial drink; they were also used in divination and rune oracles. In late Antiquity the figure of the Germanic seeress (called in Old Norse a *seiðkona* or *völva*), was already known for her wondrous abilities throughout Europe and beyond its borders (one was even active in Egypt!). These seeresses—of whom Albruna and Weleda are

Sacred Plants of Our Ancestors

BLACK HENBANE, AN INGREDIENT IN TRUE PILSNER. (ENGRAVING, NINETEENTH CENTURY)

two famous examples—fell into a prophetic trance with the help of such magical substances and shamanic techniques (Delorez). Sacred plants were used in medicine to exorcise harmful spirits, that is, to heal insanity and madness. Other plants were used to increase the fertility of humans, animals, and fields. Love potions were not reprehensible, but instead something sacred, for they could help to spur forth creation.

Henbane and True Beer

Black henbane *(Hyoscyamus niger)* contains various tropane alkaloids that can lead to extreme changes in consciousness (euphoria, hallucination, trance, delirium). These powerful characteristics have been recognized by all peoples and thus henbane has been considered a "plant of the gods" since very early times (Heiser 1987). Today henbane—known in the German vernacular as *Prophetenkraut* (prophet's herb), *Zauberkraut* (magic herb), or *Nifelkraut* (fog herb)—is one of the rare, and therefore protected, plants of Europe. It is more commonly found in the warmer Mediterranean-type climates of countries such as Greece, Portugal, and Spain. In Germany and Denmark it rarely ever appears anymore. It is still occasionally found in Norway. It prefers loamy, nitrogen-rich soil in remote areas, and is often located growing near cultic sites and in the vicinity of convent ruins. Because of its scarcity, the Germanic peoples cultivated henbane in gardens (Höfler 1990). Famous henbane gardens were grown in places whose current names still attest to their former status: Pilsensee (henbane lake), in the regions of Bilsengarten (henbane garden) and Bilstein (henbane stone), and in the Czech city of Pilsen (henbane).[2] The pre-Indo-European natives of the Alps knew of henbane. They placed the small, strongly intoxicating henbane seeds in the urns of their deceased tribal brothers and sisters (Graichen 1988: 69). Henbane was also well known to the Celts. They called it *Belinuntia* or *Beleño*, names which indicate it was sacred to Bel, the god of the sun, oracles, and medicine. The Gaelic Celts also used the herb in the preparation of arrow poison and for the killing of the elders, which is where the German common name *Altsitzerherb* (an herb for *Altsitzer*, or those who can no longer work and are dependant upon others) comes from. At their own request, aged and frail people were sent first on a trip, and then to the beyond, with a brew of henbane (Höfler 1990).

The Germanic peoples used henbane for magical and religious rituals, medicine, and love magic. The consciousness-altering powers of the herb were so skillfully employed that, depending on what was needed, they could lead to insights, healing, or romantic yearnings. When possible, the herb was to be harvested by a naked girl who was consecrated to the magical spirit or the divine nature of the plant. Henbane stood under the dominion of the fertility god Donar/Thor (the Romans connected it with their own thunder god, Jupiter). For this reason it was used for weather magic. When the land was suffering from a drought, a stalk of henbane was dipped into a spring. The drops that clung to it were then sprinkled onto the sun-parched earth. Bishop Burchard of Worms (ca. 965–1025) described a heathen henbane weather magic ritual of the tenth century:

> During a period of incessant drought the girls gathered together, stripped one of their playmates naked and searched for *belisa* (i.e., henbane). The naked girl had to pull it out with her right hand, and it was then bound to the small toe of her right foot. Afterward some of the girls, with sticks in their hands, led the naked one to the nearest stream and sprinkled her with water. Doing this was supposed to call down the desired rain. Then the girl, who had to now walk backwards like a crab, was led back to

where they had begun. (Quoted after Bräunlein 1986: 55)

Henbane's most important religious role is in the Germanic libational offering to honor the thunder god Donar/Thor. Already in the first century C.E., the Roman historian Tacitus wrote that the Germanic peoples have always been heavy beer drinkers. They drank many different kinds of beer: lighter beer for daily enjoyment, strong beer for the ram and buck sacrifices, heavy Yule beer for the winter solstice. There was also beer for weddings, the harvest, binding ceremonies, and for friendship. The Germanic beers were all top-fermented and brewed without hops. They were brewed with barley malt, *bierbrot* (bread soaked with water, used to start the fermentation), and honey (Gaeßner 1941). In order to make the brew strong and intoxicating, marsh rosemary *(Ledum palustre)*, bog myrtle *(Myrica gale)*, or above all henbane was added (Maurizio 1933). The name "pilsner," currently used to denote modern hoppy beer, came from henbane, which was formerly known in German as *pilsener krut* (henbane herb). Henbane beer was a potent intoxicant, aphrodisiac, and could reveal visions of divine splendor. A beer like this would not make you tired and sleepy, as a hopped beer does. It was stimulating and inspired the imagination, inducing heavenly trips and causing the henbane fairies to introduce themselves. The "true pilsner" is the only beer that makes you thirstier, the more you drink!

Not Only Rope Got Twisted From Hemp

Hemp (of which there are three species: *Cannabis sativa, Cannabis indica,* and *Cannabis ruderalis*) has been used for around 10,000 years for fiber, food (the seeds and their oil), medicine, and as an intoxicant. It is one of the oldest—perhaps *the* oldest—cultivated plants of the human race. The drugs derived from hemp (hashish, marijuana) are very mild euphorics. They stimulate the associative imagination and put the user into a euphoric state for 2–3 hours, which is characterized by aphrodisiac feelings and changes in the experience of the time-space continuum.

The most ancient archeological discovery of hemp seeds *(Cannabis sativa)* was found at a dig done at the stratum of the band ceramics culture in Eisenberg near Thuringia (Renfrew 1973: 163). Thus, the earliest evidence of hemp culture (approxi-

GERMANIA, THE PERSONIFICATION OF THE GERMAN REVOLUTION OF 1848, HOLDS A HEMP BRANCH AND SWORD. (PAINTING BY PHILIPP VEIT, 1848)

THE WHITE GARDEN POPPY.
(ILLUSTRATION FOR "THE HERBAL"
OF JOHN GERARD, 1633)

mately 7,500 years old) is found on the soil of present-day Germany! Hemp has been established as part of Germanic culture from before the fifth century B.C.E. It was cultivated in fields, often together with flax. Hemp was sown, tended, and harvested by women (Höfler 1990: 98). The workings of the love goddess Freya were recognized in hemp. Sowing and harvest were conducted in her honor with an erotic ritual, a *Hochzeit* —a "high time."[3] In the feminine flowers lay the eroticizing and love-generating power of Freya (Neményi 1988). Those who became intoxicated from them experienced the sensual joy and aphrodisiac ecstasies of the love goddess. From archeological digs it has been discovered that the Germanic and Celtic tribes were already placing female hemp flowers (marijuana) in the graves of their dead 2,500 years ago (Kessler 1985).

The Garden Poppy's Got It

Most people believe that the poppy *(Papaver somniferum)* originally came from eastern Asia and that the opium produced from it was a discovery of the Chinese. Both beliefs are incorrect. Poppies were cultivated in the eastern Mediterranean region. Opium was discovered by the Minoans (on Crete) and the ancient Greeks, and used medicinally, ritualistically, and hedonistically in many different ways. Poppies, and the knowledge of how to prepare opium (by making incisions in the immature capsules), came very early to the Celtic-Germanic regions. In the pile dwellings on Lake Constance and in Switzerland (e.g., at Robbenhausen), which date back around 4,500 years, cakes with poppy seeds as well as incised capsules have been found (Seefelder 1987).

The Germanic peoples planted poppies in poppy fields or *Magenfeldern* (stomach fields) which were considered convalescing and healing fields and were known as *Odâinsackr* (Old Norse, "field of the living"). There Odin/Wotan, the god of healing and ecstasy, practiced his greatest marvels. Dissolving all fears, stimulating the imagination, and facilitating psychic abilities, the poppy juice (=opium) also protected one from harmful spirits, bloodsucking vampires, and the mischievous Prussian gnome known as the Nickel-Kobold or Nickelruh (Höfler 1990).

In our own century, poppy juice dissolved in wine continues to be used in German folk medicine as a remedy for sleep, pain, and anxiety. Perhaps these folk-medicinal uses have their roots in a Germanic drinking tradition in which opium was added to mead.

The Fruits of the Valkyries

The atropine-containing belladonna *(Atropa belladonna)* is called *tollkirsch* ("crazy" or "lusty cherry") in German. Because it is also known as *Wutbeere* (rage berry) in German (Hirschfeld and Linsert 1930: 157), the intoxicating, hallucinogenic plant is placed under the dominion of Odin, the "raging." The plant, which causes death in higher doses, is also connected to Odin as the god of death, and to the valkyries as the spirits of death. The beautiful and seductive valkyries were the daughters of Odin and Erda—in other words, of heaven and earth. They were the goddesses of the wind, who carried the souls of heroes who had fallen in battle, or others who had died honorably, to the divine fortress of Valhalla. Those chosen by the valkyries are then allowed to delight and intoxicate themselves with the divine mead until the end of the world, or more precisely, until the cyclical renewal of the universe. In the lower Rhine regions, belladonna is called *Walkerbaum* (valkyrie tree). It is said that everyone who eats of the berries will fall prey to the valkyries (Perger 1864: 182f).

Belladonna is said to open the gateway to Valhalla, thus to an alternative state of consciousness.

Fly Agaric and Other Flying Mushrooms

In many German-speaking regions the expression *"der hat wohl Narrenschwämme gegessen"* ("he must have eaten fool's mushrooms") has been preserved into modern times.[4] This refers to someone who has been living out his foolishness, craziness, or insanity. The name is a folkloric memory that mushrooms exist which can put a normal person into an extraordinary state of consciousness. Many indigenous mushrooms of Europe such as liberty caps *(Psilocybe semilanceata)* contain the same active ingredients as the famous Mexican magic mushrooms *(Psilocybe mexicana)* (Hofmann et al. 1963; Jordan 1989). These native European mushrooms are just as capable as the Mexican species of revealing the splendidly colorful visions of a different, higher, or truer reality. They can answer questions, provide solutions, and fill the individual's life with meaning. But they can also reveal the depths of the individual soul in the form of demons and horrific images. Those who are afraid of themselves are easily made foolish by the mushrooms. Those who wish to further expand themselves will find true allies. We know that the Germanic peoples added mushrooms to their ritual beer or mead (Lohberg 1984: 66). It is only likely that the mushrooms would imbue the drink with the power of divine revelation—for those who drank in the circle saw the gods descend among them.

We know of one mushroom that was consecrated to Odin, the god of ecstasy: fly agaric *(Amanita muscaria)*. Fly agaric has a very long shamanic tradition in northern Eurasia. Its intoxicating qualities were used culturally for shamanizing, divination, and dreams (Bauer et al. 1991; Rosenbohm 1991). According to Germanic conceptions, fly agaric arose when Odin rode through the air with his horse on a wild hunt at the time of the winter solstice. The foam from his horse's nostrils fell to the ground, fertilizing and impregnating it. After nine months—thus, at the end of August or beginning of September—the earth bore forth the bright red, phallic fly agaric (Pursey 1977: 80). These mushrooms are able to help the soul to fly, and to bestow it with the visionary gift of the divine. Odin had two ravens who were called "thought" and "memory." They fed themselves from the mushroom which since

AN AGE-OLD CONNECTION EXISTS
BETWEEN MUSHROOMS AND OTHER REALMS.
(ILLUSTRATION BY EDMUND DULAC FOR
SHAKESPEARE'S "THE TEMPEST," 1906)

Antiquity has been called *Rabenbrot* (raven's bread) in German vernacular. Perhaps this mushroom can make the thoughts of our ancestors more understandable, in that it once again sets our suppressed memories free.

This brief overview should be sufficient to illustrate that the use of mind-altering drugs is not originally "culturally alien" to

Europeans. Our ancestors have known them and used them in a meaningful way for centuries. It was only by the suppression of our native tradition that the misuse—in other words, the uprooted use—of psychoactive substances was brought about.

(Translated by Annabel Lee)

An earlier version of this article appeared under the title "Was schon den Alten heilig war" (What Was Already Sacred to the Ancients) in Esotera (10/91). This translation is of a subsequent version, "Die heiligen Pflanzen unserer Ahnen," which appeared in the Festschrift collected in honor of Albert Hofmann entitled Das Tor zu inneren Räumen: Heilige Pflanzen und psychedelische Substanzen als Quelle spiritueller Inspiration *(Gateway to Inner Space: Sacred Plants and Psychedelic Substances as a Source of Spiritual Inspiration), edited by Christian Rätsch (Löhrbach: Edition Rauschkunde, 1996). It appears here by kind permission of the author.*

Translator's Notes:

1. In his Ring Cycle operas based on the Nibelungen stories, Wagner merged aspects of Freia (Freya) and Idunn, the latter of whom was actually the goddess in the ancient Germanic myths who tended the apples of eternal youth.

2. *Bilsenkraut* is the German common name for henbane.

3. *Hochzeit* = marriage or wedding; literally *hoch* = high, *zeit* = time.

4. *Narrenschwämme*, literally "fool's mushrooms," is one of the many German common names for fly agaric (*Amanita muscaria*).

Sources:

Bauer, Wolfgang, et al. *Der Fliegenpilz: Ein kulturhistorisches Museum* (Cologne: Wienand Verlag, 1991).

Bräunlein, Peter. "Vom Zauber der Pflanzen in der mitteralterlichen Heilkunst" in the exhibition catalog *Kreutter-Kunst* (Freiburg: 1986), pp. 55–77.

Delorez, R. L. M. *Götter und Mythen der Germanen* (Einsiedeln, Zurich, Cologne: Benziger, 1963).

Flattery, David S., & Martin Schwartz. *Haoma and Harmaline*

[Near Eastern Studies, vol. 21] (Los Angeles: University of California, 1989).

Gaeßner, Heinz. *Bier und Bierartige Getränke im Germanischem Kulturkreis* (Berlin: Veröffentlichungen der Gesellschaft für die Geschichte und Bibliographie des Brauwesens, 1941).

Graichen, Gisela. *Das Kultplatzbuch* (Hamburg: Hoffmann & Campe, 1988).

Heiser, Charles B. *The Fascinating World of Nightshades* (New York: Dover, 1987).

Hirschberg, Magnus, and Richard Linsert. *Liebesmittel* (Berlin: Man Verlag, 1930).

Höfler, Max. *Volksmedizinische Botanik der Germanen* (Berlin: VWB, 1990 [reprint from 1908]).

Hofmann, Albert, et al. "Présence de la psilocybine dans une espèce européene d'Agaric, le *Psilocybe semilanceata* Fr. Note(*) de MM" in *C. R. Acad. Sc.* (Paris: 1963), pp. 10–12.

Huber, E. *Das Trankopfer im Kulte der Völker* (Hannover-Kirchrode: Opperman, 1929).

Jordan, Michael. *Mushroom Magic* (London: Elm Tree Books, 1989).

Kessler, Thomas. *Cannabis Helvetica* (Zurich: Nachtschatten, 1985).

Lohberg, Rolf. *Das große Lexikon vom Bier*, 3rd. expanded edition (Stuttgart: Scripta, 1984).

Maurizio, A. *Geschichte der gegorene Getränke* (Berlin: Paul Parey, 1933).

McKenna, Terence. *Food of the Gods: The Search for the Original Tree of Knowledge* (New York: Bantam, 1992).

Müller-Ebeling, Claudia. "Wolf und Bilsenkraut, Himmel und Hölle—Ein Beitrag zum Thema Dämonisierung der Nature" in Susanne G. Seiler, ed., *Gaia—Das Erwachen der Göttin* (Braunschweig: Aurum, 1991), pp. 163–182.

Neményi, Géza von. *Heidnische Naturreligion* (Bergen an der Dumme: Johanna Bohmeier Verlag, 1988).

Perger, K. Ritter von. *Deutsche Pflanzensagen* (Stuttgart and Oehringen: August Schaber, 1864).

Pursey, Helen L. *Die Wundersame Welt der Pilze* (Zollikon: Albatross, 1977).

Rätsch, Christian. *Lexikon der Zauberpflanzen aus ethnologischer Sicht* (Graz: Akademische Druck- und Verlagsanstalt, 1988).

Rätsch, Christian. "Bridges to the Gods: Psychedelic Rituals of Knowledge" in *Annali dei Musei civici* 6 (1990), pp. 127–138.

Renfrew, Jane. *Paleoethnobotany: The Prehistoric Food Plants of the Near East and Europe* (New York: Columbia University Press, 1973).

Rosenbohm, Alexander. *Halluzinogene Drogen im Schamanismus* (Berlin: Dietrich Reimer Verlag, 1991)

Schultes, Richard E., and Albert Hofmann. *Plants of the Gods* (New York: McGraw Hill, 1979). Revised edition, with Christian Rätsch (Rochester, Vermont: Inner Traditions, 2002).

Seefelder, Mattias. *Opium—Eine Kulturgeschichte* (Frankfurt an der Main: Athenäum, 1987)

Siegel, Ronal K. *Intoxication: Life in Pursuit of Artificial Paradise* (New York: Dutton, 1989)

Storl, Wolf-Dieter. *Vom rechten Umgang mit heilenden Pflanzen* (Freiburg: Hyperion, 1986).

Wasson, R. Gordon. *Soma, the Divine Mushroom of Immortality* (New York: Harcourt Brace Jovanovich, 1968).

Wasson et al. *Der Weg nach Eleusis* (Frankfurt on the Main: Insel, 1984).

Weil, Andrew. *The Natural Mind*, revised ed. (Boston: Houghton Mifflin, 1986).

Wohlberg, Joseph. "Hoama-Soma in the World of Ancient Greece" in *Journal of Psychoactive Drugs* 22 (1990), pp. 333-342.

Zinberg, Norman. *Drug, Set, and Setting: The Basis for Controlled Intoxicant Use* (New Haven: Yale University Press, 1984).

Witchcraft Medicine
Healing Arts, Shamanic Practices, and Forbidden Plant
CLAUDIA MÜLLER-EBELING, CHRISTIAN RÄTSCH, and *WOLF-DIETER STORL*

Witchcraft Medicine takes the reader on a journey that examines the women who mix the potions and become the healers; the sorceress as shaman. The authors offer an in-depth investigation of the outlawed wild medicine of witches which does more than make one healthy, it creates lust and knowledge, ecstacy and mythological insight.
$24.95, paper, 272 pgs., 8 x 10, three 8-page color inserts
158 b/w illustrations, ISBN 0-89281-971-5
AVAILABLE OCTOBER 2003

Shamanism and Tantra in the Himalayas
CLAUDIA MÜLLER-EBELING, CHRISTIAN RÄTSCH, and *SURENDRA BAHADUR SHAHI*

After over eighteen years of field research the authors present this comprehensive overview of shamanism based on the knowledge and experience of the many different tribes of Nepal.
$49.95, hardcover, 320 pgs., $8^1/2$ x 11
605 color and b/w illustrations, ISBN 0-89281-913-8

Plants of the Gods
Their Sacred, Healing, and Hallucinogenic Powers
RICHARD EVANS SCHULTES, ALBERT HOFMANN, and *CHRISTIAN RÄTSCH*

World-renowned anthropologist and enthopharmacologist Christian Ratsch provides the latest scientific updates to this classic work. Numerous new and rare photographs complement the completely revised and updated text.
$29.95, paper, 208 pgs., $7^5/8$ x $10^1/2$
400 color and b/w illustrations, ISBN 0-89281-979-0

Marijuana Medicine
A World Tour of the Healing and Visionary Powers of Cannabis
CHRISTIAN RÄTSCH

This detailed visual record of cannabis culture explores the therapeutic, historical, and cultural uses of this plant in traditions from around the world.
$24.95, paper, 224 pgs., 8 x 10, 16-page color insert
150 b/w illustrations, ISBN 0-89281-933-2

INNER TRADITIONS BEAR & COMPANY
One Park St., Rochester, VT 05767   800•246•8648
www.InnerTraditions.com   orders@InnerTraditions.com
Please add $4.50 S/H for one book, $5.50 for two books, FREE SHIPPING for three or more.

The First Northern Renaissance: The Reawakening of the Germanic Spirit in the Sixteenth and Seventeenth Centuries in Germany, Sweden, and England

Stephen Edred Flowers

Introduction

The Germanic peoples have been working to reawaken their pagan heritage and their pagan values for over seven hundred years. At first, they held onto their pagan virtues well into the Middle Ages. But as soon as these values had been suppressed by the increasing establishment of ideas rooted in Christian theology, there arose attempts to reawaken archaic indigenous cultural patterns. These old patterns never actually died out. They merely fell dormant, awaiting certain stimuli to reawaken them. The term *renaissance*, which literally means "rebirth," implies some sort of "death" which may have actually never occurred. Overt and conscious attempts to reawaken Germanic cultural values begin in the fifteenth to seventeenth centuries, a time often referred to in Germanic Studies as the Renaissance-Reformation period.

This article stems from the second volume of a larger work which is a projected three-volume study entitled *The Northern Dawn: A History of the Reawakening of the Germanic Spirit*. The general underlying concept for this is the tracing of historical attempts to reawaken Germanic cultural patterns from the beginning of the disestablishment of these ideas in the Middle Ages to the middle of the twentieth century. In order to perform this complex task in a coherent manner, a certain intellectual lens, or framework of understanding, had to be developed. This framework is elaborated upon in the first volume of *The Northern Dawn*. First, it had to be established what the phrase "Germanic culture" even means. Without knowing what the basic Germanic cultural values are, it is impossible to recognize them as they are historically reawakened. Additionally, the story of the diminution, or disestablishment, of these values—usually synonymous with the Christianization process—had to be discussed. The body of the work then deals with the reawakening of Germanic culture. In order for this reawakening to take place it was determined that four elements had to be in place to a greater or lesser extent: desire (the will to reawaken the culture), freedom (the psychological and/or political liberty to engage in this activity), sources (upon which to base the work authentically), and methods (by which to analyze the sources productively). Certain fields of Germanic culture had to be addressed systematically. These fields are law (politics, economics), literature, religion, language, and material culture. Readers of my previous contribution in volume one of *TYR* will remember that an integral culture is composed of a complex of factors. Separating one of these factors from the rest can only be done provisionally with a specific, limited purpose in mind. This is why the *Northern Dawn* project cannot be characterized simply as a "history of the revival of Germanic religion." An integral culture does not isolate one aspect of itself from other aspects. The trend towards this disintegration in our modern culture is directly traceable to the advent, first of Christianity, and then of the Enlightenment, with its idea of universal progress based on rationalism. Finally, it must be noted that Germanic culture, which in ancient times could be spoken of as a whole possessing only organic tribal divisions, must in historical times be considered in three major cultural spheres: the German, English, and Scandinavian.

During the Middle Ages, Germanic culture survived in the vibrant forms of (secular) heroic myth as well as in (ecclesiastical) religious ritual.[1] Although the ancient Germanic values continued to exist in various sheltered corners of the medieval world, they were rapidly diminishing under the direct influence of Christian theology. National traditions throughout Europe were put at an overwhelming disadvantage by medieval political theory which was essentially based on the Pauline formula "For there is no power but of God" (Romans 13:1). This theoretically and effectively placed the secular kings under Church authority. The kings had previously derived their authority from the national divinities which manifested in the blood of the aristocratic folk of the tribes, from among whom the kings were elected. Christian political theory taught that the God from whom political power was derived was universal (international) and that His will was expressed through the international agency of the Church. This theory placed all indigenous national cultures in a precarious position.

The medieval, Church-dominated, theoretical cultural framework would not last, however. The Middle Ages themselves crumbled due to a variety of Church-inspired calamities. These included the economic collapse of Europe, which fell from its superior position during the Roman Empire, to a place where it could perhaps be considered the most backward region of the world by around 1350. Additionally, Europe suffered ultimate military defeat at the hands of the Muslims, who not only repelled the Crusaders' invasions (by 1291), but who were also beginning to overrun eastern Europe in the fifteenth century. Intellectually, Europe had been greatly impoverished and crippled by the ideological influence of the medieval clerical culture.

These and other failings played no small role in the rise of the critical questioning of established ideological norms in Europe during the fifteenth century. In Italy, this critical questioning was answered positively in the form of what would come to be known as the Renaissance. To oversimplify a bit, the Renaissance was essentially a rebirth of the philosophies and aesthetics of the pagan classical world.[2] The Renaissance in Italy was universalized by later humanists. However, in its origin it was mainly an expression of Italian cultural nationalism (centered in various city-states in the Italian peninsula). By restoring a pagan-based culture they thought that they might find the key to the restoration of their lost cultural glories.

In Italy, this pagan restoration was relatively simple in a theoretical sense. The Italian libraries were full of books of pagan wisdom in languages easily read by the new academicians, such as Greek and Latin. New attitudes and methods were exported from Italy to other parts of Europe. North of the Alps, in Germany and beyond, these ideas echoed as "Northern Humanism." Humanism is seen as a "revolt against religious limitations on knowledge, with a revival of classical learning and a stress on man's enjoyment of this existence."[3] The impetus towards a true Northern Renaissance, based on northern cultural models, was strongly present. The inner or psychological freedom to pursue such a venture was reserved to an elite few, while outer or political freedom remained a sporadic and fleeting commodity throughout the age. Moreover, the type of sources readily available in the South for such a "rebirth" were almost utterly lacking at this time for the Germanic world. However, such sources began to be collected, edited, and published in the North in a flurry of scholarly activity inspired by humanist thinking. The major manuscript of the *Poetic* or *Elder Edda (Codex Regius)* was only discovered in Iceland in 1643. The methods of understanding the texts and other sources were also rather impoverished, but some important theoretical and methodological foundations were laid in the Germanic cultural sphere at this time, for example the *experientia ac ratio* of Paracelsus. This would be an age of great enthusiasm and expectation but also one fraught with fanaticism and often still mired in the shadow of medievalism.

For the purposes of this article I will address the topics of myth, religion, mysticism, and law among the Germans, Swedes, and English during this period. By "myth" I intend to indicate the legendary tales of origins, heroes, and apocalypse; while, here, "religion" is limited to formal expressions of cult and theology of the period. "Mysticism" is the often heterodox and subjective expression of what would otherwise be called religion. "Law" conveys ideas of political organization and theories of sovereignty.

Myth

During the Renaissance-Reformation period in the Germanic world, myths and legends abounded in learned and popular writings. The invention of the printing press in Germany in the middle of the fifteenth century led to more widespread literacy—especially in the Protestant areas of northern Europe in the sixteenth century. This supply of affordably printed works fed the popular demand for material concerning heroes and the legendary past. These myths can be said to fall into three general categories: 1) the legends of the ancient Germanic world and ancient Germanic ethnography; 2) tales drawn from the archetypal characters of medieval history; and 3) "Germanized" versions of biblical narratives.

The main sources for the legendary Germanic past during this period were the historical and ethnographic works of the ancient Roman historian Cornelius Tacitus (55–117 C.E.). Chief among these were his *Annals*, *Histories*, and *Germania*.[4] These had survived the medieval period and, with the rebirth of classical learning, new attention was being paid to ancient Greek and Latin works. The most striking figure from this material was Arminius (Hermann). The Germanic form of his name would probably have been Harmannaz. He was a Cheruskan war-leader, who is credited with being the (Roman-trained) general who conducted a successful defensive military campaign against the Roman

The First Northern Renaissance

AN 1897 REPLICA OF THE HERMANN MONUMENT
IN NEW ULM, MINNESOTA.
(PHOTO COURTESY OF THE CITY OF NEW ULM)

legions under Varus in 9 C.E. The chief source for this history is the *Annals* of Tacitus. This war is said by Tacitus to have ended in a final massacre of the Romans in the *saltus Teutoburgiensis*—or Teutoburg Forest. The Romans were virtually wiped out to the last man, and this early defeat is thought to have once and for all discouraged the Romans from ever trying to invade Germany much to the east of the Rhine or north of the Danube again. Starting from the period of the Protestant Reformation, the image of *Germania contra Romam* conjured a powerful nationalistic paradigm. This served the contemporary struggle of Germany to free herself from Roman religious authority and so struck a deep chord in the national psyche. The most ferocious fighter against Rome at this time was not Martin Luther, but a far less well-known warrior-poet named Ulrich von Hutten (1488–1523), of whom I will have more to say later. Ulrich wrote a dialog entitled *Arminius* (1529), which celebrated the exploits of the ancient Cheruskan war-leader. This work was intended to provide a heroic ideal to the German Emperor Maximilian I (1493–1519). The emperor had named Ulrich *poet laureate* in July of 1517. This dialog inaugurated a virtual Arminius cult in Germany, which reached its zenith with the erection of the *Hermannsdenkmal* (Hermann monument) in 1875, but would continue to echo strongly well into the twentieth century.[5]

Historical emperors of the medieval period became the objects of strong mythologizing tendencies. The principal myth in this regard was that of Emperor Barbarossa ("Redbeard"). These myths conflate two different Emperors: Friedrich I (Barbarossa, 1152–1190) and Friedrich II, "the Antichrist" (1211–1250). The main outline of this myth is that the once and future (and final) emperor sits slumbering in a hollow mountain somewhere in Germany. This was usually identified as the Kyffhäuser mountain in Thuringia. (An alternative is the Untersberg, near Salzburg.) The emperor's lair is guarded by ravens, and it is said that he will awaken and return to the world in the hour of the nation's greatest need. Then he will hang a shield on a barren tree, and at once set forth to destroy the Church and the clergy. This particular myth was exceedingly popular in vernacular circles, but was understandably discouraged in learned ones. Again, this myth was to echo right into the nineteenth and twentieth centuries, when the awakened emperor was once more awaited as a national savior.[6] In 1896 an elaborate monument was erected to this idea on the Kyffhäuser.

Because the mythology of the biblical narrative had been so deeply ingrained—especially in learned circles where classical languages dominated—it would continue to exert a great influence even in times when the orthodox interpretations of these narratives were becoming increasingly unpopular. Typically, the biblical myths are accepted in their broad outlines, but they are explicitly "Germanized" in that biblical figures are identified as being Germans, and often the location of the biblical narrative is transported from the Levant to northern Europe. One of the most noteworthy mythographers of this type, identified only as the "Alsatian Anonymous," wrote a work entitled *Das Buch der Hundert Kapitel* (The Book of a Hundred Chapters, 1509). In it, he flatly states that Adam *ist ein teutscher man gewesen* ("Adam was a German man"). So, too, were all the biblical heroes. The Alsatian Anonymous also predicts that in the future there will come an emperor named Friedrich who will exterminate the clergy and establish a new chivalric order called the Brotherhood of the Yellow Cross, and that his empire will last a thousand years.

This whole mythic tradition is interesting especially for its vital aspects. These were no mere tales for entertaining bored workers or children—these were paradigms for radical action. The myths of the national past—whether based on events in distant pagan times, the medieval period, or Germanized biblical narratives—all gave meaning to the present and served as either a call to future action, or provided hope for a better time to come.

Religion

During the sixteenth and seventeenth centuries, the Germanic cultures of northern Europe were wracked with questions of a religious nature. Since the advent of the medieval model of a separation of secular and ecclesiastical authority, "religion" had become a specialized and discreet part of life increasingly separated from the greater whole. This, according to what we know of ancient Germanic culture, was an idea especially foreign to the Germanic attitude towards life.[7] By "religion" I mean to indicate a formalized and established ideology and set of outward practices or ritual, intended to be adhered to by mass populations. This contrasts with mysticism, which addresses such spiritual issues in a more individualized and subjective manner. Viewed from this perspective it will be seen that the tenets introduced by Protestantism at first tended to encourage a mystical direction, and that this drift was an essentially "northern" characteristic.

Earlier Christianity—medieval Roman Catholicism—had at one point been heavily Germanized. This is convincingly argued in James C. Russell's *The Germanization of Early Medieval Christianity*. The process of Germanization hinged primarily on outer ritual and other practices, which were made to accord with pagan Germanic practice, so that the essence of the inner life of the newly Christian Germanic peoples would have some continuity. By the fifteenth century, however, traces of the old pagan spirituality were almost entirely obscured in the world of religion. The two chief contributions of official Protestantism to the restoration of the true Germanic spirit are the reemphasis on the role of the individual soul in the process of spiritual development (or in Christian terminology, "salvation"), and the reintroduction of the king as the official "high priest" of the religion.

The Protestant Reformation started in earnest in the first quarter of the sixteenth century. Its most effective single leader, the German churchman Martin Luther, set a certain chain of events into motion when he nailed a series of ninety-five theses of protest against Roman Catholic practices and tenets on a church door in Wittenberg, Germany on 31 October 1517. By 1521 he had been excommunicated, and the Reformation was underway. By 1540 most of Germanic northern Europe—Scandinavia, England, and the northern half of German-speaking central Europe—had embraced one form of Protestantism or another. Curiously—and tellingly—those parts of Germany that had in ancient times been part of the Roman Empire remained part of the Roman Catholic sphere, while those regions and peoples that had never been conquered by ancient Rome were the areas wherein the revolt against medieval Rome was strongest and most successful. Luther had not been the first to raise a questioning voice against Roman religious hegemony[8]—he merely gave concrete and organized form to centuries-old trends. Luther's doctrines were in fact very much watered down when compared to the radical ideas that were in the air at the time, such as those of Ulrich von Hutten.

The main tenets of "Lutheranism" are that man is saved by three things alone: God's grace, faith, and scripture. In the first term, God's grace, Luther asserts his adherence to Augustinian orthodoxy, but in the latter two terms he opens the door to a subtle aspect of re-Germanization. By faith, Luther opposed the Catholic idea that outer works were surer signs of God's grace than any mysterious inner spiritual state, as implied by faith. By scripture, Luther intended to indicate that all the faithful should be able to read the holy scriptures (the Bible). This meant that a) the Bible would have to be translated into German (from Latin, Greek, and Hebrew); and that b) a more universal literacy would have to be encouraged among the general population. The ultimate consequences of all this were more far reaching and profound than Luther himself might have foreseen.

The Germanic elements in the Protestant Reformation were both subtle and, eventually, in some instances even detrimental[9] to the process of the reawakening of the indigenous Germanic spirit. The fact that Protestantism was essentially a Germanic cultural phenomenon—that it occurred exclusively within the Germanic-speaking realm—gave it, de facto, a certain intrinsically Germanic stamp. But consciously, Luther saw his ideal paradigms stemming not from Germania, but from so-called "primitive Christianity." The systematic translation of the Bible into the vernacular Germanic tongues—German (1522), Danish/Norwegian (1524), Swedish (1527), English (1535), and Icelandic (1584)—gave new prestige to these languages and ultimately to literatures produced in them over the centuries.

As the Roman Catholic Middle Ages had been ideologically dominated by an overtly Christian elite (the clergy), all efforts to devolve that ideological hegemony back to other elements of the culture, such as the individual or the king (state), can be seen, in some sense, as re-paganizing. In Germanic pagan times, each individual actively participated in his or her own spiritual development and the king (or head of the family) was the "priest" as well. Turning the focus away from an outward emphasis on a non-organic, professional, and international priesthood toward an inner emphasis on the individual's relationship to divinity and toward a national priesthood with a national church, is an implicit move towards a subjective inwardness (German: *Innerlichkeit*). The invisible inner life of the individual becomes the paramount theater of spiritual activity. This "turning inward" is reflected in a mystical way (as the individual reflects on his own soul) and in a nationalistic way (as the people becomes once more aware of its spiritual importance).

The individual could now again be an active agent in the religious "ritual," as the Protestant rite provided for preaching in the common vernacular of the people and the singing of the laity, and in the process of "salvation" in the form of the inner experience of faith and the understanding of God's will provided by reading the Bible in one's own language. It is curious to note that these Protestant reforms of the sixteenth century were so clearly mirrored by the "heretical" practices of the (Arian) Church of the Gothic people more than a millennium earlier. The Goths were roundly condemned by Roman Church authorities for translating the scriptures into their own language (the Gothic Bible of Ulfilas), and for allowing the laity to sing during services. They were supposed to have set holy words to popular "sea shanties"—which is virtually identical to the later charge that Luther wrote hymns to "tavern tunes." From our perspective, all this is only interesting because of its paradigmatic effect of unconsciously refocusing the religious life in ways harmonious with the old pagan structures.

Of all the reforms instituted by Protestantism, the one that made the most immediate impact was the restoration of the king to his role as high priest, or "head of the Church." This was perhaps a brilliant political ploy by the Protestants who took advantage of the historical antagonism between the Roman Church and the secular lords. Finally, with Protestantism the northern kings could be rid of meddling from Rome, and the wealth accumulated by the Church in their respective countries over the centuries could be "nationalized" as the king's property. This, like so many of the Protestant reforms, began with what appeared to be a good idea, but soon degenerated into corruption. As the king continued to be chosen by the Christian-inspired practice of primogeniture, rather than the pagan idea of election from among a large body of aristocrats, the quality of the kings was often questionable. Yet they now ruled with a freer hand and increasingly hid behind the idea of their supposed "divine right" to rule.

In the northern Germanic realms during the Renasissance-Reformation period, the religious revolution of Protestantism opened the door to ideas that would only indirectly manifest themselves in overt revivals of paganism. The individual soul embedded in the cultural context of its nationality became an active agent of its own salvation, just as the soul of the king became the focus of national salvation. These ideas fundamentally grew out of mystical roots that had been cultivated in German soil from the days of paganism through the Middle Ages (e.g., Eckhart, Tauler, and Süse). These roots would eventually flower in the Romanticism of the eighteenth and nineteenth centuries.

Mysticism

Mysticism, "a type of religion which puts the emphasis on immediate awareness ... [and] direct and intimate consciousness of Divine Presence,"[10] is a predictable outgrowth of the combination of religion and the new emphasis on the individual in Protestantism. Mysticism is a universal phenomenon in the history of religion. The specifically Germanic character of the mysticism found in the sixteenth and seventeenth centuries in northern

Europe is rather difficult to confirm. On the one hand, this period was one of extreme paucity of information on "native" Germanic traditions, yet it was a time of conspicuous mystical activity and thought among men of Germanic heritage and in areas of northern Europe where Germanic languages were spoken. The Germanic traits of mysticism in this time and place are perhaps rooted not so much in external symbols, but in methods of approach.

For our purposes, the most dominant thinker in the northern European Renaissance is Theophrastus Bombastus von Hohenheim (1493–1541), better known by his academic moniker, Paracelsus. Born in Switzerland, he studied in various monastic and mining schools, received a bachelor's degree in Vienna and studied medicine in Ferrara, Italy, where he received his doctorate in 1516. Paracelsus traveled continuously throughout central Europe during the course of his life. He remained Roman Catholic, although many of his friends and sympathetic colleagues were northern European Protestants. Paracelsus was a lifelong critic of the entrenched theories of medieval medicine—which amounted to little more than the application of recipes found in ancient manuals. The help provided to patients by cures derived from these manuals simply amounted to a hastening of inevitable death. As an act of protest against the academic establishment, Paracelsus burned a volume of Avicenna's canon of scholastic medicine. This occurred in Basel on 24 June (St. John's Day) 1527. This began a period of conflict with established academic and political authorities. By the end of his life his practical medical successes and eloquence in writing and in speech had largely vindicated him and restored his reputation.

The written work of Paracelsus fills twenty volumes in the modern edition. It is largely alchemical and magical in nature (with a focus on medical applications). But it also includes large sections on philosophy, religion, and even political life. He often taught and wrote in his native German, at the time a significant departure from the exclusive use of Latin in such contexts. The essential methodological approach of Paracelsus, and the thing which set him apart from his contemporaries and at odds with the "authorities" of the past, was his insistence on the formula of *experientia ac ratio* ("trial and reckoning"), in other words, experimentation and the subjecting of the results to rational analysis. Coupled with this was his focus on the idea that the philosopher, or "researcher," must forge a union between himself, his soul, and the "object" of his research. This element of his method clearly separates him from pure empiricism. It is this constellation of methodological ideas that strikes us as most notably Germanic.

The ideas of Paracelsus spread like wildfire throughout northern Europe. Individual alchemists, magicians, physicians, and reformers were inspired by his ideas, but they also clearly lie at the root of the seventeenth-century Rosicrucian movement. Rosicrucianism became a code for an international "think-tank" made up of a network of mystical Protestants. For this reason, although Paracelsus is overtly acknowledged in official Rosicrucian literature, it is noted that "Theophrastus [=Paracelsus] ... was none of our Fraternity,"[11]—that is, he remained a Catholic.

In Scandinavia, perhaps the most important "Paracelsist," and even Rosicrucian, was Johan Bure (Johannes Bureus, 1568–1652).[12] Bure was born into a family of Lutheran pastors. He studied at Uppsala and Stockholm. As a young man he developed an interest in mystical teachings and magic. At the same time he first took notice of the runes when his attention was drawn to a runestone situated in the church at Riddarholm, near Stockholm. From this time on he began to study the runes on all levels. This was synthesized with Bure's mystical work. As a friend and teacher of two Swedish kings, Karl IX and Gustavus Adolfus, Bure was at the nexus of the international Protestant intelligentsia. He himself refers to the year 1613 as the time when he "received knowledge concerning the hidden truth," and after finding this truth, it was his duty "to become its apostle." The Rosicrucian manifesto, not published until 1614, circulated in manuscript from as early as 1612.[13] But Bure would not have been dependent on written sources, as he was personally connected with thinkers from all over northern Europe.

Bure is of special interest to us, of course, because he was the first renewer of esoteric runology. However, true to his Paracelsist roots, he was not merely a fantasist—he was first a scientist, then a philosopher. In his runic studies he not only saw a key to inner knowledge, but he also correctly read and interpreted actual runic monuments in his native Swedish countryside. As such he is a precursor to post-modern, esoteric runology.

In order to understand the nature of Bure's esoteric runology, let us examine a portion of it. According to Bure there are ordi-

The First Northern Renaissance

JOHAN BURE (1569–1652).

nary runes and then there are the fifteen *adalrunor*, or "noble runes," which are said to be inscribed on a cubical stone which fell from heaven as a sign of the powerful divinity to act as the mediator between God and man. On three sides of the cube are inscribed five staves, organized in the form of a cross. The forms of the staves of the *adalrunor* are often quite different from the "ordinary" versions of the staves. The difference is often a matter of rotating the stave ninety degrees, or the use of the rare Hälsinge rune-forms for U: ⌐ and R: ⌐ . In the first quintet the five signs appear:

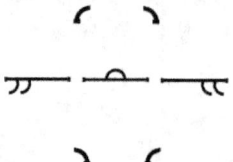

The three central runes ᚦᚢᚠ (T-O-F) refer to the triune divinities: Thor-Odin-Frigg. According to sixteenth-century "tradition," Sweden inherited these gods from Noah and his son, Japhat. Bure insists that only later did Asiatic masters of magic (Swedish: *sejd*) and wizards (Swedish: *tollare*) arrive pretending to be incarnations of the true gods. But the true religion of the ancients held sway for a much longer time in the North than in southern Europe. Bure, like many other mythologists of his time and earlier, used the Old Testament as a text for basic data—coupled with a primitive understanding of Saxo Grammaticus and perhaps of Snorri's *Edda*, copies of which had surfaced in the mid-1500s.

One of the innovations of the religion instituted by the "wizards" was that instead of a triune godhead, the people should worship Thor in life, Frigg at birth, and Odin in death. Here, Bure wishes to maintain the supposed "primal monotheism" of the ancestors and ascribe pantheism to a later, decadent, phase of history. As Bure interprets the staves:

⟨rune⟩ is the most free and functions everywhere and in everything. This is the highest and most powerful force, and it is equated with the Norse god Thor. According to Bure, this force is actually androgynous. He points to an image of Thor found in Uppsala which is masculine in the upper body, and feminine below. (Later commentators have identified this image as a badly damaged early depiction of Christ.) Thor is linked with Jove, and hence to Jehovah. The icon shows the door of a lodge at the horizon. It is flanked by ⟨rune⟩ and ⟨rune⟩, Odin and Frigg, who, with outstretched arms, show the way to the door.

⟨rune⟩ is the *adalruna* of Odin, the son of Thor, according to Bure. This interpretation of Odin as Thor's son was common in the early studies of Norse myths, which were heavily influenced

The First Northern Renaissance

by comparisons with classical mythology. To Odin belongs all property and estate, and all offices of state. The name Odin is equated with Latin *fatum*, "divine foresight." This linkage comes through the Swedish word *öde*, "fate." This *fatum* is seen as the origin of all created things. The originators of the runes concealed Odem, or the "blood-red one," Ådam, behind the image of Odin—or Mars, the destroyer.

ᛏ is on the left side of Thor, and hence on the day after his day. This signifies Frigg (or Fröja), the daughter of Thor and wife of Odin. Bure identifies Freyja (Fröja) with Frigg and says that the Swedish ancestors worshiped the true breath of holiness under the name of Fröja. This is further identified with the spirit that "moved upon the face of the waters." (Genesis 1:2) This is the one who distributes all good gifts.

Below the horizon and outside the door are the twins (U-R), which appear as ram's horns ᚅ—ᚱ. They indicate the password to the whole divine work, which emanates from above and which is in perpetual motion and expansion. Bure indicates that everything emerges from the one, and returns to the one, and cites a comparison of three biblical passages (Daniel 7:10, Matthew 13:41 and 22:30) as a key.

But above the horizon the twins (R-U) are paired inside the door in this way: ᚱ ᚢ , which is characterized as a password to eternal rest and union with the highest God. Here, Bure cites the "Egyptian Trismegistus." Those chosen by god are of two kinds, the one are those who migrate, the other those who are still, and these are the highest holiness of souls.

From this brief overview of Bure's esoteric runology, it is clear to see the limited degree to which he was aware of the historical Germanic tradition, and the degree to which he remained dependent on biblical mythology. It is also clear that he is extremely interested in reawakening the meaningfulness of the pre-Christian divinities for his people.

Mystics and scholars such as Paracelsus and Johan Bure did not content themselves with idle speculation, and with a retreat into their inner worlds. What they saw within, they sought to actualize in the world.

Law and Politics

As culture is indeed a holistic concept, factors such as mysticism and politics, as far apart as they might seem to the modern mind, are not so distinct in reality. This was a period referred to by Fredric Jameson as the "heroic modern"—a time when the split between the signifier and the signified was not so great as it would eventually become.[14] Spiritual concepts easily drove themselves into the world of politics and statecraft. For the northern European world, this drive was largely consumed with the idea of restoring the natural, and hence national, rights of the folk.

At the dawn of the sixteenth century the religious establishment learned to despise Luther, but there was a man they feared far more—the aforementioned Ulrich von Hutten (1488–1523). Ulrich was a true "Renaissance man." He was an aristocrat, knight, scholar, and poet who urged an open "revolt against the property and might of the Roman Church itself."[15] Ulrich was trained as a knight and entered a monastery in 1499, which he left six years later. He studied in Frankfurt an der Oder (where he contracted syphilis). In 1506 he received his baccalaureate. 1511 finds him in Vienna, where he met Conrad Celtis and began a series of "illegal lectures." Ulrich was acquainted with Mutianus Rufus, who had introduced the pagan ideas of the Italian Renaissance held by Marsilio Ficino and Pico della Mirandola north of the Alps. Wheelis says of Hutten that he "moved in a bohemian, satirically oriented circle whose view of life approached the pagan."[16] He sought to restore Germanic national life based on the ideals reflected in the account of the Germanic peoples in the works of Tacitus. His radical attacks on the Church earned him an especially fearsome reputation—one which he seemed to embrace. A favorite motto of his was "Let them hate us, as long as they fear us."[17] Hunted by Church authorities, Ulrich was eventually isolated on the island of Ufenau in Lake Zürich where he remained under the protection of the Swiss reformer Zwingli. There he died from complications of syphilis.

Ulrich von Hutten was an "applied humanist." Knowledge was seen not as an end in itself, but as a means to action.[18] His ultimate aim was to restore what he thought to be the primitive piety of the very early Christians and the primitive virtue of the early Germans as described by Tacitus. He wanted to reestablish an austere, moral, and independent Germany, which he thought should be "ruled by a benevolent and humanistically educated aristocracy."[19] Among Ulrich's most important works was the previously mentioned dialog entitled *Arminius* (1529).

Ulrich was a firebrand who struck terror into the hearts of the religious establishment with his radical plan of armed action. However, even his apparently benign scholarly activity was recognized by the establishment as a danger to the status quo.

In England, the Society of Antiquaries was founded in 1572. The radical changes actually effected by the humanists of this circle would be deep and far reaching. This humanistic, scholarly society was founded in the wake of the firm establishment of Protestantism in England in the middle of the reign of Elizabeth I, but became, among other things, a center for political reform based upon the discoveries of its members concerning the true history of the English people. This was the beginning of a new "age of absolutism" in the history of the English monarchy. The English have had a long history of resisting absolutist rule by monarchs, at least since the time of the Magna Carta. The age of increasing absolute rule by the kings and their increasing claims to "divine right" were met with reactions from the people who insisted ever more strongly on the necessity of the monarch sharing sovereignty with the collective representatives of the aristocracy and people—since the thirteenth century known as the "parliament."

Strict monarchical hierarchy with a single, all-powerful ruler, who was succeeded only by his eldest son (or in a few cases, his eldest daughter), was a byproduct of Christian theories of politics. The ancient Germanic peoples had sacral kingships, war-leaderships, and primitive republics as models for the exercise of sovereignty. One thing all three models had in common, however, was that a collective body of tribal elders or aristocrats *(principes)* were the primary repositories of sovereign power—and it was by their collective advice and consent that kings or war-leaders were elected from their own number. For this reason, the political urge to devolve power back to the collective body can be seen as an implicit drift away from a Christian basis of political and legal theory back to a more indigenous and pre-Christian model.

The origin of the concept of a limit being placed on monarchical power was, according to the researches of the Society of Antiquaries, rooted in Anglo-Saxon ideas concerning these restrictions on the power of the king. These originally Anglo-Saxon ideas were applied politically as they were increasingly rediscovered through the English Antiquaries' researches.

In 1628, John Pym argued in the Petition of Right that the rights being asserted by the parliamentarians were those that had been established earlier by the Saxons. He maintained that these had been broken, but that nevertheless they remained intact—surviving the Conquest. The parliamentarians were simply "demanding their ancient and due liberties, not suing for any new."

The home of Sir Robert Cotton (1571–1631) in Westminster housed an enormous library, which became a meeting place of dissident parliamentarians. The library was a repository for Anglo-Saxon manuscripts that had been collected from various places around the country. Scholars began learning the language of these manuscripts, and absorbing the ideas to which they gave expression. One of the things that research by these scholars clearly showed was the alternative "myth" of English origins, which maintained that the Angles, Saxons, and Jutes were Germanic tribes who had invaded the island beginning around 450 C.E. This myth also had the advantage of reflecting some definite historical fact, as opposed to the fanciful medieval myths of English origins, which had the English descended from a lost Israelite tribe, or a wandering Trojan![20] Cotton was imprisoned in 1629 for treasonous behavior by Charles I. In 1630, his library was "sealed" as a hothouse for sedition! Nowhere in history has it been clearer just how threatening to the status quo the learning of the true roots of a culture can be.

After several more generations many of these same ideas would be used by some of the "founding fathers" of the American republic. Most notable among these was Thomas Jefferson, who would also argue that the rights for which he fought were first expressed in the laws of the Anglo-Saxons.[21]

Several things are clear from the observation of the use of political and legal ideas rooted in the Germanic past during the Renaissance-Reformation period. First, it is obvious that at that time politics and law were still seen as a part of the greater whole of culture. It had not yet been entirely separated from the daily fabric of life and segregated into a discreet compartment the way it would be in more modern times. In this, a meaningful comparison can be drawn between politics and religion which shared a similar fate in modernism. Second, it is obvious that when the Germanic cultural paradigm began to remanifest itself generally, some did not hesitate to try to apply the paradigm in a political and legal way. It was this remanifestation of the Germanic paradigm, more than its reassertion in the "religious" sphere, that would affect the shape of the modern world.

Conclusion

The first Germanic renaissance followed a medieval period that at first saw the widespread preservation of Germanic cultural values in the guise of Christian symbols and institutions. At the very instant when Christianization was complete, the impetus to reawaken the slumbering forms of native northern European myth, religion, mysticism, and law began to grow stronger and be felt throughout the cultures of the Germanic countries. When we compare this "renaissance" to what occurred in Italy during these same centuries, we see vast differences. These differences can generally be accounted for by the fact that the ancient texts of the Germanic peoples remained largely undiscovered or unappreciated at the time. However, the renewed interest in northern antiquities struck extremely deep roots that remain vibrant to this day. Akin to the regular beating of a hammer on hot iron, from that day to this, there has been a steady, eternally recurring, interest in the often hidden, deep cultural paradigms of the Germanic peoples, who ultimately gave this culture its tongue, its myths, and its law.

This article is based on an address given to the Woodharrow Institute on 12 January 2003. A greatly expanded and revised version of this text will also appear as a chapter in the second volume of The Northern Dawn.

Notes:

1. James C. Russell, *The Germanization of Early Medieval Christianity* (Oxford: Oxford University Press, 1994), chronicles the Germanization of ecclesiastical forms of Christianity. For a summary of the continuity of the heroic culture see Stephen Edred Flowers, *The Northern Dawn: A History of the Reawakening of the Germanic Spirit*, vol. 1 (Smithville: Rûna-Raven, 2004), chapter 4.

2. The term "renaissance" as applied to the intellectual histo-

ry of fifteenth- and sixteenth-century Italy was not really developed into a historical term until the middle of the nineteenth century. However, it is very true that thinkers on both sides of the Alps during this time thought of their work as ushering in a period of renewal after a time of decay. This renewal was, moreover, largely based on the reapplication of pagan models of thought.

3. Dagobert Runes, ed. *Dictionary of Philosophy*, 15th ed. (Patterson, N.J.: Littlefield Adams, 1963), pp. 131–32.

4. All of these works by Tacitus have been conveniently translated in Penguin editions.

5. For a study of the figure of Arminius see Rainer Wiegels and Winfried Woesler, eds., *Arminius und die Varusschlacht: Geschichte—Mythos—Literatur* (Paderborn: Schoningh, 1995).

6. For an overview of the mythology of the Kyffhäuser, see Dietrich Kühn, *Sagen vom Harz und vom Kyffhäuser* (Weimar: Wartburg Verlag, 2002), and for the political movement surrounding this idea see Marc Zirlewagen, ed., *Kaisertreue—Führergedanke—Demokratie; Beiträge zur Geschichte des Verbandes der Vereine deutscher Studenten* (Cologne: SH-Verlag, 2000).

7. See the first volume of *The Northern Dawn*. Our earliest indication that there was no "religious" office separate from the "secular" comes with Caesar's statement that that Germans "have no druids" (*De bello gallico* 6:11), and this trait continues down to Iceland on the eve of Christianization where we find the *goðar*, whose functions are as much "secular" as they are "religious."

8. The way had been prepared for Luther's reforms by the German mystics and other reformers such as John Wycliffe in England and John Hus in Bohemia. Just prior to Luther's efforts, Germany was swept with a wave of popular piety. But none had the organizational skills necessary to mount a true reform movement.

9. The high estimation of individual freedom and religious autonomy, as well as economic independence, further encouraged all manner of idiosyncratic religious interpretations. The final result of this last point can be seen in the cacophony of Protestant Christian sects in America today. These characteristics also made freelance, or entrepreneurial, witch-hunting and other forms of religious persecution for individual and state profit increasingly possible.

10. Runes, *Dictionary of Philosophy*, p. 203.

11. Quoted from the English translation of the *Fama*

Fraternitas published in 1652, but circulated in manuscript form decades earlier.

12. For more on the life and work of Johan Bure, see Stephen E. Flowers, *Johannes Bureus and Adalruna* (Smithville: Rûna-Raven, 1998).

13. Frances A. Yates, *The Rosicrucian Enlightenment* (Boulder: Shambhala, 1978), p. 41.

14. See Steven Conner, *Postmodernist Culture* (Cambridge, Mass: Blackwell, 1989), pp. 46–47.

15. Sam Wheelis, "Ulrich von Hutten," in *The Renaissance and Reformation in Germany*, ed. G. Hoffmeister (New York: Ungar, 1977), p. 112.

16. Ibid., p. 118.

17. The original Latin phrase is *oderint dum metuant*, which more literally translated would be "let them hate so long as they fear." It is ascribed to the Roman tragic poet Lucius Accius (170 B.C.E.). This was also thought to be a favorite saying of the Emperor Caligula.

18. Wheelis, "Ulrich von Hutten," pp. 121–22.

19. Ibid., p 123.

20. These three different myths concerning the origin of the English are discussed in some detail in the first volume of *The Northern Dawn*. See also the discussion by Léon Poliakov, *The Aryan Myth* (New York: New Meridian, 1974), pp. 37–42.

21. The second volume of *The Northern Dawn* will take up Jefferson's ideas, and those of other American revolutionaries, in more detail. See also Stanley R. Hauer, "Thomas Jefferson and the Anglo-Saxon Language," *Publications of the Modern Language Association of America*, 98:5 (1983), pp. 879–95.

Eis & Licht

apocalypic pagan folk & pop music

OSTARA
-ultima thule-
CD, lt. first edition

Ultima Thule - in ancient times, the furthest point North - represents the realm of the extremities, the non plus ultra of existence.

WALDTEUFEL
-eines gottes spur-
10inch vinyl, gatefold

Four brand new tracks from the well known project. Pagan chants and percussion.

CAWATANA
-struggle for wisdom-
CD, digipak

Pure and powerful neo-folk from Hungary. Strong and melodic. Limited to 700 copies.

DARKWOOD
-weltenwende-
10inch vinyl, gatefold

Dedicated to those who gaze within, who eternally seek, who create, and who constantly doubt.

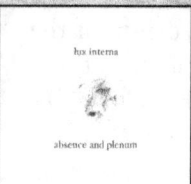

LUX INTERNA
-absence and plenum-
CD, digipak

Apocalyptic Folk about pain, love, hate, and motion from the U.S.A. The new L. Cohen?

OSTARA
-kingdom gone-
CD, digipak

Formerly STRENGTH THROUGH JOY, OSTARA now play pure Folk-Pop. Stunning!

SCIVIAS
-...and you will fear death not- CD, digipak

The topic of the CD is the decline of the last traditional empire: Japan.

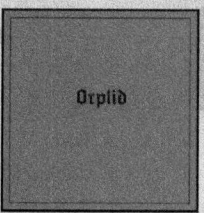

ORPLID
-geheiligt sei der toten name- MCD, digipak

Orplid honor all the soldiers who have died in numerous wars all over the world. 20 min.

VARIOUS ARTISTS
-eisiges licht-
CD

Our label "best of" for a very good price. Order **now for only $/€ 4,-** incl. airmail in Europe! With LEGER DES HEILS, CAWATANA, OSTARA, CAMERATA MEDIOLANENSE, SONNE HAGAL, DIES NATALIS, FORSETI, LUX INTERNA, DARKWOOD and SCIVIAS.

Visit our homepage with information about all our releases and artists. Mp3 files from each record are available. In our onlineshop you will find a huge selection of the finest Neofolk releases. We accept Paypal.

Eis & Licht
P.O. Box 160 142
01307 Dresden
mailto: eislicht@gmx.de
http://www.eislicht.de

Our distribution in the U.S.: www.tesco-distro.com

Three Decades of the Ásatrú Revival in America

Stephen A. McNallen

More than thirty years ago, I pledged my loyalty to Odin and the other deities of the Vikings. What followed in the ensuing decades was a persistent and ever-evolving attempt to revive an archaic European religion. That struggle, on a deeper and wiser level, continues to this day.

If it is true that we learn more from our mistakes than from our successes, then the reawakening of Germanic religion in America has much to teach us. My private devotion became a movement—at first narrow, then broader and better informed—with implications for all who care about the direction of our culture and the fate of the European peoples in general.

This narrative is a personal one, based on my experiences as the founder of three successive organizations devoted to the practice and promotion of Germanic religion, or Ásatrú. It is a report of my own history and lessons learned, and makes no claim of being an encyclopedic account.

What is Ásatrú?

The word *Ásatrú* comes from the Icelandic and means "those true to the gods." In the strictest interpretation, it is the religion of the Vikings. More generally, it refers not just to pre-Christian Scandinavian beliefs and practices, but to the indigenous religion of all the Germanic peoples.

I try to avoid terms like "pagan" or "heathen" in describing Ásatrú, as these words have a generally negative connotation. Instead, I identify Ásatrú as an expression of "native European religion" comparable to, for example, the religion of the American Indians or any other identifiable ethnic or racial group.

To understand the evolution of Ásatrú in the United States, we need to address the split between two opposing camps:

The *folkish* viewpoint maintains that there is an innate connection between ancestry and religion. The race, tribe, or nation is linked to the gods in a unique relationship; gods and people might be thought of as expressions of each other. In this world-

STEPHEN A. MCNALLEN, DRIGHTEN OF THE ÁSATRÚ FOLK ASSEMBLY.
(PHOTO BY EVE FOWLER, COLLECTION OF THE AUTHOR)

view, the essence of a religion is not transferable outside the group.

The *universalist* camp believes the opposite—that any religion is open to, and valid for, anyone who wants to follow it. Religion is completely separate from issues of ancestry. According to universalists, the deepest understanding of Ásatrú is accessible to anyone on the planet, regardless of descent.

I am a strong proponent of folkish belief. For me, "universalist Ásatrú" is a contradiction. All indigenous/native/pagan religions—not just Ásatrú—spring from the soul of a particular people and represent the collective experience of that people. Such organic religions are not items to be purchased "off the shelf" in the spiritual marketplace; rather, they are an integral part of who and what one is.

This conviction has not exactly won me accolades from the politically correct, even though the folkish standpoint is antitotalitarian, respectful of other races and cultures, and celebrates the uniqueness of all peoples. It seems to me that this is the very essence of "diversity"—but perhaps that word has a different meaning to the ideology-commissars who define our society.

American Indian scholar Vine Deloria, now a professor at the University of Colorado, expressed an essential folkish idea in his book *God is Red*, when he suggested that it might be natural for different groups to have different religions. When I sent Dr. Deloria some of our literature, I received a letter of thanks and approval in return. At least one chapter of the American Indian Movement has used our material to steer white "wannabes" away from Indian spirituality, and towards a path more suited to people of European heritage.

The Viking Brotherhood—The Beginning

I decided to follow the gods of the Vikings in either 1968 or 1969, during my college years. This decision arose from two things: my perception that the God of the Bible was a tyrant and that his followers were willing slaves, and an admiration for the heroism and vitality of the Norsemen as depicted in popular literature.

This pagan epiphany did not spring from the leftist/hippy/Age-of-Aquarius counterculture of the 1960s. Quite the opposite! I was attracted to the Vikings by their warlike nature, their will to power, and their assertion of self. My own views bore no resemblance to "peace, love, and good vibes"; I was a cadet in the Reserve Officer Training Corps and aspired to a career in the US Army's Special Forces.

If my allegiance to the Æsir and Vanir (the two families of Nordic deities) did not originate in the hippy/Left counterculture, neither did it come from the racially tinged writings of the Australian, Alexander Rudd Mills, nor from Canadian Else

Christensen, nor from the early-twentieth-century German rune mystic Guido von List (as at least one Marxist critic has alleged). In those early days, my interest was driven by my romanticism, and by my youthful desire to do brave deeds.

My devotion to Odin and the other gods and goddesses remained a private and lonely faith for about two years. As far as I knew, I was literally the only person on Earth who stood alongside the elder gods.

Soon, however, I felt the need to find others like myself. I took out advertisements in *Fate* magazine and other "pagan-friendly" publications under the (rather embarrassingly dramatic) name of the "Viking Brotherhood." In the winter of 1971–72, the first issue of *The Runestone* saw print. I produced it with a rickety typewriter and a mimeograph machine, and the first run was of eleven copies.

So far as I have been able to ascertain, the Viking Brotherhood was the first organization in the United States devoted to the elder faith of the Germanic peoples. In 1972, the Internal Revenue Service recognized it as a tax-exempt religious organization.

Two or three months after this publishing debut, I reported for active duty as an Army officer. I was off to attend the infantry officer course, then to earn my parachutist wings and the black-and-gold Ranger tab. *The Runestone* limped along, gradually improving in quality and reaching between one and two hundred subscribers. I was astounded at its success! Who could have imagined there were so many other people out there who loved the old gods? The consuming obligations of Army life occupied me for the next four years, and the Viking Brotherhood remained a miniscule organization, devoid of grander ambitions, until its transformation in 1976.

The Viking Brotherhood in Retrospect

The Viking Brotherhood was focused on the image of the warrior, and on the assertion of individual will and freedom that the warrior epitomizes. In many ways it was a reflection of where I was at that point in my life. A photograph of me taken in that era shows a serious young man. His eyeglasses betray the scholar within the infantryman's uniform. No doubts fog his face; the self-exploration and introspection of the 1960s did not sway him from his

MCNALLEN (LEFT) AND VALGARD MURRAY OF THE ÁSATRÚ ALLIANCE.
(COLLECTION OF THE AUTHOR)

chosen course. He is a romantic and a warrior, sincere and well meaning but largely ignorant of his own depths. He has a capacity for intellectual and spiritual breadth, but it is by no means fully tapped. In a way, that photograph was not only Steve McNallen; it was the Viking Brotherhood itself.

I would evolve, and so would Ásatrú, in the years to come. Many aspects of the complex and rich Nordic belief system—the feminine, the magical, the agricultural, the broader Indo-European context—were largely ignored. I was just beginning to shift out of this narrow vision during the period from 1972 to 1976.

It was in about 1974 that I began to realize that there was an innate connection between Germanic paganism and the Germanic peoples. I had resisted the idea as being somehow racist, but I could not ignore the evidence. Within a year or two I had shifted from a universalist to a folkish position—even though neither of those terms would enter our vocabulary for many years.

The Ásatrú Free Assembly

After my release from the Army in 1976, I moved to Berkeley, California. I had learned the term "Ásatrú" from *Hammer of the North*, a book by Icelandic scholar Magnus Magnusson. Finally, I had a name for my beliefs! The Viking Brotherhood soon became the Ásatrú Free Assembly, or AFA.

In Berkeley, we met in the back of Dick Johnson's insurance agency on University Avenue. Dick took the religious name of Aluric. Twenty years later, in the New Jersey Pine Barrens, I befriended another man who had taken the name Aluric (and for the same reasons as Dick). By coincidence, this "new" Aluric had worked at a pizza parlor a few blocks from Dick's office during the years we were meeting there—but never knew of us.

During the ten years of the AFA's existence we devised a religious calendar, composed and performed a multitude of rituals, and published booklets and audiotapes. Beginning in 1980, the AFA hosted an annual event called the Althing (a tradition which Valgard Murray of the Ásatrú Alliance has continued down to the present day). Local congregations, or "kindreds," were formed around the country.

We established several special interest groups or "guilds" to meet the needs of warriors, women, and brewers. Each of these guilds had its own newsletter, and a richly varied Ásatrú literature soon began to proliferate. The existence of a guild dealing with rocketry and space travel testified to the fact that we were not locked into the distant past. (For a few years it was customary to open each Althing with a rocket launch, just to remind ourselves that the Faustian reach expresses itself differently in each age.)

The Ásatrú Free Assembly held to a middle ground on racial issues. On the one hand we were proud of our European heritage, and we actively espoused the interests of European-descended people. On the other hand we opposed totalitarianism and racial hatred, convinced that decency and honor required us to treat individuals of all racial groups with respect. Forces from either extreme periodically tried to budge us off this position, but we successfully held our ground.

When the AFA crumpled in 1986, the reason had nothing to do with racial politics (contrary to many reports). I was working as a peace officer in the county jail, and my wife kept books for an oil company. She and I were logging around sixty hours and forty hours per week, respectively, on Ásatrú-related matters. We knew we could not continue putting out this effort without financial compensation, which would allow us to cut back on these mundane jobs. When we approached the membership, the general reaction was negative. Some accused us of trying to "establish a priesthood" or of being "money hungry." Surprised and bruised by this rejection, we tried cutting back on membership services to make the job more manageable. This in turn caused more complaints among some AFA members.

We soon realized this was a losing battle. We were at the end of our financial and emotional resources. The AFA was disbanded, with the ashes turned over to Valgard Murray, leader of the Arizona Kindred, who used them as the foundation for the Ásatrú Alliance.

Looking Back on the Ásatrú Free Assembly

The Ásatrú Free Assembly had evolved far beyond the old male-dominated, warrior-oriented Viking Brotherhood: we honored the goddesses along with the gods. Women, originally rare in our ranks, played an important part in our activities. The AFA understood that warriors have a role, but that they are only part of a healthy community. The continuity between Germanic religion and the broader Indo-European family was acknowledged. I coined the term *metagenetics* to refer to the link between spirituality and heredity, and we produced a body of literature that served as a valuable foundation for the future.

It is important to realize that all the things we did were new. There was no model on which to base our actions. Liberal revisionists have attempted to minimize the role of the AFA, claiming that we were only one of many groups extant at that time, but this is not true. For all practical purposes, the AFA *was* Ásatrú in America until the mid-1980s.

The Wandering Years

Disappointed by our experience with the Ásatrú Free Assembly, my wife and I eventually moved to a semi-deserted mining town in the mountains of California, earned teaching credentials, and tried to find meaning in our lives without the AFA. I taught science and mathematics to junior high school students, visited exotic countries during the summer, and tried to forget about organized Ásatrú.

I interviewed Tibetan resistance fighters in northern India, gave blót to Thor in a high Himalayan pass, and spent time in the jungles of Burma. Some of the articles I wrote during this period were published in *Soldier of Fortune* magazine. These experiences helped me to develop sympathies not just for my own people, but for others around the world. To this day I am active in the Tibetan freedom struggle, and AFA publications have given me a chance to voice support for Burmese, Nigerians, and southern Sudanese—all working for the independence and freedom of their respective tribes, nations, or ethnic groups.

Even in my travels I could not escape the gods. I was sitting in a guerrilla camp in Burma, talking with a young German who worked as a physical therapist most of the year, but spent his summers teaching Karen freedom fighters how to be snipers. The German saw my Thor's hammer amulet and asked me about it. I explained its religious significance—at which point he produced a similar one from under his shirt. Years later, in Bosnia, I was to see hammers worn by some of the young men in the international section of the Tomislav Brigade.

I also joined the Army National Guard during this period. My unit was called up during the Rodney King riots in Los Angeles. I am no doubt one of very few men in America to have stood on the famous corner of Hollywood and Vine with a loaded M-16 rifle. One of the best things about these years—indeed, about my life—has been the chance to work with soldiers, doing a job I loved.

I never lost my love for the gods, either, but it was very difficult to do any religious work in my wandering years. Even a simple prayer before meals was painful, too much a reminder of the past. I was scarred, and angry, and bitter.

But I got over it. Healing always comes—and sometimes circumstances force our hands.

The Ásatrú Folk Assembly

Until the collapse of the Ásatrú Free Assembly in 1986 there had been no significant universalist presence in the movement; the AFA dominated the scene with a solidly folkish ideology. With the AFA gone, the universalists found an opportunity to establish themselves.

In 1994, I saw signs that the politically correct faction was making inroads into territory long dominated by the folkish. I decided to reenter the fray by organizing the Ásatrú Folk Assembly—which became known as "the new AFA," as distinct from the Ásatrú Free Assembly, or "old AFA."

This had been brewing for some time. Already, my scars healing, I had begun writing again, putting out small, digest-size versions of *The Runestone* for interested readers. I suppose, looking back, that my eventual return was inevitable.

Our new organization soon made original contributions to the Ásatrú scene. *The Runestone* and the guild newsletters became thicker and more professional than ever before, and for a while we arranged for a distributor to stock them on newsstands.

One of our more daring experiments was the "Ásatrú Community Church," which offered public services every other Sunday. In our own way we were trying to carry out Edred Thorsson's dream, expressed in the pages of *A Book of Troth*, of having a *hof* or building for worship in every major city in the country. The Community Room of the Nevada County Library was a far cry from a building of our own, but it was a start!

We designed the format to be comfortable for people with Christian backgrounds, but at the end of a year we had little to show for our efforts. In looking back, I can see things we could have done to make the Ásatrú Community Church more successful, and someday we may try it again.

The most important thing about the Ásatrú Community Church was that it tried to reach beyond the usual target audience, to the public at large. I am convinced that Ásatrú must do this if it is ever to be more than a tiny cult on the fringe of American life.

Kennewick Man

The AFA's greatest fame, or notoriety, came with the Kennewick Man case.

When a set of Caucasian-looking bones was found in the shallows of the Columbia River, the anthropologist who examined them thought they must be the remains of a White settler. When radiocarbon dating showed them to be about 9,300 years old, it was time to take a second look at American prehistory.

As the skeleton was found in the city of Kennewick, Washington, the media quickly dubbed its original owner

"Kennewick Man." The name stuck.

The US Army Corps of Engineers (on whose property they had been found) decided to turn the bones over to local Indian tribes under a law called NAGPRA—the Native American Graves Protection and Repatriation Act. Since the skeleton did not seem to be Indian, and since it was far too old to have been the ancestor of the recent and historically mobile tribes in the area, this was simply politically motivated pandering on the part of the Corps of Engineers.

The AFA filed suit to stop the hand-over. Since there was a very considerable chance that these were the remains of an ancient European, it was only right that a native European religious organization should have a say in what happened to them.

We were of course outgunned from the very beginning. Our lawyer, working *pro bono*, was up against the entire massed legal might of the government. They had millions of dollars to spend; we had at most a few thousand. They had White guilt and political correctness on their side; we were identifiably members of the genocidal, oppressive European race.

The AFA didn't have a chance, but we scored a few points. We were the first to contest the government's definition of "Native American" as anyone whose remains were here before 1492. We noted that any Viking burials—such as those of Leif Erikson's colony, for example—would be turned over to the nearest Indian tribe under those guidelines. Much later, Judge Jelderks used precisely the same argument to demolish the government's faulty definition.

The controversial case earned the AFA a huge amount of publicity, relatively speaking. Hundreds of newspapers over the next few years carried articles about us, and several books published since then have mentioned our role. Some of the reporters got things horribly wrong, and the leftist press was quick to insert absurdities, but not all the publicity was bad.

There were incredible inaccuracies—so incredible that some of them really ought to be called lies. One commonly heard statement was that we had said Kennewick Man was a Viking, or that he was Nordic. This was completely false. Another writer tried to claim that a prominent Christian Identity figure was an AFA spokesman, which is ludicrous to anyone familiar with the American Right. Perhaps the strangest article accused us of being a racist cult based on a belief in the lost continent of Atlantis!

The fact is, if the American media wants to lie about you, they will simply do so and there is not a lot to be done about it. People who urged us to sue did not stop to ask themselves where we would get the hundreds of thousands of dollars to take such a case through the courts.

One result of the Kennewick Man case is that scientists are finally taking a serious look at the possibility that ancient Americans might have migrated to this continent via the "Atlantic Crescent," an equivalent to the Bering land bridge over which Mongoloid peoples crossed. Dr. Dennis Stamford plans to publish a book outlining this theory, and the evidence supporting it, in the near future.

Soon after the discovery of the Kennewick Man skeleton, a group of leading scientists sued to be able to study Kennewick Man. As things now stand, Judge Jelderks has ruled in their favor, and against giving the skeleton to the Indians. Appeals have been filed and the legal process grinds on.

Tribal Ásatrú

Beginning in the late 1990s, the AFA began promoting the idea of *tribalism*—developing our own organic social structures patterned after the Germanic and Celtic tribes.

This tribalist initiative received little support in the Ásatrú community, which remains too individualistic, too disdainful of leadership, and too enamored of the idealized Viking image to buy into the concept. Ultimately, for all the talk of intentional communities and tribes, the necessary level of dedication and cooperation simply was not there. There were exceptions to this generalization, notably the very tribal Theodish movement (an Anglo-Saxon heathen group), but we did not succeed in swaying the movement as a whole.

Nevertheless, we must eventually develop our own tribe-like systems of social support, made up of networks of families and extended families and designed to take care of our needs and welfare. If the Mormons can do it, why can't we? The twenty-first century will be a time of turmoil, resource competition, and social stress. Under these hard-time conditions, the tribal model will serve Ásatrú much better than the less hierarchical ideal that currently prevails.

By mid-2001, the AFA was facing great challenges. This was

partly a replay of the problems that brought down the old AFA in 1986: our organizational structures were top heavy and time consuming. The organization was too large to be manageable with the resources we had, but too small to allow for a paid staff.

On top of this, we were under assault. One of the AFA's key members became angry over an unintended slight, and launched a campaign of lies and insinuations against us. Private emails were forwarded from our members-only list to so-called "anti-hate groups." There was nothing in this material implicating the AFA in any wrongdoing, but we could no longer guarantee our membership privacy. The government itself had grown hostile to "Odinism" in the paranoia surrounding the turn of the millennium, and some of this repressive atmosphere still hovered like a bad odor.

Weighing the problems of infiltration and betrayal, along with the realization that running a membership organization was too burdensome for our volunteer staff, the AFA did away with membership and other parts of our structure, leaving only the core of our activity. This radical surgery saved the AFA, and we did not succumb as we had back in 1986.

However, organizational simplification could not hide the fact that Ásatrú in America simply was not working as it should. Though the AFA had weathered the storm and continues to function today, I quietly stepped back into the shadows and began a long, painful reevaluation of our movement.

Evolution

During these upheavals, it was hard for me to maintain focus. I floundered from idea to idea, with little results to show for all my thrashing about. With the AFA at least partly neutralized by diminished resources and conflict, I began to look to the world of politics for solutions to the problems of our time. If I couldn't change the world with religion, perhaps political action would prove a better tool!

For years I had been a member of a group called the European American Issues Forum. The president of the organization resigned for health reasons, and I ended up filling his shoes. The EAIF was a great idea—a genuine, non-racist civil rights group for Americans of European descent—but in practice it was unworkable. The basic premise was simple: the social and political system could be made to respond to the needs of European-Americans just as it had responded to the demands of other racial groups. It took me a while to realize that no amount of letter writing or protesting was going to win any concessions from our opponents until there was a massive change in consciousness.

Perhaps it was no coincidence that I was diagnosed with colon cancer a few months into my presidency. My tenure as EAIF president had made me a frustrated, cynical, angry man. I am by nature a warrior monk, not a politician.

My illness forced me to consider the course my life was taking. The cancer was only a physical manifestation of something else that was going wrong. To get some guidance, I decided I would think of my upcoming surgery as a symbolic death and rebirth, with the idea of "pushing the restart button" on my life.

I was hardly out from under the anesthetic when I knew with certainty that my path was supposed to be spiritual rather than political. For now, I can best serve the European peoples by helping my brothers and sisters recover their collective soul. Until we remember who and what we are, no political remedy can touch the disease eating away at our insides.

Within a few weeks I had resigned from the presidency of the EAIF.

A Critical Reflection

It is easy to make mistakes when one is doing something that has never been done before. I certainly made my share of errors, as did the rest of us. All one can do is try to see the mistakes clearly, and correct them.

It is easy to dwell on the negative and overlook the good. Reading the remarks that follow, one could conclude that Ásatrú in America has been a haven for hobbyists, fools, and the insincere. That would not be an accurate assessment, though goodness knows all three are plentiful in our ranks. Alongside them, though, are intelligent, serious, and thoughtful men and women who give us high hope for the future.

Looking back at the last thirty years, here are some things we should have done differently—as well as matters we intend to remedy in times to come. My comments apply both to the three organizations I established, and to many (but not all) of the other individuals and groups making up Ásatrú today:

—The narrow focus on the Vikings. It was a mistake to focus so strongly on the Norse experience. The Scandinavian sea rovers were indeed tough, courageous, and enterprising, and these traits deserve our admiration. But the Vikings were hardly typical of Germanic prehistory. They were ultimately cosmopolitan, and their culture incorporated a mass of non-native elements, which grew with time. Kinship loyalty and the ancient freedoms were all too often discarded if they interfered with the pursuit of gold and power, trade replaced heroism, and royal ambition (encouraged by the Church) ate away at the old traditions of the folk.

Instead of being "Norse centered," we would have done better to use the Germanic tribes as models (which, indeed, the AFA began doing in the late 1990s). The tribes demonstrate a better balance between the needs of the individual and the group, as well as a greater connection to kin and soil. Besides, only a relatively small number of Americans have Scandinavian ancestry—while most can identify with the Germans and Anglo-Saxons.

—Lack of hierarchy and a disregard for leaders. Our romanticized, historically incomplete picture of the Vikings hurt us in another way: it seduced us into thinking we did not need leaders or hierarchy. Ásatrú today has too many mediocre men and women who, believing "we are all equal," have no notion of the bond between leaders and followers so central to Germanic society.

This anarchic tendency must be replaced by the spirit of our ancestral tribes, where the chieftain, the aristocracy, and the freemen existed in an interplay of powers, similar to the "checks and balances" found in the original Constitution of the United States.

—Historical anachronisms. A third malady afflicting Ásatrú is the penchant for adopting Viking Age clothing and mannerisms. Many followers of Ásatrú wear Norse tunics or Viking dresses when they gather among themselves. Swords and axes, too, are common accessories at some events. It's not hard to figure that many worthwhile people have turned away from us in disgust because they expected to find a religion, and found a historical reenactment group instead.

—Lack of dignity and reserve. Related to the "dress up" syndrome is a lack of seriousness and a proper dignity among many of us.

"The Holy Powers must have had plans for us." McNallen today. (Collection of the Author)

We have exposed our most sacred rites to the glassy eye of the media (I was guilty of this, particularly during the Kennewick Man case). We have invited the curious and those not a part of our religious fellowship to take part in our ceremonies. This air of openness exposes us to public scoffing, and allows the Holy Powers themselves to be ridiculed.

Indigenous cultures do not generally allow outsiders free access to the Mysteries. We need to emulate the American Indians and other groups, enforcing what I call "a holy reserve" in regard to the Sacred. That which is open to all is respected by none.

Apart from safeguarding our private relationship to the Holy, there is the more general question of mature behavior. What must people think when, surfing the Internet, they see photos of an Ásatrú group making an obscene gesture at the camera, or out-of-shape people sporting low-class T-shirts, or scruffy individuals pouring beer through their beards? The fact that such images exist tells us that there is something wrong with the way Ásatrú is being practiced in this country.

—*Lack of philosophical depth*. We have studied the *Eddas* and sagas. Beyond that, we know the work of Georges Dumézil, Edgar Polomé, and the excellent popularizations of H. R. Ellis Davidson. But until we can hold our own in debate with the Jesuits or in the pages of the *New York Times Review of Books*, we will not be taken seriously. What does Nietzsche have to say to our topic? How does our idea of the holy compare to that of

Rudolf Otto? Are the gods only Jungian archetypes? Does the work of British biologist Rupert Sheldrake confirm our own ideas on kinship affinity? How do the writings of Alain de Benoist and Tomislav Sunic impact us? In short, verses from the *Hávamál* will not suffice to express our beliefs to a sophisticated world.

De Benoist reminds us that we cannot ignore the fact that Christianity has dominated us for more than a millennium. It is an error to think that we can simply pick up where we left off a thousand years ago. The Christian interregnum must be addressed, using the intellectual tools that have developed in the intervening time—and this means examining our beliefs and expressing them in intellectually compelling ways.

—*Marketing to the wrong audience*. While we have attracted many intelligent and thoughtful people, we have also drawn far too many marginal individuals. We have not made a systematic effort to bring in more or less ordinary people—those looking for ancestral European roots, for fellowship with their own kind, for a sacralized vision of the world, or simply for a way to live good and rewarding lives. Ásatrú has the spiritual power to recruit educated, financially successful men and women with functioning lives, if only we present it properly. It is time to tailor our message to this end. Instead of advertising among survivalists, pagans, and the political fringe (all of which occupy miniscule and marginalized niches in our society) we need to reach out to young families, college students, business executives, and the creative thinkers who shape our world.

—*Under-capitalization*. Ásatrú has been trying to change the world with pitifully insignificant resources. The traditional way of starting an Ásatrú organization has been to put up a web site, offer a newsletter and a stock of books for sale, and hope that enough money comes in to keep the organization alive. We have to do better than that. In the business world, more new companies fold because of under-capitalization than for any other reason. Why should a religious organization be any different?

To make Ásatrú viable in the modern world, we need not only new ideas of the kind outlined in the above paragraphs, but serious funding. Volunteer, unpaid, part-time staff, despite the best of intentions, cannot yield the results we must have if we are to make a difference.

We must find philanthropists to help us plant the seeds of a cultural revolution—and we must be worthy of their generosity.

Conclusion

The rebirth of Ásatrú was accompanied by an intriguing synchronicity. In England and Iceland, Canada and the United States, four organizations dedicated to the religion of our ancestors were founded within a few months of each other. None knew of the others' existence at the time; only later did they establish communication. A wind was blowing through the branches of the World Tree, marking a new chapter in the evolving saga of the European peoples.

The Holy Powers must have had plans for us. We have not yet succeeded in our task. However, thirty years is nothing in the lifetime of our people, or in the lifetime of the gods. We can still become worthy vehicles for the Shining Ones, and lead our folk to what Dr. Stephen Flowers has so eloquently called "the way back to right."

I look at the fading photographs and yellowing newspaper clippings of the last thirty years, and I do not recognize the man I was. He was young, and sure of himself, and it seems impossible that he would not have succeeded in bringing the sons and daughters of Europe back to their spiritual heritage. But I can see inexperience and lack of maturity in his unlined face, too—and then I do not regret my gray hairs and the wrinkles around my eyes.

I look again, and I know that the man I see in the mirror is far more dangerous to my enemies than the clueless fellow looking at me from the photo album.

I grin a wolfish grin. The best is yet to come.

The Lost Philosopher

The Best of
Anthony M. Ludovici

EDITED BY
JOHN V. DAY

In the first decades of the twentieth century, Anthony Mario Ludovici (1882-1971) was one of Britain's most celebrated intellectuals.

One of the first and most accomplished translators of Nietzsche into English and a leading exponent of Nietzsche's thought, Ludovici was also an original philosopher in his own right.

Without a graduate degree or university professorship (indeed, without any need of them), Ludovici went over the heads of academia and directly addressed the educated public, supporting himself entirely by his writings.

In nearly forty books, including eight novels, and dozens of shorter works, Ludovici set forth his views on metaphysics, religion, ethics, politics, economics, the sexes, health, eugenics, art, modern culture, and current events with a clarity, wit, and fearless honesty that made him famous.

After World War II, however, Ludovici fell rapidly into obscurity. Why? Because Ludovici was a passionate, principled defender of aristocracy and conservatism and a fierce, uncompromising critic of egalitarianism in all its manifestations: Christianity, liberalism, Marxism, socialism, feminism, multiculturalism, crass commercialism, a debased popular culture, and the denial of biological differences between individuals and races, as well as the envious hobbling of the gifted and the sentimental coddling of the mediocre and botched.

Thanks to this volume, however, the lost philosopher has been found again, and far from seeming antiquated, his ideas are even more radical, relevant, and challenging in our day than in his own.

The Lost Philosopher collects Ludovici's thoughts on nine topics—Religion, Conservatism, Liberalism, Men and Women, Eugenics, Health, Education, Economics, and Art—in the hope that our times might catch up to Ludovici's philosophy.

Praise for *The Lost Philosopher*:

"Of all unjustly ignored authors, Anthony M. Ludovici is certainly the one who today most deserves to be remembered. In his works, as imposing in quantity as in quality, this profoundly original philosopher never ceased to offer opinions on the most various subjects (from religion and education to art, eugenics, and the relations between the sexes) that are perfectly opposed to contemporary 'political correctness.' Even those who will disapprove of his remarks will be able to recognize their prescient character. For collecting in this volume the most significant pages of Ludovici's works, John V. Day without a doubt deserves the gratitude of all free spirits."—Alain de Benoist, author of *On Being a Pagan* (Ultra, 2004)

Ordering Information:

ISBN 0-9746264-0-6
Cloth edition limited to 500 numbered copies.
v + 305 pages.
Printed on acid free paper.

Price: $30.00
California Residents: Add 7.75% sales tax
(for a total of $32.33).
U.S. Orders: Add $5.00 for postage.
Foreign orders: Add $10.00 for postage (Air Mail).
Send check or money order made payable to ETSF to:

ETSF
1678 Shattuck Ave, #330
Berkeley, CA 94709-1631
USA

www.etsf.org
lostphilosopher@etsf.org

Ludwig Fahrenkrog and the Germanic Faith Community: Wodan Triumphant

Markus Wolff

During the first decade of the twentieth century, various personalities concerned with the spiritual future of the German people, and indeed of all Germanic peoples, began to call for a renewal of religion and spirituality. The success of Richard Wagner's opera cycle *Der Ring des Nibelungen* had inspired considerable interest in the old Germanic legends, and Nietzsche's devastating critique of Christianity further contributed to an environment in which writers, artists, and thinkers began looking to the pre-Christian past for inspiration. Even earlier, in 1885, the novelist Felix von Dahn had concluded the introduction to his collection of Nordic sagas by emphasizing that "this pantheon of gods and its lore is the mirror image of the magnificence and splendor of our own people." As growing numbers of Germans grew dissatisfied with the state of religious affairs, political divisions, and the negative effects of the industrial revolution, all sorts of idealist and utopian movements appeared, offering their visions of a revitalized and respiritualized future.

Around the turn of the century various periodicals, like *Heimdall* and Ernst Wachler's *Iduna*, started to address the questions of religion and identity. Then, in 1906, an Austrian writer named Adolf Weber, writing under the pseudonym of Riemann, published the 96-page book *Allvater (Wodan) oder Jehovah?* (Allfather Wotan or Jehovah?) It is a highly charged—though somewhat convoluted—rant against dogmatic Christian precepts, which Riemann sought to replace with a vaguely pantheist worldview more suited to the German spirit. This simultaneously new and ancient conception of the divine he called "Allfather," after one of the *Eddic* descriptive names for Odin/Wotan. Riemann was later the first Hochwart (High Warden) of the Gesellschaft Wodan (Wodan Society), which soon evolved into the Austrian branch of the Germanische Glaubens Gemeinschaft (Germanic Faith Community [GGG]). His tract remained obscure, although it was one of the writings that directly influenced the artist Ludwig Fahrenkrog to call for the organization of a group based on this new religiosity.

LUDWIG FAHRENKROG, SELF PORTRAIT.

Ludwig Fahrenkrog was born on 20 October 1867 in Rendsburg, a small northern German town near the Danish border. A talented artist as a child, he began his career illustrating catalogs and newspapers, while also working as a decorative painter. Beginning in 1887, he studied at the Berlin Royal Art Academy under Anton von Werner, Woldemar Friedrich, and Hugo Vogel, receiving five primary awards, including the state prize for art. After marrying his wife Charlotte (with whom he was to have four daughters and a son), he moved to Barmen, Westphalia in 1898, where he had accepted a teaching post at the School of Arts and Crafts, a position he was to hold until 1931. Fahrenkrog's prolific artistic career ran parallel to his religious endeavors. He became a professor in 1913. In 1925 he was appointed a guest professorship at the Dakota University in Mitchell, South Dakota, and in 1928 he received the first prize at the Glass Palace exhibition in Munich.

By the early 1890s, it was clear that Fahrenkrog would not become just another bourgeois artist. He was chastised by the Academy for failing to display any Italian influence in his painting *Jesus vor Pilatus* (Jesus Facing Pilate), and his 1901 work *Jesus predigent* (Jesus Sermonizing) shows the savior as a stern, beardless, Balder-like figure, and was also criticized. In 1898, Fahrenkrog completed the oil painting *Lucifer's Lossage von Gott* (Lucifer's Renunciation of God), which already pointed the way to a new awareness of the religious question. Fifteen years later, he included the work in a slim volume entitled *Lucifer: Dichtung in Wort und Bild* (Lucifer: Poetry in Word and Image). Here, Lucifer speaks in tones reminiscent of the German anarchist philosopher Max Stirner: "We choose our own property: the right to freedom! The empire of the spirit wants only masters, not slaves." As Fahrenkrog put it elsewhere: "Now, what else can freedom mean except: I have become aware of my being and reign and obey my self ... the self-redeemers are no ascetics ... their will has nothing to do with misunderstood lust, nor with misunderstood morals" (*Selbsterlösung: Jungdeutsche Religion* [Self-Redemption: Young German Religion]). This renunciation of Christian principles led Fahrenkrog to the possibility of an identity that is at once both new and ancient. In the account of his spiritual development, *Geschichte meines Glaubens* (The Story of My Faith), he formulated his idealistic goal of a *völkisch* awakening: "When we find ourselves, we are at home, and thus also ready to welcome others."

Stylistically, Fahrenkrog's art is grounded in the academic tradition of solid craftsmanship, while at the same time being profoundly influenced by the revolutionary artistic movements of the time: German Art Nouveau or Jugendstil (*Jugend*-style, so named after one of its most influential publications) and Symbolism. Many of his works are reminiscent of Hans Thoma, the popular master of the German mythological landscape and its fairy tales, although Fahrenkrog was also capable of great flights of fancy and inventiveness when the subject demanded it. The strongest connection between Fahrenkrog and Symbolists like Klinger and Stuck, is his insistence on the religious nature and mission of art. Yet he went further than any of his contemporaries by actually participating in the founding of a new religious movement.

Fahrenkrog was one of those people who, encouraged by the audacious thinking of Nietzsche, was shaking off the old moral constraints while retaining a love for his people and nation. This life-affirming yet principled outlook made him part of the *völkisch* movement that was beginning to form at this time. The word "*völkisch*" in general denotes an eagerness to cultivate features typical of one's own nation and people, while attempting to curb the material and spiritual influence of other peoples and nations. While the movement included many different religious outlooks, brands of nationalism, and various reform movements (such as nudism and vegetarianism), the search for a genuine native religiosity was central. Yet only a relative few were truly ready to leave all traces of the dominant religion behind.

Part of this hard-to-define movement was a curious figure named Wilhelm Schwaner (born 1863 in Waldeck) who had compiled one of the standards of the neo-heathen movement, the *Germanen-Bibel: Aus heiligen Schriften germanischer Völker* (The Germanic Bible: Compiled from Sacred Writings of the Germanic Peoples), which was published in 1904. The book was comprised of various quotes and short excerpts from a variety of German and Scandinavian poets, philosophers, and scientists. In 1905 Schwaner founded the Bund Deutscher Volkserzieher (League of German Populist Educators), which aimed for broad educational reforms and which since 1897 had also been publishing the journal *Volkserzieher*, a sounding board for his quasi-religious sociopolitical ideas. It was in this publication that Fahrenkrog made some of his first efforts toward founding a religious group. In 1907 and 1908 he published his two "Germanic Temple" essays, the first of which idealistically envisioned a cultic community and a Germanic temple where the group would hold services. The second, dated 22 March 1908, already called for the formation of a "German religious community" and ends on this soaring note: "And whoever it be that has the power shall work and further inspire to free us from oriental myth and to unify everyone's longing into a symbol of our faith, in which religion and nature, art and science, find a home: the Germanic temple!" While Fahrenkrog would never see the construction of a real edifice inspired by his idea, these essays at least ignited a passionate flame that would give impetus to a small movement.

In 1907 the aforementioned Gesellschaft Wodan also came into being. In addition to Adolf Weber, its founders were Adolf Kroll and Dr. Ernst Wachler, the latter an influential figure who had already sown many seeds to rekindle the Germanic religion, and who would play an influential role in the GGG. Born in 1871, the year of German unification, Wachler had studied literature and theater. Dissatisfied with the stuffy cosmopolitan literary scene, he had demanded a new kind of popular outdoor theater that would stand in bright contrast to the "wilted and colorless nature" of contemporary urban theatre. Around 1902 he contacted the Wagnerian painter Hermann Hendrich, who had been the primary mover behind the Walpurgishalle, an impressive wooden sanctuary modeled after Norse architectural styles and situated at the famous Hexentanzplatz (Place of the Witches' Sabbath) near Thale. The relationship inspired Wachler to conceive a plan for the first outdoor theater, the Harzer Bergtheater (Harz Mountain Theater), which was built in four months and inaugurated in 1903 with a play by Wachler called *Walpurgis—ein Spiel zur Frühlingsfeier* (Walpurgis—A Play to Celebrate Spring). The poster featured an image of Wotan, surrounded by his ravens.

For a few years these somewhat loosely formed groups were organizationally dependent upon Fahrenkrog's Deutscher Bund für Persönlichkeitskultur (German League for the Culture of the Personality), whose publication *Mehr Licht!* (More Light!) bore the Thor's hammer as its emblem and covered such topics as religion, family life, and education. But the young movement did not remain idle. In 1908 Schwaner and his cohorts erected a fire altar called the "Hermannstein" on Schwaner's land. It consisted of an imposing stone platform with an inlaid metal Thor's hammer, and was situated on top of a hill. To reach it, visitors first had to walk through a wooden gate decorated with runes and sunwheels. Wachler and Fahrenkrog issued a wealth of writings probing

Ludwig Fahrenkrog, "Allfather."

LUDWIG FAHRENKROG, "BALDUR."

issues relating to a revival of the Germanic faith (a good example is Wachler's article "Can the *Edda* Be Our Religious Book?"). In 1912 Schwaner himself created a complementary magazine called *Upland*, to be included with the *Volkserzieher* and which was named after the small religious group that had gathered around him. It was also the organ for the new Deutsche Religionsgemeinschaft (German Religious Community [DRG]), the logo of which was a superimposition of Schwaner's curved swastika and Fahrenkrog's hammer design. The second issue bore a drawing by Fahrenkrog announcing the consecration of the Hermannstein on 26 May 1912, a date that also marked the inauguration of the new organization.

The Pfingsten (Whitsuntide) meeting at which this took place was a momentous one. For five days, like-minded people came together to meet, listen to guest speakers, and go on hikes to special places in the surrounding area. At this point Fahrenkrog and Otto Sigfrid Reuter, the *völkisch* author and founder of the Deutscher Orden (German Order), were collaborating closely, which helped make the event a success. Reuter had attracted attention with his Riemann-inspired, but more refined, 1910 manifesto entitled *Sigfrid oder Christus?* He later helped found the *völkisch* commune Donnershag in 1919, and wrote works on the *Edda* and Germanic skylore.

The most significant act of the Pfingsten gathering occurred on the third day, when the Hermannstein fire altar on the Ermensberg was consecrated. After speeches by Schwaner, Fahrenkrog, and Philipp Stauff, Karl Engelhard recited his "Fire Blessing," the last two lines of which are: "*Wotan-Wotan-Wotan-Seele! Dir sich unsre auf ewig vermähle! Wotan!*" (Soul of Wotan! Join together forever with our own! Wotan!). According to eyewitnesses, the event was deeply experienced by all the participants and can perhaps be regarded as the first public invocation and sacrifice to Wotan in modern Germany. As Schwaner later wrote, "When 80–100 people remain in a religiously exalted state of mind for five days, can there be a sure proof that the mood was authentic and not just an intoxication?" Schwaner's doubts must have been significant, for he left the GGG soon after to propagate the "Germanization" of Christianity, thereby joining a movement which later proved very popular during the 1930s.

Two months later, the first Althing of the DRG was convened in Thale, near Wachler's mountain theater. At this Althing,

Fahrenkrog's sacral play *Baldur* was performed for the first time. The setting must have been impressive. "Surrounded by the German mountains, ancient Germanic heritage spoke in dulcet tones to the audience. The natural scenery corresponded perfectly to the content of the piece, down to the ancient sacrificial stone," noted F. V. Meier-Gostenhof in the 1917 special Fahrenkrog issue of the magazine *Die Schönheit*. Here it was decided to change the name to Germanisch-Deutsche Religionsgemeinschaft (Germanic-German Religious Community [GDRG]), since Otto Sigfrid Reuter did not attend the meeting, signifying the first schism in the organization. Reuter did not support the attempt led by Kroll and Weber to reintroduce a cult of the old gods. He and some others thought this would expose them to public ridicule, and they decided to espouse a general promotion of the German "essence" instead. Reuter also did not approve of Wachler's partly Jewish ancestry, and wanted to exclude him from the movement's activities. Fahrenkrog would not have this, and so Reuter and his cohorts split off, retaining the older DRG name until they changed it to Deutschgläubige Gemeinschaft (Association of the German Faithful [DGG]) in 1915. The DGG exists to this day. Later authors associated with the DGG continued the non-dogmatic and somewhat blurry line of argument in reference to reviving the ethics of the *Edda*. In 1926, Alfred Conn advocated the cultivation of an "*Eddic* sentiment" instead of an "*Eddic* creed." He also emphasized that "a German Faith is nothing without freedom of conscience, which alone can impart nobility to man." After the split, Adolf Kroll noted that the main difference between the two factions lay in the "fully conscious continuation of the faith of our own Germanic forefathers" by the GGG, whereas Hunkel's and Reuter's followers were too vague in their definition of their faith.

A year later, again at Thale, the GDRG changed its name to its final form: Germanische Glaubens-Gemeinschaft (Germanic Faith Community [GGG]). Here the famous ten points were agreed upon, which were later published in their compendium, *Das Deutsche Buch* (The German Book). These are:

1. We acknowledge the powers of the spirit and of life which permeate the cosmos and our being.

2. We also recognize in the cosmos the shape-giving pow-

ers of life, which cause the variety of all manifestations and therefore also acknowledge all special phenomena *(Sondererscheinungen)* as necessary manifestations of life's powers.

3. Since the truth and meaning of existence naturally lies in the manifestations themselves, it is therefore the purpose or task of all manifestations to fulfill themselves.

4. Thus we recognize the purpose and function of our existence—created as a seed in us and awaiting fulfillment—as lying within us.

5. Consequently, we believe and know that a Germanic religion can only be created by a Germanic people.

6. To us, religion is the pure, world-affirming relationship of a soul joyful in deed and discovery with the beings of the cosmos and with their revealed and manifested forms.

7. Our realization and experience of the gods as ultimate truths and beings and as forces working in and through us is both a knowledge of an ethical law within us, and the reason for our trust in their guidance, as well as the cause of our faith in the higher destiny of the Germanic people.

8. From such a realization also springs our will to do good, the will to purity, truth, and justice, to self-redemption and self-fulfillment, and thus also the will to free, ethical action, up to and including self-sacrifice.

9. Therefore, in the contemplation of our own being as the active field of special manifestations of the gods working through us and in keeping this essence and being healthy and strong, developing it further and upwards towards ever purer and more noble forms and goals, we see the loftiest purpose of every Germanic person within and outside of German borders.

10. But beyond the grave we trustfully gaze to eternity, whence we came. Our task is to fulfill this existence—to

determine it is the right and power of the gods that permeate the cosmos and ourselves, in time and in eternity.

The constitution also included such points as a division into "Hausgemeinde" (Hearth), "Ortsgemeinde" (local Kindred), "Gau" or "Stamm" (District or Tribe), and "Gemeinschaft," and the prerequisites for membership (Germanic ancestry, dedication to Germanic faith, no membership in any other religious association). The rules regarding the Thing were also agreed upon and gave both men and women (even if married) over eighteen the right to vote. Furthermore, the Gesellschaft Wodan and Nornenlogen (Lodges of the Norns) were incorporated into the GGG, and Fahrenkrog's drama *Wölund* (Wayland) saw its world premiere on the stage of Wachler's Bergtheater. In addition to having them performed, Fahrenkrog published his Germanic plays in lavish editions, complemented with his own illustrations and decorative ornaments.

On 11 October 1913 the Volkserzieher contingent did manage to make an appearance at the momentous Youth Movement meeting on the Hohe Meissner mountain, declaring, according to Walter Laqueur, that they "regard Germany, not Palestine, as the promised land." At this time, a good portion of the GGG's membership was made up of participants in the Youth Movement. The *völkisch* artist Fidus, Fahrenkrog's lifelong friend and also a GGG member, drew the cover illustration for the Hohe Meissner event program. The *Wandervögel*, as the Youth Movement was called, naturally veered towards a romantic outlook of Germanic prehistory and its religion (one of the movement's typical literary heroes, Helmut Harringa, reads *Beowulf* and the *Edda*, seeing "everything Nordic and Germanic" as "the incarnation of true heroism, loyalty and every other high ideal," according to Laqueur), since they were engaged in rebellion against their strict Christian environment. The main activities of these youth groups were hiking and camping excursions, during which they cultivated a revival of traditional and new folk songs and folk dances.

During these years, Fahrenkrog's art had matured and taken on its final style. Whether the medium was pen, crayon, or oil paint, the results were always the mirror of the artist's soul-searching within his ever-widening heathen perspective. While drawing from the vocabulary of Symbolism and Art Nouveau in his extravagant moments, Fahrenkrog otherwise firmly followed in the

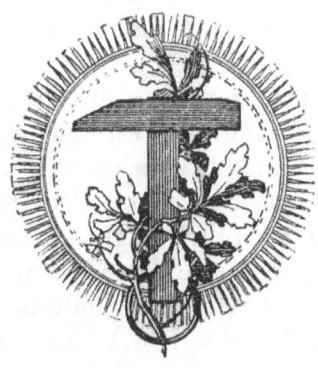

GGG Hammer Insignia.

footsteps of populist painters such as Hans Thoma. Like Fidus, he had prints and postcards made of his most popular works and worked on numerous book illustration projects. George Mosse mentions that during this time Fahrenkrog also executed drawings of Baldur and Thor for the strange *völkisch* apostle Tarnhari, who sold them as "small pictures that could be used as stamps." Together with Fidus, Franz Stassen, and Hermann Hendrich, Fahrenkrog was part of a group of artists favored by the Life Reform and Youth Movements. And though, unlike these other *völkisch* artists, he did not take part in the exhibits sponsored by the Werdandibund (Verdandi League) whose aim it was "to preserve the uniqueness and strengthen the spiritual power and soul of the German people through the arts," this statement is certainly in line with what Fahrenkrog wanted to achieve.

In 1914, the GGG invited all Germanic religious and *völkisch* groups to its "Pfingstfahrt" (Whitsuntide excursion) in Thale. The five-day gathering was marked by hiking, folk song and dance, and a ceremony on the Feuerfelsen, which began with readings from the *Edda* and concluded with each participant tossing a log in the fire and reciting a "fire saying." The meeting also incorporated the first formal Althing of the GGG.

The first world war interrupted the activities of the GGG to such an extent that the second Althing could only be held in 1919, again in Thale. The third Althing was held in Detmold in the fabled Teutoburg Forest in 1920. Here, the main tenets of the GGG were formulated in the three tenets: *"Gott in uns"* ("God within ourselves"), *"Das gute Gesetz in uns"* ("The law of good in ourselves"), and *"Selbsterlösung"* ("Self-redemption").

At the fourth Althing in Dresden, the participants witnessed a

"THE GERMAN BOOK," AN OFFICIAL PUBLICATION OF THE GGG.

typical outdoor "German Baptism" of young Siegfried Retzlaff. After the naming and sprinkling with water, the GGG hammer was raised to conclude the rite, and a young oak was planted in Siegfried's honor. At the fifth Althing, the GGG could note with satisfaction that its membership had doubled from the year before, and that it had won members in Sweden, Holland, Austria, and Czechoslovakia, thereby becoming in effect a pan-Germanic organization. During this time the GGG consolidated its thought in the slim volume called *Das Deutsche Buch*, which went through several editions. It contained sections written by Fahrenkrog,

Kroll, and others. A section entitled *"Das Germanische Jahr"* (The Germanic Year) listed the Germanic names for the months and days as well as names for all the Sundays of the year: "These are assigned according to the metaphors of the gods in the *Edda*. The first quarter [of the year]—becoming—tells of the creation; the second—blossoming—of the amorous affairs of the gods, etc., up until Balder's death; the third—the ripening—of the deeds of the gods; and the fourth—the wilting—tells of the fates of the heroes and the Nibelungs and the demise of the world." The "High Feasts" included the summer solstice and Yuletide, and certain other holidays were adopted such as the Scandinavian "Helig Thorsdag," the sixth Thursday after Easter, which was renamed "Hamarsheimt" (The Return of the Hammer). To the GGG, this day commemorated "the rebirth of Germanic faith and its ways."

At the sixth Althing in Berlin in 1923, Fahrenkrog used the occasion to clarify the spiritual position of the GGG in his speech:

> We want to build! The ruins are all around us as well as in our hearts but we also carry the faith in rebirth. Our task: to grow from a seed into a world ash [tree] through our blood and spirit. Decline of the Western world? We are alive! To no one's benefit and to no one's harm, we just want to be ourselves ... That is why we are not an anti-Semitic association that exists because it despises the Jews—no, we are important and worthy enough to exist for our own sake. And even less are we a Semitic association or otherwise a supporter of foreign ways ... No, we of the GGG are Germanic people, and only Germanic people ... That is why we are not a political party and furthermore see the party system as a hindrance to the ascent and united will of all Germanic people. We only know the well-being of all Teutons through self-determination, a self-determination that grows from the inside outward ... in a peaceful, organic manner, like the growth and development of a German oak.

The same Althing saw the heathen wedding of a young couple, consecrated with the following hammer blessing, replete with thinly veiled sexual symbolism:

Thor's hammer, crash through the gate of flames to the

blessed grounds! Coax life from the dark womb, life in the sacred hour! Blood should be blood, and flame should be flame, life should find life and woman her man!

The seventh Althing in Munich featured *völkisch* author Rudolf John Gorsleben reading his new *Edda* translations as well as demonstrations by the Augsburg *völkisch* gymnasts "Der Einheerer"—their name, of course, referring to Odin's departed warriors. During the proceedings, Fahrenkrog emphasized that the Germanic faith is not a religion of weakness, but rather one of strength and courage. These were timely words, for Fahrenkrog's own strength was to be tested in the following years.

After a long period of growth and harmony, the GGG was almost torn apart by several momentous events in 1925. During this year, Fahrenkrog's vision of a Germanic temple seemed on the verge of becoming a reality. Richard Stein, Fahrenkrog's stepson, had designed a *Halgadom* (actually a Listian term for a sacred temple or place) that the GGG wanted to erect at Witzenhausen an der Werra as a "visible expression of our indigenous religion." Several of Fahrenkrog's paintings, such as *Allvater* (Allfather) and *Segnender Baldur* (Baldur the Blessing Giver) were to be part of the interior decoration. The city had already provided a free parcel of land for the project. Immediately, various Christian and Judaic groups and the local archbishop protested the plans (two alarmist book accounts of the neo-heathen phenomenon by Christian authors had come out recently as well). There were also opposing voices inside the GGG which insisted that the Germanic faith should be practiced outdoors, and not inside a temple. All these obstacles resulted in the postponement of the project; in fact, it was never built and the chance to erect a visible monument to the reborn faith was lost. At the same time, a quarrel erupted between Adolf Kroll and Fahrenkrog over the application of the ancient myths. A commentary in the GGG publication *Weihwart* (Sacred Warden) summarizes their respective positions:

> For the contemporary German, who lives in different conditions than his ancestors did thousands of years ago, Fahrenkrog puts the emphasis on the inner experience of God, in the sense of Meister Eckhart, Jacob Böhme, Goethe, etc., and predicts that in time a new mythos will

arise from this foundation. Adolf Kroll, as an *Eddic* researcher, wholly builds his conception of the Germanic faith and mythos on the *Edda*. Both views naturally have room to coexist and function within the GGG. As much as I value Kroll's *Eddic* researches, I see a danger of our exclusive adherence to the *Edda*, resulting in a unilateral development into a dogmatic church.

While Fahrenkrog put forth his theses in an impartial essay, Kroll unfortunately replied with thinly veiled personal attacks against the artist. Fahrenkrog later put his position this way:

> Just because one does not place one's faith in the *Edda* in the sense that the Adventist places his faith in the Bible, by no means does this indicate that one is opposed to the *Edda* ... Fundamentally speaking, I have a deep love for the *Edda*, as can be seen in my *Baldur* and *Wölund* dramas. But the research and interpretation of these myths must be a free pursuit, otherwise we cannot advance.

Various intrigues followed between different factions, mostly in regard to the continued attempts to rejoin with the DGG, thereby uniting the movement further. In the end, Fahrenkrog and his supporters won out, and ejected several groups and individuals from the organization. But the talks with the DGG came to nought, since the inner schisms in the GGG placed them in a less-than-favorable light.

All these thwarted efforts and prolonged arguments and divisions had sapped Fahrenkrog's energy to the breaking point. For a brief time in 1927 at least, the now sixty-year-old activist abdicated his Hochwart post and took a break. But the next year he was back and invited guests to the tenth Althing at his house in Barmen, seeking to emphasize the "enjoyment of community" in his invitation.

The following years saw several further furtive attempts to unite the various factions of the Germanic faith movement. All failed because of the unwillingness to compromise, basic incompatibilities, and personality clashes. In 1931, the Nordungen, the Nordische Glaubensgemeinschaft (Nordic Faith Community) under Dr. Wilhelm Kusserow (after WWII the leader of the Artgemeinschaft [Kindred Community]), and the GGG joined in the formation of the Nordisch-Religiöse Arbeitsgemeinschaft (Nordic Religious Working Association [NRAG]), founded by Norbert Seibertz and Graf Ernst von Reventlow as a countermeasure to the various nationalist Christian groups. In 1933 this association joined the Arbeitsgemeinschaft der Deutschen Glaubensbewegung (Working Association of the German Faith Movement), which was led by Professor Jakob Wilhelm Hauer, the noted Indo-Germanic scholar who had left the Church thanks to Fahrenkrog's inspiration. But Hauer also allowed some Christians to join and aimed to undermine the independence of the organizations, and so the "Nordics" (who numbered only 3,000 of the 100,000 members) departed barely a year later.

The German Faith Movement, like most other endeavors of its kind, was not exactly encouraged by the new regime. Unlike other organizations, the GGG was not forbidden altogether, in part because of Fahrenkrog's international status as an artist. But it had to endure several curtailments of its freedoms. In 1936 it was forbidden to hold public meetings, thereby cutting off its main means for winning new members. In 1938 the GGG was forbidden to use the swastika, which had been the group's symbol since 1908, because the NSDAP claimed its exclusive use as a symbol of the party and the German state. Hence, Fahrenkrog changed the curved swastika into a sunwheel. This follows a general pattern in the NS regime. For instance, in an effort to appeal to *völkisch* elements, they had initially sponsored the so-called *Thingspiele* (Thing Plays) but then proceeded to outlaw the word *Thing* in 1935 because the National Socialists did not want to "resort to such outmoded and dead words, dating from gray prehistoric times which are not able to bolster the difficult present-day political struggle" (quoted by Klaus von See). As the party consolidated its power, it also streamlined its use of language and symbolism. According to Géza von Neménji, Fahrenkrog was also reluctant to use the "Heil Hitler!" greeting in his letters, a gesture which precluded any further success or recognition in the NS regime. A large exhibit of his paintings was forbidden by the propaganda ministry in 1934. On the other hand, he was allowed to take part in the third traveling exhibit of the German Art Society in 1943. During the 1930s he was honored by his hometown of Rendsburg, and became honorary Master of the Hamburg Painters Guild. Unfortunately, his fellow traveller Ernst Wachler met a grimmer fate, and died sometime in 1944 or 1945 in a concentration camp in Czechoslovakia.

Ludwig Fahrenkrog himself passed away in 1952 in Biberach an der Riß, a week after his eighty-fifth birthday and that year's GGG Althing, where he had bidden farewell to his friends and associates. He pointedly summarized his achievement as an artist and writer in the following poem:

Condensed Life Story

Gray days crawled along the earth
Silent and sullen
and creeping fog made me ill
day in and day out.

Then across the plain hailed the storm
—It destroyed everything.—
So I swung my arms
And defended myself.

Still:
My vision grew ever darker, full of blight.
Then I went on the attack
And it became light!

The new German postwar society was marked by an unprecedented break with the past, allowing outside influences to replace indigenous values at a rapid rate. After the experience of the Hitler regime, the chances for a group that championed Germanic ideals were slim. After Fahrenkrog's death, Ludwig Dessel became the new Hochwart and Althings continued to be held until 1955, while the GGG magazine *Germanen-Glaube* was published until 1960. But by 1964 the GGG had ceased to exist as a registered association and most of its remaining members had died.

A few decades later, as part of the renewed interest in alternative lifestyles in general and paganism in particular, new groups sprang up to continue the work of the old GGG. In order to promote the artistic heritage of the founder, an admiration society, the Freundeskreis Ludwig Fahrenkrog, was founded in 1982, as was the Heidnische Gemeinschaft (Heathen Association), a related group that continued Fahrenkrog's religious activities. One of the main leaders of this group was Géza von Neményi, who at this time was also very active in reconstructing the pagan tradition according to actual historic sources—a kind of "orthodox heathenism." The fruits of this labor were gathered together in Neményi's major work *Heidnische Naturreligion* (Heathen Nature Religion). Its 450 pages contain reconstructed rituals ranging from a hammer blessing to a burial rite. The book is appropriately dedicated to Snorri Sturluson, the collector and author of the *Prose Edda*. In 1991, after consulting Ludwig Dessel, Neményi reactivated the GGG and reestablished its magazine *Germanen-Glaube*, whose covers often feature Fahrenkrog's artwork. The new GGG is an amalgam of the different streams of thought within the GGG, following in Kroll's footsteps when it comes to the practical aspects of the religion, while still invoking Fahrenkrog's spirit and retaining the ten points of the original constitution. Neményi remains the GGG's leader (now called "Allsherjargothi," following Old Norse terminology, rather than "Hochwart"), writes meticulously researched, in-depth articles for *Germanen-Glaube*, and guides the religious life of the group. He has stepped on the toes of many would-be heathen spiritual leaders by insisting on the need for stringent formal training and initiation within the realm of a Germanic priesthood. In early 2003 his important new book on the runes, *Heilige Runen: Zauberzeichen des Nordens* (Holy Runes: Magical Symbols of the North), was issued by a major German publisher. It stands as one of the few modern books on the subject by a practicing heathen *Gothi* or priest, and places the runes in the context of Germanic religion and culture, instead of treating them as disembodied symbols.

BRONZE RITUAL HAMMER OF THE GGG.

In conclusion, the GGG can be regarded as one of the first Germanic religious societies that resurrected and put into practice elements that today have become widespread among the Ásatrú community and other Germanic neo-heathens. It was definitely among the first groups that regularly practiced religious rites which at least partially (in accordance with the still-limited historical knowledge of the time) based on old Germanic pagan rituals. The GGG held annual Althings and used a special bronze Mjölnir, or Thor's hammer, in its rites. Its primary movers managed to publish numerous periodicals promoting their worldview, and even to create sacral spaces and places for the group's members to gather. And the spiritual path of its founder Ludwig Fahrenkrog represents a perfect example of an inner transformation from Christianity to what he thought was a more authentic German faith.

I gratefully acknowledge the help of Géza von Neményi, who generously provided me with materials, including his many articles on the history of the GGG in the publication Germanen-Glaube, *which were major sources for this article. I would also like to thank Daniel Junker, whose excellent study of the GGG inspired this revised version of my original article, which appeared in* Vor Tru *59.*

Selected bibliography of works by Ludwig Fahrenkrog:

Geschichte meines Glaubens (Halle/S.: Gebauer-Schwetschke, 1906).
Baldur (Stuttgart: Greiner & Pfeiffer, 1908).
Selbsterlösung (Leipzig: Fahrenkrog-Verlag, 1912).
Lucifer: Dichtung in Bild und Wort (Stuttgart: Greiner & Pfeiffer, 1913).
Aufsätze zum Germanenglauben (Leipzig: Fahrenkrog-Verlag, 1914).
Wölund (Stuttgart: Greiner & Pfeiffer, 1919).
Nornegast (Leipzig: Wilhelm Hartung, 1920).
Die Godentochter (Leipzig: Wilhelm Hartung, 1921).
Gott im Wandel der Zeiten, six vols. (Leipzig: Wilhelm Hartung, 1923–1930).
Das Deutsche Buch (Berlin: Kraft und Schönheit, 1922).
Die Schönheit magazine, 2nd Fahrenkrog issue (Dresden: Verlag der Schönheit, 1927).
Das Goldene Tor: Dichtungen in Wort und Bild (Leipzig: Fahrenkrog-Gesellschaft, 1927).
Germanische Mythologie (Heidelberg: Winter, 1934).

Further sources:

Conn, Alfred. *Die Mythen der Edda* (Hamburg: Gustav A. Schmidt, 1926).

Dahn, Felix von. *Walhall: Germanische Götter- und Heldensagen* (Kreuznach: R. Voigtländer, 1885).

Ehrhardt, Ingrid and Simon Reynolds, eds. *Kingdom of the Soul: Symbolist Art in Germany, 1870–1920* (Munich, London, New York: Prestel, 2000).

Engelbrecht, Kurt. *Ludwig Fahrenkrog: Seine Schöpfungen und ihre Bedeutung für unser Volkstum* (Dresden: Verlag der Schönheit, n.d.).

Hubricht, Emil. *Buchweiser für das völkisch-religiöse Schrifttum* (Freiberg i. Sa.: Hubricht, 1934. Reprinted Toppenstedt: Uwe Berg, 1983).

Junker, Daniel. *Gott in uns! Die Germanische Glaubens-Gemeinschaft* (Hamburg: Verlag Daniel Junker, 2002).

Laqueur, Walter Z. *Young Germany: A History of the German Youth Movement* (New York: Basic, 1962).

Merk, Anton. *Franz Stassen 1869–1949* (Hanau: Museum Hanau, 1999).

Mosse, George. *The Crisis of German Ideology* (New York: Grosset & Dunlap, 1964).

Neményi, Géza von. *Heidnische Naturreligion: Altüberlieferte Glaubensvorstellungen, Riten und Bräuche* (Bergen/Dumme: Kersken-Canbaz-Verlag, 1988).

Neményi, Géza von. *Heilige Runen: Zauberzeichen des Nordens* (Munich: Heyne, 2003).

Pflanz, Michael. "Dr. Ernst Wachler" in *Der Runenstein*, Wonnemond/Brachmond (1994).

Reuter, Otto Sigfrid. *Sigfrid oder Christus?* (Leipzig: Neuer Verlag Deutsche Zukunft, 1910. Reprinted Toppenstedt: Uwe Berg, 1976).

Riemann. *Allvater (Wodan) oder Jehovah?* (Berlin: H. Walter, 1906. Reprinted Bremen: Faksimile Verlag, 1995).

Rohling, Elke. *Hermann Hendrich: Leben und Werk/ Life and Work* (Billerbeck: Selbstverlag Werdandi, 2001).

Schnurbein, Stefanie. *Religion als Kulturkritik* (Heidelberg: Carl Winter, 1992).

See, Klaus von. *Barbar, Germane, Arier* (Heidelberg: Carl Winter, 1994).

Ulbricht, Justus. "'Doch diesmal kommt von osten nicht das licht': Zum Nordlandmythos der völkischen Bewegung," in *Wahlverwandschaft: Skandinavien und Deutschland 1800–1914* (Berlin: Jovis, 1997).

Various, *Harzstadt Thale* (Quedlinburg & Jena: Verlag Dr. Bussert, 1997).

Weißmann, Karlheinz. *Druiden, Goden, Weise Frauen* (Freiburg: Herder, 1991).

To Each His Own

I do not like your dark church!
I prefer the bright shining sun!
And my own women are a thousand times
more dear to me
Than your painted Madonna.

And the son that my wife has given me
Is a thousand times more dear to me
Than your gilded crucifix,
With its contorted arms and legs.

Overall, I do not like what is alien to this world
What is cold, wilted and lifeless.
I love life, and joy, and light
And the blood, surging and red.

—Ludwig Fahrenkrog

(Translated by Markus Wolff)

The Friedrich Hielscher Legend:
The Founding of a Twentieth-Century Panentheistic "Church" and Its Subsequent Misinterpretations

Peter Bahn

For decades, the life and work of the writer, religious philosopher, and scholar Dr. Friedrich Hielscher (1902–1990) have given rise to all manner of speculative misinterpretations. This holds especially true with the genre of popular "esoteric" literature, in which Hielscher has repeatedly been a subject for the wildest speculations and assertions. By the beginning of the 1960s, an extremely negative "Hielscher legend" had already arisen, with even bolder embellishments being added to it all the way up to the present day. This legend is, however, virtually light years away from Hielscher's actual actions and intentions, and devoid of any reference to reality.

In order to get to the bottom of these speculations, and to determine their sources of origin, it is first necessary to examine the course of Hielscher's life. Regarding the years up to 1954, this can be ascertained not least of all via his autobiography.[1] Concerning the subsequent time period there exist—in the literature, at least—only scattered, fragmentary bits of information that are difficult to access.[2] By contrast, the extant archives relating to Hielscher are much more fruitful, especially his literary estate[3] and his correspondence with Ernst Jünger, which lasted from 1926 to 1986.[4]

The son of a textile merchant, Friedrich Hielscher was born on 31 May 1902 in Plauen, Vogtland, and grew up in Guben, Niedersaulitz. At the age of seventeen he graduated from the Humanist High School in Guben. Immediately following his final exams, he joined a Freikorps unit that took part in resistance battles against Polish groups in Upper Silesia.[5] His unit later became part of the German army. In March 1920, Hielscher refused to participate in the Kapp putsch, and retired from the military.[6] He then began to study law at the University of Berlin and also attended lectures at the College of Political Science.[7] These political science studies brought him into close contact with Theodor

HIELSCHER IN FREIKORPS UNIFORM. (COLLECTION OF THE AUTHOR)

Heuss, with whom he formed a lifelong friendship.[8] In Berlin, Hielscher joined the Normannia student dueling corps, and up until the 1970s he was active as an authority on the group's history, as well as a sought-after lecturer in regard to the Kösener Assembly.[9]

While the short period in the Freikorps was marked much more by aspirations toward independence and adventure than by concrete political visions,[10] during the course of his studies in Berlin Hielscher gradually became more politicized. Following a temporary affiliation with the Reichsclub of the national-liberal German People's Party[11] he gravitated toward the circles of the "leftists of the Right" and the "new nationalists." These small circles, which were centered around certain journals and publishing projects, endeavored to bridge the gap between the intellectual background of the socialist workers' movement and that of traditional nationalism.[12] At the same time, he crossed paths with personalities such as the cultural philosopher Oswald Spengler[13] and Nietzsche's sister Elisabeth Förster-Nietzsche, the latter acquaintance coming about due to Hielscher's numerous stays at the Nietzsche archive in Weimar as part of his promotional work.[14] In 1926 Hielscher completed his degree with a thesis entitled "Die Selbstherrlichkeit: Versuch einer Darstellung des deutschen Rechtsgrundbegriffes" (Sovereignty: An Attempt at a Description of the Basis of German Law), for which he was awarded a dual doctorate, summa cum laude, in legal philosophy and legal history.[15] But he found his subsequent bureaucratic, regimented job as a legal clerk to be such an ordeal that in November 1927 he was discharged at his own request from the civil service.[16] For the rest of his life he lived as a scholar—after a fashion, largely—from the proceeds of publications, lectures, and occasional research commissions.

Hielscher, who had by now developed a close personal contact with Ernst Jünger, was active from 1926 on as a contributor to the various journals connected to the national-revolutionary "new nationalism." His first essay appeared at the end of 1926 in the magazine *Neue Standarte—Arminius: Kampfschrift für deutsche Nationalisten*. With its title, "Innerlichkeit und Staatskunst" (Inwardness and Statecraft), he indicated from the start that he was not concerned with superficial political activity, since things did not rest "at the beginning of a new departure, but rather at the end of the old collapse."[17] This collapse could only be overcome by a new "faith," "which will bear the German future and without which the new work will not be begun."[18]

With the emphasis of this early text on the fundamental importance of a new faith, a trait had already emerged in Hielscher's work that rapidly intensified, and which would remain predominant until the end of his life. Hielscher thought "politically" only in a secondary and transitory way; he was much more concerned with the derivation of a new "statecraft" from religious concepts. This was already clear by the end of the 1920s from his correspondence with Ernst Jünger. Accordingly, in November 1929 he sent Jünger an extensive religious-ideological "declaration of faith" *(Bekenntnis)*, and in another letter a few weeks later spoke of the necessity for an "invisible church" to come into being which would be effective in terms of both faith and politics.[19] Living at the time in the seclusion of a parsonage in the Lausitz area, where a former school friend was serving as a Protestant clergyman, Hielscher worked on his book *Das Reich*, which was published in 1931.[20] This was preceded by the first issues of a periodical of the same title that Hielscher had edited since September 1930. A circle of followers, loyal to Hielscher as a *spiritus rector*, gradually formed around the journal and from among the readership of the book, which had sparked considerable discussion. Until 1933 this circle was primarily drawn from the ranks of the Youth Movement and national-revolutionary youth groups.[21]

The unity of faith and politics postulated by Hielscher, of "inwardness and statecraft," was not without consequences for the structure and activity of his circle. In the years between 1932 and 1935 the association grew, in Hielscher's words, both "as a resist-

A PHOTOGRAPH OF FRIEDRICH HIELSCHER TAKEN AROUND 1930.
(COLLECTION OF THE AUTHOR)

ance against the rabble, and as a church."[22] Hielscher always considered the NS movement to be "rabble," against which he stood in a diametrical opposition for religious-ideological reasons. In fact, the circle around Hielscher saw itself both as an "embryonic church" with the corresponding ritual activities, and as an "embryonic state" with the task of resisting National Socialism,[23] although it is unlikely that all the politically active members of the circle participated with the same intensity in the church-oriented, religious aspects of the group. Altogether, the circle consisted of about fifty persons, whose names can be determined from the archives relating to Hielscher.[24]

The activities of the circle, both as a "church" and as a resistance group, were carried out on the basis of an extraordinarily complex religious-ideological system. This had not been borrowed by Hielscher in finished form from other sources, but was developed successively from specific, fundamental axioms. Of central importance was the idea of faith as an unquestionable "basis of the deed," and thus as the primary leitmotif for every human action.[25] On a subordinate level to this meaning of faith in general (i.e., of a faith as such), Hielscher placed his own concrete theology with its special perspective on God, the gods, and man— a perspective which he defined as "heathen."

The starting point was the panentheistic perception of God as the "Eternal One, in whom everything is contained."[26] Thus, God was not external to the world, but rather the world was in Him; he was not the Creator, but rather the one who (from out of himself) continually creates. Hielscher connected this to various notions. From Nietzsche's understanding of the world as "will to power," he extrapolated the idea of becoming one "with the eternally becoming world."[27] Out of this could "be sensed ... an awareness of God."[28] At the same time, he returned specifically to the thought of the early-ninth-century heretic and scholar Johannes Scotus Eriugena, according to whom, "God is everything that is eternal and which has become."[29] Eriugena also described God as a "manifold unity within himself."[30] This idea exclusively and completely dominated the religious convictions of Hielscher and his circle until the end of the 1930s, before being expanded (with conceptions that were systematically derived from the aforementioned thinker) to include "gods" or "celestial messengers," who as personal "particularities" *(Besonderungen)* of the "almighty and one true God" appeared as mediators between the latter and human beings. In this regard, polytheistic elements found in German classicist thought (especially in the works of Goethe and Hölderlin)—but clothed by Hielscher as gods from German mythology ("Wode," "Thor," "Loki," "Freya," "Sigyn," etc.)—were taken up and incorporated structurally.[31] As a "soul," the human being was also nothing other than one of the "particularities" emanating from the fullness of the one true God. For Hielscher, this consequently led to a rejection of modern Western conceptions of the autonomous individual: each "soul" (i.e., each human being) receives "its own essence at every moment from God."[32]

Out of these basic conceptions, from the start of the 1930s the Hielscher circle developed a belief system that continually differentiated itself through new manifestations, as well as a church-oriented liturgical practice with ceremonies for the cycle of the year and the course of life. With the inauguration of Hielscher's new apartment in Falkenhain near Berlin on 27 August 1933 came the church's first official "observance" *(Andacht)*. This was henceforth considered to be the actual founding date of the church, which Hielscher named the "Unabhängige Freikirche" (UFK), the Independent Free Church.[33] This was followed by liturgical elaborations, oriented extensively upon the folkloric, mythological, and religious-historical studies done by members of the group; almost exclusively, these studies were distributed internally. By 1941, they were able to complete an annual sequence of heathen rituals consisting of twenty-four ceremonies.[34] Each ceremony was dedicated to one of twelve German gods, and was (as Ernst Jünger hinted in an entry in his *Paris Diaries* in October, 1943, written after a meeting with Hielscher) combined with diverse symbolic correspondences—signs, trees, flowers, animals, foods, drinks, and "inherent colors" and "apparent colors" *(Wesensfarben und Erscheinungsfarben)*.[35] At the same time, as head of the UFK, Hielscher also performed baptismal and wedding ceremonies for members of his circle, later followed by the group's first funerals.[36]

Structurally, the liturgy of specific UFK religious services—with their invocations, prayers, songs, and readings—also contained elements that could definitely be found, in this or a similar fashion, among communities of the Christian faith. The differences lay primarily in terms of content, which within the UFK was distinguished by the Germanic pantheon of gods and the "one true God" arching over it. But there was something further. In his autobiography, Hielscher expressly described himself—drawing an explicit distinction with Ernst Jünger—as a "mystic."[37] The meaning imbued to the ceremonies within the UFK stood, therefore, in a very specific context. Hielscher emphasized accordingly that with these ceremonies "the church would celebrate the dominion of the celestial in this space and in this time"[38] and spoke of a "returning from the ceremony to our daily duties with new energy and power."[39] This was reminiscent of a mystical understanding of religion, which viewed the inner, contemplative experience of the numinous as a source of energy, especially for the individual believer taking part in the ceremonies.

For Hielscher and his circle, the resistance against National Socialism was nurtured by religious sources. It was much less a criticism of the individual political steps taken by the NS regime—although here, too, Hielscher developed various dissenting positions, the discussion of which is beyond the scope of the present essay—than a rejection in principle. Due to its lack of a transcendental connection, NS rule was viewed by the Hielscher circle as a decayed level of statehood, a form of mob rule that—not least on account of its biological racial ideology—had become enslaved to "matter" and to the purely material. To Hielscher, infiltration and subversion-from-within seemed a feasible path of resistance, though in light of the numerical weakness of his circle this strategy rapidly came up against limiting factors. While members of the Hielscher circle were able to occupy some middle-level positions in the army, in counter-intelligence, and in the SA and SS, there was very little—besides gathering information and occasionally offering help to individual victims of political persecution—that could be done.

One exception was the influence exerted on the Ahnenerbe, the SS research organization founded on 31 July 1935, and of which Wolfram Sievers, a younger friend of Hielscher's and also a member of the UFK, came to be the administrative leader.[40] Beyond its original aim of furthering the study of "Spiritual Prehistory" *(Geistesurgeschichte)*[41] the Ahnenerbe, an object of prestige for Heinrich Himmler, gradually subdivided into new research departments related to art history, the natural sciences, medicine, and even technology.[42] As a result of the later involvement of the medical departments in the barbaric human experiments conducted by the SS, Sievers, who despite his religiously motivated disapproval of these incidents had found himself unable to openly take action against them, was sentenced to death at the Nuremberg trials and hung.[43] Hielscher—who had, under the protection of his friend,[44] even received temporary research commissions from the Ahnenerbe concerning folkloristic and cultural-historical matters—attempted unsuccessfully until the end to gain a pardon for Sievers. Immediately prior to the execution, he visited Sievers in prison and celebrated a religious farewell ceremony with him, according to the observances of his heathen church.[45] It was this event in particular that later gave cause for a number of extravagant speculations.

When it was feasible, Hielscher took advantage of his activities for the Ahnenerbe, which were occasionally combined with research trips, in order to help people who were being politically or racially persecuted,[46] and to cultivate contacts with various groups within the anti-Nazi resistance.[47] In September 1944 he was arrested by the Gestapo in connection with the attempted assassination of Hitler by Count Von Stauffenberg, imprisoned for some months, and tortured. It was Sievers's intervention at that time which led to his being released on "probation to serve at the front," and ultimately saved his life.[48]

After 1945 the Hielscher circle ceased any further political activity and concentrated exclusively on religious pursuits within the parameters of the UFK. Basing his outlook on a cyclical view of history and employing seasonal terminology, Hielscher believed that mankind found itself in a historical "winter" (which had begun around 1800 with the French Revolution and the rise of industrialization) amid which one had to proceed from a fundamental "impossibility of the state," necessitating a conceptually new construction of the state. In contrast, the "church in winter" was seen as the "root of spring, and first step of the Reich,"[49] and the new focus of its pursuits appeared to be the next logical step. For decades, this remained the work of the UFK. And as it had during the Third Reich, in the Federal Republic of Germany the UFK maintained its nearly complete isolation from outsiders. From the 1950s through the 1980s, UFK activity was characterized by annual "church days," home celebrations, and the amassing of a wealth of internal compositions that exist in hectographic form; above all, these deal with questions of theology and historical philosophy.[50] The advancing age of its members (for newer, younger ones could hardly be brought into the fold) and two "church crises," in 1969–70 and 1983–84,[51] finally weakened a circle which had never been especially strong—so much so that in the years preceding Hielscher's death in March 1990, the UFK consisted primarily of himself and his wife, Gertrud.

In conclusion, it can be emphasized that Hielscher, who emerged from the politically motivated national-revolutionary current of the Weimar period, had already by the end of the 1920s turned to religious themes in an intensified way, and as a result of this tendency had created his own "heathen" church. At first glance, the UFK seems comparable with numerous other contemporary *völkisch* religious initiatives, but it differed from them with its formulation of a strictly axiomatic theological system and a consequent rejection of all racial-biological, and therefore materialistic, conceptions. Hielscher and his circle disapproved of the NS system from the outset, but attempted to make use of their positions, through the infiltration of specific institutions (the Ahnenerbe in particular), as part of a resistance effort. By doing so, Hielscher came into life-threatening conflict with the Gestapo. After 1945 he withdrew almost completely from public view, and aside from his activities with the student dueling society and the publication of his autobiography, he concentrated solely on cultivating the mystical-contemplative practices of his church.

In the place of this accurate record, which can be verified completely through literary evidence and archives, from 1960 onward a web of misinterpretations, speculations, and legendary formulations began to develop that no longer bore any relation to Hielscher's actual life and work. Nevertheless, it is necessary to go into the matter, for much of what the broader public, both inside and outside of Germany, came to know about Hielscher in recent decades has been influenced and clouded by these legendary formulations. An unbiased analysis of Hielscher—and especially of his theological system, which contains some extremely remarkable elements—can hardly take place as long as a bramble of negative myths obstructs the necessary access.

At the root of the legendary formulation was the book *Le matin de magiciens* (The Morning of the Magicians) by Louis Pauwels and Jacques Bergier, first published in France in 1960 and soon translated into various languages. The authors' basic intent was to point out certain aspects of mundane reality that lay outside of the current rationalistic and positivistic explanatory model. Against this backdrop they outlined—and not, ultimately, in a detailed manner—various "dark" and "bizarre" sides to the intellectual history of the twentieth century and suggested (actual or speculative) historical references. Of particular interest was the purportedly esoteric or "occult" background of National Socialism. It was inevitable that in this context, Heinrich

Himmler's predilections for Germanic mythology and for the rituals of the traditional *Männerbünde*, the history of the NS Order Castles, and the relevant research activities of the Ahnenerbe would also be brought up.[52]

Proceeding from the now publicly known farewell ceremony prior to Wolfram Sievers's execution—described not least of all by Hielscher in his own autobiography—Hielscher found himself in the sights of Pauwels and Bergier as well. They initially introduced him as Sievers's "spiritual teacher,"[53] which of course had a certain plausibility, due to Sievers's membership in Hielscher's religiously motivated resistance circle. But in the face of the sufficiently researched organizational history of the Ahnenerbe,[54] much more far-fetched was the factual assertion in the same paragraph that the founding of this organization could actually be traced back to the "private initiative" of Hielscher,[55] who had moreover been bonded in a "mystical friendship" with the Swedish explorer Sven Hedin. What we are to make of this "mystical friendship"—which is neither alluded to in Hielscher's autobiography (where he often wrote readily and extensively of his encounters and friendships with various personalities) nor in his literary estate—is a question that Pauwels and Bergier leave unanswered. Yet the imaginative detour to Hedin's earlier explorations in Central Asia provided perfectly for the elaboration of a National Socialist "secret doctrine," apparently influenced by the Far East, the genesis and establishment of which Sven Hedin—and Hielscher along with him—were alleged to have been substantially involved.[56]

Pauwels and Bergier did, in fact, concede a few sentences later that Hielscher was never a National Socialist, but claimed that a connection existed via his commonality "with the 'magic' doctrines of the Grand Masters of National Socialism."[57] But it was specifically with this explicit ascription of "magical" ideas to Hielscher, that Pauwels and Bergier revealed how little they actually knew about his religious-cosmological system, for Hielscher had always disapprovingly opposed the concept and practice of "magic." This he emphasized not least of all in his autobiography, which had been available since 1954 (and was therefore quite accessible to Pauwels and Bergier). In it, denoting a characteristic difference between his worldview and that of Ernst Jünger, he classified his personal perspective as a mystical one, whereas Jünger's was magical.[58] And there is yet another source for this rejection of magic that was stringently deduced from Hielscher's religious-cosmological system, according to which it is not possible for the human being "to approach the gods, to seal their blessing, to rise up to them."[59] On 11 December 1956 Hielscher wrote to Friedrich Georg Jünger, the brother of Ernst Jünger, that magic was the "unsuitable, but always culpable attempt using earthly means, namely those of sorcery, to force the Celestial into one's service." White magic was even more reprehensible than black magic, since the white magician was guilty of "desiring to subject a good spirit," rather than an evil spirit, "to one's own will."[60]

But Pauwels and Bergier were unconcerned with all of this. Far removed from any sources concerning Hielscher's life and work, they ultimately attributed to him "an important role in the drafting of the [National Socialist] secret teachings,"[61] this cold and cruel doctrine allegedly transmitted by Sven Hedin from Asia, which lay behind political events and in the authors' view could alone explain the actions of the protagonists of National Socialism and especially the SS. Far-reaching conjecture of this sort, pulled out of thin air and spread internationally via the Pauwels and Bergier book in large editions, established an ideal, fertile soil in subsequent years for even further-reaching speculations and increasingly foolhardy claims concerning Hielscher's role during the NS era.

A typical example in this regard is the book *The Spear of Destiny* (published in Germany as *Die Heilige Lanze*) by British author Trevor Ravenscroft, in which Hielscher—naturally again without a shred of evidence and as a result of the "method" of fully unrestrained yarn-spinning—is once more built up as having been the spiritual leader of the Ahnenerbe organization, and "the most important single figure in Germany after Adolf Hitler himself."[62] "The Führer," according to Ravenscroft, asked Hielscher for advice "in all occult matters" and in the event of a German victory in World War Two, Hielscher "may well have become the High Priest of a new world religion that would have replaced the Cross with the Swastika."[63] Finally, Ravenscroft also imagined he knew that it was none other than Hielscher who had developed a mysterious "Ritual of the Stifling Air" by which select members of the SS "took oaths of irreversible allegiance to Satanic powers."[64] The fact that even in the second, revised edition of his book[65] Ravenscroft was still writing "Friedrich *Heilscher*" instead of

"Friedrich *Hielscher*" is probably indicative of the command of facts and sources possessed by this and some other authors in the genre.

Another English-speaking writer, Gerald Suster, approached the subject in a similar manner. In a book bearing the sensational title *Hitler: Black Magician* he felt compelled to write that Hielscher had already founded the Ahnenerbe in 1933, after which it received recognition as an "official" organization in 1935.[66] According to Suster, Hielscher influenced the SS in particular, and to a much higher degree than had generally been known.[67] Suster, too, was guilty of lacking any evidence for these claims, let alone references to sources that could be verified bibliographically or via archives. The bibliography of his 222-page book is limited to less than two full pages. Although the bibliography contained neither Hielscher's autobiography nor the serious scholarly literature on the Ahnenerbe, the British edition of Pauwels's and Bergier's *Le matin des magiciens*, published in 1964, is found once again to be one of the primary sources.[68]

The same speculative associations, for the most part making direct and explicit references to Pauwels-Bergier and Ravenscroft, are also to be found in the voluminous book *Das Schwarze Reich*, credited to the obviously pseudonymous author "E. R. Carmin," which claims to reveal the considerable influence of all sorts of secret societies on the politics of the twentieth century. The book appeared in 1994 from a small publisher in the Rheinland area, passed relatively unnoticed at first, but a gained wide circulation three years later when it was issued in paperback by the famed Heyne Verlag in Munich. "Carmin" not only seized once more upon the usual legendary formulations of his literary antecedents, such as the "mystical friendship" between Hielscher and Sven Hedin, but also busily concocted—as an additional, original ingredient to the burgeoning Hielscher legend—connections between Hielscher's clandestine church (the name of which, however, he did not know) and Alfred Rosenberg's desire for the creation of a national Reich church.[69] In passing, "Carmin" also describes Hielscher's primary historical-philosophical work *Das Reich* as a "novel,"[70] throwing a revealing light in every respect on this kind of contemporary "historical" research.

A thoroughly unique contribution to the "Hielscher legend" which not only drew upon, but heavily contributed to previous speculations, was made by the Chilean author and ardent Hitler

HIELSCHER IN THE 1980S AT HIS HOME, THE
RIMPRECHTSHOF. IN THE BACKGROUND ARE VISIBLE
CULTIC IMAGES RELATING TO HIS CHURCH.
(COLLECTION OF THE AUTHOR)

admirer Miguel Serrano with his book *Das Goldene Band: Esoterischer Hitlerismus*. This first appeared in Spanish in 1978 and was published in a German translation in 1987. In it, Serrano set out to detail an extensive spiritual line of tradition, including doctrines of Hinduism, medieval alchemy, the Templars, the Cathars, and Rosicrucians, that led directly to an "esoterically" interpreted National Socialism in which a surviving Adolf Hitler lives on at the South Pole. Amid this Hielscher, of all people, respectfully called "the initiate" by Serrano, was placed on par with the "highest and unknown leaders of Hitlerism" and even elevated all the way to being a "spiritual leader of the SS."[71]

Serrano's bibliographical appendix, too, lacked any trace of Hielscher's autobiography, the other texts published by Hielscher, and the relevant material that rests in archives. But *Le matin des magiciens* turns up once more in the sources given—this time in its 1963 Spanish translation.[72] This again underscores the leading role played by Pauwels and Bergier for decades as the catchphrase-providers for an entire genre of literature. The various attempts to demonize Hielscher's life and work in terms of a bizarre "black" esotericism (as in the works of Pauwels and

Bergier, Ravenscroft, Suster, and "Carmin") intersect here with Serrano's attempt to make use of him in the context of an "esoteric" and "Tantric" Hitlerism. For all of these authors, their common ground is one of sheer (but obviously deliberate) speculation, which absolutely and most painstakingly avoids any critical analysis of verifiable sources.

Completely excised, in turn, was of course any examination of Hielscher's actual positions, and especially the fundamental elements of his religious-cosmological system. At best, fragments and conceptual shreds were extracted, willfully misinterpreted, and inserted into contemporary historical contexts to which they were in fact diametrically opposed. This was especially true in the case of the little that was known (such as from Ernst Jünger's diaries) concerning Hielscher's heathen free church, and which was later eagerly interpreted as an indication of Satanic "rites" and "secret doctrines." Hielscher's strict, life-long refusal to allow a broader audience access to the dogma and liturgy of his church was—from his point of view—logical and well founded. It was based on the assumption that it was precisely in light of negative experiences with the Third Reich that the small circle of those faithful to him should be protected, and that in general only a few persons were mature enough in soul and character to grasp the UFK's axiomatically constructed belief system, intuitively as well as mentally.

Unintentionally, however, this clandestine position encouraged the unhindered growth of legends and in the end turned out to be counter-productive. Only after an open examination, based upon existing sources, of the motivations, spiritual foundations, and actual practices of Hielscher's circle—which still existed until the 1980s—will these legendary formulations be cleared away and allow for the reclamation of a fertile and thoroughly interesting aspect of the intellectual history of the twentieth century.

(Translated by Michael Moynihan and Gerhard)

This essay first appeared under the title "Die Hielscher-Legende: Eine panentheistische 'Kirchen'-Gründung des 20. Jahrhunderts und ihre Fehldeutungen" in the German journal Gnostika *(Lothar-von-Kübel-Str. 1, D-76547 Sinzheim, Germany), issue 19 (October 2001), pp. 63–76. This new version, translated into English and with enlarged bibliographic references, is published in* TYR *by kind permission of the author.*

Notes:

1. Cf. Friedrich Hielscher, *Fünfzig Jahre unter Deutschen* [Fifty Years among Germans] (Hamburg: Rowohlt, 1954)
2. Here the following articles should be mentioned in particular: Marcus Beckmann, "Dem anderen Gesetz gehorchen: Zum Tode Friedrich Hielschers," in *Fragmente* 6 (1990), pp. 4–13; Werner Barthold, "Die geistige Leistung Friedrich Hielschers für das Kösener Corpsstudentum," in *Einst und Jetzt: Jahrbuch des Vereins für corpsstudentische Geschichtsforschung*, vol. 36 (1991), pp. 279–82; Karlheinz Weißmann, "Friedrich Hielscher: Eine Art Nachruf," in *Criticón* 123 (January/February 1991), pp. 25–28; Peter Bahn, "Glaube—Reich—Widerstand: Zum 10. Todestag Friedrich Hielschers," in *Wir selbst: Zeitschrift für nationale Identität*, nos. 1–2 (2000), pp. 21–33; Peter Bahn, "Ernst Jünger und Friedrich Hielscher: Eine Freundschaft auf Distanz," in *Les Carnets Ernst Jünger*, no. 6 (2001), pp. 127–45.
3. This is the Friedrich Hielscher Deposit in the Schwarzwald-Baar District Archive (Villingen-Schwenningen); an electronic index of the archive is currently in preparation. Henceforth abbreviated SBDA.
4. This is found among the Ernst Jünger documents at the German Literature Archive in Marbach; there are also additional Hielscher letters in other collections of unpublished papers, such as those relating to Friedrich Georg Jünger.
5. Cf. Hielscher, *Fünfzig Jahre*, pp. 21–29.
6. Cf. Hielscher, *Fünfzig Jahre*, p. 31.
7. Cf. Hielscher, *Fünfzig Jahre*, pp. 33–35.
8. Cf. Hielscher, *Fünfzig Jahre*, pp. 45–47.
9. Cf. Hielscher, *Fünfzig Jahre*, pp. 35–38, and Barthold, 1991. Regarding Hielscher's dueling society activities cf. also Hermann Rink, "Friedrich Hielscher" in Thomas Raveaux and Marcus Beckmann, eds., *Veritati: Festschrift für Friedrich Hielscher zum 85. Geburtstag* (Würzburg: Self publ., 1987), pp. 19–22.
10. Cf. Hielscher, *Fünfzig Jahre*, pp. 21–22.
11. Cf. Hielscher, *Fünfzig Jahre*, pp. 41–44.
12. Concerning this current in general, and Hielscher's—partial and marginal—role in it, cf. among other works: Karl O. Paetel, *Versuchung oder Chance? Zur Geschichte des deutschen Nationalbolschewismus* (Göttingen: Musterschmidt, 1965; new edition, Koblenz: Bublies, 2000); Otto-Ernst Schüddekopf,

Nationalbolschewismus in Deutschland 1918–1933 (Frankfurt/Berlin/Vienna: Ullstein, 1972); Louis Dupeux, *Nationalbolschewismus in Deutschland 1919–1933: Kommunistische Strategie und konservative Dynamik* (Munich: Büchergilde Gutenberg, 1985); Susanne Meinl, *Nationalsozialisten gegen Hitler: Die nationalrevolutionäre Opposition um Friedrich Wilhelm Heinz* (Berlin: Siedler, 2000). The biographical-bibliographical standard text in this subject is Armin Mohler, *Die Konservative Revolution 1918–1932: Ein Handbuch*, third edition, enlarged with a supplemental volume also containing corrections (Darmstadt: Wissenschaftliche Buchgesellschaft, 1989). Hielscher, whom Mohler correctly describes as a characteristic "system builder" among the national revolutionaries, is detailed on p. 450.

13. Cf. Hielscher, *Fünfzig Jahre*, pp. 82–83.

14. Cf. Hielscher, *Fünfzig Jahre*, p. 84.

15. Cf. Hielscher, *Fünfzig Jahre*, p. 105. His dissertation, which contained many references to the thought of Nietzsche and Spengler, appeared in book form in 1930, published by Frundsberg-Verlag, Berlin.

16. Cf. Hielscher, *Fünfzig Jahre*, p. 111.

17. Cf. Friedrich Hielscher, "Innerlichkeit und Staatskunst," in *Neue Standarte—Arminius: Kampfschrift für deutsche Nationalisten*, issue of 26 December 1926, pp. 6–8. Cited here and below from the reprint on pp. 335–38 of *Jahrbuch zur Konservativen Revolution* 1994 (Cologne: Anneliese Thomas, 1994), p. 335.

18. Cf. Hielscher, 1926 (1994), p. 337.

19. Cf. the letters from Hielscher dated 28 November 1929 and 12 January 1930, in the Ernst Jünger documents at the German Literary Archive.

20. Cf. Friedrich Hielscher, *Das Reich* (Berlin: Das Reich, 1931).

21. On the formation of the Hielscher circle and its efforts during the NS dictatorship, cf. Rolf Kluth, "Die Widerstandsgruppe Hielscher" in *Puls: Dokumentationsschrift zur Jugendbewegung*, no. 7 (December 1980), pp. 22–27.

22. Cf. Hielscher, *Fünfzig Jahre*, p. 237.

23. Cf. Friedrich Hielscher, "Die Entwicklung unserer Kirche" (The Development of Our Church), typescript in the SBDA, Hielscher documents, no. 73, p. 1–2.

24. Cf. Friedrich Hielscher, "Bericht über die unterirdische

Arbeit gegen den Nationalismus" (Report on the Underground Work Against Nationalism), typescript in the SBDA, Hielscher documents, no. 140 (with directory of persons belonging to the circle).

25. Cf. Friedrich Hielscher, *Die Selbstherrlichkeit: Versuch einer Darstellung des deutschen Rechtsgrundbegriffes* (Berlin: Frundsberg, 1930), pp. 63–64.

26. Cf. Letter from Hielscher dated 28 November 1929, in the Ernst Jünger documents at the German Literary Archive.

27. Cf. Hielscher, *Die Selbstherrlichkeit*, 1930, p. 83.

28. Cf. Hielscher, *Die Selbstherrlichkeit*, p. 81.

29. Cf. Johannes Scotus Eriugena, *Über die Einteilung der Natur*, trans. by Ludwig Noack (Hamburg: Felix Meiner, 1994), p. 325.

30. Cf. Eriugena, *Über die Einteilung der Natur*, p. 324.

31. Cf. "Die 1. Klasse des heidnischen Glaubensunterrichts während der Schule" (The First Class of the Heathen Religious Instruction in the School) typescript in the SBDA, Hielscher documents, no. 15 (probably authored by Hielscher).

32. Cf. the letter from Hielscher to Alfred Schaeffer dated 23 January 1931, in the Walter Ehlers collection at the German Literature Archive.

33. Cf. the SBDA, Hielscher documents, no. 81, and the public document of the Triberg notary dated 6 July 1966 concerning a sworn statement of Hielscher's on the founding of the "Unabhängige Freikirche" in the year 1933 (copy in private possession of the author).

34. Cf. Friedrich Hielscher, "Die Entwicklung unserer Kirche," p. 2.

35. Cf. Ernst Jünger, *Strahlungen II: Das zweite Pariser Tagebuch*, *"Kirchhorster Blätter: Die Hütte im Weinberg,"* paperback edition (Munich: Deutscher Taschenbuchverlag, 1988), pp. 172–73. (entry of 16 October 1943). Ernst Jünger himself was incidentally never a member of Hielscher's church, but was one of the very few outsiders informed of its existence and development by his old friend Hielscher. The various letters and enclosures from Hielscher to Jünger even into the 1980s should be noted in this regard (cf. the Ernst Jünger–Friedrich Hielscher correspondence in the Ernst Jünger documents at the German Literature Archive).

36. Cf. Hielscher, "Die Entwicklung," p. 2.

37. Cf. Hielscher, *Fünfzig Jahre*, p. 117.

38. Cf. Friedrich Hielscher, "Der Aufbau der Kirche" (The Building of the Church) typescript no. 16 in the Hielscher documents at the SBDA, p. 18.

39. Cf. Hielscher, "Der Aufbau," p. 18.

40. Cf. Michael H. Kater, *Das "Ahnenerbe" der SS 1935–1945* (Stuttgart: Deutsche Verlagsanstalt, 1974), p. 38.

41. Cf. Kater, 1974, p. 27. On the original connotations of the institution's name, see Joscelyn Godwin's article on Herman Wirth in this issue of *TYR*.

42. Cf. Kater, *Das "Ahnenerbe,"* p. 215.

43. For a critical assessment of Sievers's role cf. Kater, *Das "Ahnenerbe,"* pp. 317–19, and the earlier more positive depiction of Sievers in Alfred Kantorowicz, *Deutsches Tagebuch*, Pt. 1 (Munich: Kindler, 1959), pp. 496–507.

44. Cf. Kater, *Das "Ahnenerbe,"* p. 323.

45. Cf. Hielscher, *Fünfzig Jahre*, pp. 453–54

46. Cf. Hielscher, *Fünfzig Jahre*, pp. 444–47.

47. Cf. Friedrich Hielscher, "Die Hielscher-Gruppe 1933–1945: Bericht über die unterirdische Arbeit gegen den Nationalsozialismus" (The Hielscher Group 1933–1945: Report on the Underground Work against National Socialism) in *Jahrbuch zur Konservativen Revolution* 1994 (Cologne: Anneliese Thomas, 1994), pp. 329–34, as well as the description by Kluth (1980).

48. Cf. Hielscher, *Fünfzig Jahre*, p. 402–26.

49. Cf. Friedrich Hielscher, "Die Entwicklung," p. 3.

50. The typescripts are found in the Hielscher documents at the SBDA.

51. Material on the cause and course of the "church crises" that were linked to the split can be found in copious quantity under the keywords "1. Kirchenkrise" (first church crisis) and "2. Kirchenkrise" (second church crisis) in the Hielscher documents at the SBDA. The "Freie Kirche," which was dissolved in the 1990s, emerged from out of the "first church crisis" around Dr. Rolf Kluth, temporary director of the State and University Libraries in Bremen and a member of the Hielscher circle since the 1930s; in comparison, the "second church crisis" did not lead to the formation of a new group, but rather to the actual implosion of the UFK.

52. Cf. Louis Pauwels and Jacques Bergier, *Aufbruch ins dritte*

Jahrtausend: Von der Zukunft der phantastischen Vernunft, paperback edition (Munich: Heyne, 1982), pp. 379–90. This material appears on pp. 200–10 of the American edition, published under the title *The Morning of the Magicians* (New York: Stein & Day, 1963).

53. Cf. Pauwels and Bergier, *Aufbruch*, p. 389. This appears on p. 206 of the American edition.

54. Here the standard work by Kater (1974) should be cited in particular. This well-researched history of the Ahnenerbe organization, however, is limited by the broad omission of an analysis of specific research projects worked on by the Ahnenerbe, whether in regard to the realm of intellectual history, or that of specific technological developments.

55. Cf. Pauwels and Bergier, *Aufbruch*, p. 389. This appears on p. 206 of the American edition.

56. Ibid.

57. Ibid.

58. Cf. Hielscher, *Fünfzig Jahre*, pp. 115–17.

59. Cf. Hielscher, *Fünfzig Jahre*, p. 115.

60. Letter in the Friedrich Georg Jünger documents at the German Literary Archive.

61. Cf. Pauwels and Bergier, *Aufbruch*, p. 390. This appears on p. 207 of the American edition.

62. Cf. Trevor Ravenscroft, *Die heilige Lanze: Der Speer von Golgotha*, 2nd edition (Munich: Universitas, 1996), p. 265. This appears on p. 259 of the American edition of *The Spear of Destiny* (New York: G. P. Putnam's Sons, 1973).

63. Ibid.

64. Ibid.

65. *The Spear of Destiny* originally appeared in Great Britain in 1972 and was not translated into German until 1988!

66. Cf. Gerald Suster, *Hitler: Black Magician*, 2nd edition (London: Skoob, 1996), p. 182.

67. Cf. Suster, *Hitler*, p. 184.

68. Cf. Suster, *Hitler*, pp. 211–12.

69. Cf. E. R. Carmin, *Das schwarze Reich: Geheimgesellschaften und Politik im 20. Jahrhundert*, paperback edition (Munich: Heyne, 1997), pp. 143, 701.

70. Cf. Carmin, *Das schwarze Reich*, p. 700.

71. Cf. Miguel Serrano, *Das Goldene Band: Esoterischer*

Hitlerismus, German edition (Wetter: Teut-Verlag, 1987), p. 245.

72. Cf. Serrano, *Das Goldene Band*, pp. 373–98.

We Call Your Wolves

We call your wolves
And call your spear
We call all twelve
Down from heaven to us here.
Above all we call You.
Now comes the wild hunt,
Now let the horn resound,
For the dead do not lament.
The enemy has fallen
Before the morning breaks.

The prey has no name,
The enemy no face,
The carcass no seed,
Righteous is the court of justice.
The harvest is past,
The chaff is daily sold,
The ravens now demand
The portion they are due.
The hunt has begun:
Now, Lord, your salvation
sustains us!

—Friedrich Hielscher

(Translation by Gerhard and Michael Moynihan)

Herman Wirth on Folksong

Joscelyn Godwin

There are two groups of people, neither of them large, who know who Herman Wirth was. One group has heard that in 1935 he was one of the founders of the Deutsches Ahnenerbe, and that is enough for them. The other group knows what Wirth meant by *Ahnenerbe* ("ancestral heritage"), and something of the history of that institution.[1] The Ahnenerbe, as Wirth conceived it, grew out of his researches of the 1920s, published in the large volume *Der Aufgang der Menschheit* (The Rise of Mankind) and developed in the even larger *Die heilige Urschrift der Menschheit* (The Sacred Primordial Script of Mankind).[2] These are monuments of what Wirth called *Geistesurgeschichte*,[3] mainly based on rock-carvings and inscribed artifacts gathered from the northernmost regions of the globe. Wirth deduced from his study of this corpus not only a coherent symbology and indeed mankind's first writing, but also the witness to an ancient matriarchal, monotheistic[4] culture that flourished in prehistoric times throughout the Arctic circle. He believed that when geological and climatic changes forced this ancient race to leave its Arctic homeland, it spread southwards in all directions, bringing its spiritual and cosmological legacy and mingling it with that of the other races it encountered. The peoples of northern Europe were its most direct descendants.

Wirth pursued his research with an unshakable conviction of his own rightness, fueled with nostalgia for his Arctic Ur-race: for their spiritual awareness without religious dogmatism, their honoring of the feminine principle, their peaceful way of life. These ancestors and their high paganism were the models he hoped to promote through his institute. By 1934 he was making plans for a "Germanic cultural landscape"—a sort of theme park or open-air museum—in the Kieferwald outside Berlin, which he was already calling "Deutsches Ahnenerbe."[5] In 1935, the adoption of this title for a state-sponsored institution, with Wirth himself as its president, must have answered his wildest hopes. But Wirth's notions did not coincide with those of Heinrich Himmler and his sycophants. Wirth was steadily marginalized until his resignation in December 1938,[6] and spent the rest of the National Socialist era as an internal exile, forbidden to lecture or publish. The subsequent deeds of Ahnenerbe functionaries are therefore not to be laid to his charge.

This phase of Wirth's work finds its appropriate context in the centuries-long "Atlantis Debate," that is, the debate over whether high civilization existed in prehistoric times; and, if the evidence indicates that it did, then where did it flourish, and how did it come to an end? Plato, of course, situated it in the mid-Atlantic Ocean, and so did Ignatius Donnelly, the reviver of the debate in recent times.[7] Today's theories, given a powerful charge by the re-dating of the Sphinx of Giza, on geological grounds, to pre-dynastic times,[8] propose locations for Atlantis ranging from the Bahamas to Antarctica, and suggest a comet, a shift in the earth's crust, or an emanation from the center of the galaxy as the cause of its demise. Wirth belongs with that sub-group of Atlantologists who find evidence of high culture in the North, in Arctic or even polar regions: a strain of the debate that I have treated elsewhere.[9]

If this quest for the prehistoric mind was the reason for Wirth's ill-fated flirtation with the Schutzstaffel, how did he get started on it? It began as early as 1911, immediately after Wirth obtained his doctorate, with a project of photographing the strange carvings that decorated the old farmhouses of Friesland, in the northern Netherlands.[10] He resumed the project after World War I, during a period of high-school teaching in the Friesian town of Sneek, and became convinced that these carvings of wheels, ladders, swans, etc., had a symbolic significance, which he felt sure went back to pre-Christian times, and perhaps to a deeper antiquity still, if the *Oera Linda Book* (see below) was to be believed. As he searched the scholarly literature for parallels and for possible explanations of their meaning, he realized that he was dealing with something much larger than a regional folk-art. Fate had handed him the end of an Ariadne's thread that led back to a vastly ancient and widespread tradition, even to the discovery of the earliest writing of mankind.

Why did Wirth notice these sixteenth- and seventeenth-century carvings and think them significant, when no one else had paid any attention to them? The short answer is that he was in quest of his own ancestral heritage, as a Dutchman, and was thus alert to any relics of it. In particular, he had come to see folk art as superior, in a way, to so-called "high art." This brings us to the starting-point of Wirth's intellectual journey, and to the main subject of this article, which is his doctoral dissertation and first

HERMAN WIRTH, APRIL 1958, WITH "PALMPAASKEN," A SCANDINAVIAN FOLK OBJECT WITH SYMBOLS OF THE RETURN OF LIFE: SWANS, WHEEL, ODAL-RUNE, TREE OF LIFE.

book, *Der Untergang des Niederländischen Volksliedes* (The Decline of the Dutch Folksong).[11] And having cursorily worked back to that point, I must now sketch his early life.

Wirth was born in Utrecht on 6 May 1885 to Ludwig Wirth, a German from the Palatinate region, and a Dutch mother, Sophia Roeper Bosch.[12] Ludwig Wirth, a Doctor of Theology, was a teacher at the Gymnasium (select high school) and a *Privatdozent in Germanistik* (private tutor in German Studies) attached to Utrecht University. Herman's mother died in 1891, his father remarried, and the boy was raised by a strict Calvinist grandmother and aunt.[13] Here is Wirth's account of his education:

> I attended and graduated (1904) from the State Gymnasium in Kampen and immediately applied myself to Germanistik and historical studies at the University of Utrecht, taking the candidates' examination (for high-school teaching) in both faculties in 1908. Meanwhile in 1906 and 1907 I had pursued musicological studies in Leipzig, under Professor Hugo Riemann among others. After my candidates' examination I continued my studies while working as a high-school teacher, until on the recommendation of the Dean of the Philosophical Faculty, my respected teacher Professor J. W. Müller, I was appointed Lecturer in Dutch Language and Literature by the Philosophical Faculty of the Friedrich-Wilhelm University in Berlin, and received confirmation from the

Ministry of Culture in August 1909.[14]

As a doctoral dissertation, *Der Untergang des Niederländischen Volksliedes* is an anomaly. Thoroughly interdisciplinary, it has elements of literary history and criticism, comparative literature, sociology, history, and musicology. Moreover, the whole aim and tone of the work is opinionated and polemical in a way that no modern doctoral candidate could get away with.[15] The young scholar uses his study of folksong to present a revisionist view of his national history, driven by two purposes: to debunk the myth of the Dutch seventeenth century as a Golden Age, and to reveal the dreadful effects of the Calvinist religion.

Viewed more narrowly as musicology, Wirth's work was revisionist (for its time) in the way that he viewed the introduction of polyphony—the thing that most distinguishes the Western musical tradition from that of every other civilization. Its origins are inaccessible, but the question was whether polyphony came from folk music, or whether it was an invention of church musicians. Folk music, as an oral tradition, was almost never written down, whereas medieval churchmen were in command of music notation, hence the first to record any development, no matter where it came from. Consequently music historians have always overemphasized the written tradition of "art music" and been inclined to credit it with every innovation. Wirth is of the opposite opinion. He says that church music, like its ancestor, Greek music, was confined to the monophonic (one-line) singing of plainchant, at a time when folk music was already using polyphony; we know this from early chroniclers who write of people singing in harmony, especially in the Celtic regions (pp. 56–57[16]). Wirth states outright that "Polyphony is to be regarded as a property of the Germanic people" (p. 56), and supposes that it came to England with the Danish and Norwegian invaders, and was there refined. Based on later English sources, he guesses that early folk polyphony favored the intervals of thirds and sixths, which were arrived at naturally, in contrast to the fourths and fifths of theoretically-based church polyphony; that this preference led to *fauxbourdon* (singing in parallel first-inversion chords); and that it was from the latter that true polyphony emerged (pp. 58–59). Nineteenth-century musicology had indeed established that the English liking for the sounds of *fauxbourdon* spread after 1400 to Burgundy and the Netherlands and led, by the end of the fifteenth century, to a harmony based on triads and already containing the principles of tonality (the major and minor keys). Wirth's contribution was to bring out the role of folksong in this evolution. He summarizes it thus: "The role played by English music in Netherlandish culture from the end of the fourteenth century is that of a savior. It freed folk art from the fetters of the unnatural high art of the Church, and made possible a fruitful penetration of churchly abstraction." (p. 71)

A lifelong pagan, in the original sense,[17] Wirth always takes the side of the folk against the Church, with what he regards as its "abstract" doctrinal concerns, and against the artificial life of towns and cities which became ever more dominant, especially in the Netherlands, as the Middle Ages drew to a close. He sees folksong, and folk art in general, as having the virtues of honesty, naturalism, and a straightforward acceptance of the facts of human life. To explain the contrast, he uses a subtle distinction based on two Dutch words for "worldview": *Wereldanschouwing* and *Wereldbeschouwing*. The former, perhaps translatable as "looking at the world," is "that unconscious, unreflective activity which we know from the animal, the child, and the so-called 'natural man,' and which folksong expresses by keeping within the world of sensory appearances, by lacking and eliminating abstraction, speculation, and by its '*sensorification*' of abstract, speculative elements." (p. 4) In contrast to this is the normal Dutch term for "worldview," *Wereldbeschouwing* (perhaps "looking round the world"), which Wirth says "rests on a reflected, abstract activity, which does not allow the world of appearances in its relative reality to act directly upon itself, but beholds it in the light of a speculative idea, and thus receives it at second-hand through speculation." (p. 5) This distinction is fundamental to Wirth's philosophy, and to his reconstruction of the psychological history of mankind.

As Wirth tells it, the effect of folk music on the art music of the Netherlands (and everywhere else) was permanent and positive. In consequence, "the sixteenth century stands completely under the sign of folk art"; it is marked by the decisive adoption of major and minor and the rejection of the church modes that were "forced on us Germans," and by the instrumental dances that derived from folk minstrelsy (p. 96). Not by chance did this coincide with the collapse of faith (i.e., the Reformation) and the supplanting of the Christian ascetic ideal by that of Antiquity (i.e., the Renaissance). Concerning the latter, Wirth was all for pagan naturalism as against Christian abstraction, or as he says, "Pompeii versus Ravenna." (p. 94) The trouble was that in the

Netherlands and Germany, the Renaissance was preceded by the Reformation. "This explains the fact that the inner problem of the Renaissance, which is the contact with a unified, sensual world whose basis is the law of nature, and the consequent liberation of the individual and of the body, the reclaiming of the freedom of life, the relinking with the world of appearances, never came out in poetry, so that we find only an outward form, a form of social convention whose basis is a social class-distinction." (p. 93)

This raises the social problem that looms so large in Wirth's story. He tells of how the flood of capital gained through trade created a gulf between rural and city dwellers. The latter, anxious to slough off any taint of peasant ancestry, rejected folk art, music, and poetry, adopting instead an artificial high culture imitating French and Italian humanism. From what Wirth says, and illustrates with many examples (pp. 144ff.), by 1600 everyone in the prosperous towns of the Netherlands belonged to a "Rhetoric Academy" (a sort of literary club) and was writing bad poetry in a classical vein, while congratulating themselves on how sophisticated they were. I cannot fully appreciate the Dutch poetry that he quotes in order to reveal its vapidity, its artificiality, and its prurient humor, but it is clear enough that he is waging war on one of his nation's sacred cows: the myth of the seventeenth century as its Golden Age. "I feel it my moral duty," he says, "to reveal the inside of this society, so that the reader will no longer admire this legendary cultural epoch." (p. 149)

Like all Traditionalists—and Wirth, after his own fashion, was a Traditionalist—Wirth is nostalgic for the nobility. He contrasts it with the Amsterdam patriciate, "that particularistic, self-satisfied caste with its un-national interests and its haughty detachment from the entirety of the folk. It is a historical fact that the true nobility, which through its agrarian base always remains in contact with the flat land, is much more folkish and much more strongly rooted in the people than the patrician, the *bourgeois-gentilhomme*." (p. 140)

But the people and their traditional way of life had a still worse enemy in Calvinism, that branch of the Protestant Reformation which in Wirth's opinion far outdid the Catholic Church in ruining the life, the psychology, and the creativity of his countrymen. With its hostility to all sensuous enjoyment, Calvinism was not welcomed by the comfortable and worldly patricians of the cities, but it found a fertile field of evangelism in the small towns and villages, and among the farmers and peasantry. Here it set out, with a series of synodal decrees (cited on pp. 176–179), to eradicate every folk tradition and to clothe every sensual pleasure with guilt. In their dour worship, the Calvinists did away with symbolism, imagery, and all music except the droning of unaccompanied psalms (p. 181). Wirth's loathing for them is patent. Perhaps it had something to do with his Calvinist grandmother and aunt.

For all his emotional involvement in the topic, Wirth does not simply divide phenomena into good and bad, but has a scale of relative values that enables him to censure something in one context, then commend it in another. His approach to the Renaissance is an example. The aping of classical Antiquity by the Dutch poetasters seems to him artificial and absurd, yet the classical principles in themselves are praiseworthy: "In Greece, all the great natural forces are sacred, and man is not split into beast and spirit." (p. 147) Although far from being a Freudian, Wirth recognizes that repressing natural sexual impulses leads to their irruption in obsessive and perverse forms, and he sees symptoms of the latter in the poetry of the Golden Age. "The Christian-ascetic ideal has done a great deal of harm in this regard, and the depravity of sexual life, the forced unnaturalism, is to be attributed to it; in this respect, the dogma of the 'immaculate conception' may well qualify as a source of 'immorality.'"(p. 148)

His view of Catholicism, which here seems hostile, is similarly nuanced. Whereas in Dutch history, the Catholic Church is normally cast as the villain in view of the cruel oppression of the Netherlanders by Spain, Wirth barely mentions this. The legacy of Catholic Christianity may be bad, but in comparison with the more lasting influence of Calvinism it looks to him positively benevolent. He favorably compares Catholic asceticism, which is largely restricted to those choosing a monastic life, to the Calvinist version, in which everyone is expected to be an inner ascetic (p. 112). In this context Wirth quotes his contemporary, the sociologist Max Weber, on the "replacement of an easy outward yoke by the perpetual regimentation of all aspects of life." (p. 116) Weber's concept of the "Protestant ethic" was evidently one of the guiding thoughts behind Wirth's version of Dutch history.[18]

Although Wirth is writing about Dutch folksong, his glance continually strays across the frontiers. He looks to Catholic Flanders (now Belgium) in the South, where social conditions were much less repressive of the folk and their arts; and he looks east to Germany, the land of his father and eventually his chosen *Vaterland*. Up to the eighteenth century, the two lands were culturally alienated, for all that "Dutch" and *Deutsch* were essentially the same people, speaking dialects of the same tongue. The prosperous Netherlanders regarded their German neighbors merely as useful *Gastarbeiter* for low-paying jobs (p. 254). According to Wirth, it was music that acted as the first bridgehead between the two peoples (p. 271). One reason for this was the dawning realization of how fortunate the Germans had been in their Reformation: while the Netherlands had Calvin, Germany had Luther—and J. S. Bach. Although no friend of dogmatic theology, Wirth appreciates Luther's humility, as opposed to the Calvinists' complacency in being "saved" (p. 111), and most of all, he admires the Lutheran musical tradition (p. 207). Whereas in the Netherlands, all authentic art was squeezed out of existence by the dual (and mutually hostile) forces of Calvinism and patrician culture, in Germany it enjoyed a perpetual renewal.

Wirth sees folk music and art music as two streams existing simultaneously, one constant, the other changing. Folk music, from whatever period, always strikes one with a sense of innate familiarity (p. 238). Art music, on the contrary, is ever-changing, bound as it is to broader cultural developments; hence the parade of historical styles. But it keeps going back for renewal to the perennial springs of folk art (p. 2). I have already mentioned some of Wirth's examples of this, in the fertilization of Continental art music by the English school after 1400, and in the instrumental dances and songs of the sixteenth century. As it continued in later centuries, after the "abstraction" of the Bachian period came the folksong-influenced music of Bach's sons, the Mannheim School, Haydn, and Mozart. Later it was Wagnerism that called forth the reaction of Brahms, who went back to folksong to discover "the organic logic of inner form." (p. 18) Wirth accuses Wagner and the modernists (remember that he is writing in 1910) of "metaphysical backwardness" and of leaving no room for the listener's fantasy as they seem to say: "I will *make* you feel this, because it is the *only* truth!" He adds the revealing comment: "They are like philosophers who pretend to explain everything with their system; they do not know that the world is in fact only our representation, and that something completely different from what we think lies behind things." (p. 19) The return to folksong, on the other hand, is the consequence of cultural development, wherein "we return consciously to the sense world and the deepening of the sensory, instead of getting lost in the formless supersensible." (p. 19)

At the end of the book, Wirth concludes that no renewal of folksong and all that it represents is possible without an inner rebirth of all participants, to overcome the forces that have divided the folk and destroyed not only its art but its national life. "A folk without its own life is like a man without an ego, without individuality or independence." (p. 302) But more than ever before, it must be firmly based on the sense world. There is no room today for elves or goblins: others factors must be valued and poeticized. Thus, he concludes, we face the difficult problem of creating a new folk art. He ends with the clarion cry: "The future now belongs to the nation!" (p. 303)

Wirth's dissertation received a surprising number of reviews, most of them warmly favorable.[19] An Italian reviewer wrote that "Such a work is among the few that raise aesthetic study, so despised these days, to a true science of the arts."[20] Most reviewers wondered at the scope of the work, belying its modest title. "...the whole book reads almost as a cultural history of Holland,"[21] said one, while others went more deeply into its implications:

> This book strikes a different tone from that which we are used to hearing from modern hyper-aesthetes and the obsessively specialized average scholar. It not only deserves to be read for scholarly purposes by literary historians and critics within their four walls, but to find an echo and an effect in the widest public sphere. The practical consequences that could arise from such a book can hardly be anything but a blessing for the collectivity.[22]

This comes from a long, serious review by the German folksong specialist Arthur Kopp (1860–1918). He criticizes Wirth's anti-Wagnerism, his one-sided anti-Calvinism, and the many misprints in Latin and French quotations, but appreciates and shares the global implications of Wirth's work. Kopp writes:

> Using the example of the Netherlands, [Wirth] shows that folk art is the lasting foundation of every healthy cultural development of a people; of their scientific and artistic, moral and social blossoming; of the true prospering and

unfolding of all creative forces; of real improvement and authentic culture. Above all, the rural population, with its native and rooted quality, has everywhere proved to be the carrier of good, solid folk art and folk culture. When it is completely oppressed or subjugated by urban culture—as it was by the commercial world of Amsterdam in Holland, and, thanks to the dominance of Holland, in the whole United Provinces—then instead of true art and education, what prevails and alone is possible is the parasitic, meretricious, uncontrollably fermenting "culture" of the big city population, in which the stuck-up parvenus and the uncultivated rabble are the most influential, if not the only arbiters.[23]

Kopp adds that the same goes for Berlin, and, thanks to the dominance of Prussia, for the whole of Germany, in whose big cities, thanks to an "international plutocracy," indigenous culture is completely shut out.

During the ten years following the publication of *Untergang*, Wirth threw himself into musical activities of many kinds. He planned a second volume of the work, which would consist of musical examples.[24] Beside his responsibilities at the University of Berlin, for which he compiled Dutch grammars and vocabularies,[25] he was constantly giving lectures, slide presentations, and lecture recitals in Germany and the Netherlands. Some of these were about Dutch folksong, while others were aimed at making the music of the Netherlands better known inside the country and outside it. For a multimedia presentation on "Flanders and its People," he arranged the musical examples for large orchestra.[26] He made editions of Renaissance dances that included the choreography, not just the music.[27] The Dutch musicological society published his edition of dances from the first decade of the seventeenth century, in which Wirth recognized a blend of the madrigal style with the tunes of itinerant folk musicians.[28] During World War I he published *Old Netherlands Army Marches* and a volume of *New War Songs*.[29] After the war, he became a leader in the *Trekvogel* movement—the Dutch version of the German *Wandervögel*. The movement, which aimed to get city children out to hike and explore the country, would have appealed to Wirth for its outdoor orientation, its clean-living morality, and for the importance of singing (*Vögel*=birds!) among its activities.[30]

HERMAN AND MARGARETHE WIRTH, CA. 1920, DRESSED
FOR AN EARLY MUSIC CONCERT WITH A THEORBO LUTE.

Towards 1919 Wirth prepared a course of articles or lectures, probably with a view to a professorship of music history that never materialized.[31] They include "Ancient Germanic Musical Instruments, Their Migrations and Their Fate, Comprehensively Illustrated"; "The Musical Instruments of the Middle Ages" (a slide-lecture); "Studies of Instruments in Flemish Paintings;" and four articles on the origin of the trombone. After the war, Wirth and his wife Margarethe Wirth-Schmitt formed a small early music ensemble which went on tour, presenting songs and dances in period costume. She played the theorbo (a seventeenth-century lute with extra bass strings) and he the contrabass lute.[32]

From all this activity it is plain that Wirth is an unrecognized pioneer of two important musical movements of the twentieth century. First, he belongs to the initial phase of the early music revival, in all of its three aspects: unearthing and performing the music of the pre-Bach period; discovering and if necessary building the appropriate instruments for this music; and researching performance practices through literary and iconographic sources. Thinking of this movement, I am struck by the parallels between Wirth and one of its most prominent figures, Arnold Dolmetsch (1858–1940). A voluntary immigrant to England, Dolmetsch, like Wirth, was a vegetarian with a reputation for eccentricity and a belief in the moral value of early music. There are photographs of Dolmetsch, too, got up in knee-breeches for concerts in which he was assisted by his family. After World War I he founded a workshop for building harpsichords, clavichords, viols, and recorders, and in 1925 he started the Haslemere Festival, the first festival dedicated to authentic performance.

In another contemporary parallel from the English-speaking world, Wirth's concern to rescue his nation's folksong resembles that of Ralph Vaughan Williams (1872–1959), who urged his countrymen to return for their inspiration to folksong, and to the music of the time before foreign domination. Like Bartók in Hungary, Vaughan Williams collected folksongs from the men and women who were still singing them, and used these melodies in his own works, as did Gustav Holst, Peter Warlock, Percy Grainger, and many other English composers. Most influentially, Vaughan Williams included folksong melodies when he compiled *The English Hymnal* (1906), which became the musical equivalent of the King James Bible: the fount of melody known to every English schoolchild and churchgoer. This attunement of the national ear is probably why folksong continued to be favored by English composers, through Benjamin Britten right up to the end of the century, with Harrison Birtwhistle and Peter Maxwell Davies. I suppose that one could count this as another example of Wirth's principle of the perennial renewal of art music through contact with folk music. In any case, Wirth's idea of musical and national renewal through the return to early music and folksong seems to have been realized in the British Isles more successfully than anywhere else. Having spent my schooldays in the England of the 1950s, I can confirm the effects of folksong, maypole and Morris dancing, *The English Hymnal* and the music of the Anglican Church, on the national consciousness of my generation.

It was a different story in the German-speaking lands, which hardly needed to be urged to cultivate their own native talents in music. The history of Wagnerism, post-Wagnerism (Strauss,

Mahler, Bruckner), and the Second Viennese School (Schoenberg, Berg, Webern) does not concern us here, unless one follows Wirth's principle in identifying the folksong revival of the inter-war years as a wholesome reaction to it. Rather than influencing composers, as it did in Britain, this revival addressed the young. Three examples of it are the prominent use of folksong in the *Wandervögel* movement, in Rudolf Steiner's Waldorf Schools, and in Carl Orff's system of musical education. After being suppressed during the National Socialist era (which, however, continued to cultivate folksong in its own youth movements), all three movements flourish in Germany to this day, with the result that children involved in them grow up with a rich fund of folksong: something that cannot be said of many other nations.

Returning to the young Wirth and his aspirations, these clearly belonged within the folkish nationalist movements of the period that ended effectually with World War I. Unlike the brand of nationalism that led to that war, this was a non-aggressive return to folk roots and local traditions, rejoicing in the "otherness" of every people but preferring to cultivate one's own ethnic heritage. It was in part a reaction against industrialization, the materialistic religion of progress, the decline of the crafts, and the marginalization of the countryside. Politically it tended toward a national or regional socialism; and Wirth, like other folkish types, initially saw in the movement that assumed that label a haven for his aspirations.[33]

The most negative reaction to Wirth's dissertation was a long and searching review by the philologist J. F. D. Blöte, who pinpoints the contradictions in Wirth's one-sided story. These, he says, "may have their basis in the fact that the author has specific hypotheses in view, without asking himself whether his material is sufficient to support these hypotheses."[34] Blöte's words, sad to say, might serve as the epitaph to all of Wirth's enterprises. *Untergang*, though of all his works it has the best claim as scholarship, already betrays the tendencies that would come to full flower in *Der Aufgang der Menschheit, Die Heilige Urschrift der Menschheit*, and, catastrophically, in Wirth's edition of the *Oera Linda Book*: an eighteenth-century manuscript that Wirth believed to contain genuine mythological material going back to the sixth century B.C.E. and supporting the theories of *Aufgang*.[35] In his replies to the attacks on the *Oera Linda Book*, he dug himself ever deeper into historical implausibilities, after which no one in the academ-

HERMAN WIRTH, CA. 1978, OUTSIDE A HESSIAN HOUSE
WITH TRADITIONAL SYMBOLIC DECORATION.

ic world would take him seriously.

But I take Wirth seriously, for at least two reasons. First, because he is an example of a distinct human type, whom I have described elsewhere. The following passage was written in a context of esotericists and occultists, but, *mutatis mutandis*, it holds good for Wirth:

> The search for universality runs risks that are just as serious as those of more limited fields, albeit of another order. A person often sets out on this search after some kind of spiritual revelation, or at least some profound psychological experience. Perhaps the illuminate has a glimpse in which the entire cosmos seems to explain itself. No one, he feels, can ever have had such a revelation of divine secrets! He believes himself invested with a sacred mission; he must tell his fellows about these unknown or forgotten truths, for their own good. Alas, the world does not want to know about them. Faced with such ingratitude, the illuminate turns inward and cultivates the precious seed that God or Providence has bestowed on him. He

HERMAN WIRTH'S EXHIBITION "DER LEBENSBAUM IM GERMANISCHEN BRAUCHTUM" (THE TREE OF LIFE IN GERMANIC CUSTOMS), BERLIN, 1935, SHOWING THE SURVIVAL OF ANCIENT SYMBOLS IN FESTIVE BREADS.

builds his revelation into a system that explains the cosmos and uncovers the hidden causes of things. Wrapped up in the fascinating developments of his intuition, he loses contact with other ways of thought, which in any case he rejects. Does he end by becoming a sage, or a paranoiac?[36]

Wirth is a particularly interesting example of this type, because he was not an occultist or an esotericist. Although with his later researches into prehistory he seems to rub shoulders with Theosophists, Anthroposophists, and the like, he was never given to what he spurned as "abstract" speculation. The key to his philosophy resides in the *Wereldanschouwing* which he defines at the very beginning of *Untergang* and associates there with a "conscious return to the sense world and the deepening of the sensory." Its corollary is the observation that has already been quoted: "that the world is in fact only our representation, and that something completely different from what we think lies behind things." Fifty years later, his empiricism had not changed, but he felt freer to emphasize its non-materialistic aspect, granting that the objective world includes "parapsychological phenomena," and that man possesses (or once possessed) the capability of perceiving "things beyond time and space," as in telepathy, and so on.[37] Such thoughts lead to a kind of secular mysticism, more akin to the nature-based, non-theistic philosophies of the Far East (Taoism, Zen Buddhism) than to any Western school.

Second, I happen to like studying this type because he sees things differently from the run-of-the-mill scholar or the academic time-server. He is touched, however lightly, by the fire of genius, which allies him not with scholars—for no scholar is a genius—but with artists, epic writers, composers, architects, and men of action. More often than not—and Wirth is a case in point—music has a part to play in his makeup. Like Kepler with his planetary geometries and harmonies, or Goethe with his metamorphosis of plants, he transcends the barrier that separates science from art; and one no longer worries about whether the creative artist is "right" or "wrong."

Such a person may turn out to have been on the right track after all. In Wirth's case, his theory of "light from the North" receives support from recent carbon-14 dating, recalibrated by tree-rings. This has proved that the megalithic cultures of northern Europe long preceded those of Egypt and the Near East, thereby upsetting a whole basket of assumptions about cultural diffusion.[38] Here Wirth resembles his contemporary Alfred Wegener, whose theory of continental drift was ridiculed for decades (including by the later Ahnenerbe, which preferred Hörbiger's World Ice Doctrine), but is now accepted as a valid geological hypothesis. Wirth's account of prehistoric religion, like most other efforts to penetrate the inner world of early man, is probably off the mark—but what is the "mark" in this regard? His privileging of the feminine and his image of a primordial matriarchy, while incompatible with the *Männerbund* mentality of the Schutzstaffel, resurface in the anthropology of Marija Gimbutas. I do not know whether or not this happened through the direct influence of Wirthian ideas during her doctoral study in Tübingen (1945–46), but Gimbutas's alternative prehistory, while much more acceptable in the scholarly world, has a remarkable similarity to Wirth's. Gimbutas's ideas in turn trickled down into contemporary feminist, "Goddess"-oriented strains of neo-paganism and Wicca.[39]

One purpose of this article has been to make a first documentation of the musical side of Herman Wirth, about which much remains to be discovered.[40] My overview of his dissertation is intended to show how the seeds of his subsequent and more famous work were already present when he was in his twenties. For example, his ascription of the invention of polyphony to preliterate musicians adumbrates his theories of a *heilige Urschrift*, a symbolic script preceding the era of hieroglyphic and alphabetic writing. His interpretation of history not as progress but as *Untergang* would expand from the scale of a few centuries in Holland to many millennia of world history. In his late work *Um den Ursinn des Menschen* (1960), Wirth suggested a Hegelian model for the latter.[41] The "thesis" is the prehistoric era (given as 40,000 B.C.E. or at least 13,000–3,000 B.C.E.), called *Mann- und Frau-Zeitalter* (Man and Woman Age). In *Untergang*, the equivalent thesis would be the beginningless state of pure folksong and folk art. The "antithesis" is the historical era since 3,000 B.C.E., a *Mann-Zeitalter* of unbalanced masculinity that begins with the nomadic incursions and goes on to develop kingship, priesthood, state gods, absolutism, feudalism, clericalism, capitalism, and finally proletarian class warfare, ending with the "break-up" of the Russian Revolution in 1917. On the very much more modest scale of *Untergang*, the antithesis would be the so-called Golden Age of Dutch culture, with its patrician and Calvinist dominance. Thirdly, in the Hegelian model, comes a "synthesis" of the two contraries. This is what Wirth was calling for in 1911 with his idealistic hopes for the "inner rebirth of all participants" for the healing of music, culture, and society, and his conviction that "the future belongs to the nation." Fifty years later, in *Ursinn*, he was postponing the synthesizing era till the third millennium. Then, maybe, would come another *Mann- und Frau-Zeitalter* with a fulfillment of philosophy, a naturalism, and a renewed awareness of the *All-Kraft* (universal energy), leading to a new humanism and its humanity.

Notes:

1. The intricate history of Wirth's relation with the Ahnenerbe is told in Michael Kater, *Das "Ahnenerbe" der SS 1935–1945: Ein Beitrag zur Kulturpolitik des Dritten Reiches* (Stuttgart: Deutsche Verlags-Anstalt, 1974). Some further biographical information is in H. Wirth, *Um den Ursinn des Menschseins* (Vienna: Volkstum-Verlag, 1960); Eberhard Baumann, ed., *Verzeichnis der Schriften, Manuskripte und Vorträge von Herman Felix WIRTH Roeper Bosch von 1908 bis 1993 sowie der Schriften für, gegen, zu und über die Person und das Werk von Herman Wirth von 1908 bis 1995* (Toppenstedt: Uwe Berg Verlag, 1995), p. 9; E. Baumann, *Der Aufgang und Untergang der frühen Hochkulturen Nord- und Mitteleuropas als Ausdruck umfassender oder geringer Selbstverwirklichung (oder Bewusstseinsentwicklung) dargestellt am Beispiel des Erforschers der Symbolgeschichte Professor Dr. Herman Wirth* (Passau, 1991).

2. *Der Aufgang der Menschheit* (Jena: Eugen Diederichs, 1928, reprinted Horn, 1993); *Die heilige Urschrift der Menschheit* (Leipzig: Koehler und Amelang, 1931–36, reprinted Frauenberg, 1979; Horn, 1993). The latter title provocatively echoes that of the German Bible, *Die heilige Schrift*, implying that mankind's original script, or scripture (*Schrift* means both), was another and a more ancient one.

3. *Geistesurgeschichte* translates as "prehistory of the spirit" or "of the mind," or even as "intellectual prehistory." The original title of the Ahnenerbe was "Studiengesellschaft für Geistesurgeschichte, Deutsches Ahnenerbe." See Kater, p. 11.

4. Monotheistic not in the sense of devotion to one personal god, but in acknowledging a single principle behind existence which Wirth calls *das Gott*, using the neuter rather than the masculine article.

5. Joachim Günther, "Germanische Kulturlandschaft—dicht bei Berlin: Gespräch mit Herman Wirth über seinen Plan eines Nationalparkes 'Deutsches Ahnenerbe,'" in *Die Unterhaltung*, 4 January 1934. I am grateful to Michael Moynihan for access to this illustrated newspaper article.

6. In Wirth's letter of resignation from the Ahnenerbe, he declared his conviction that "the repeated emphasis on an official warrior-band ideology is not the beginning of a new age, but the end of the old one." See Wirth, *Ursinn*, p. 50.

7. Plato: *Timaeus* and *Critias*, I. Donnelly, *Atlantis, The Antediluvian World* (New York: Harper Bros., 1882, many reprints).

8. Robert M. Schoch with Robert Aquinas McNally, *Voices of the Rocks; a Scientist Looks at Catastrophes and Ancient Civilizations* (New York: Harmony Books, 1999).

9. J. Godwin, *Arktos: The Polar Myth in Science, Symbolism and Nazi Survival* (Grand Rapids: Phanes Press/London: Thames & Hudson, 1993, reprinted, Kempton: Adventures Unlimited, 1996). See also my "Out of Arctica? Herman Wirth's Theory of Human Origins" in *Rûna* 5 (2000), pp. 2–7.

10. See Wirth, *Ursinn*, p. 44.

11. Wirth's dissertation was accepted by the Philological-Historical Section of the Philosophical Faculty of the University of Basel on 24 May 1910. It was published by the academic press of Martinus Nijhoff, The Hague, 1911, in two versions: (1) *Der Untergang des Niederländischen Volksliedes* (Abschnitt V: Das "Goldene Zeitalter" und sein Ausgang) *Inaugural-Dissertation zur Erlangung der Doctorwürde Eingereicht der philosophische Fakultät der Universität zu Basel von Herman Felix Wirth aus Utrecht (Niederland)*, 132 pages; (2) *Der Untergang des Niederländischen Volksliedes von Dr. H. F. Wirth mit Beilagen*, 357 pages. Version 1 is identical in all except front-matter and pagination to Part Five of Version 2.

12. Hence Wirth's occasional use of his full name in Dutch style, Herman Felix Wirth Roeper Bosch.

13. Baumann, *Verzeichnis*, p. 8; information on Ludwig Wirth from Wirth's "Vita" in *Untergang*, Version 1, p. [1].

14. Translated from Wirth's "Vita" (see previous note). Wirth taught at the university in Berlin until the summer semester of 1919, as documented in the regular faculty and lecture lists (Baumann, Verzeichnis, pp. 83–91). From 1922 he taught Dutch and Geography at the Gymnasium of Sneek (Baumann, Verzeichnis, pp. 6–7). In 1923 he moved to Germany and settled in Marburg, which remained his home until after World War II.

15. Wirth's Doktorvater (thesis advisor) was Prof. John Meier (1864–1953), a prolific scholar of German folksong, folk art, and philology. Meier's presence in Basel probably explains why Wirth chose that university for his dissertation.

16. All page references are to *Untergang*, Version 2.

17. Derived from Latin *paganus*, a countryman, as opposed to

the Christianized urban masses.

18. In a review written the year after *Untergang*, Wirth reproaches another author for neglecting Weber's "ground breaking" work. See H. Wirth, review of L. Knappert, *Geschiednis der Nederlandsche Hervormde Kerk gedurende de 16e en 17e Eeuw*, in *Zeitschrift des Vereins für Volkskunde* 21 (1911), pp. 427–29.

19. Baumann, *Verzeichnis*, pp. 83–88, lists twenty-five reviews.

20. "L. Th.," review of *Untergang* in *Rivista musicale italiana* 18 (1911), p. 453.

21. Ernst Schultze, review of *Untergang* in *Zeitschrift für Sozialwissenschaft*, 1914, p. 807.

22. A. Kopp, review of *Untergang* in *Zeitschrift für deutsche Philologie* 44 (1912), pp. 378–83; here p. 379.

23. Ibid.

24. Baumann, *Verzeichnis*, no. 449 is "Unpublished songs of the seventeenth–nineteenth centuries," vol. 2 of *Untergang*, announced but never published.

25. Baumann, *Verzeichnis*, nos. 24, 28.

26. Baumann, *Verzeichnis*, nos. 34–35, give the score as published by Breitkopf & Härtel, Leipzig, 1917, and the parts as existing in manuscript.

27. See Baumann *Verzeichnis*, nos. 450, 458.

28. Dr. Herman Felix Wirth, ed., *Orkestcomposities van Nederlandsche Meesters van het begin der 17de eeuw*. Amsterdam: G. Alsbach/Leipzig: Breitkopf & Härtel, 1913 (Vereeniging voor Nederlandsche Muziekgeschiedenis, vol. XXXIV). Wirth's comment on p. 12.

29. *Altniederlandische Armeemarsche* (Berlin: Bote & Bock, 1915); Baumann, *Verzeichnis*, no. 26. *Ein Hähnlein wollen wir rupfen: Neue Kriegslieder* (Jena, 1916); Baumann, *Verzeichnis*, no. 29.

30. See Baumann, *Verzeichnis*, nos. 42, 44–50.

31. Baumann's *Verzeichnis*, nos. 464–80. In December 1916, Kaiser Wilhelm II named Wirth "Titular Professor" at the Brussels Conservatory (see Kater, *Ahnenerbe*, p. 12), and promised him a chair in musicology there. After the liberation of Belgium, this was of course impossible.

32. See "Mein Leben ist immer geistliche Revolutionsarbeit gewesen: ein Gespräch mit Prof. Wirth," *Humus* 1–2 (Löhrbach, 1979), pp. 127–32; description of the ensemble, p. 128. Photograph of the Wirths circa 1920 in Baumann,

Verzeichnis, p. 355.

33. For Wirth's analysis of this, see *Ursinn*, pp. 83–84, 91–92.

34. J. F. D. Blöte, review of *Untergang* in *Anzeiger für deutsches Altertum und deutsche Litteratur*, 36 (1913), pp. 258–61; here p. 259.

35. H. Wirth, ed. *Die Ura Linda Chronik; übersetzt und mit einer einführenden geschichtlichen Untersuchung* (Leipzig: Koehler & Amelang, 1933). Among the flood of reactions (see Baumann, *Verzeichnis*, pp. 180–259) was the devastating criticism by the philologist Arthur Hübner: *Herman Wirth und die Ura-Linda-chronik* (Berlin: De Gruyter, 1934).

36. J. Godwin, *Music and the Occult: French Musical Philosophies 1750–1950* (Rochester: University of Rochester Press, 1995), p. 50.

37. Wirth, *Ursinn*, p. 118.

38. See Colin Renfrew, *Before Civilization: The Radiocarbon Revolution and Prehistoric Europe* (New York: Knopf, 1973).

39. I am grateful to Michael Moynihan for pointing out this connection.

40. *Die Musik in Geschichte und Gegenwart*, 2nd ed., Sachteil vol. 7, p. 193, gives a short but tidy estimation of the historical position and influence of Wirth's dissertation. To go much further would require research into surviving archives in Austria and Germany, and into printed sources (e.g., concert reviews) in Dutch, in order to discover what competence Wirth possessed as performer and composer, what contacts he had with other musicians, and whether music played any part in his life after the 1920s. This would establish whether he made any real contribution to the early music and folksong revivals.

41. *Ursinn*, pp. 114–15.

The photographs in this article appear in Eberhard Baumann's bibliographical Verzeichnis *of writings by and about Herman Wirth, published by the Uwe Berg Verlag (Toppenstedt, 1995; see note 1 for full citation).*

WWW.FERALHOUSE.COM

LORDS OF CHAOS: NEW EDITION!
The Bloody Rise of the Satanic Metal Underground

By Michael Moynihan and Didrik Søderlind

"Black Metal's 'medieval Satanism' is the logical fulfillment of Christianity's worst apocalyptic fantasies, or at least the ones the media have irresponsibly legitimized."
—*Vor Tru*

6 x 9 • 404 pages • illustrated • ISBN: 0-922915-94-6 • $18.95

RUNNING ON EMPTINESS
The Pathology of Civilization

By John Zerzan

"[John Zerzan's] unrelenting questions and careful analysis point us toward the necessary goal: the unmaking of civilization."

5 1/2 x 8 1/2 • 214 pages • ISBN: 0-922915-75-X • $12

SEXUALITY, MAGIC AND PERVERSION

Francis King

Out of print for decades, with copies selling for as much as $300 by antiquarian dealers, Mr. King investigates the use of sexuality by Western and Eastern religions and occult traditions.

5 1/2 x 8 1/2 • 204 pages • ISBN: 0-922915-74-3 • $16.95

TO ORDER FROM FERAL HOUSE:
Shipping: US: $4.50 first book, $2 each additional book; Canada: $9 first book, $6 each additional book; other countries: $11 first book, $9 each additional book. Money order or check in US dollars drawn on a US bank. Feral House, PO Box 39910, Los Angeles, CA 90039.

Musical Ammunition: An Interview with Allerseelen's Gerhard

Joshua Buckley

The first time I encountered Allerseelen was on an obscure cassette-only release I discovered in a catalog devoted entirely to experimental, limited-edition tapes—strange, hybrid recordings utilizing Brion Gysin's cut-up techniques, hypnotic, occult-inspired atmospheric music, and painfully abrasive power electronics. But even in that underground milieu, where sexually and politically transgressive themes are practically de rigueur, Allerseelen's music stood out. One side of the tape consisted of field recordings of the ritual drumming processions held annually in the Spanish village of Calanda; the other featured a sampling of Allerseelen's own compositions. Combining clattering, electronically generated dissonance with heavy bass lines and pulsating, techno-inspired rhythms, it was a sound distinct enough to be almost immediately recognizable. I was intrigued.

Later, I began receiving a series of tracts written and published by the man behind Allerseelen, who at the time was referring to himself simply as "Kadmon" (in the Kabbalistic tradition, Adam Kadmon is the "primordial man" who emanates the world). These unusual journals—part research papers, part spiritual autobiography—were almost impossible to categorize. Ranging over a wide array of subjects, they were filled with information gleaned from Kadmon's extensive readings in primary and secondary texts. But more than that, they contained personal observations, meditations, and travel diaries, the subjective nature of which gave each issue a perspective difficult to obtain elsewhere. One issue dealt with the work of avant-garde musician and Kabbalistic shaman Z'ev; another focused on the experimental short films of counter-culture icon Kenneth Anger. More often, though, Kadmon's research turned towards various aspects of Western esotericism: Gnosticism, the Cathars, and the Greco-Roman Mysteries. The now infamous "Black Magic" issue was devoted entirely to scatological rites in various mystical traditions, and especially to the use of excrement in the alchemical "Great Work." Or, in other words: Holy Shit.

But there have been other reasons for Kadmon's notoriety.

GERHARD MEDITATES ON THE PEAKS.
(PHOTO COURTESY OF GERHARD)

Both his music and his writings have at times delved into a detailed examination of the German *völkisch* subculture, which many scholars have associated with the rise of totalitarianism. One issue of the journal *Aorta* featured an article on the Jugendstil artist Hugo Höppener (Fidus), who was also a *völkisch* hippie and nudist, while another contained a biography of the SS Grail researcher Otto Rahn. In his academic potboiler *Black Sun: Aryan Cults, Esoteric Nazism, and the Politics of Identity* (New York: NYU Press, 2001), Nicholas Goodrick-Clarke has characterized Kadmon as an out-and-out fascist "inspired by a dark romanticism, the occult and mythical and chthonic elements of European culture." While the reality is undoubtedly far more complex, Kadmon has nevertheless complicated matters by describing himself as part of a "conservative avant garde." It should be remembered, however, that the German word *konservativ* carries entirely different connotations than the English and American "conservative." In the sense that Kadmon uses the term, it is a reference to the Conservative Revolutionaries, political theorists like Ernst Niekisch, Othmar Spann, and Oswald Spengler. Though undoubtedly men of the Right, these were also individuals who harbored a deep, aristocratic contempt for Nazism and other populist fascist movements.

In recent years, Allerseelen's music has departed considerably from the noisy, industrial harshness that marked their earlier releases. Kadmon, who now goes by his birth name Gerhard, has also abandoned the "cassette culture" of which the group was once so much a part. New albums have appeared in beautifully realized compact disc editions, and the music itself has risen to similarly high production standards. There is also little that remains of Gerhard's "dark romanticism" on the excellent *Venezia* album. Though still heavily percussive and driven by a throbbing beat, Gerhard's minimalist lyrics (some of which have been borrowed from Ezra Pound and Rainer Maria Rilke) are joyously exultant paeans to feminine sensuality, good wine, and Italian opera. Hardly the sort of material one would expect from a man planning the next *Anschluss*—regardless of what Nicholas Goodrick-Clarke might think.

I decided to begin the interview that follows by asking Gerhard about his experiences with the Vienna Actionists. Mainly active during the 1960s, the Actionists courted infamy with their shocking public performances. Although in some ways similar to the "Happenings" then popular with other artists, the Actionists' willingness to test the boundaries of the human body by staging mock castrations and executions, engaging in gender play, and utilizing blood and other bodily fluids in their performances, distinguished Actionism as one of the most confrontational art movements of the last century. Although representative figures like Hermann Nitsch originally interpreted this work in terms of its therapeutic and cathartic aspects, Nitsch later adopted a more mystical stance. Actionism, he would explain, was calculated to "trash the violently imposed subject-object divide and … bring people towards an awareness of the Whole." This interpretation was probably inevitable, considering Actionism's preoccupation with the "Great Themes" of birth, death, dissolution, and regeneration. These are, of course, the same concerns that run throughout the music of Allerseelen.

Tell me about your background as a performer and musician. Specifically, I'm curious about your work with the Vienna Actionists and the music group Zero Kama.

Even in the days of my youth, living near the mountains in Upper

Austria, I was already fascinated by Surrealism and Symbolism, and I loved the poetry of Antonin Artaud, Baudelaire, and Rimbaud. In Berlin, I became acquainted with the music of groups like D.A.F. and Einstürzende Neubauten. At some point I obtained a copy of Re/Search's *Industrial Culture Handbook*, which inspired my interest in American underground culture—especially the avant-garde books by William Burroughs and the films of Kenneth Anger. It was around this time that I began exploring ways to record my own music.

During my military service, I spent a lot of time in Vienna with Michael DeWitt of Zero Kama. I played kettledrums during rehearsals, but was never involved in any of his recordings or live performances. He did use some material I recorded in Sicily, near Aleister Crowley's Abbey of Thelema at Cefalu, for a 10" record for the French music label Athanor. Those early years in Vienna were strange, intense, and magical. My nights were taken up with military duties. I was listening to a lot of Balinese Gamelan and Tibetan music, as well as to industrial/ritual groups like Psychic TV and 23 Skidoo, who were giving concerts at the time. All of this undoubtedly influenced my own recordings.

I was also fascinated by the Vienna Actionists and Hermann Nitsch's O. M. Theater [Orgies Mysteries Theater]. I interviewed Nitsch for my magazine *Aorta*; the issue was devoted to the Viennese artist Rudolf Schwarzkogler. I did have the opportunity to play kettledrums once for the O. M. Theater—it was a three-day-long baptism of blood and wine, held at Nitsch's castle in the Weinviertel region north of Vienna. Interestingly enough, this was close to an artificial hill called the Gaiselberg, where the Austrian ariosophist Guido von List once spent a night invoking the goddess Ostara.

My passion for Nitsch's work was an essential experience; now it is part of my past. I learned what I could from his blood-soaked art, but I'm no longer that interested in his work. I am still fascinated, though, with some aspects of the more esoteric, introverted art of Schwarzkogler.

Was your interest in esotericism in general, and the Western esoteric tradition in particular, latent in these early explorations?

In a certain way, everything was there in latent form. My fascination with Surrealism and Symbolism opened my eyes to the sacred sciences, to the occult, alchemy, magic, and mythology. I was—and still am—fascinated by the beautiful, colorful Tarot cards that Aleister Crowley created with Lady Frieda Harris. Hermann Nitsch's work also has a certain occult lineage, to the extent that his performances were inspired by the rites of Dionysus, Cybele, and Mithras. I've always been interested in shamanism. One of my first cassettes was called *Autdaruta*. This was the name of a shaman from Greenland who lost his powers when he was baptized as a Christian—which I consider to be an important lesson!

Books and poetry have always been very important to me. There is an occult bookshop in Vienna where I discovered Otto Rahn's poetic books on the Cathars and the Grail, as well as Julius Evola's books on alchemy. It was also there that I first came across Rudolf Mund's book on the Austrian occultist and poet Karl Maria Wiligut, which contained a series of mystical poems Wiligut had written in 1937. I immediately felt compelled to record songs based on these poems—it was a challenge and a necessity. [These poems appear on the Allerseelen album, *Gotos=Kalanda*.—Editor's note] The music was a strange blend of industrial and ritualistic elements, although it is a bit noisy for my tastes now.

My passion for traveling was likewise inspired by books and authors—especially Jack Kerouac and the other Beat writers, not to mention Arthur Rimbaud, who was quite an adventurous traveler himself. I have embarked on many "magical mystery tours" over the years. These have been quests in both an esoteric and an exoteric sense—searching for cromlechs, dolmens, menhirs, and Roman churches in beautiful landscapes like Catalonia, Corsica, Menorca, and Tyrol. I am fascinated by these visible manifestations of an invisible, hidden world: the sacred underground of Europe. I consider these places to be power points.

That seems to be something you've tried to capture on some of the more recent recordings: the magic of certain places.

I like to take a lot of photographs during my travels, and if the places have especially impressed me with their magic and beauty these often end up on the covers and in the booklets accompanying my CDs. In some respects, each album symbolizes a particular journey—to a place, a sanctuary, a castle, or an island. I also devise a specific color scheme for every release. The chestnut-brown *Gotos=Kalanda* disc contains various photos of the

Wewelsburg castle in Germany. *Stirb und Werde*, which is flaming red in appearance, is filled with images of the Externsteine in Westphalia, where Kenneth Anger also filmed scenes for his movie *Lucifer Rising*. *Neuschwabenland* refers to the mythical utopian state created by the Germans near the South Pole, and I utilized deep-blue photographs of ice and oak leaves to evoke it. Obviously, the *Venezia* album contains images of this surrealistic city—which to me is like a psychedelic bridge between East and West, land and sea, dream and reality. The title of the CD *Abenteuerliches Herz* refers to a book by Ernst Jünger. It is rendered in blood red and depicts the megalithic Taula monuments on the Balearic island of Menorca, where I happened to be staying when Jünger died. These megaliths look like giant Thor's hammers, or mushrooms cast in stone.

For the emerald-green *Sturmlieder*, I discovered a strange building in Bremen, Lower Saxony—the astonishing Haus Atlantis. This was built by the architect and artist Bernhard Hoetger, and is based on ideas derived from the researcher Herman Wirth. The façade incorporated a strange wooden sculpture of Odin hanging on Yggdrasil, the world ash, surrounded by a circle of runes. But unlike most depictions of this god, where he appears as a divine king, hierophant, or warrior, Hoetger's Odin is more like an African fetish—an archaic entity. I am still fascinated by this mysterious artwork. Unfortunately, the sculpture was destroyed during the war, although the Haus Atlantis still stands in the center of Bremen. And their archive now includes a copy of the *Sturmlieder* disc.

A lot of the newer material seems to have been influenced by your travels in southern Europe—particularly Italy and Spain. From a geographical standpoint, has living in Austria given you a special appreciation for the intersection of northern, southern, and eastern European cultures?

Austria is in some ways the heart of Europe. Perhaps this explains why so many artists and occultists have been born in this country—which was once an enormous empire. Many veins, from the East and West, North and South, flow into this heart—and also into mine. One theory has it that Tyrol derives its name from the gods Tyr and Odal. High up in the Tyrol mountains I visited a site containing various archaic inscriptions—some experts claim that they are Etruscan, while others believe them to be runes.

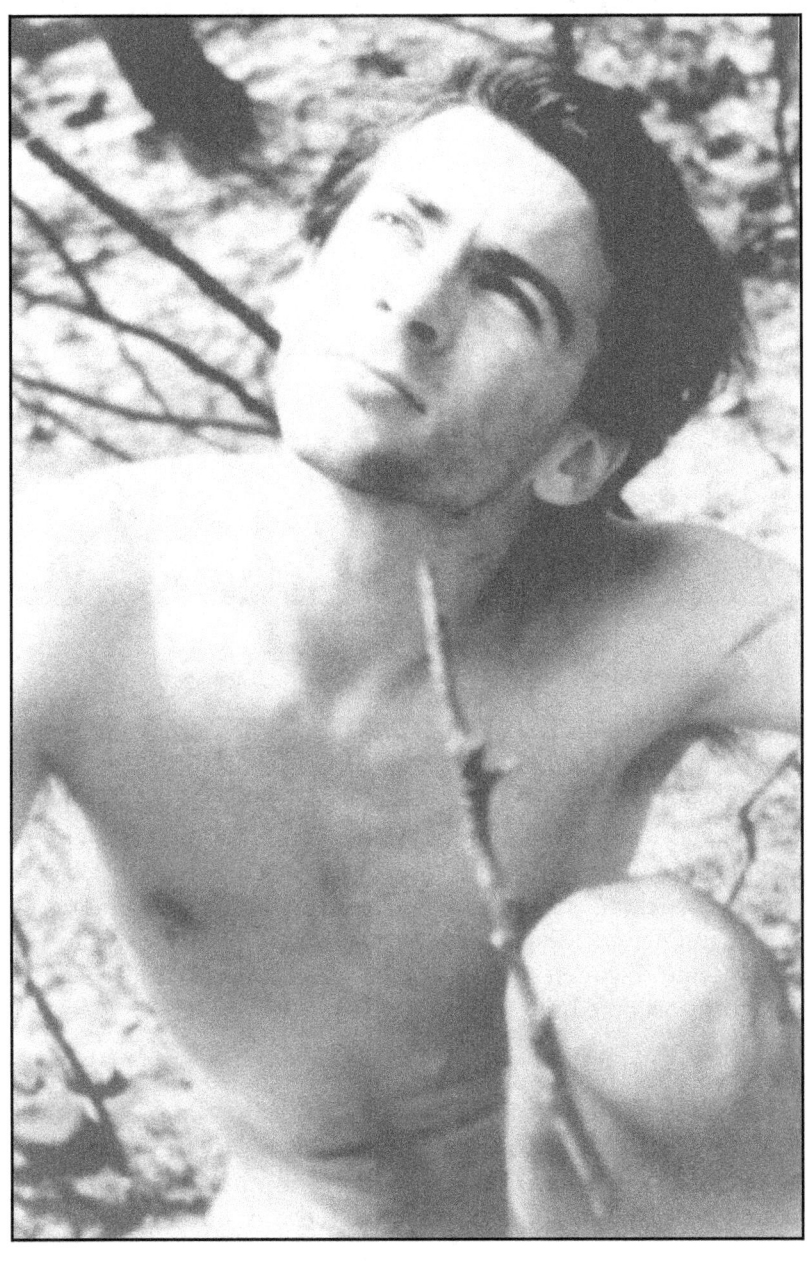

GERHARD IN CROATIA.
(PHOTO BY CLAUDIA ORTHOFER)

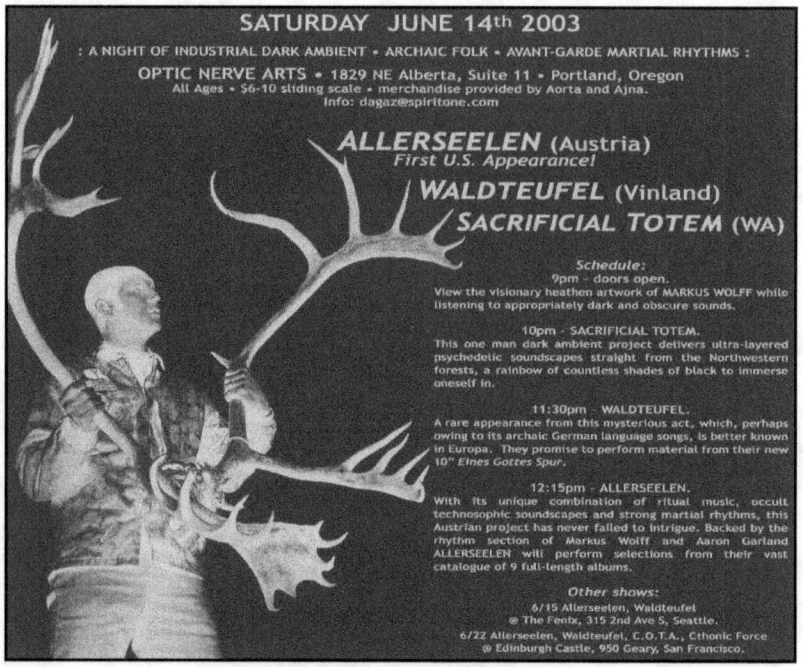

FLYER FOR RARE ALLERSEELEN CONCERTS IN
PORTLAND, SEATTLE, AND SAN FRANCISCO.

Both worlds met in Tyrol, where tribes from the North and South lived together. And both of these worlds, both of these influences, meet in my work. I am a child of the monarchy; I have German, Slavic, and Roman blood in my veins. Each predominates at different times. Once I recorded one of Friedrich Bernhard Marby's rune songs along with a slow-motion flamenco piece. The result was a unique melding of a German song with an Andalusian touch—and of course, these two worlds met in the past, when the Visigoths occupied the Iberian Peninsula.

Over the last few years, your music seems to have incorporated more feminine aspects—not only with the inclusion of female vocals, but also with the move towards more melodic song structures, and away from the violent abrasiveness of your earlier recordings. Has this been a deliberate progression?

Actually, I think the earlier recordings, based as they were on melancholic or shamanic sample-loops, had a certain "yin" aspect with their emphasis on the chthonic, the underworld. But then my passion for electronic rhythms came to the forefront, and the music became much more "yang" influenced. The *Neuschwabenland* CD had to have an icy, iron character with masculine, martial elements. The *Venezia* album was far more influenced by things that might be associated with the feminine: imagination and dreams, mirrors, water, the night. Of course, my desire is for these qualities to achieve some kind of balance in my releases.

I do not think that there are really deliberate progressions in art—the artist is always a tool of his work. Music is seductive, both for the listener and for the composer: I listen to a particular sound, and I fall in love with it. It's like falling in love with a woman, a poem, or a landscape. The muses and I are seducing each other.

I work in a very intuitive way. As such, the songwriting process is often very easy—like Nietzsche's *gaya scienza*. The sounds interact in the darkness of my room like children playing in a garden. New games are created. This is how the best songs are written.

One thing I find interesting about your albums is the juxtaposition of magical and archaic themes with electronic music—you once described your style as "technosophical." Do you feel that the technological apparatus of modern society can be reinvested with the sacred? Do you see this as part of your overall project?

That is the challenge of this century, and it might be the only chance that we have—a strange blend of sacred science and *gaya scienza*, of holy quest and *dolce vita*, which must unfortunately be based in the dark-gray and black magic of industrialism. My access to modern technology is very surreal. I sometimes feel like an alchemist: scanning and sampling, sending and receiving images, words, and sounds at the click of a button. Perhaps one day I will discover a way to translate words into images, images into sounds and vice-versa. My music has always been an alchemical process, with strange imaginings and manifestations melting into one another, with phoenixes being burnt and rising again from the ashes, and maybe some scarecrows too.

There is an old magician who is always with me whenever I

record—together we create sounds and songs. He has only one ear, his skin is black like an Ethiopian warrior, and his name is Ensoniq EPS 16+. He is the black heart of Allerseelen. Sometimes this sorcerer is tired, sometimes he is sick, sometimes his magical tools don't really work. One day he will die, and I'm unsure as to whether or not I will find another who has the passion and patience to continue this musical work with me.

Venezia is full of references to sleep and dreams. How important have dreams been in charting the course of your own life?

The city of Venezia itself is like a dream, a vision that has become reality. That is why it has been so admired by artists all over the world. I hope that some traces of this magical world have survived in my recordings.

In my youth, I always wrote down all of my dreams in diaries. I still have them. Even now, they seem like the adventures of a stranger in a strange land. I have always been fascinated by these manifestations of a hidden universe. Nevertheless, it has become more and more difficult for me to remember my dreams at all—they are almost a *terra incognita*. If they continue to influence me now, they do so subtly.

You recently halted production of your journals *Aorta* and *Ahnstern*. Despite their obscurity, they seem to have been surprisingly influential—the "Schwarze Kunst" issue, for example, was recently reproduced in its entirety in the American anthology *Apocalypse Culture II*. Did any of your publications cause you problems with the European authorities? I imagine the issues dealing with more *völkisch* themes might have precipitated some controversy.

Actually, even more people saw my writing in the book *Lords of Chaos*—it includes my "Oskorei" essay about violent archaic rites in the Norwegian countryside. This essay also appears in the German translation of the book.

Since I published the journals in bilingual editions, people from all over the world were able to read them. There were twenty issues of *Aorta*, and nine issues of *Ahnstern*. I consider each one of them to be like a seed, and many of them seem to have fallen on fertile ground. There were readers who continued my researches, my quests. So it was fruitful work, but time consuming. Therefore, I've decided to stop writing, and concentrate solely on my music. The journals are almost completely sold out and I have no intention of reprinting them. However, my comrades from the labels Ajna and State Art will publish a bilingual book and CD anthology containing most of the texts, as well as new material by Allerseelen.

I have never really had any problems with the authorities, although I was once asked to come to the Austrian Ministry of the Interior to show them copies of my publications. This was fine, though, as they ended up buying them for their archives. My concerts have been banned on occasion, primarily because of the *Gotos=Kalanda* material, and the fact that Karl Maria Wiligut was part of the Ahnenerbe. These troubles will no doubt continue, as I am currently working on a CD compilation for my Aorta label based on a poem by Friedrich Hielscher—who was also a member of the Ahnenerbe.

What do you hope the average listener might experience when listening to an Allerseelen CD? It's obviously going to be highly subjective. But to the extent that you are capable of influencing the people who hear your music, what would you hope that that influence might be?

I want the same divine sparks that have flashed in my soul to leap into the souls of the listeners. I want them to be electrified by the same artists and poets, the same dreams and visions that have been so important to me. Sometimes, if the music is beautiful and powerful enough, this is precisely what happens. Sometimes it doesn't.

Music has always had a dual nature for me—it can be medicinal and healing, but it can also serve as ammunition. This is why I love powerful rhythms. Music has helped me tremendously in my own life, encouraging my confidence, my passion, my patience, and my strength for the eternal warfare that is existence. My desire is that my own music might have the same effect on some of the people who hear it. Only in this sense is music magical. I am always pleased when people tell me that my songs have been helpful or useful in some specific situation. Then, suddenly, I know that it makes sense to create these songs, and that what I'm doing has meaning.

Allerseelen CDs can be purchased in the United States from:

The Ajna Offensive, P.O. Box 3003, Ashland, OR 97520
<www.theajnaoffensive.com>

Reviews: Books

Nutrition and Physical Degeneration by Weston A. Price, D.D.S. Softbound, 524 + xxx pages, illustrated, with index. La Mesa, Calif.: Price-Pottenger Nutrition Foundation, 2000 (first published in 1939). ISBN 0-87983-816-7.

Nourishing Traditions by Sally Fallon with Mary G. Enig, Ph.D. Revised second edition. Softbound, 674 + xii pages, with index. Washington, D.C.: New Trends, 2001. ISBN 0-9670897-3-5.

Throughout written history there has been much speculation about the perceived decline of the human race. But it would be hard to dispute that the most rapid degeneration of mankind has come in the last century, and seems to be accelerating. This can be seen everywhere, often manifesting in stark contrasts, such as the abysmal existence eked out by most of the world's inhabitants versus the decadent consumption enjoyed by the remainder of the population. Dwindling natural resources are reflected in a sinister explosion of empty abundance: throwaway books and other ephemeral media published at the expense of the trees, the endless deluge of plastic, the literal mountains of garbage. The disappearing wilderness areas and the vanishing animal species, particularly key predators, simultaneously bear witness to an increase in certain rodents and insects. But one of the most obvious signs of decline, in the Western world at least, is easily revealed by a casual glance at one's fellow citizens—it is the appalling state of people's physical and mental health. In the 1930s this type of human deterioration was blamed by many on miscegenation.

The dentist Dr. Weston Price thought differently. He believed that nutritional factors were a leading element in the onset of degenerative health problems. "My investigations have revealed that these same divergencies from normal are reproduced ... while the blood is still pure." (p. 2) From 1936–38 Price surveyed fourteen different isolated racial groups and found that physical degeneration occurred in each of them as soon as they were exposed to the modern Western diet and left behind their ancestral ways of eating. In other words, Price suspected that

TWO BROTHERS FROM THE ISLE OF HARRIS. THE YOUNGER, LEFT, USES MODERN FOOD AND SUFFERS DISFIGURING TOOTH DECAY. THE OLDER, RIGHT, EATS ONLY TRADITIONAL FOODS. (FROM "NUTRITION AND PHYSICAL DEGENERATION")

something else was going on—something internal. The very food people were consuming was causing their drastic decline in vitality and viability. In all groups, Price found the rapid degenerative process to be consistent with that of the general populations of Europe and America.

Throughout the civilized world, poor nutrition manifested itself visibly in the poor condition of people's teeth. Price relates this physical disintegration to the increase in psychological problems. At the time Price was conducting his researches, proper functioning of the brain was thought to be genetically predetermined, and not influenced by biological factors. Price's data indicated, however, "that associated with disturbances in the development of the bones of the head, disturbances may at the same time occur in the development of the brain. Such structural defects are usually not hereditary ... They are products of the environment rather than hereditary units transmitted from the ancestry." (pp. 3–4)

Price examined small, isolated, and homogeneous populations and their modernized counterparts, including Gaelic people in the Inner and Outer Hebrides, Aborigines, Indians of the high Peruvian Andes, Swiss dairy farmers in remote valleys of the Alps, African tribes, Eskimos, Polynesians, and various Native American tribes. The groups that had no or little contact with modernized Western food—that is, processed foods, in particular flour and sugar—enjoyed rugged health; lived long lives free of disease; had teeth that were straight, white, and free of cavities; produced healthy babies with ease; and were not plagued by psychological disorders or criminal behavior.

As soon as they were exposed to a modern Western diet, however, people of the same racial stock, regardless of where they lived, experienced rampant tooth decay; narrowed facial structures; poor health and disease; infertility; and psychological disorders and criminality. This happened rapidly, even within the same generation: older children born to parents who still ate a traditional diet were much healthier than the younger ones born after the family had moved to more urban environments, or had been exposed to modernized foods.

In the chapter "The Progressive Decline of Modern Civilization" Price addresses the correlations between biology, ethics, morals, physical health, and nutrition. He cites a variety of source literature, from criminal studies to reports on the lack of good Italian tenors due to the changes in facial structure. Supporting his belief in the significance of dental health, he quotes Earnest Hooton's book *Apes, Men and Morons:*

> I firmly believe that the health of humanity is at stake, and that, unless steps are taken to discover preventatives of tooth infection ... the course of human evolution will lead downward to extinction ... human teeth and the human mouth have become ... the foci of infections that undermine the entire bodily health of the species ... [D]egenerative tendencies have manifested themselves in modern man to such an extent that our jaws are too small for the teeth which they are supposed to accommodate ... Let us go to the ignorant savage, consider his way of eating, and be wise. Let us cease pretending that tooth-brushes and tooth-paste are any more important than shoe-brushes and shoe-polish. It is store food which has given us store teeth. (p. 12)

Price's quest for isolated racial groups brought him to the Gaelic people living on the northern islands of Scotland:

> Stories have long been told of the superb health of the people living on the Islands of the Outer Hebrides ...

> These stories have included a description of their wonderfully fine teeth and the stalwart physiques and strong characters. They, accordingly, provide an excellent setting for a study to throw light on the problem of the cause of dental caries and modern physical degeneration ... The basic foods of these islanders are fish and oat products with a little barley. (p. 44)

These foods have served the northern man well for centuries and are even mentioned in the Eddic "Lay of Harbard" when Thor boasts to Odin (disguised as a ferryman) of the good meal he enjoyed:

> Ferry me across,   and you'll have a fine breakfast—
> the basket on my back   holds the best of foods.
> I took time to eat   before I traveled,
> stuffed myself   with herring and oatmeal.

While the diets of the isolated groups he studied greatly varied, Price found certain unifying factors. These included attention to traditional ways of eating; a high intake of animal protein, fats, and organ meats; and the use of lacto-fermentation. Needless to say, the food they ate was also fresh and locally grown, raised, or caught.

Price was also impressed with the family planning practiced by so-called primitive people. He not only saw the quality of physical and mental health decline when a woman has too many children, but also observed that too many children are a burden to the earth's fertility. He believed that a mother needs several years to rebuild her body before having another child, if it is to be a superior one. He goes on to point out that the call for overbreeding "is the demand of war-lords for larger families—more men to man the guns—more men for fodder. There also remains the primitive feeling that the nation is the strongest that has the largest population. Obviously this is no longer true." (p. 466)

In his 1938 foreword (hence the outdated use of terms such as "savages") to Price's book, Earnest Hooton points out:

> Since we have known for a long time that savages have excellent teeth and civilized men have terrible teeth, it seems to me that we have been extraordinarily stupid in concentrating all of our attention upon the task of finding

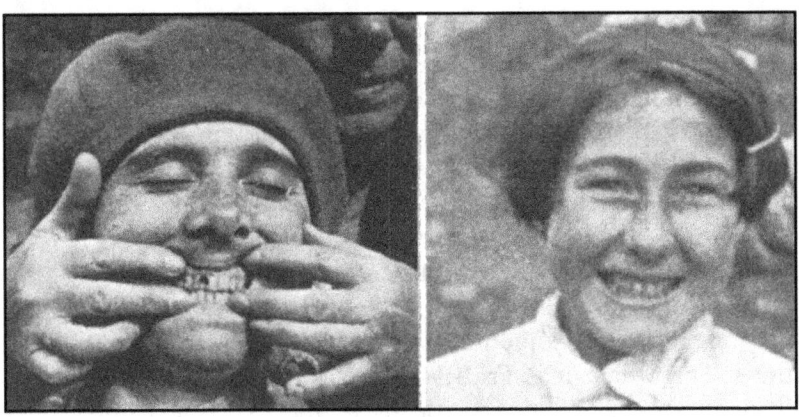

MODERNIZED GAELIC WITH RAMPANT TOOTH DECAY CONTRASTED WITH "PRIMITIVE" GAELIC.
(FROM "NUTRITION AND PHYSICAL DEGENERATION")

out why our teeth are so poor, without ever bothering to learn why savage teeth are good. Dr. Weston Price seems to be the only person who possesses the scientific horse sense to supplement his knowledge of the probable cause of dental disease with a study of the dietary regimens which are associated with dental health. (p. xx)

The foreword to the 1989 edition by Abram Hoffer, M.D., again questions why this important work has been ignored, suggesting that when medicine turned to the new "wonder drugs," corticosteroids and antibiotics, it left clinical nutrition behind to wither on the vine. Very simply put, "Dr. Price found that people eating fresh, whole foods, uncontaminated by additives such as sugar and salt, grown on soils still rich in essential minerals, grew and maintained healthy jaws and teeth. In modern terms, people should consume foods they have adapted to for over 100,000 years, because these foods are essential for health." (p. xxix) Confirming Price's warnings from a half-century earlier, he continues:

Recent intergenerational research in animals and people has shown that, on a uniformly poor diet, the offspring of each generation deteriorates more and more ... We do not know what the final stage will be in human deterioration. I suspect that many of the people with psychiatric disorders today, the addicts, the high degree of violence, the tremendous number of depressions and tension states, and a great number of physical degenerations such as diabetes, arthritis, etc., are the modern manifestations of this continuing degeneration. ... I shudder to think of the final outcome. ... In my own practice I am now seeing children who are the second generation of junk-consuming peoples. The results are obvious and depressing. (p. xxx)

The problems come not only from poor food, but also from the soil in which it is grown—soil that is now greatly depleted throughout the world. This leads to food with less nutritional value, which in turn causes grazing animals to suffer a similar fate to the humans who may later consume them at the dinner table. Already in the 1930s ranchers were noticing the drastic effects of soil depletion on the ability of their herds to reproduce. Ranchers whose animals used to produce nearly 100% healthy offspring, almost all of which were of sufficient physical quality to breed, were getting approximately forty calves per hundred cows annually, and of these only around ten were fit for reproductive purposes.

Nourishing Traditions is a modern companion to this book. The authors reiterate Price's research, substantiate it with modern scientific studies, and add further information about what they consider to be healthy nutrition. This book contains numerous quotes from studies which question the standard American diet as recommended by the American Medical Association and also the ones recommended by the alternative health food proponents. The AMA diet includes low-fat, high-carbohydrate, and processed foods (for instance margarine instead of butter). The alternative diets are usually vegetarian and rely heavily on soy products. The book contains good information on how to prepare food in the manner that Price recommends. There are recipes for basic traditional foods such as bone soup, lacto-fermented beverages and vegetables, advice for selecting and cooking organ meats, along with recipes for other, more familiar foods. This reviewer recommends using the information from both of these books as a guide to choosing healthy recipes from good cookbooks such as *The Joy of Cooking* or *The Old World Cookbook*, which was reviewed in volume one of *TYR*. The latter has many good recipes for traditional foods; they are easy to follow, and in my experience so far, they have always turned out a tasty meal. If you are fortunate, your own family's recipes can also be a great source of common sense and good nutrition.

The most important message from these books is that we are literally what we eat, as are our children who receive the foundation of their health through their mothers and fathers. The best general guideline is to eat what one's ancestors did for thousands of years. Seek out fresh and local food. Enjoy simply processed, whole foods, such as meat, eggs, whole milk, vegetables, and whole grains; highly processed foods such as soy milk, margarine, precooked, processed, and canned foods should be avoided. Americans eat some of the oldest, stalest food in the world. Use your nose: throw away food that is stale or rancid. Olive oil, which has been used for millennia, is the most stable vegetable oil. Modern canola oil quickly goes rancid, whereas the much-maligned lard has a very long shelf life.

Both of these books ignore two important factors that separate us from our ancestors: the level of their physical activity and the quantities of food they ate. The physical activity was abundant; the servings of food were not. While indeed they ate thick slices of dense bread with equally thick slices of cheese, they usually ate no more than *one slice* and that would suffice until the main warm meal at midday. Supper was small. To this day, many Europeans and some American farmers still eat in this manner, but increasingly the main meal is eaten at night, just before bed. Worse yet, nowadays all meals could easily be considered "main meals" in terms of their unnecessarily large proportions. The accompanying beverage of choice—soft drinks (bubbly, artificially colored sugar-water sold to consumers at obscene profits), drunk in America literally by the liter, contributes greatly to the problems. "What's wrong with soft drinks? Just about everything..." (*Nourishing Traditions*, p. 51).

The situation with physical exercise is equally deplorable: most people get little exercise beyond walking down an office hallway, or taking a few steps to their cars. The modern world has created so many "labor-saving" devices that those endeavoring to maintain their physical strength frequently must resort to expensive labor-making devices such as treadmills and stair-masters.

Weston Price's original research revealed how quickly overt physical and mental decline can set in as a result of modern eating practices. It has not been all that long since he published his major work on the subject, but the situation now is probably far worse than he could have ever imagined. If these trends continue, modern man will simply collapse under his own morbidly obese weight, and no amount of medicine will save him. But rest assured of one thing: great profits will be made by the medical industry in their futile attempt to save a sinking human ship.

Annabel Lee

Viking Age Iceland by Jesse Byock. Softbound, 447 pages + xxi with illustrations, bibliography, and index. New York: Penguin, 2001. ISBN 0-14-029115-6.

Modern heathens, and those who wish to duplicate Germanic social institutions, often find themselves looking to Viking Age Iceland (800–1100 C.E.). Besides Iceland's undeniable romantic appeal, the reasons are largely practical: because of Iceland's geographic isolation, Germanic culture and religion survived there long after continental Europe had succumbed to the Christian conversion. Still, it should be remembered that the same factors which contributed to the comparatively long survival of paganism in Iceland (isolation from the mainland, climactic conditions, etc.) distinguished Icelandic culture as anomalous in other ways, as well. As Byock argues quite convincingly, Iceland's situation was unique, and many of Iceland's social and cultural institutions were innovations designed to adapt to an environment quite different from the one left behind by the region's immigrant inhabitants. The Icelandic political system—often idealized as utopian by proponents of small-scale, participatory democracy—differed substantially from other Germanic social arrangements and, according to Byock, would have been impracticable elsewhere.

Part of Byock's approach, which will be familiar to readers of his other books, involves looking to Iceland's rich store of saga material as an important historical source. This would seem an obvious step. But surprisingly, modern historians have largely ignored the sagas. In part, this is due to the extreme difficulty one encounters separating fact from fiction in these sweeping, epic narratives. But more particularly, Byock describes how a small cadre of Icelandic scholars, the "bookprosists," worked to change the perception that the sagas were based on oral traditions that reflected actual history. The reasons for this are complex. In the mid-twentieth century, Iceland was still extricating itself from Danish control, and many Icelandic intellectuals were actively involved in cultivating a distinct national identity. While nineteenth-century nationalists in other parts of Europe had embraced folktales, fairy tales, and other purportedly oral traditions, the fashion had shifted by the time of the bookprosists. It now seemed more profitable, at least from a nationalistic standpoint, to treat the sagas as strictly literary creations. But in downplaying the sagas' roots in oral traditions, it also had to be admitted that their value as historical documents was negligible. Not surprisingly, the bookprosists' attempts to co-opt the sagas as "literature" never caught on with the farmers and other ordinary Icelanders—who had always held their written heritage in high esteem, anyway. These men, many of who still lived on the farmsteads described in the sagas, and whose own lives were not so far removed from the lives of the sagas' protagonists, would continue to take the sagas' historical veracity at face value.

Iceland was settled in the ninth century by *landnámsmenn* (land-takers) who arrived from Scandinavia, and especially Norway. But there were other immigrants as well. Vikings from Celtic settlements brought their Gaelic wives (and slaves) in tow, and some of the settlers themselves were of Celtic origin. These founding settlers were of tremendous significance for Iceland's subsequent development. They laid the groundwork for the Free State period, and established patterns of land use and farming. As for Iceland's image as a Nordic utopia, it might be noted that these farming techniques were disastrous for the Icelandic ecosystem—and wrought significant changes in the land and climate over time. By the tenth century, resource depletion had become a major problem, and a number of native species had been hunted to extinction.

Although Viking Age Iceland has often been described as a commonwealth, Byock prefers the "Free State" *(Fristat)* designation favored by modern Swedes, Danes, and Norwegians. Despite the fact that the early Icelanders adopted some of the apparatus of statehood (and especially, a national legislature), they rejected most forms of governmental centralization. They had no kings, political chieftains had no defined territorial units on which to levy taxes, and there was a comparative lack of strictly defined social hierarchies. The situation in other parts of the Viking world was moving in precisely the opposite direction. In Norway, for example, government was becoming more centralized and hierarchical. It is impossible to say how much of this was an organic development, in response to the new environment and social setting, and how much of it was deliberate. Clearly, Iceland's founders *did* set out to create a new society that would, in their eyes, correct the excesses of the systems they had left behind in mainland Scandinavia.

Under the Free State, Icelanders gathered annually for the Althing, which brought together the *goðar* (chieftains; singular form *goði*) and their thingmen for two weeks in June. The site was hallowed by the *allsherjargoði*, or "supreme chieftain," a sovereign with little power, whose office, like the modern British monarchy, was mainly symbolic. For judicial purposes, Iceland was divided up into four quarters, and representatives of each quarter conducted "quarter courts" at the Althing. More importantly, the Althing provided a time for the *lögrétta*, or law council, to meet. Anyone could propose new laws, or amendments to old laws, by taking a position at the Law Rock. The *Grágás*, or Free State laws, began to be written down in 1096. Perhaps the strangest aspect of the Icelandic system was that—despite having a highly developed legal apparatus—there was no centralized method of enforcement. A judgment might be pronounced against a criminal aggressor, but it was up to the victim, or the victim's family or other advocates, to see that it was carried out. Obviously, a lone individual might have little success against a powerful or influential enemy. His only hope would be to appeal to a *goði* for support. Conversely, the *goði's* power hinged on his ability to gather around him a large group of thingmen who had likewise sought his protection, and agreed to side with others who did the same. It would not be a stretch to say that Iceland under the Free State consisted of an intricate web of these "advocacy alliances," which in some ways were not dissimilar to modern protection rackets. Byock's occasional references to the Sicilians are, in this light, instructive.

The free farmer who aspired to a *goðorð* (chieftaincy) had to compete in a sort of market economy in which the political office of chieftain, and even seats on the *lögrétta*, was for sale to the highest bidder (this is why taxation was, for the most part, unnecessary). As a *goði's* following grew, he could demand greater dividends from other free farmers who sought his advocacy. Help in a particularly difficult matter could cost a farmer the inheritance

THINGVELLIR TODAY.

rights to his land, and could ultimately enable a chieftain to amass large stores of wealth. It could also produce sexual rewards. Concubinage was common in early Iceland, and was a source of further *goðar*-thingmen alliances. A chieftain would often look after the kinsmen of his concubines, and the arrangement could be advantageous for the concubine, as well. A folk saying from this period states: "Better a good man's *frilla* (concubine), than married badly."

The fluidity of alliances that characterized the advocacy system meant that feuds tended to be short-lived, since they seldom gave rise to long-term hatreds between families and kin groups that formed more permanent alliances. On the other hand, these more organic bonds could be jeopardized when family members in the service of competing chieftains were forced into conflict. Yet despite the popular image of the bloodthirsty Viking, violence as a whole was limited in Free State Iceland. More often than not, even potentially violent conflicts could be diffused by a sufficient show of force (or the ritualized combat of judicial proceedings), and the pragmatic motivations of advocates prevented the degeneration of simple disputes into protracted, "Hatfield and McCoy"–type conflicts.

As has often been the case, the end of the Icelandic Free State, and Iceland's status as a sovereign nation, was preceded by spiritual colonization. It has often been remarked that the conversion of Iceland was relatively peaceful. Still, it should not be forgotten that—in practice—the "lambs of Christ" acted more like lions when they encountered non-believers. Iceland was no exception. Stefnir Thorgilsson, one of the first Norwegian missionaries to Iceland, violently attacked the pagan temples, and was forcibly exiled by the angry Icelanders. Norway's Christian king, Olaf Tryggvason, next sent a priest named Þangbrand. Although somewhat more successful than his predecessor, Þangbrand reacted to any criticisms of the new faith by having the insolent party killed. When these efforts failed, Olaf stepped up his campaign. He closed off Norwegian ports to Icelandic traders, financially crippling Iceland. Worst of all, he took the children of prominent pagan Icelanders hostage, proclaiming that they would be released only if their parents repented of their heathen ways. When the Althing convened later that year, hostilities between recently converted Christians and those who still clung to the old religion were escalating. But civil war was ultimately averted with the decision to convert *en masse*. Within 250 years, Iceland would also lose its political independence. The decision to submit to the Norwegian king, however, had less to do with Christianity than it did with Iceland's unraveling social fabric. Perhaps inevitably, competition between rival chieftains, and the rise of the *stórgoðar* (or "big chieftains"), had become unmanageable. Centralization was the necessary antidote, and for this the newly Christianized Icelanders looked to Norway.

The end of the Free State highlights the inherent weakness of the Icelandic system, although it had managed to persist for a considerable span of time. While in no way ideal—at least not in the sense that modern heathens often make it out to be—Free State Iceland was a fascinating social and political experiment, from which we still have much to learn.

Joshua Buckley

***

Runes and Germanic Linguistics **by Elmer H. Antonsen. Hardbound, 380 + xxii pages, with bibliography and index. Berlin and New York: Mouton de Gruyter, 2002 (Trends in Linguistics Studies and Monographs 140). ISBN 3-11-017462-6.**

Most students of runes will have started with a popular book on the esoteric side, but it is essential to study the academic texts in addition, if only so that one may see in which areas the esoteric studies fall short. I was fortunate enough to study runology with Prof. Michael Barnes at University College London, but such courses are rare and becoming rarer, which means one must undertake this study alone. Any book with a good bibliography can act as a guide, and Antonsen's is no exception.

Antonsen has written several academic works which argue that the runes are not inherently magical, and *Runes and Germanic Linguistics* brings together many of his major articles in one handy volume. Of course, he discounts the runes' magical significance here as well, but he does inform the reader of alternative arguments and where these might be found. I disagree with Antonsen about his perspective for many reasons—not least of which is that, wherever one finds mention of runes in the ancient literature, they are referred to as "magical"—but nothing hones the intellect better than trying to find the flaws in an alternative theory to one's own.

This volume is written in an easy style of English (probably because Antonsen is a non-native speaker) but it uses many arguments based on the complexities of Germanic grammar that will certainly be a bit much for the average reader. However, one must start somewhere, and this book is certainly on the more accessible side of the really serious works in the field.

Challenging reading for anyone serious about the study of runes.

Ian Read

The Disenchantment of the World: A Political History of Religion **by Marcel Gauchet. Hardbound, 228 + xv pages, with bibliography and index. Princeton: Princeton University Press, 1997. ISBN 0-691-04406-6.**

Like another French intellectual, Alain de Benoist, Marcel Gauchet's historical anthropology reveals Christianity as the source of most "modern pathologies." Unlike de Benoist, however, Gauchet sees no way out of the modern condition. He is both a liberal and a democrat, but is honest enough to recognize that Enlightenment values of individual autonomy and reason, though widely established, have not been actualized without considerable expense. Furthermore, Gauchet does not see these values as the result of an inevitable historical progression. On the contrary, he is quick to acknowledge there are other ways of conceiving the world which, though fraught with problems of their own, might nevertheless be equally valid.

Reversing ordinary historical assumptions, Gauchet points to Karl Jasper's Axial Age (800 to 200 B.C.E.) as the point at which religion began to *lose* its hold over humankind. Christianity in particular is a "religion for departing from religion." To understand this seemingly incongruous assertion, it is important to explain how Gauchet defines religion in the first place, and especially the sort of "primitive" religious consciousness that is, for him, religion's purest manifestation. Whereas in modern societies, man attempts to gain self-possession by dominating nature (including *human* nature), a genuinely religious society is one in which man gains self-possession precisely by "consenting to dispossession." To put it another way, modern man realizes himself by negating (changing) his reality. In a religious society, on the other hand, man "negates his own negativity." That is, by submitting to the received order of religion, the religious man utilizes his energy to *constrain* his energy (recall, for example, the Delphic injunction against hubris). Gauchet calls this "the principal of mobility placed in the service of immobility."

This "immobility" is due to the fact that pre-Christian religions located the founding acts, whereby the gods instituted both the natural and the human order, in the inaccessible past. An order so constituted cannot be the subject of debate, nor does it leave room for innovation. It simply *is*. This being the case, it remains only for man to work to maintain the laws, customs, and traditions that have been handed down from one generation to the next. He is also significantly restricted in his relationship with nature. The cycle of the seasons, plant and animal life, and sexuality have also received their structures from the founding acts of the gods (who, unlike the Christian God, do not enter into history). Therefore, to tamper with or defile the natural world becomes the ultimate transgression. Another consequence of this system is the marginalization of political leadership. The chieftain or tribal leader has very little freedom to act on his own whims and aspirations. He becomes a simple functionary, whose role it is to make sure that the received order is maintained. All this is to say that pre-Christian religious societies were conservative to an extent difficult for us moderns to comprehend. Moreover, this conservatism was able to sustain itself for thousands of years, providing an essential framework for people whose lives remained virtually unchanged from generation to generation. Relatively speaking, modern society—with its radically different orientation—is merely a speck on the historical timeline.

So what exactly occurred during the Axial Age that allowed such a drastic inversion to take place? Perhaps even more fundamental than the rise of the monotheistic, major religions, was the rise of the state in Egypt and Mesopotamia—without which, Gauchet contends, the simultaneous religious revolutions of this period would not have been possible. No longer was the role of the leader simply to maintain an absolute law, based in a mythical past. The founding law now had its "representatives, administrators, and interpreters." As such, it became possible to contest. The immanent presence of the gods, incarnated in an absolute, terrestrial order, had been lost. It was now feasible to conceive of a radically transcendent god, wholly outside and above the natural order. Paradoxically, the more powerful this god becomes, the more alien he becomes; it is the idea of a transcendent god that would eventually enable man to establish *himself* as lord and master of the immanent world.

Following Nietzsche, Gauchet believes that Judaism's positing of a god beyond the world of man and nature was partially inspired by the Jewish peoples' military defeats and dispossession. While an immanent god could only have been imagined as sanctioning these defeats, a transcendent god could be absolved of responsibility. However, Judaism still struggled to maintain a tangible connection with its god through the Covenant. But this, too, was undermined by the teachings of Christ, who inaugurated Christianity by declaring that the Christian god was the god of all men. Historically, Gauchet tells us, the tremendous power of the Church in the terrestrial sphere is irrelevant. Its very role as mediator between the immanent and the transcendent is symptomatic of religion's deep decline. In pre-political societies, when the gods had been wholly present, the idea of mediation, or explanatory Theology, was completely unnecessary. When the Reformation finally challenged the Church's ability to act as mediator at all, the last strand uniting man to the divine was snapped. Modernity had begun.

But Gauchet never denies that modern people continue to harbor certain spiritual impulses, and he is open to the idea, proposed by William James and others, that this may be a fundamental human need. Nevertheless, the highly subjective and individualistic nature of modern spiritualities (think, for instance, of the extreme diversity and decentralization of the New Age) precludes them from being religious in the sense that Gauchet defines the word. A real religion permeates the social space, providing a mandate for the preservation of both the social and the natural order. Modern "religions" are impotent to do either. Moreover, the secular varieties of religion, the all-encompassing ideologies of the nineteenth century, have similarly failed in their attempts at articulating new societal frameworks that can be sustained for any length of time. Without the founding acts of the gods, localized in the distant past, society can only direct its attentions towards a future that is both uncertain and unknowable. In the end, Gauchet seems unsure as to whether or not the freedoms we enjoy following the departure of the gods are worth the extreme angst and anxiety that these freedoms entail. But he is utterly pessimistic about our ability to "think our way" back into religion.

For modern proponents of pagan and tribal religions, this is a serious consideration. If, at the outset, these "pagan spiritualities" must begin as articles of personal belief, how can they then come to occupy the larger cultural and political arenas? For if pagan gods are immanent gods, then somehow they must do so. It is a difficult question, and I certainly do not know the answer.

Gauchet provides much food for thought regarding reactionary movements that have traditionally disdained religion for various reasons. In particular, I am thinking of deep ecology and "green" anarchism (which, despite the fact that these movements' adherents like to think of themselves as progressives, harbor deeply reactionary elements). Part of this hostility is undoubtedly the legacy of leftist materialism, and part of it is a reaction against Christianity's inherent hostility to nature. But, as Gauchet has demonstrated, Christian otherworldliness is the very *antithesis* of religion. A religion of the primordial type, with its strict checks on man's ability to tamper with the social and natural order, could place much-needed limits on modern humanity's project of dominating the earth. This is exactly what deep ecology would like to achieve, and it is difficult to imagine that such a "revaluation of values" will ever be brought about by intellectual arguments alone.

The Disenchantment of the World is a dense and difficult book, but a rewarding one as well. Gauchet is one of the few contemporary philosophers bold enough to propose an all-encompassing historical anthropology and explanatory analysis of the birth of modernity. While this is by necessity filled with questionable generalizations, it is also, on the whole, a surprisingly satisfying account.

Joshua Buckley

The New Ecological Order **by Luc Ferry. Softbound, 159 + xxix pages, with index. Chicago and London: University of Chicago Press, 1995. ISBN 0-226-24483-0.**

With the passing of the Age of Ideologies, a considerable gap has opened up between conventional notions of what constitutes the Left and the Right, and the actual dichotomies that would now seem to distinguish various political movements from one another. Virginia Postrel, who writes for *Wired* and the *Los Angeles Times*, has proposed that we ditch our old assumptions about the "Left" and the "Right," and that it might now be more appropriate to speak of "stasists" and "dynamists." The latter are those who, like Postrel herself, are oriented entirely towards the future, the overcoming of human nature, and the transformation of the world into a field of ever-greater and as-yet-unimagined possibilities (Postrel is an unabashed cheerleader for the technological society—and, although it's a cheap shot, I can't help but point out that she even *looks* like a cheerleader). Stasists, on the other hand, are those who cling to the notion that there are certain institutions (both natural and human) worth preserving, and that it might at least be prudent to exercise some caution before surpassing them in favor of an undefined future. Feminism provides us with one example. Simone de Beauvoir and other "traditional" feminists argued that women were not, in their essence, defined by their femininity, and could thus attain any of the possibilities that had previously been open only to men. But most contemporary feminists assert just the opposite: that femininity is the essence of womanhood, that there is a valid, "feminine" way of

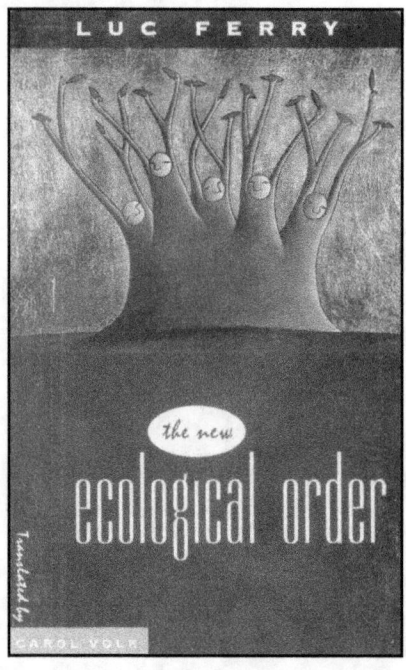

perceiving the world, and that women should celebrate their essence as women, rather than emulating men. While feminists who embrace this position would never dream of describing themselves as conservatives, they are most certainly stasists. Conversely, American conservatives—with their boundless faith in the free market and the ingenuity of Big Business—are dynamists. But so are liberals who cling to the idea that advances in science and technology will eventually lead to a world in which organic inequalities and human suffering, once accepted as the wages of Original Sin, will be done away with once and for all. Obviously, there is a need for a new categorization that takes these overlaps and distinctions into account.

Luc Ferry traces the conflict between Postrel's stasists and dynamists (terms he himself never uses) back to the Enlightenment, and the Romantic reaction that followed it. The Enlightenment view, which is Ferry's own, was that man is distinguished from the natural world by the freedom to constitute his own essence. This position has been represented in the twentieth century by (among others) Jean-Paul Sartre, and his particular variant of Existentialism. The Romantics countered with their belief that man can only be fully himself by remaining *rooted* in the national, cultural, and linguistic traditions from which he has sprung. He can transcend these traditions to some extent (there have always been cosmopolitans who have done just that), but he does so at the risk of losing what he *is*. Ferry is distressed that liberalism has succumbed to a similar tendency, and seems to have betrayed its origins in the Enlightenment. Following the inhumanities of colonialism, which was to some extent motivated by the idea that indigenous peoples could be transformed into good Europeans with a little education and encouragement, most liberals now subscribe to the idea (once the sole province of the Right) that indigenous and "primitive" peoples should be left alone to be what they *are*, fundamentally. Ferry finds this "respect for diversity" especially troubling in that it presupposes that human cultures are diverse because they are different in their essence. He asks us to consider how this is really any different from the racist's conviction that there is a Jewish "essence," an Aryan "essence," and so on. For Ferry, what makes us human is our ability to choose whatever essence we like.

Following this thread, Ferry devotes an entire chapter to the "ominous parallels" between liberal attitudes about maintaining diversity to certain strands of thought inherent to Nazism. Almost all of the examples he cites are excerpted from the writings of Walther Schoenichen, who held the Chair for the Protection of Nature at the University of Berlin. Schoenichen emerges as a major defender of original folk-groupings and cultures, and writes passionately against the violent displacement of the Sioux, the South American Indians, and the South African bushmen. It is somewhat shocking to hear a committed Nazi condemning in no uncertain terms "the white man, the great destroyer of creation: in the paradise he himself is responsible for losing, he has paved only a path of epidemics, thievery, fires, blood, and tears." But Ferry's use of Schoenichen as an example is misleading, because Schoenichen's case *is* such an anomaly. Presumably, we are supposed to infer that his stasist desire to maintain distinct, indigenous cultures (voiced in words which could have been uttered by any modern liberal) must somehow lead straight to the gas chambers! But considering that Schoenichen was a relatively marginal figure—whose principles stand in stark opposition to those embraced by the architects of the Final Solution—it is somewhat difficult to understand why Ferry has gone this route at all. Certainly, the Nazis did subscribe to the idea that the Jews and other non-Aryans were essentially different and unassimilable *as* Aryans. But this kind of thinking would seem to merit a healthy respect for and acknowledgement of Jewish uniqueness. The fact of Nazi barbarity towards outsiders indicates that Nazism was little concerned with "diversity" in the sense that Schoenichen—let alone modern liberals—would use that word.

Throughout the course of the book, Ferry lumps the animal rights movement together with deep ecology, although he acknowledges there are fundamental differences between the two.

Most deep ecologists, for example, are not vegetarians. Philosophically, vegetarianism can be seen as an attempt to transcend man's nature as an omnivorous, predatory animal. For the deep ecologist, however, it is precisely this tendency to remove man from the natural order that is at issue. What unites these movements, at least in Ferry's view, is the desire to bestow legal rights on plants and animals, thus widening the social contract to encompass endangered species. Man's special status as a legal subject (or so Ferry's argument goes) is the result of his uniqueness as the only creature capable of freely creating its own essence. Granting the same status to trees and birds is to deny man the privileged position that this autonomy confers. This denial of human freedom can only lead, or so Ferry would have it, to ideas like racial and cultural determinism.

It is indeed true that deep ecology denies man any "special status" in relation to other beings, or indeed, to Being itself. But I don't think that this necessarily follows from a denial of man's existential freedom. It is precisely man's status as the anti-natural being, as the being that is capable of transcending the natural order, that has allowed us to so ruthlessly despoil the earth. What deep ecology *does* advocate is that we leave behind our anthropomorphic assumptions, and recognize the sacred interconnection of all living things. It naturally follows that we must also recognize the fact that human life—seen from this non-anthropomorphic perspective—may not be any more "sacred" than the life of a spotted owl or an old-growth tree. In this sense, deep ecologists have even denounced the use of the word "environment." So describing the natural world reinforces the Judeo-Christian assumption that "the world" is simply a field for human action, and does not possess value in and of itself. In the face of a worsening ecological crisis, deep ecologists like Arne Naess ask us to "think like a mountain," or to adopt the Heideggerian injunction to "let Being be." Asking that we change our thinking is hardly a denial of our freedom to think, or a recourse to the idea that we are wholly defined by our natural or biological makeup.

Ferry's belief in human freedom, and particularly the human freedom to constitute our own essence, is accompanied by the completely unfounded conviction that—somehow—our free choices will enable us to overcome virtually any obstacle. He is a stalwart believer, for instance, in the dynamist conviction that, left to its own devices, the free market will eventually correct its own excesses. The folly of this position seems obvious. Human choices are typically so short-sighted that to wait for a time in which it becomes economically viable to "fix" the environment, is to wait for a time in which it will be far *too late* to actually do so (and, in fact, that time may have already come and gone). But Ferry's optimism is typical of the humanist persuasion. While his assertion that man's "special" status is the result of his existential freedom may be defensible, one wonders how the belief that this freedom will lead to man's "doing the right thing" inevitably follows. Why, for example, should we believe that human innovation and creativity can keep pace with human destructiveness? Despite the impressive scope of our achievements, is it not conceivable that Western civilization's unbounded hubris will ultimately lead to the complete despoliation of the planet, our own, and all other human cultures?

In the face of overwhelming evidence that this is exactly what is happening, it is a question that Ferry, and other liberal intellectuals, seem incapable of answering.

Joshua Buckley

The Imperative of Responsibility: In Search of an Ethics for the Technological Age by Hans Jonas. Softbound, 255 + ix pages, with index. Chicago: University of Chicago Press, 1985. ISBN 0-22-640597-4.

The German philosopher Hans Jonas (1903–1993) formulated a set of ethical principles for a world in which man has severed all links with nature, and thus lost any feeling of responsibility towards the future of life on the planet that he calls home. Jonas's primary work, *The Imperative of Responsibility* may serve as a guide for anyone who understands that man is a part of nature, and not above it.

Jonas was a student of Husserl, Heidegger, and Bultmann. Whereas Heidegger conceived of man as being "thrown into" the midst of a strange and hostile cosmos, Jonas asked whether this wasn't simply a new version of the old Gnostic belief that situated man outside of nature. Although he began to realize early on that such a belief did not make sense, even in strictly biological terms, it would be decades before Jonas was able to formulate his own philosophy. In 1933 he emigrated from Germany to England, and two years later he moved to Palestine. During the Second World War, he served as volunteer in the British army; in 1948–49 he engaged himself in the First Arab-Israeli War. In 1949 he moved to Canada, where he became a professor at McGill University in Montreal. From 1950 to 1954 he lectured at Carleton University in Ottawa, and after 1955 at the New School for Social Research in New York.

Jonas's approach is not anti-modern, although he does break with the modern, Cartesian tendency to distinguish between the body and the soul. It is, rather, a modest attempt to articulate an ethics of a technological—and therefore modern—civilization. Why modest? Jonas observed man's development of knowledge with considerable scepticism. On the one hand, he saw that science (or better, the scientific industry) produces an unbelievable degree of "knowledge," but on the other hand, he realized that this knowledge does not lead to wisdom. This was not a new observation, but Jonas emphasized—like few philosophers of his time—the need for reflection as a prerequisite to research. He stressed that there is obviously no reason to place man above nature, and no reason why man's intellectual abilities should be considered as noble when they result in the destruction of mankind and the planet.

Modesty should be a means of coping with man's incredible power to change the world. Jonas named three decisive developments that could radically influence, endanger, or even deny future life: the extension of human life, behavior modification, and genetic engineering. Although scientists are quick to enumerate what they claim are the advantages of such technological developments, they ignore their potentially nightmarish possibilities. Of course, most people will agree that technology should be used to alleviate sick or disabled people of their pain and disabilities. But if, for example, genetic engineering is successfully employed to make people function more effectively in one way (for example, to alleviate depression), what will happen if this same technology is used to make people function more effectively in another way—to make them conform as unquestioning citizens, or rather, as servants?

Jonas realized that dreams of immortality and the mastery of nature have accompanied mankind since its beginnings, and have evolved from utopian fantasies into a possible reality that is now close at hand. He believed that the relentless exploitation of nature was a result of an anthropocentric ethics, and especially the Hellenistic/Jewish/Christian ethics, which placed man above nature, allowing him to regard himself as more worthy than other forms of life. He attempted to develop a "planetary ethics of responsibility." He emphasized that science itself is far too limited to explain the world in all of its detail, and thus can never serve as the basis of an ethical system. He even dared to consider nature as "sacred," which meant that he integrated elements of metaphysical belief that had been consequently disputed or denied by modern philosophers.

What are some of the important implications of Jonas's theory?

1. Scientific research must have limits. Jonas realized that the modern production of knowledge provides the basis for an almost unstoppable process of development. Jonas was convinced that even the scientific discovery of nature was but the first step towards the *manipulation* of nature. Therefore, the process of knowledge-production cannot be seen as isolated, but must be judged in terms of its foreseeable results. In an interview, Jonas pointed out that knowledge about the human body's reaction to radiation has been gained at too high a price, if it must first necessitate a catastrophe like Hiroshima.

2. We must learn to judge technical interventions into nature by their possible negative consequences. Furthermore, we must not only consider short-term, but also long-term consequences. The imperative of responsibility should make us aware of future generations who should have the same right as preceding generations to live on a planet that has not been totally exploited.

3. It is only if we regard nature as sacred and as worthy of protection from mankind's exaggerated opinion of itself, that we can act responsibly not only for ourselves, but also on behalf of future generations and other life forms.

All of these ideas obviously lead to a vehement critique of many previously established technological standards, and standards for life in general, but this is far too much to be covered in a small review whose purpose is simply to provide an introduction to Jonas's philosophy.

Jonas won many awards, among them the peace prize of the Deutsche Buchhandel (German Booksellers Society) in 1987. His critique of scientific amorality is naturally interpreted by many scientists—and by the economically powerful lobbies that support them—as a "horror scenario" that is far from reality. Nevertheless, Jonas's critique is based on a legitimate perspective regarding the process of research. Even with the very best of intentions, scientific innovations might still have fatal consequences. Erwin Chargaff, who discovered the decisive rule that allowed the human genetic code to be deciphered, has reached similar conclusions. He is now one of the harshest critics of genetic engineering, and of the belief that the application of such technologies will make life more comfortable.

Hans Jonas passed away in 1993, but his thoughts should remain with us for as long as we do not give up the hope of inhabiting a world in which man and nature are no longer opponents.

Thor Wanzek

Cassiodorus, Jordanes and the History of the Goths: Studies in a Migration Myth by Arne Søby Christensen. Hardbound, 391 + xi pages, with bibliography and index. Copenhagen: Museum Tusculanum Press, 2002. ISBN 87-7289-7104.

One of the more potent myths in European history belongs to the Goths, the loose confederation of fearsome Germanic tribes most famous for sacking Rome when the empire could no longer maintain its overextended dominion. Traced back earlier in time, the dark history of the Goths soon becomes a fog of legends about their obscure origins in the far North. The Gothic Myth veers into equally uncertain and uneasy pathways when followed forward to the modern age. Subsequent applications of the word "gothic" as a descriptive term for everything from medieval architecture to romantic poetry, horror literature, and even aspects of contemporary music and fashion, are all in some way related to the barbarian legacy of the Goths—and this is only another dimension to a myth which is, by its very nature, far more than the sum of its parts.

The history of the Goths has been a subject of heated scholarly debate for centuries, not to mention a question laden with political implications for those claiming to have inherited the blood of the ancient gothic kings. Across Europe from Spain to Scandinavia, Gothicism as an ideology has assumed various forms

Woodharrow Institute for Germanic and Runic Studies

The present cultural environment has proven itself rather unsupportive of traditional knowledge and as each day goes by this lack of support seems to increase. Those who have an interest in the preservation, promotion, and growth of education in the traditional cultural knowledge relating to the Germanic and Indo-European peoples now have a means to help remedy this kind of progressive cultural decay. It is the goal of the Woodharrow Institute to promote traditional fields of academic study relating to Germanic and Indo-European studies. It is our belief that the preservation of these studies where we find them, and their restoration where they have disappeared, will be of great benefit to society at large. It is our lack of awareness of our "culture of origin" that has led us to boredom within and conflict without. It is the goal of the Woodharrow Institute to provide access to academic and scientific research and methods to its general membership.

Educational Curriculum

Woodharrow implements its goals with a variety of effective means: First among these is the establishment of an educational curriculum in a full spectrum of traditional cultural studies, e.g., languages, literature, history, religious and mythic studies, and scientific runology. Woodharrow Institute courses are taught by individuals objectively qualified to teach at the college or university level. The Woodharrow Lore-House, or school, will specifically provide organized classes in the following fields: Language (German, Modern Scandinavian dialects, [Old] Icelandic and Old English), Cultural Studies (Indo-European culture, history of religious ideas, Germanic culture in the Roman Age, Migration Age, and Viking Age, Germanic myth and religion), Literature (history of Germanic literature before 1500, Old Norse poetry and prose, Old English poetry and prose, the Eddas, Romanticism and Neo-Romanticism), and Runology (older, younger and medieval, Anglo-Frisian and modern). Entry into the Lore-House is possible by application and the payment of a set yearly fee, which gives the student unlimited access to courses and resources.

Library / Archive

One of the main projects of Woodharrow is the development of a well-organized and sizable library collection of books, journals, offprints, and other archival material relating to Germanic, Indo-European, and runological studies. Libraries around the world have begun to neglect the collection of materials in these fields and so it becomes increasingly necessary for us to do it. It is hoped that a library facility can soon be erected and the collection moved to a location where it can be made available to the membership at large.

It has often been noted that the academic libraries around the world hold tremendous amounts of information that often proves extremely difficult to access for many who are interested in the material and who would greatly benefit from access to it. It is the goal of Woodharrow to collect such material and make it available to those who will be able to use it. The educational curriculum is, however, the essential key to being able to use this material, as much of it will be in languages other than English.

The library is the laboratory of our school. Here we can learn of the ideas of scholars who have gone before us, and carry out a dialog with them. This library will become a permanent collection and will be passed on to future generations of members of the Woodharrow Institute. They will depend to a great extent on what we are able to collect and organize for them now. If we neglect this task, even more information will be lost in the future. Woodharrow accepts tax-deductible donations of books and other material for the library.

Lectures and Classes

At present the Institute offers monthly talks in Smithville, Texas. We also offer lectures and classes to the public on a wide variety of topics of general interest. Among these are: "Our Mysterious Original Way of Writing: an Introduction to Runology," "Our Ancient Tongue: the Beauty of Old English," "Our Ancient Heritage and Destiny," "Our Ancient Heritage and its Importance for Today." Members of the Woodharrow speakers' bureau can present these and other topics to the general public, clubs and associations, or to public and private schools.

Runestone Project

Under the aegis of Woodharrow the "Runestone Project" seeks to re-establish the concrete expression of deep cultural values by erecting authentic major runestones in North America. These stones will be created according to traditional methods and techniques and will have as their underlying purpose the same motives that caused our ancestors to raise such stones in antiquity: memory of the dead and continuity of the deep values of our unique culture—as well as the everlasting fame of the carvers. These stones can be carved by rune-masters on a commission basis, or simply erected by the qualified masters.

The "Woodharrow Letter" and "Symbel"

The quarterly newsletter of the Woodharrow Institute is entitled the "Woodharrow Letter." This contains news of the Institute and its work in the preservation and restoration of Germanic studies, as well as shorter articles and reports on substantive issues in Germanic and runic cultural studies.

The annual journal of the Woodharrow Institute is called "Symbel." It acts as a forum for the presentation of the results of research in the fields of Germanic and runic studies, as well as other academic fields relating to Indo-European studies which might have played a part in the development of the Germanic cultural tradition. Articles which appear in "Symbel" will concentrate on mythology, religion, and the history of ideas. A major feature of the journal will be translations of older scholarly articles from German and the Scandinavian dialects, as well as reprints of older articles in English. Both The "Woodharrow Letter" and "Symbel" are available exclusively to members of Woodharrow.

Membership

What is needed at this time is for each and every person who feels it to be of vital personal importance to preserve and promote traditional knowledge and education in the ancient cultural values of the Germanic and Indo-European peoples to support the Woodharrow Institute. By becoming a member of Woodharrow you will be lending your tangible support to this worthy cause. Membership in the Woodharrow Institute is open to any and all individuals and families with an interest in the preservation and promotion of traditional cultural knowledge and values.

To become a member of the Woodharrow Institute, send a contribution (minimum $35.00, $25.00 for students with official student identification) to our offices, or write for a membership form to:

The Woodharrow Institute
Post Office Box 557
Smithville, Texas 78957
USA

Runa@texas.net

and made varying impact. Whether perceived in a positive or negative sense, the barbarian Goths have always had a remarkable power to capture the minds of men, much as they might have at one time seized and occupied an enemy stronghold.

The most famous historical text that recounts the story of the Goths was written by the sixth-century figure of Jordanes, who was at least partly of Gothic descent. This text is *De Origine Actibusque Getarum*, more commonly referred to as the *Getica*. Jordanes, in turn, allegedly based his account on a much longer (and now lost) treatise by an earlier writer, Cassiodorus, who had written his Gothic history at the request of no less than King Theodoric, a mighty ruler who became the stuff of legend. Up through the nineteenth century, Jordanes's work was accepted almost entirely at face value. In more recent times historians have found many reasons to question it. Nevertheless, most experts on Gothic history would rather not dispense with the book entirely, for despite its numerous problems and dubious statements, it contains a certain amount of material that is available nowhere else. The task for the modern historian of the subject, then, is to compare and corroborate this material with archeological, linguistic, and other historical evidence in order to see what still may be of relevance. Scholars such as Herwig Wolfram and Peter Heather, both of whom have written extensively on the Goths, have done exactly this.

Arne Søby Christensen, a history professor at the University of Copenhagen, would prefer to consign Jordanes to the dustbin once and for all, and hopefully deflate and discredit much of the Gothic Myth in the process. To this end, Christensen has done an extremely concerted job of deconstructing Jordanes's *Getica*. He makes countless valid points about why the account is at times unreliable, maybe even terminally so. His analysis is detailed and unrelenting; sometimes its repetitive assault takes on a near hypnotic quality. But it also often makes for fascinating reading, and is so thorough that it functions as a useful guidebook to the important textual material supporting and surrounding the Gothic Myth—whether from ancient sources or the heaps of modern academic secondary literature. Christensen provides extensive running footnotes and painstakingly translates almost all of the foreign language citations. Worthy of mention, too, is that his book is eloquently written, beautifully typeset, and exquisitely produced by the Museum Tusculanum Press. Its production values are far above most academic books these days, which only rarely justify their exorbitant price tags.

Christensen's study makes it quite clear that the foundations of the Gothic Myth do not necessarily rest on hard facts. Is there any reason, though, why they should? No mythic history can technically withstand the scrutiny of a modern scholar on such an obsessive mission as this. But no matter, for mythic histories exist in their own mysterious realm—one which lies entirely outside the quantifiable world of facts and figures. They are passed down like a Promethean flame through the imaginations of men, and they will continue to spark anew, sometimes when it is least expected. Despite years of inquests and autopsies—and Christensen's razor-sharp scalpel is only the most recent to be applied—the Gothic Myth is alive and well, and any belief in its imminent demise is surely presumptuous.

Michael Moynihan

Northern Lights: Following Folklore in North-Western Europe, edited by Séamas Ó Catháin. Hardbound, 377 + xxi pages, with illustrations and index. Dublin: University College Dublin Press, 2001. ISBN 1-900621-63-0.

Now in his seventies, the Swedish scholar Bo Almqvist devoted his career to the discovery of parallels between Celtic and Norse folklore. Although this has long been a topic of interest for those involved with Indo-European studies, Almqvist and his students believed that the extent of cultural interaction between these peoples in the eleventh and twelfth centuries has been largely ignored. It was during this period that Norse settlers, the remnants of earlier Viking expeditions, were integrated into Celtic society. At the same time, these settlers maintained ties to their Scandinavian homelands, thus insuring that mutually influential lines of cultural transmission remained open. Significantly, it was at this time that the Irish literary renaissance came about, while in Iceland, prose literature was beginning to take shape. In both of these traditions, there is ample evidence for cultural cross-pollination.

Northern Lights was assembled in Almqvist's honor, and so comprises twenty-eight academic articles devoted to this line of inquiry (although some of the essays deal only with some particular aspect of Celtic or Norse folklore, independent from Almqvist's context of Nordic-Celtic interaction). Obviously, it is impossible to summarize each contribution to this wide-ranging anthology, and I will not attempt to do so. (I should also mention that a handful of the essays are in Gaelic, and so are beyond my powers of comprehension altogether.) I will mention many of these briefly, and then pass on to a few ideas that seem particularly worthy of comment. Considered in its entirety, this is a valuable book—although some of the material included may be too specialized for many readers—peppered throughout with fascinating and useful information.

Editor Séamas Ó Catháin contributes an essay on parallel horse-dancing customs in Iceland and Ireland. He speculates that the Icelandic *vikivaki*—a banquet that featured a horse dance (or *hestleikur*)—might be related to Morris dancing, and other customs found in the British Isles. In one form or another, the horse seems to play a role in almost all of the Irish seasonal festivals, including Lúnasa. In "Mists, Magicians, and Murderous Children," Terry Gunnell explores the grim mythology relating to the Black Plague, which developed in Iceland between 1402 and 1495. Rory McTurk examines structural similarities between Snorri's prose *Edda* and the Middle Irish prose collection *Acallam na Senórach*. Both are presented as framed narratives, and each in its own way attempted to reconcile pagan and Christian traditions. There is also a substantial amount of material here relating to folk music. This is not surprising, considering the importance of music, particularly for the Irish—contributor Tom Munnelly reports having once seen the folk singer Edmund "Quizzer" Hoare singing "The Lady Leroy" in his sleep! Munnelly offers many such fascinating anecdotes as he recounts his career as a "songcatcher," or collector of traditional tunes. Among other things, he ruminates on the damaging effects recorded music has had on oral traditions, and the ideal setting in which to experience a song first hand. Some of his informants, for example, could only perform while engaged in housework or other chores, the times during which they ordinarily practiced their repertoire. H. R. Ellis Davidson (whose book *Myths and Symbols in Pagan Europe* is also devoted to Norse and Celtic comparative mythology) weighs in with an interesting piece on the significance of dreams in Celtic and Nordic culture. Post-Freud, dreams are typically thought of as emerging from an unconscious where unrealized hopes and fantasies lie buried. But in traditional societies, dreams were primarily divinatory. They were omens. Before the battle of Stamford Bridge, one of Harald's soldiers dreamed of a troll woman who rode on a wolf's back, devouring the corpses of the slain. Significantly, the heathen gods lived on as recurring dream motifs, long after they had ceased being honored during waking hours. In *Flóamanna Saga*, Thor appears in a dream to rebuke his followers for abandoning him for Christ.

Jóan Pauli Joensen provides us with an excellent article on Faroese wedding customs. For most modern people, holidays and rites-of-passage pass by with nary an acknowledgement. Those customs that are celebrated have been co-opted by greeting card companies and the marketing efforts of corporate retailers. But weddings involving the whole community, which lasted for days and incorporated complex rituals with a considerable historical lineage, emphasized the fact the marriage was the glue that cemented society together—and was more than just an arbitrary sexual and romantic compact between two individuals. Perhaps a return to this more solemn attitude might stem the tide of divorce and broken homes. For the Faroese islanders, weddings involved an array of ritualized dances, and a ceremony in which the participants accompanied the newlyweds to the nuptial bed (a common practice, which stresses that sex and reproduction are attended by communal responsibilities; even the New England Puritans utilized the custom). But it was the ritualized drinking—in which guests often consumed massive quantities of alcohol—that eventually brought down the wrath of the Church. The righteous indignation of the temperance movement would put an end to these traditions toward the close of the nineteenth century.

The volume concludes with Bodil Nildin and Jan Wall's "Beliefs and World View of a Swedish Crofter" (a crofter was a farm worker who was allowed a cottage in exchange for his labor). The folklorist Rudolf Lundkvist met a crofter named Johannes Rössberg around the turn of the century. Rössberg was an anomaly even then; a man for whom wood spirits, changelings, and water horses were very real presences. Rössberg relates how he once rescued a frog from his plow, because he suspected it might be one of the Hill People in disguise. Later, he says, the frog returned in the form of a young woman to express its gratitude. Like many rustics, Rössberg also had an intense fear of the dead.

Lundkvist relates one incident in which a mentally ill laborer died under Rössberg's watch. Rössberg went to considerable lengths to guard the man's corpse—lest it should reawaken.

It is no longer our lot to live in a world populated by spirits—whether malevolent or beneficent. But for all that, it is a lonelier place to be.

Joshua Buckley

Nationalism and the Nordic Imagination: Swedish Art of the 1890s **by Michelle Facos. Hardbound, 234 + xviii pages, with illustrations, bibliography, and index. Berkeley and Los Angeles: University of California Press, 1998. ISBN 0-520-20626-6.**

As a movement, National Romanticism flourished in Ireland, Belgium, Hungary, Poland, Russia, and especially Scandinavia, where it reached its pinnacle towards the close of the nineteenth century. In Sweden as elsewhere, the National Romantics' primary concern lay in preserving Swedish cultural identity from the fragmentation and dislocation they anticipated (and experienced) as a fundamental byproduct of modernity. Unlike the *völkisch* movement in Germany, however, the National Romantics were never simply reactionaries, nor could they be accused of the crude nationalistic chauvinism that characterized their German counterparts. Like William Morris and John Ruskin in England, they embraced the social reforms then sweeping Western Europe (women's suffrage, economic equality), while simultaneously seeking to preserve their own Nordic identity. Thematically, it was these dual political commitments that inspired their art. Nevertheless, National Romanticism never succumbed to the ideological overstatement of Soviet "social realism" or the bellicose pan-Aryanism of Nazi neo-Classicism. With its emphasis on creativity and intuition (and with an inevitable nod to Wagner), National Romantic art was an art that "sought to communicate on the level of music."

Like other nineteenth- and early-twentieth-century movements concerned with national identity, the National Romantics were consistent in celebrating the virtues of the peasantry. It was among the peasants, and not among the cosmopolitan bourgeoisie, that the line of cultural and national continuity had most maintained its integrity. But the peasantry embodied other values as well. Inspired by Nietzsche, National Romanticism rejected the otherworldliness of Christianity, and strove to invest the here-and-now, the immanent world of day-to-day experience, with sacred value. Although the peasantry has always represented the most naïvely pious segment of the population, they are also the most in tune with the natural rhythms of life. Even Nietzsche, for all his railing against the decadence of modern people, was the quintessential Western intellectual: sickly, neurotic, and sexually repressed. The peasant, or at least the peasant as imagined by the National Romantics, was a product of the land, physically hardened by the elements, comfortable with his own physicality, and noble and incorruptible in his bearing. Not surprisingly, this somewhat fanciful depiction of the agrarian working classes signified an even deeper desire to identify with nature itself. Ecological concerns (and particularly the growing threat posed by deforestation) soon joined the litany of other ills National Romanticism sought to address. An etching by Gustaf Ankarkrono (for Valdemar Lindholm's book *When The Forest Dies*) is significant, not least of all for its contemporary relevance. Standing solemnly amid a field of tree stumps, Ankarkrono depicted a gravestone inscribed: "Here lies Norrland's independent country folk. Corporations erected this monument."

Aesthetically, National Romantic art was united by its guiding spirit, and was never a recognizable "style" in the sense that Impressionism or Cubism might have been. From its inception, the National Romantics were self-consciously determined to distinguish themselves from French art, despite their admiration for French painters like Gauguin. Gauguin's engagement with Tahitian and other native traditions—motivated by his desire to reinvigorate Western culture by returning to the primitive vitality of its origins—mirrored the National Romantic fascination with Swedish folk culture and the peasantry. National Romanticism also embraced many of the themes then defining French Symbolism: imagination, dreams, history, legend, and myth. Still, National Romanticism was antithetical to Symbolist decadence and elitism, and while Symbolism drew heavily on its Greco-Roman heritage for inspiration, National Romanticism was strictly concerned with Scandinavia's mythic past. The overlap with Symbolism grew more pronounced as the rift with

THE LIBRARY AT LILLA HYTTNÄS.

Naturalism widened. Invariably, the latter had proven too limited to convey the ineffable and otherwise inexpressible aspects of the Nordic "folk soul"—a concept only approachable through abstraction. Individual artist's flirtations with Swedenborg and spiritualism exacerbated this tendency, as did an interest in paganism. Vibrant depictions of the Neolithic dolmens and menhirs rising up evocatively from the Swedish landscape were common. The National Romantic author Verner von Heidenstam's 1905 novel *The Tree of the Folkungs* chronicled the northern tribes' resistance to Christianity, and celebrated paganism as the true folk religion of the Scandinavian peoples.

But while many of those associated with National Romanticism have faded into obscurity, one name in particular has stood the test of time: Carl Larsson. Arguably the most famous Swedish painter of any school or era, Larsson's charming depictions of ruddy-cheeked Swedish children (and especially his own) continue to captivate the imaginations of modern viewers. Yet it was the Larsson home, Lilla Hyttnäs, which best exemplified the National Romantic project.

Historically, the home was what tied a man to his native land and it was the center of the life of the people, the place where one lived, loved, and died. It was important, then, that the home provide its inhabitants with a sense of rootedness in their own folk and culture, as well as providing them with a means to express their individuality. The Larsson home succeeded admirably on both fronts. The joint creation of both Carl and his wife Karin (whose participation reflected the National Romantic conviction that the most authentic relationship between the sexes was one of equilibrium), the Larssons were driven by the belief that one's immediate environment played a central role in shaping one's character. They built their own furniture, utilizing techniques perfected for centuries by peasant craftsmen. They covered their walls with decorative paintings and borders, a custom also passed down by generations of Swedish folk artists. Still, it is important to emphasize that this never degenerated into mere pastiche—the key was allowing oneself room for self-expression, within the confines of tradition. Even the children were encouraged to contribute. Stylistically, Lilla Hyttnäs fluctuated between the rustic peasant decor of its surroundings, and two eighteenth-century aristocratic fashions, Rococo and Louis Seize. This attempt to transcend class—at least in the realm of design—was emblematic of the National Romantic longing to articulate a Nordic identity that would cut across economic lines. Another Nordic quality Larsson sought to express was simplicity. Though his "folk home" was embellished throughout with bright colors and beautiful objects, it maintained an earthiness and a connectedness to the surrounding countryside. Larsson was also fervent in denouncing factory-produced and foreign-made accoutrements. "Become again simple and dignified," he wrote in *A Home*, "be awkward rather than elegant; dress in leather, fur, and wool; make household goods compatible with your heavy body; at the same time, let your hand naturally carve or paint on your furnishings the embellishments it can. Then you will be happy in the feeling of being yourself." Contrast this with the cheap manufactured décor of most modern homes, yet another reminder of the bland uniformity of global consumer "culture."

Nationalism and the Nordic Imagination is a welcome exploration of a folkish movement that succeeded in implementing its ideas in the real world, without falling victim to ideological or political excess.

Joshua Buckley

The Pagan Dream of the Renaissance by Joscelyn Godwin. Hardbound, 292 pages, illustrated, with bibliography and index. Grand Rapids: Phanes Press, 2003. ISBN 1-890482-84-6.

Joscelyn Godwin is an accomplished scholar in a number of disciplines, as anyone who has read his articles in *TYR*—or better yet, one of the many books he has written, edited, or translated—will be well aware. He is foremost a scholar of music, in particular its esoteric or metaphysical implications, but is also an authority on the history of theosophical (using the term in a broad sense) religious currents in Western culture. Godwin has translated important texts in these areas, but his most recent endeavors have related to the Renaissance, most notably with the first complete translation into English of the famous illustrated novel *Hypnerotomachia Poliphili* (The Strife of Love in a Dream), written by the monk Francesco Colonna (1433–1527) and printed by Aldus Manutius. This curiosity cabinet of a book is a wonder to behold, and bibliophiles everywhere should be grateful to both Godwin and his publisher, the venerable Thames & Hudson, for bringing forth an edition that so closely follows the contours of the original, even down to its artful typographical embellishments and idiosyncracies. It was presumably the charms of the *Hypnerotomachia* that also helped seduce Godwin into undertaking his work on the present volume.

The Pagan Dream of the Renaissance addresses a familiar topic—the resurgence of interest in the classical pagan gods during the Italian Renaissance—but from a specific perspective that makes the past come alive in an especially vibrant way. This is neither a study of Renaissance literature nor art per se. The focus here is on how the dreamlike, "poliphilic" longing for a pagan Golden Age manifested in the visual aesthetics of ornament and illustration,

THE GREAT MOTHER
NOURISHES HER GARDEN.
(DIANA OF EPHESUS,
VILLA D'ESTE)

and particularly man-made monuments, garden designs, and statuary, not to mention animated outdoor pageants and the musical dramas that later evolved into modern opera. Such romantic dreams of being pagan are of course just as alive today as they were in the fifteenth century, and many of the pageants and activities of the Renaissance aesthetes that Godwin relates would undoubtedly turn even the most ambitious and theatrically inclined modern neo-pagans green with envy.

While the notion of a Golden Age is often equated with a time of lost innocence, this is clearly a Christian idea. A pagan Golden Age is something else entirely. Pointing to the Platonic notion that earthly eros reflects the heavenly contemplation of universal beauty, Godwin proceeds to catalog an astonishing array of subtly heretical artistic expression that had freed itself from the confines of what was hitherto almost exclusively a Church-dominated territory. While the Church undeniably served as a patron for some of the arts, it also narrowed the scope of artistic expression down to a boring procession of the same tired old iconography. This forced artists to paint either portraits of the wealthy or endless—and often uninspired—variations on the Madonna and Savior, the Crucifixion, and other prescribed biblical themes. It was this "suffocating conformity," to use Godwin's phrase, that the poliphilic dreamers so boldly sought to escape. And the Church, no stranger to lavish excesses, largely turned a blind eye to the pagan imagery that became rife during the Renaissance (or else let its eyes be dazzled by these same earthly delights). At the heart of the pagan dream is the desire—which some might label Neoplatonic at root—to manifest a microcosmic reflection of an "imaginal" world governed by eternal laws of beauty.

After his detailed survey of how the pagan dream spurred the development of various Renaissance artforms, Godwin relates some of its latter-day manifestations at Louis XIV's Versailles and Ludwig II's fantastic castles. From this point forward, the pagan dream would only occasionally resurface, in a far less extravagant manner, in the writings of poets and philosophers. And while a glimmer of the dream was alive (as it always will be, so long as men walk upon the earth), its tenor had changed. As Godwin writes, "The need still existed for escape into an alternative world of the imagination, but it was no longer from the tyranny of a religion in which fewer and fewer people believed, and which had worn out its claws and teeth upon itself."

Godwin concludes by taking a look at how the pagan dream has been received in more recent times. When twentieth-century Traditionalists such as Ananda Coomaraswamy, René Guénon, or Julius Evola passed judgment on the Renaissance, they generally deplored it as a grandiose, humanistic step in the ongoing despiritualization of the world. Despite Godwin's admiration for the ideas of these men (he has translated works by the two latter figures), he correctly points out that their views too often succumb to easy and simplistic moralizing—exemplifying a wish to return to an age when the tyrannical power of religion had not yet cracked sufficiently to allow for any escape routes.

In the age of mass-market books that quickly end up pulped or become landfill, works like those of Joscelyn Godwin are to be treasured. *The Pagan Dream of the Renaissance* is no exception. Perfectly in accordance with its subject matter, it is a sensuous book. Godwin's prose seems more fluid than ever, and he delights in pointing out the tantalizing details of the various manifestations of his theme. Beautifully designed by Phanes Press and lavishly illustrated with artwork and photographs (a number of which were taken by the author), the book is full of imaginal wonders. The only thing that a reader might long for is that some of these images could have been reproduced in color. But really this just points to the fact that to fully experience these total environments, one must visit them in person.

The objects and productions documented in this book represent in many ways a magical reclamation of creative expression.

Such art was considered an aesthetic end in itself, but this also entails a definite functionality. And despite its debt to the pagan classical world, it may be "modern"—or even "postmodern"—in the sense of drawing at whim from all manner of past traditions, styles, and iconography. Sadly, there is very little art being made nowadays that can claim to evoke this kind of atmospheric wonderment. A poliphilic creation is not only the product of an artist's inner vision, but it holds the intoxicating power to entrance the viewer, or the visitor to the places where the art has been erected, and to seduce them into this very same realm, at least for a few fleeting moments. Except possibly in your own nightside dream world, it is unlikely you will be similarly charmed anywhere else.

Michael Moynihan

The Indo-Europeans by Jean Haudry. Washington, D.C.: Scott-Townsend, n. d. Softbound, 165 pages, with bibliography and multiple indexes. ISBN 1-878465-28-7.

There are many approaches toward reconstructing various aspects of Indo-European culture and the Indo-European worldview. Jean Haudry explains that his own work in this direction might best be described as "linguistic paleontology." This approach has been particularly fruitful (though the results are always attended with controversy) in proposing an original, Indo-European homeland, or at least a geographical area from which the Indo-European migrations might have begun. Through comparative linguistics, it is possible to isolate certain words relating to natural phenomena (types of animals, trees, plants, etc.) which point—with some degree of certainty—to a specific locale. Haudry devotes the final chapter of the present volume to this line of inquiry. However, he is mainly concerned with matters of ethics and belief, and at the reconstruction of what he calls a "virtual culture." By examining personal names, for example, we can surmise what virtues were held in esteem, or what sort of life a family might have hoped for its child to lead.

This is very much in keeping with Haudry's assertion that Indo-European society was oriented primarily toward the political. Georges Dumézil has famously demonstrated the tripartite structure of the Indo-European social hierarchy (priests, warriors, and herder-cultivators). It is significant that this structure was furthermore projected onto the gods themselves. Tripartition also recurs as a narrative framework in epic poetry, in medical formulas, and in more metaphysical doctrines, such as the three *Gunas*, or components of the soul, in the Hindu tradition. In a similar manner, Indo-European cosmogonic myths—though often difficult to interpret—appear to be concerned mainly with the establishment of political order. Against a primordial chaos, the founding acts of the gods can be seen as inaugurating an inviolable metaphysical structure based on "differentiation, hierarchy, and supremacy." As with other traditional cultures, Indo-European society was deeply conservative. With its origins firmly ensconced in the mythic past, the political and metaphysical hierarchy (tripartition) could not be called into question. At the same time, Indo-European religion was completely devoid of missionary fervor. Each social grouping had its own gods and rites that it guarded jealously. Thus, there was a tolerance for the beliefs of others. Religious wars and campaigns aimed at converting groups with different cults or initiatory orientations had no place.

Nevertheless, this religious pluralism should in no way be interpreted as implying that the Indo-Europeans were individualistic in the modern sense. What was important was an individual's place within the hierarchy, and his specific clan and familial allegiances. In ethical terms, this was a "shame culture." The best a man could hope for in this life was to have his exploits ("the fame of a dead man's deeds") celebrated in verse, which could then be recited with pride by his descendants. Conversely, the worst punishment that could befall a man was to be satirized. Satire, insofar as it dragged down the reputation of a man's entire family and clan, was often a reason for suicide. Indo-European poetry was characterized by its reliance on strict forms and "right expression"—it has been described by Benveniste as an "aristocratic style." This brings us to another important dimension of Indo-European ethics: the importance of truth and the carrying out of one's oaths and (usually familial and clannic) obligations.

One seemingly paradoxical aspect of Indo-European ethics is the Indo-European attitude towards wealth. On the one hand, we find the accumulation of possessions by the warrior aristocracy celebrated as a noble goal. A man's greatness can in part be inferred from the possession of great wealth. On the other hand, the third function's preoccupation with business affairs was looked upon as contemptible. The distinction, according to Haudry, is mainly historical. The wealth of the warrior was accumulated through conquest (cattle raids and land-taking), and was thus the product of a martial bearing, bravery, and prowess-at-arms. With the appearance of money, however, economic pursuits became the province of an altogether different segment of society. Wealth could now be amassed through the far less reputable practices of usury and business. An interesting corollary is to be found in the doctrine of the Ages, found in Hesiod and adopted in our own time by the Traditionalist school of René Guénon and Julius Evola. In the beginning, the first function (with the values that this function embodies) is in the ascendant. Following a long period of historical dissolution, however, the third function becomes more and more prominent. In this final stage, society—dominated by Nietzsche's "Last Man"—is geared entirely towards the production and consumption of material goods, physical security, and sensual comforts. Modern American society, for example, is a society almost entirely oriented towards these "third function" pursuits.

Joshua Buckley

The Encyclopedia of Indo-European Culture, **edited by J. P. Mallory and D. Q. Adams. Hardbound, 829 + xlvi pages, with illustrations and multiple indexes. London and Chicago: Fitzroy-Dearborn, 1997. ISBN 1-884964-98-2.**

Compiling an encyclopedia on a particular subject is undoubtedly a daunting task. When that subject is an entire culture, the scope of relevant material is even more formidable. In the case of the volume at hand, the intricacies are compounded further: the subject in question is, in fact, an "*ur*-culture" that subsequently spread out over millennia and developed into numerous disparate and distinct branches—some ancient and extinct, and others that extend unbroken into modern times. Taking all this into consideration, one can begin to imagine the depth and importance of what is referred to by the heading of "Indo-European culture."

It is not surprising, therefore, that there have been relatively few encyclopedic works that deal with Indo-European language and culture; two of the most notable are Julius Pokorny's *Indogermanisches Etymologisches Wörterbuch* (Indo-European Etymological Dictionary, 1959) and the earlier *Reallexikon der indogermanischen Altertumskunde* (Encyclopedia of Indo-European Antiquities, 1917–23) by O. Schrader and revised by A. Nehring. While much of the cutting-edge research into ancient European philology, archeology, and so on, has always been conducted and published in continental Europe, the study of the ways in which these relevant findings are reflective of an older Indo-European culture has had a healthy pedigree in the English-speaking world, and scholars residing in the United States have made especially strong contributions to the field. Judging from the list of contributors who have provided entries for this volume, the *Encyclopedia of Indo-European Culture* can be seen as the latest manifestation of this admirable legacy.

The encyclopedia is comprised of hundreds of alphabetically arranged entries referring to mental concepts, physical objects, key mythological elements, archeological researches, organic substances, cultural expressions, and so forth. The editors also provide a useful list at the outset which organizes the specific entries into a number of more general classifications such as "Activities," "Anatomy and Natural Functions," "Animals," "Emotions," "Food and Drink," "Law," "Mind," "Religion and Comparative Mythology," "Speech," "Time," and "Sense Perception," just to name a few. It is through an awareness of these fundamental elements that one may gain deepened insight into the essential web of beliefs that underpinned Indo-European culture and social institutions.

Entries tend to focus either on a lexical basis (aiming toward the reconstruction of Proto-Indo-European words), or may concern archeological and cultural matters. Given the intrinsic interconnection of language and culture, however, both types of entries continually overlap: a lexical entry might provide the linguistic background for a specific object or concept via a list of etymologically related words in various Indo-European tongues that refer to it (thus strongly hinting at its cultural implications). Conversely, a general entry might offer a succinct exposition of a concept in terms of Indo-European comparative mythology, archeological evidence, or other sources (while making frequent reference to relevant vocabulary). Whenever possible, general bibliographical sources are give for the subject entries. In this sense the book is a veritable goldmine for both the student and scholar alike, especially as it synthesizes a vast range of academic literature and allows for a relatively thorough grasp of the general state of Indo-European studies at the beginning of the twenty-first century.

Although guided under the able direction of J. P. Mallory, a work on the level of the *Encyclopedia of Indo-European Culture* could only be produced through the diligent cooperation and collaboration of a wide variety of scholars. It will never be truly "complete," since the ongoing study of the Indo-European past continues to enliven and expand our range of knowledge. As with any project of this breadth, the contents can at best provide a substantial framework, for which further work in all areas will continue to help shade in missing details, reveal new correspondences and connections (and new conundrums), and open up new avenues of study and interpretation. This process can already be seen in the fact that *The Journal of Indo-European Studies* has published two substantial commentaries on the book (see *JIES*, vol. 26, 1+2, pp. 279–288; and vol. 27, 1+2, pp. 105–163), both of which offer various suggestions for refinements and additions while at the same time praising the tremendous accomplishment which the book represents. Hopefully this encyclopedia will continue to remain in print, and be revised and updated for new editions in the coming years.

For the layman who wishes to gain an understanding of Indo-European culture, important surveys such as J. P. Mallory's *In Search of the Indo-Europeans* and Shan M. Winn's *Heaven, Heroes, and Happiness* will provide a sound basis. A weighty reference work like the *Encyclopedia of Indo-European Culture* is not the ideal place to start. But once a handle on the subject has been gained, then this volume will become a powerful tool for deeper investigations. It should be noted that Calvert Watkin's magnificent *American Heritage Dictionary of Indo-European Roots* fulfills a similar function with regard to linguistics, especially in relation to modern English.

While the archeological study of ancient cultures and the examination of extinct languages may seem like isolated pursuits, relevant only to the most specialized of specialists, the case of Indo-European shows how shortsighted such an assessment would be. It is through diverse work in innumerable areas that an informed glimpse into the early manifestations of Indo-European culture has been achieved, and it is via the continued cross-pollination of these disciplines that further revelations will arise. This likewise holds true for the study of specific later traditions, for example the Germanic or Celtic religious and social structures, and it is thus essential to have a basic understanding of their earlier Indo-European roots, as well as of their varied cultural cousins.

The adage that "you have to know where you have been to know where you are going" is more relevant than ever in the modern age. We are inundated with a dizzying flow of superfluous information and given unprecedented opportunities for almost unlimited movement, and it is easy to lose track of one's bearings. The most important core of these bearings, in both a figurative as well as literal sense, can be traced back to the worldview of our ancestors—a worldview that often still impacts upon our present, living reality. The *Encyclopedia of Indo-European Culture* represents a scholarly achievement of immense value for anyone who desires to understand the fundamental origins of ourselves and our culture, as well as that of a number of other related cultures, and we owe a debt of real gratitude to its editors and contributors.

A publication of this type, primarily aimed as a reference work for libraries, will certainly be cost-prohibitive for the average reader. It is therefore suggested that you request your local library to purchase the book for their permanent holdings, which will allow both you and others in your area to take advantage of everything that this seminal distillation of scholarship has to offer. Considering that the *Encyclopedia of Indo-European Culture* simultaneously illuminates and facilitates a greater understanding of the ancient cultural streams that resound right up to our present world, this volume deserves to be made accessible to the widest possible readership.

Michael Moynihan

Essays on Vedic and Indo-European Culture by Boris Oguibénine. Hardbound, 257 + xi pages with notes and index. Delhi: Motilal Banarsidass, 1998. ISBN 81-208-1499-1.

For Boris Oguibénine, a professor of Sanskrit and South Asian Studies at the University of Strasbourg, each branch of the Indo-European "family" places its emphasis on a different aspect of culture. The Romans, for instance, were politically oriented, and Dumézil has demonstrated that the most recognizable Indo-European elements are to be found in the founding myths of the Roman State. Vedic man, on the other hand, was deeply religious. The Vedas, the oldest extant Aryan sacred texts, deal mainly with sacrificial practices. The institution of sacrifice, it would seem, was what bound Vedic society together.

Oguibénine's essays are difficult reading and, like most scholarly books dealing with Indo-European culture, rely heavily on complex linguistic arguments that the non-academic reader must accept at face value. These difficulties are worth enduring, however, since there are a number of insights here that the student of Indo-European origins will profit by. As a *TYR* reader, I will assume that you might well fall into this category.

Vedic sacrificial rites, like those in other cultures, were designed to establish a link between the macro- and microcosm, and reflected the traditional belief that human beings had an important part to play in the maintenance of right cosmic order. Sacrificial rites also bound the community together. Vedic man's identity was shaped largely by the distinction between sacrificial participants, and the non-Aryan, non-sacrificing "others" on the periphery of society. Oguibénine discusses at length the relationship and social status of those who did participate in the sacrifice, the patrons who sponsored the rites, as well as the poet-priests who recited the sacrificial formulas. Of particular interest is Oguibénine's discussion of the Vedic warrior's place within this nexus. The Indo-European warrior, a component in the famous Indo-European *Männerbund*, is characterized as "one who is so self-willed as to show no regard for reasonable constraints, whether these be imposed by moral or religious obligations, the claims of fellow-feeling or compassion, the superior power of others, or the limitations of one's own body." Indra, the Vedic warrior god *par excellence*, is the protector of the community, and the bold subduer of the non-Aryan hordes. But he is also hopelessly addicted to the intoxicating soma, and prone to other sorts of excess. I will add a rather crude observation of my own: it is probably fair to say that, in practice, the *Männerbund* was not unlike the modern phenomenon of the "outlaw" biker gang. These were men you desperately wanted on your side in a combat situation. In times of peace, however, it was best to keep them as far away as possible from the women, children, and other more vulnerable elements of the community. In Germanic culture, the *Männerbund* always had this marginal, "outlaw" status, despite the heroism and unflinching bravery of individual warriors. Oguibénine argues that Vedic society was able to overcome this alienation of the second-function warrior more successfully. It was the cattle-raiding warrior who procured the sacrificial booty, thus entering into an integral relationship with the first-function poet-priest. In fact, the warrior's actions in battle were considered a part of the sacrifice, and the sacrifice itself—insofar as it laid down a dividing line between law-abiding Aryan and lawless non-Aryan—was often conceived of in martial terms.

The sacrificial linking of macro- and microcosm was generally described in terms of a "binding together" of elements within the terrestrial world to their divine, archetypal, counterparts. Oguibénine spends considerable space explicating the verbal formulas concerning the all-important soma sacrifice, which linked the embodied, "real" soma to the otherworldly, divine soma. There are many allusions to soma as a "steed" or "eagle" with the power to carry the soma-sacrificer beyond the immanent world, and into the world of transcendent essences. But I would contend that the metaphors in question might be more than just an attempt to explain the process by which the world "above" and the world "below" are brought into harmonious conjunction. There exists an entire cottage industry of books that have speculated as to what "soma" might have been. Clearly, it was an intoxicating, mind-altering beverage of some sort, and the powers attributed to it would further lead us to believe that it was far more potent than mere mead or beer. If soma was a drug, and particularly an entheogenic drug, than it seems likely that allusions to soma as facilitating travel between worlds were more than just symbolic. ("Soma," the Vedas tell us, "knows the way to the gods.") Like the henbane and belladonna witches' salves of the European Middle Ages, a strong dose of soma might have transported its imbiber to other dimensions in a very real sense. Strangely, Oguibénine entirely ignores the idea that soma's power as world-traversing "steed" or "eagle" might have been more than just symbolic.

The final essay in this collection deals with "primitive Vedic yoga." The word yoga is derived from the Sanskrit *yuj*, which means "to yoke" or "to harness." The poet-priests who officiated at the Vedic sacrificial rites were exercising yoga when, by reciting the appropriate formulas, they attempted to bind together the human order of their patrons to the divine order of the gods. This interpretation has survived among contemporary yoga practitioners. In *The Gita According to Gandhi*, Mahadev Desai writes: "[Yoga] thus means the yoking of all the powers of body, mind, and soul to God; it means the disciplining of the intellect, the mind, the emotions, the will, which the yoga presupposes; it means poise of the soul which enables one to look at all aspects of life evenly." As a linguistic and (to a lesser extent) religious concept, Oguibénine has identified Indo-European parallels in Sanskrit, Vedic, Hittite and Roman culture.

Joshua Buckley

The Nibelungen Tradition: An Encyclopedia, edited by Francis G. Gentry, Winder McConnell, Ulrich Müller, and Werner Wunderlich. Hardbound, 375 + xxvi pages, with index. New York and London: Routledge, 2002. ISBN 0-8153-1785-9.

Given the enduring fascination—not only of scholars, but also artists, writers, and the general public—for the legends of Siegfried and the Nibelungen warriors, the appearance of a comprehensive, single-volume reference work dedicated to this rich subject is a welcome event. This new encyclopedia is the fruitful cooperative endeavor of more than fifty Germanic scholars of various stripes from Europe, England, America, and beyond, and it draws on much more than merely philological, literary, or historical analyses of the source materials.

The material relating to different versions of the Nibelungen stories is vast, and so rather than just present what would be an overwhelming general assembly of alphabetical entries, the editors have first subdivided these into ten major sections, beginning with the primary works themselves and then covering areas such as "Personal and Place Names"; "Themes, Motifs, Objects, and

Key Words"; scholarship over the years; the literary reception of the theme in both the German-speaking and other spheres; music, art, and film inspired in any way by the Nibelungen stories; and much more. The breadth and number of the individual entries is remarkable—clearly the product of a focussed yet farseeing editorial vision. While minute aspects of the Old Norse Eddic and saga analogues are thoroughly covered (the editors note that they may have erred here on the side of all-inclusiveness, but users of the encyclopedia will be grateful rather than disappointed to discover this), as a whole the encyclopedia is probably weighted most fully toward the continental versions of *Das Nibelungenlied* (The Song of the Nibelungs).

In these Middle High German poetic texts what had once been a pre-Christian, orally transmitted set of stories (referring back to much earlier events), evolved into an epic heroic tale set in a more contemporary medieval context. Anonymously transcribed in a series of versions beginning in the 1200s, the old stories now feature both courtly and Christian overlays, the latter coming to particular prominence in the related tale of *Diu Klage* (The Lament [of the Nibelungs]). Although these Nibelungen stories must have been immensely popular in their day—especially among the noble classes who would have had the luxury of hearing them recited in the fullest way—at a certain point after the sixteenth century they faded into total obscurity. In Germany the situation changed abruptly when more or less complete versions of the *Nibelungenlied* were unearthed in the latter half of the eighteenth century among monastery manuscripts. In learned circles, where a strong bias toward the works of classical Antiquity was already in place, the rediscovery of such homegrown Germanic works was not always met with overwhelming enthusiasm. For example, when Christoph Müller dedicated the first complete publication of the *Nibelungenlied* in 1782 to Frederick the Great, the latter rudely responded, "In my opinion, such 'poems' are not worth a rap and do not deserve to be lifted from the dust of obscurity. At any rate, I would not tolerate such miserable stuff in my library but would toss it out!" And Goethe would later comment: "I have feasted at the Homeric as well as the Nibelungen table, but nothing is more in accordance with my character than the breadth and depth of ever-living nature, the works of the Greek poets and sculptors."

Despite the sometimes lukewarm initial reactions, the attraction of the *Nibelungenlied* grew steadily over time, and the entries in the encyclopedia that chronicle this evolving reception are illuminating. In the nineteenth century, interest in the *Nibelungenlied* was given additional fuel by a prevailing desire to assert a literary tradition that reflected a "German national character" possessed of its own distinctive traits. The importance of the poems as a source of inspiration for contemporary artistic and cultural endeavors arose within this same general context, most famously in the *Ring des Nibelungen*, Richard Wagner's a remarkable operatic adaptation and conflation of both the Old Norse and continental Nibelungen stories together with his own personal vision. References to characters and events in the *Nibelungenlied* also entered the rhetorical vernacular of nationalist politicians, a trend which probably reached its apex, unsurprisingly, during the 1930s. These efforts largely focussed on Siegfried as a prototypical national warrior-hero; the fact that he is actually a bit of a clueless oaf in the *Nibelungenlied* version of the story was conveniently overlooked when political propaganda was the order of the day.

The German and American editors of this encyclopedia state that it, "like all works of the genre, is less a finished product than an ongoing enterprise." They have done a brilliant job of assembling a vast array of material into a very user-friendly form, and one that will hopefully continue to grow in scope. A few subjects which this particular reviewer thought worthy of inclusion for future editions would include, in the "Themes and Motifs" section, entries on the function of "fate" in the story and also on the literary notion of the "dark figure" (as embodied by Hagen). The section on "Art and Artists" that relate to the Nibelungen tradition is remarkably extensive, containing the full spectrum from dramatists and fine artists to obscure nationalistic hacks and modern-day fantasy novelists, although the specific achievements of the more important and innovative figures among them, such as Fritz Lang, could have been discussed in deeper detail. In any case, the existing entries always provide good bibliographic suggestions for further reading and research. Missing altogether, however, is an entry on Hermann Hendrich (1854–1931), a well-known artist in his day who produced a large array of paintings on Wagnerian themes, a significant number of which relate to the *Ring des Nibelungen*. And while the "Miscellaneous" section contains an entry on the Nibelungenhalle built in Passau in 1935, the more intriguing Nibelungenhalle in Königswinter on the Rhine was overlooked. This distinctive, iconographically rich structure, erected in 1913 on the occasion of Wagner's centenary, was a collaborative effort between the aforementioned Hendrich and the Berlin architects Hans Meier and Werner Berendt. The building still stands today and remains an evocative repository for a number of Hendrich's *Ring des Nibelungen*-inspired paintings. In an adjacent garden is a large dragon sculpture, and the Nibelungenhalle also lies on the path up to the Drachenfels, where local legend has it that Siegfried slew the giant beast.

For anyone working seriously with the Nibelungen story—in any of its myriad manifestations—this volume will be an invaluable asset. The encyclopedia's preface notes that, much like the lasting fascination for the medieval Arthurian legends, "so, too, have Siegfried, the Germanic heroes, and the bold virtue of unswerving loyalty and death before dishonor which they incorporate endured the transition from the heroic to the present, decidedly 'post-heroic' age." The publication of *The Nibelungen Tradition*—in English, no less—is a further testament to that endurance. With the paucity of heroic and grand values in both the literature and conduct of the modern world now so widespread as to be nearly ubiquitous, those who see things through older, nobler perspectives may often feel like the company of doomed Nibelungen knights trapped at the Hunnish court: all hopes of victory may be dashed, but one can still take to heart the great heroic traits of resistance and willingness to battle to the end, even if only for the sake of one's personal honor. The old world of the Nibelungen is by no means less violent and senseless than our own, but it is one that nevertheless still contained vestiges of a timeless traditional and mythic realm, which surely accounts for a significant degree of its undiminished magnetic power.

Michael Moynihan

The Lobo Outback Funeral Home by Dave Foreman. Hardbound, 226 pages. Boulder: University Press of Colorado, 2000. ISBN 0-87081-602-0.

Dave Foreman began his career as an ecologist lobbying for the Wilderness Society in Washington, D.C. But, disillusioned by years of backpedalling on the part of the mainstream conservation movement, he was eventually forced to reevaluate his tactics. Together with four friends who had reached a similar impasse, Foreman founded Earth First! in 1980. Whereas the Wilderness Society had campaigned for wildlands protection on a small scale, Earth First!ers vigorously demanded that huge wilderness tracts be set aside and closed off to human intervention. Rejecting the humanistic bias of more conservative ecologists, EF! adopted the stance that wilderness *as such* is worth preserving, not merely as a resource for human beings to exploit, but *because it's there*. In contrast to the talk-radio stereotype of the ecologist as tie-dyed, Birkenstock-wearing tree-hugger, Foreman wrote: "It is time for a warrior society to rise up out of the Earth and throw itself in front of the juggernaut of destruction, to be antibodies against the human pox that's ravaging this precious, beautiful planet."

Not surprisingly, it was sentiments like these that caused fellow conservationists to denounce Foreman as a thinly veiled (or perhaps not-so-thinly veiled) misanthrope. Although the Left has typically championed environmental issues, it has consistently evaded the fact that its own ideals of unlimited progress and the economic elevation of society's lower strata are completely incompatible with a sustainable ecological vision. The awkward efforts of "social ecologists" to reconcile environmentalism with left-leaning humanitarianism merely accentuate this discrepancy. Nevertheless, as far as the general public was concerned, Earth First!ers posed a far greater threat in the lengths they were willing to go—often risking life and limb—"in defense of Mother Earth." For his part, in 1985 Foreman compiled *Ecodefense*, a handbook instructing its readers how to pull up survey stakes, spike trees, and destroy heavy construction equipment. Ironically, a section on dealing with federal and local law enforcement would prove especially useful to Foreman himself. On 30 May 1989, a nearly three-year FBI investigation culminated in an armed raid on his suburban Tucson home. Although they had almost no evidence, the Feds gave a press conference in which they alleged that Foreman was a "terrorist" who had spearheaded plans to cut the power lines into the Palo Verde and Diablo Canyon nuclear facilities. But despite wasting nearly two million dollars in taxpayer's money, the G-men never proved a thing.

The Lobo Outback Funeral Home is Foreman's first work of fiction and, predictably I suppose, it deals extensively with ecological themes. Nevertheless, Foreman has avoided most of the pitfalls characteristic of ideological novels (think *Atlas Shrugged*, *The Turner Diaries*, or the best-selling fundamentalist Christian "rapture fantasy" series, *Left Behind*). Thankfully, the book is neither preachy nor heavy-handed and, unlike the aforementioned examples, it lacks the epic, apocalyptic tone that similarly "committed" writers tend to lapse into. Instead, this is the story of one man's struggle to live up to his principles, even though—in the end—he knows it might all be for nothing.

Jack Hunter, the book's protagonist, is a largely autobiographical portrait of Foreman himself, and his crisis of conscience is all the more believable since we can sense that it is Foreman's own. Written in sparse, two-fisted prose reminiscent of Hemingway (or Foreman's old friend, the late Edward Abbey), *The Lobo Outback Funeral Home* is that rare thing: a political novel that actually makes for compelling and entertaining reading.

When Hunter arrives in New Mexico's Diablo National Forest, he has no intention of getting involved in ecological causes; a disgruntled former lobbyist for the Sierra Club, this is precisely what he is trying to avoid. He takes up work as a farrier, and soon finds himself providing sexual services to Jodi Clayton, the frisky but cynical wife of a local politician. Hunter's real love interest, though, is MaryAnne McClellen. A tough but kittenish tomboy, McClellen works in a bar—despite holding a Ph.D. in biology. She loves the Diablo just as much as Hunter does, and soon begins utilizing her feminine wiles to lure him back into the ecological fray.

At issue is the Forest Service's plan to open up the hitherto protected Diablo's Wilderness Area to clear-cutting. Besides fattening up the coffers of the local government, it is a scheme designed to stimulate the flagging rural economy. Nevertheless, the damage done to the Diablo's already fragile ecosystem will far outlast any short-term financial gains to the town, and MaryAnne casts herself as the plan's most outspoken opponent. This only enrages the locals. But despite the tide of negative public opinion, MaryAnne and Hunter (who is becoming more and more involved, if begrudgingly) have a secret weapon. Mexican wolves, supposedly eradicated from the Diablo decades before, have begun to reappear. If MaryAnne and Hunter can prove that the wolves have reclaimed the Wilderness Area as their habitat, they can force the Forest Service to capitulate.

If there is one criticism that might be levied against Foreman's novel, it would be that many of his characters (and particularly his villains) can seem like wooden stereotypes. Buck Clayton, a demagogic conservative politician, is a one-dimensional caricature (then again, most real politicians *are* one-dimensional caricatures, so perhaps he isn't so far off the mark). The goon-like Diablo loggers and other rural folk Foreman portrays are the epitome of tobacco-spewing lumpen proletariat (Foreman's refusal to lionize the working classes has long been a thorn in the side of his leftist detractors). Many readers will find the book's conclusion, in which Hunter is forced to take on several of these especially volatile mouth breathers, rather jolting in its brutality. There are also passages where Foreman's protagonists leap onto their soapboxes at inopportune moments. When MaryAnne launches into a diatribe about birth control and her unwillingness to mother children, we know we're being propagandized with Foreman's own ideas about zero-population growth. Which is not to say that there's anything wrong with zero-, or even *negative*-, population growth.

These minor criticisms notwithstanding, this is a fun, enjoyable book, which also serves as a nice introduction to Foreman's ideas about wilderness and the realities of environmental struggle. After all, it's not surprising that a deep ecologist would harbor literary aspirations. Aldo Leopold's *A Sand County Almanac*, arguably the text that started the movement, has received just as many accolades for its beautiful prose as it has for its political import. Philosophically, deep ecology's appeal to an emotional and spiritual identification with nature owes more to nineteenth-century Romanticism than it does to scientific arguments about PCBs or global warming. Hopefully, this won't be

Foreman's only attempt to express the same, through fiction.

Joshua Buckley

Masterworks: Arts and Crafts of Traditional Buildings in Northern Europe by Nigel Pennick. Softbound, 163 + vii pages, with illustrations, bibliography, glossary, and index. Loughborough: Heart of Albion Press, 2002. ISBN 1-872883-63-X.

Before its emergence as an academic discipline in the generally accepted sense, archaeology was preceded by antiquarianism. Though inflamed by the scientific spirit of the Enlightenment, the antiquarians were men whose passionate enthusiasm for prehistory (and—understandably—the fact that they were setting out in totally uncharted territory) often resulted in wild flights of fancy. William Stukely, who along with Aubrey Burl was perhaps the greatest of these proto-archaeologists, is mainly remembered for his recklessly speculative ideas about the Druids—ideas that still crop up even in educated discussions of pre-Roman Britain.

Modern archaeology, perhaps with an element of self-consciousness about these rather inauspicious beginnings, is the rigidly empirical domain of highly technical experts. The same can be said of modern "folklore studies"—at least in the universities, where folklore has taken its place as just another academic specialty. In the beginning, however, British folklore was the province of men (and often women) who sought to reconnect with their past in a meaningful, personal way. "Merrie Olde England," or at least so these nineteenth- and early-twentieth-century romantics imagined, was a place in which life had been far richer than it was in their own time—when Dickensian workhouses and Blake's "dark Satanic mills" had already cluttered up the landscape.

Today, this spirit finds its expression mainly among writers and researchers well beyond the pale of academic acceptability—whether they be ley-hunting dowsers, psychedelic neo-shamans, or goddess-worshipping eco-feminists. Although Nigel Pennick's books are for the most part based on extensive and often difficult research (the bibliography of the present volume is particularly impressive), they will never achieve institutional "respectability,"

AN EIGHTEENTH-CENTURY SOD HOUSE OUTSIDE REYKJAVIK, ICELAND, NOW CONVERTED INTO A MUSEUM.

if only because they lack the scholar's ingrained tone of detached objectivity. Pennick is a traditionalist, for whom folklore, mythology, archaeology, and other kindred subjects are meaningful because of what they can teach us about *ourselves*. Although Pennick seldom descends into crank territory (despite a few indiscretions early in his career), he *is* willing to interpret his material in a way that no academic would consider. If one accepts the idea that traditions are worthy of being preserved—or in some cases, revived—it cannot be otherwise.

Nevertheless, *Masterworks* is not a book about how to interpret the symbolic nuances of northern European architecture. Like much of Pennick's recent work, the book focuses instead on how architecture developed as a craft, how that craft was actually practiced, and—to some extent—how these traditions might be reestablished in a modern setting. The most obvious attempt at such a revival was the English Arts and Crafts movement, but there have been others—Pennick mentions National

Romanticism, as well as the Hungarian Young Architects movement. The most contemporary of the three, the Young Architects can be seen as a reaction to the loss of traditional skills under totalitarianism, and took as their inspiration the ideas of Károly Kós and the composer Béla Bartók. The fact that these movements utilized traditional techniques in conjunction with their own creative innovations is no contradiction. While any facet of the arts and crafts must conform to certain timeless principles, there is also considerable room for individual expression. For Pennick, it is these traditional principles that are important: not a rigid adherence to static cultural forms. While modernism erred in celebrating innovation for its own sake, there is nothing wrong with innovation per se.

Modern architecture also errs in what Pennick calls its "false functionality." He is especially vehement in denouncing the use of "new materials" such as aluminum, plastics, steel, and reinforced concrete. While they may save time and money in the short run, manufactured components tend to deteriorate in a way that timber, clay bricks, and other natural materials do not. Another advantage of using traditional materials is that they can be extracted directly from the land upon which a structure is to be built. This is more than just a convenience. A building so constructed lacks the intrusive quality of modern architecture, becoming instead a living part of its surroundings. This sense of balance and harmony—exemplified in styles like the Norman farmhouse—highlights the spiritual dimension that is an integral part of any traditional discipline. Pennick also details many unconventional building materials found in historic structures. Horse skulls have been discovered underneath floorboards in Suffolk, Yorkshire, Ireland, southern Sweden, and Denmark. While it is tempting to surmise that this practice once had some cultic significance, inhabitants of such homes have explained that the skulls are an acoustic innovation, calculated to "make dancing sound better."

Other fascinating bits of folklore are scattered throughout the text. Pothooks, also known as the "wolf's tooth," were the subject of numerous customs, and were often regarded as the main haunt of the house-spirit—an idea strongly reminiscent of the Indo-European religion of the hearth. As a symbol, the pothook also turns up in medieval heraldry. Decorative techniques like pargetting could also have a symbolic significance. But Pennick discounts the tendency of *völkisch* authors like Herman Wirth to immediately equate these with magical symbols or complex bind-runes. More likely is the idea that they were craftsman's marks, the meaning of which has long since been forgotten.

There is an abundance of technical information here that will probably be of less interest to the general reader, unless said reader intends to actually implement these techniques in practice. Which, I would assume, is part of the point. In contrast to the over-specialization characteristic of modern work, traditional disciplines integrated every aspect of human nature and culture into a cohesive whole, which could then be expressed in a tangible work of art. As such, these are traditions that can only be understood from the inside—by actually participating in them.

Joshua Buckley

The Oxford Companion to Fairy Tales: The Western Fairy Tale Tradition from Medieval to Modern, **edited by Jack Zipes. Hardbound, 601 + xxxii pages, with illustrations and bibliography. Oxford and New York: Oxford University Press, 2000. ISBN 0-19-860115-8.**

The *Oxford Companions*, as anyone who has enjoyed them can attest, are far more than mere reference works. Featuring many of the top researchers in the field, each volume contains an exhaustive number of entries, articles providing historical background, overviews of current scholarship, as well as beautiful—and often obscure—illustrations. These are books best enjoyed at leisure, on holidays or a rainy Sunday afternoon. Unlike most "companions," Oxford's fascinating, imaginatively designed editions seldom wear out their welcome. The present volume is no exception.

There are a number of difficulties in defining exactly what constitutes a "fairy tale," and the *Companion* allows for a surprisingly wide scope of interpretation. Fairy tales have also been subjected to a host of different interpretations, from the structuralism of Vladimir Propp to the Freudian and Jungian approaches more popular with modern readers. The most daunting question for scholars, however, concerns the origins of fairy tales. The idea that these stories began as oral folktales or wonder-tales has considerable romantic appeal, and certainly many fairy tales rely

MICHAEL AYRTON'S ILLUSTRATION FOR GIAMBATTISTA BASILE'S
FAIRY TALE "THE KING BEAST," 1634.

heavily on motifs derived from myths, sagas, and legends with roots in oral tradition. Herder stressed this aspect of the tales with great enthusiasm, igniting a flurry of nationalistic interest. For Herder, the canonical tales had an ancient lineage in peasant culture, and were invaluable expressions of the Germanic folk-soul. This ethnopsychological approach has been no less popular elsewhere. Early interest in Norwegian fairy tales, which are filled with trolls and other elements derived from native folklore, was driven by the desire to distinguish Norwegian culture from Swedish domination. In Germany, writers like Franz Heyden and Leopold Köster emphasized the genre's *völkisch* qualities. The most famous nationalistic collectors of fairy stories, of course, were the Grimm brothers. The Grimms asserted that the tales compiled in their books were derived from "oral traditions in Hesse and in the Main and Kinzig regions of the Duchy of Hanau." But while the Grimms did record many of their stories from those told by farmers and other working people, they ignored the possibility that the tales might have been influenced by the literary fairy stories already in wide circulation.

The authors of literary fairy tales, in turn, often looked to traditional sources. The Frenchman Charles Perrault was perhaps the greatest of these literary stylists, and his versions of "Sleeping Beauty" and "Little Red Riding Hood," remain the canonical standards. Though very much a man of the Enlightenment, Perrault also believed that no project of modernization could succeed which completely turned its back on the past. "France and Christianity could progress," he wrote, "only if they incorporated pagan beliefs and folklore."

Perrault's style was also influenced by the *contes de fées* being composed in the fashionable women's salons that existed between 1690 and 1715. French collections of literary fairy tales were typically presented within framed narratives, reminiscent of the *Decameron* or Chaucer's *Canterbury Tales*. Perrault's own much-celebrated *Mother Goose Tales* (1697) is but one example. Although Italy has its own rich fairy and folktale tradition, it would not be until our own century that Italo Calvino would set down a similarly definitive collection. In the British Isles, fairy tales were most popular in Ireland and Scotland. *Fairy Legends and Traditions of the South of Ireland*, by compiler Thomas Crofton Croker (1798–1854), was an oft-acknowledged influence on William Butler Yeats. Fairy tales also became the theme of many popular folk tunes, "Thomas the Rhymer" being but one of the more well-known examples. In England, fairy tales drew heavily on the Arthurian legends, as well as *Beowulf*. Beowulf's encounter with the dragon, for example, was the model for Smaug's death in J. R. R. Tolkien's *The Hobbit*. But English fairy tale enthusiasts had to contend first with the hostility of the Puritans, and later with utilitarian dismissals of anything that smacked of the fantastic. This, in turn, inspired Romantic interest in fairy stories, which the Romantics saw as a refuge from the tyranny of reason. Lewis Carroll's nonsensical *Alice* stories were very much a part of this reaction against industrialization and the creeping anxiety that modernization was divesting human society of meaning.

Fairy tales have not fared well in America. After World War II, American troops worked to purge the Grimm Brothers' books from German libraries, because of the books' purported nationalism. (The Nazis, like the communists, had attempted to enlist the stories for political purposes.) For most modern American children, exposure to the canon has come by way of movies and television. Some of these celluloid presentations have been quite good. I can remember enjoying Shelley Duvall's *Fairy Tale Theater* series as a child in the early eighties. I was also lucky enough to have parents who read to me, and encouraged me to read on my own. Most American children, however, have discovered the few real fairy tales that they know through the popular Disney films. Disney is infamous for bowdlerizing their material and—like the occupation troops in post-war Germany—removing every trace of national and ethnic culture from the stories. Disney's regrettable animated version of Hercules, for instance, features a Greek chorus singing Negro gospel songs. The Disney preference for "happy endings" also flies in the face of tradition. It should be remembered that the original Snow White ends with Snow White's wicked stepmother being forced to dance to death in redhot iron shoes, or that Carlo Collodi's *Pinnochio* (1883) concludes with the wooden boy being hanged! Although moral watchdogs have made a career out of whining about the effects of cinematic and video-game violence on children, it would seem that the young people of earlier generations were a far sturdier sort. Of course, it is simple enough to counteract the pernicious effects of Disney-ification: turn off the television, and read to your kids. If it's an American fairy tale you want, try Baum's classic *Wizard of Oz* books. While children will delight in Dorothy's adventures in the fantastical world of Oz, it is her oft-repeated appeal to the values of family and the Kansas farm country where she grew up that they will remember: "There's no place like home."

The *Companion* deals in great depth with the presentation of fairy tales in art, music, and "serious" literature. Wagner was an admirer of Gozzi's *Fairy Tales*, and his first opera, *The Fairies*, anticipated the use of mythological and folk-traditional themes in almost all of the composer's subsequent works. Puccini, Prokofiev, Rimsky-Korsakov, and Mozart would also try their hand at various tales, like the latter's Masonic fairy tale, *The Magic Flute*. Guillaume Appollinaire, Oscar Wilde, Jean Cocteau, Herman Hesse, and the South American magical realists would likewise explore the genre. The work of illustrators like Arthur Rackham and Maxfield Parrish has significantly influenced the way most of us imagine characters like Cinderella, Snow White, and Sleeping Beauty. The famous British folklorist Katherine Briggs wrote a series of modern fairy tales, and there are few children today who haven't heard of Swedish author Astrid Lindgren's Pippi Longstocking—the strongest girl in the world. Maria Gripe, another contemporary Swedish writer, has woven motifs from Norse and medieval mythology into stories like *The Glassblower's Children* (1964). The *Companion* even includes a short entry on Anne Rice, whose erotic, three-volume take on *Sleeping*

Beauty is most decidedly *not* for children.

A friend of mine recently quipped that the horror tales of Edgar Allen Poe and H. P. Lovecraft now seem quaint in light of the horrors one can experience by simply turning on the evening news. Like the Dadaists and Surrealists—who reacted to the cold realities of World War I by retreating into the irrational world of fantasy and dreams—the imagination remains the last safe haven for those of us who find the "real world" unbearable.

The Enchanted Forest beckons.

Joshua Buckley

Nine Worlds of Seid-Magic: Ecstasy and Neo-Shamanism in North-European Paganism by Jenny Blain. London and New York: Routledge, 2002. Softbound, 185 + xii pages, with bibliography and index. ISBN 0-415-25651-8.

On first glance, it seems odd that a large, predominantly academic press would devote an entire book to the contemporary practice of "seid" (derived from the Old Norse term *seiðr*) and related shamanic techniques within the northern European heathen subculture. Ásatrú/Odinism is itself still a very marginal phenomenon, and only a few academic titles have dealt with the movement at all—usually in a fairly unsatisfactory manner. Since seid practitioners constitute a minority-within-a-minority, whose numbers probably only encompass a few hundred individuals worldwide, one might wonder why Blain feels that the subject merits such an exhaustive examination. But Blain occupies a unique position. A senior lecturer in the School of Social Science and Law at Sheffield Hallam University, she is also a seid practitioner, and a part of the larger heathen "community." This being the case, her work is not so much the product of a disinterested outsider, but an attempt by an insider to explain the social dynamics of seid-work to an audience of (mainly academic) outsiders. The results are unusual, to say the least.

One problem with Blain's book is reflective of her position within heathenism, and the ongoing debates and divisions that characterize that subculture, at least at this point in its development. The deep divide between "folkish" and "universalist" heathens (see, for example, Stephen McNallen's article elsewhere in this issue) is present here, if only by omission. Blain is herself clearly in the latter camp, and writes as if folkish Ásatrú simply does not exist—except for a few allusions to "racist" heathens, a characterization that is itself misleading. By not mentioning people like Stephen McNallen and Else Christensen, who are essentially the founders of modern American heathenism, Blain fails to put her subject in any kind of recent historical context. To the uninformed reader, it would seem that heathenism, or Ásatrú, is simply a part of the broader New Age, and is derived from similar sources. But this is simply not the case—and the distinction is an important one. For Blain, heathenism is simply "part of the patchwork of postmodernity." Another annoying feature of Blain's book is her constant attempt to demonstrate that her subject matter is relevant in terms of modern academic fashions. While questions of gender certainly play a part in a discussion of seid, Blain's efforts to frame this debate in terms of "queer theory" are highly unsatisfying. Of course, "queer studies" is very much in vogue in academic circles, at least for the time being. Blain's efforts in this direction may just be an attempt to legitimate her topic for an audience of her professional colleagues.

Blain does do a decent job of providing us with access to the deeper historical background of seid and "spae-work," and spends some time on the allusions to these techniques in the sagas. (The two terms are used more or less interchangeably by modern practitioners, although there are some slight distinctions. In the sagas, for example, spae-work seems to have had more benevolent connotations.) There is much romantic enthusiasm for shamanism—and especially Native American shamanism—in American popular culture, thanks in part to writers like Carlos Castenada. I was somewhat worried, then, that Blain would overemphasize the importance of shamanism in the North. But she does not. She distinguishes between shamanic cultures, such as are found amongst the Amerindians, and shamanistic cultures—that is, cultures in which shamanism plays some part, but is not central to the life of the community. This was clearly the case in Northern Europe. Indo-European scholars have often pointed to the suspicions aroused by any type of "sorcery" in cultures ranging from the Vedic to the Germanic. In the North, *seiðr* was always viewed with considerable ambivalence. In his book *Nordic Religions in the Viking Age*, Thomas Dubois has speculated that this ambivalence could have been because *seiðr* was viewed as "foreign." Whether

or not the practice was adopted from the Sami or Balto-Finns, or developed through cultural interaction with these peoples, the sagas and other historical material are almost unanimous in relegating any kind of shamanistic practice to suspect outsiders on the margins of society. The most complete account of an actual *seiðr* "session" is to be found in the *Saga of Eirik the Red*. It is this one description that forms the basis of most modern "High Seat" or oracular seid-work, although the account itself is somewhat patchy and open to differing interpretations.

For the most part Blain's work seems to focus on the American Hrafnar group, led by the historical fantasy novelist Diana Paxson. This is not surprising, since Blain is herself involved with this organization. The goal of "making seid" could be divination, healing, or—in one practitioner's words—"soul retrieval." The Hrafnar method utilizes singing and drumming to set a certain mood. This segues into a sort of guided meditation, in which the seid-man or woman descends through the nine worlds, eventually arriving in Hel. Practitioners describe encounters with giants and etins, the spirits of dead ancestors, and even the gods themselves. One practitioner describes being "possessed" by Woden. One area of controversy involves the use of drugs in attaining these altered states of consciousness. Gordon Wasson, for instance, has described his experiences with the Mazatec shaman Aurelia Carreras. After eating thirteen pairs of mushrooms (!), Carreras made a number of very specific predictions about Wasson's family—all of which came to pass. Although there is certainly historic evidence for drug use amongst northern European shamans (some information along these lines can be found in the article by Christian Rätsch in this issue of *TYR*), the aversion most contemporary seid-people seem to feel for this kind of experimentation seems to be motivated more by the disapproving attitude towards drug use in Western culture, generally. There is some irony here. These attitudes are very likely Christian in origin. Consciousness-expanding drugs allowed their users access to other worlds and other perspectives. This is something Christianity—which sought to limit its followers' access to "orthodox" spiritual experiences sanctioned by the Church—could simply not tolerate.

Another ambivalent aspect of seid—which Blain spends much of the present volume discussing—is its relation to gender. Traditionally, *seiðr* seems to have been perceived as "women's magic." In the sagas, male practitioners of *seiðr* are almost always reproached for their "unmanliness." There are a number of reasons why this might have been the case, and Blain's own speculations are compelling. The first involves the use of *seiðr* for malevolent purposes. The modern, Hobbesian attitude concerning crimes against persons is that vengeance should be relegated to, and carried out by, the State. But in Indo-European societies, vengeance was the responsibility of the injured party. If a man raped your wife or daughter, or interfered with your ability to make a living, honor dictated that you hunt him down and deal with him directly. Since women lacked the physical strength for armed combat, a "magical attack" was a viable option. However, for a man to resort to these techniques might have been viewed as cowardly or underhanded. Simply put, in a man-to-man conflict, to use magic was cheating.

Seiðr also involved a loss of control, and an openness to being "possessed" by outside forces. In modern society, with all of its artificial safety nets, men (à la Robert Bly) can indulge their desires to run off to the woods, sit around in drum circles, hug each other, and cry. But in traditional societies, a man had to act as protector and provider. There were very real threats that dictated that a man keep his wits about him at all times, and maintain a hard, controlled exterior. Despite Blain's fashionable claim that "gender is constructed by the community," there are solid biological reasons why masculinity has—until our own rather decadent times—assumed this form.

Why Blain feels that either of these attitudes is inherently "homophobic" is a bit baffling. Although she briefly alludes to the idea that certain aspects of *seiðr* might have historically involved passive male homosexuality—something she never really substantiates—it does not follow that something unmasculine automatically equates with men having sex with men. Nevertheless, a number of gay heathens seem to have embraced seid-work, precisely because of its "unmanly" connotations.

I will voice one final complaint, albeit a fairly minor one. Most of Blain's fieldwork seems to consist of interviews conducted over the Internet, and her book is filled with excerpts from email correspondence. Blain's subjects are discussing spiritual techniques and experiences that, according to their testimonies, have profoundly altered and shaped their own lives. I am somewhat doubtful as to whether or not this profundity can really be expressed in an email. But this may just be prejudice on my part.

All in all, this is a book that is interesting on a number of levels, and your reaction—like my own—will probably be indicative of where you stand in relation to the broader Ásatrú/Odinist subculture.

Joshua Buckley

True Hearth: A Practical Guide to Traditional Householding by James Allen Chisholm. Softbound, 116 + vii pages, with illustrations, bibliography, and glossary. Smithville: Rûna-Raven Press, 1994. ISBN 1-88-5972-02-4.

Emerging as they do out of the larger occult subculture, there is a tendency for contemporary Odinist texts to focus on magical and oracular techniques like *seiðr*. But among our ancestors, these practices were limited to a tiny minority of adepts. Then, as now, they would have been entirely inappropriate for the vast majority of people, whose identities as craftspeople, husbands, wives, and parents were far more important. Unlike Christianity and the other "Religions of the Book," what was important in heathenism was how you actually *lived* your beliefs, and not just your adherence to an unbending creed, mediated by stodgy churchmen (who had, in many ways, fled from real life altogether). Heathenism was never entirely "magickal" (and certainly not in the highly intellectualized, ritualistic sense of Western occult groups like the Golden Dawn), nor was it in any sense "orthodox." Like the Greco-Roman hearth-religion—in which each man served as priest in his family's unique ancestral cult—paganism was a living religion, given to a variety of expressions. So long as these were "true" to the gods of the folk, they were acceptable.

James Chisholm is the former Steersman of the Ring of Troth, and it was in that capacity that he originally wrote *True Hearth*. I recently had the opportunity to hear him speak at the Rune-Gild International Moot in Texas. Chisholm's lecture focused on the "personal myths" which inflamed the men who fought and died at the Alamo. The attempt to demonstrate the relevance of mythical thinking, in a context germane to the history and location of the place where the conference was being held, accords well with the spirit of Chisholm's book. *True Hearth* represents a commendable effort to reestablish the home and family as the locus of a uniquely personalized neo-paganism, a view entirely consistent with historical precedent.

The book begins with an overview of the gods and goddesses of Germanic mythology, placing particular emphasis on their specific functions within the pantheon. While many modern pagans seem to honor the gods indiscriminately, it is far more appropriate to choose one specific god who suits one's station in life. To cite an obvious example, Thor—with his stoic determination and no-nonsense pragmatism—was the appropriate god of Scandinavian working men. Other trades had their own celestial patrons, and it seems likely that there was some fluidity of allegiance as a man or woman progressed on life's journey. But other spirits were present in the household as well. Chisholm delineates these in some detail, providing us with a field guide to the "wights of the house and garden": tompts, elves, dwarves (or dark elves), and trolls. The dises (or *dísir*) became especially prominent during the Viking Age. It was important to stay on good terms with them if one wished to maintain a smoothly functioning home, as they could serve as helpmates in matters of childbearing, health, and prosperity. Another kind of "helpmate" found in many homes are the family pets. *True Hearth* features an entire chapter on the lore associated with cats, dogs, and even more exotic animals—like the cuckoo bird, whose appearance in the North ushered in the spring. Other sections cover household décor, gardening, cooking, entertainment, and ritual. An appendix on brewing mead and an extensive collection of appropriate children's names are also included. I do take some exception to Chisholm's short sixth chapter, "Welcome to the Machines" (with apologies, no doubt, to Pink Floyd). His contention that the animism of the ancients—the reverential belief that even inanimate objects like stones were possessed of souls—be applied to modern household objects strikes me as a tad off-putting. When Chisholm writes "machines work better and more harmoniously when you think of them as living beings," it seems like an unnecessary concession to the vulgarity of modernity—especially if the machine in question is a dishwasher! The fact that most people already think of machines as "living beings" has contributed significantly to the dehumanization and rootlessness so symptomatic of the modern condition.

One of the advantages of heathenism is that it is a religion any honorable man or woman—from construction worker to college professor—can understand and practice. If reconstructionist paganism is to succeed, it must succeed as a broadly cultural phenomenon or lifestyle. It must be more than just another spiritual or magical option in the postmodern grab bag that is the "New Age." One would hope that books like *True Hearth* (or Edred Thorsson's similarly oriented *Book of Troth*), might contribute toward making it so.

Joshua Buckley

Sagaman and Storyteller:
A Conversation with P. D. Brown

Joshua Buckley

Almost all traditional literature—from sagas and folktales to fairy tales—began as part of a much wider body of oral narratives. Stories were told and retold, and passed on more or less intact from one generation to the next. Any man capable of holding a packed meadhall's attentions with one of these distinguished ancestral tales could count on his share of local celebrity. Storytellers were not only entertainers, but the repositories of an entire community's history.

P. D. Brown is a modern storyteller who appreciates the gravity and history of his craft. Listening to his tales unfold, one is struck by the artistry inherent in the telling. One might also be surprised by the discovery that the printed word can have more limitations than we moderns, acclimated as we are to "book learning," have ever even considered. Hearing a myth or saga recounted firsthand—and experiencing what our ancestors must have experienced when they heard that same myth—brings the material to life in a way that the printed page simply cannot do.

Brown is part of a company of storytellers that calls itself Hand and Word. He is often accompanied by drummers and a harpist, and performs regularly in schools, theaters, libraries, and festivals throughout the British Isles. His repertoire includes tales from Norse, Anglo-Saxon, Scandinavian, Welch, Scottish, Irish, and Cornish sources—as well as traditional English ghost and horror stories. But Brown's craft is also accessible to those of us without the means to attend a performance in person—although this remains the ideal way to really experience a story. Hand and Word have produced a delightful series of compact discs, including *Fire and Ice: Ten Tales of the North*; *The Battle of the Trees: Four Traditional Stories About Trees*; and *From The Celtic Bards' Heads: Three Tales of the Island of Britain*. These are available from Hand and Word's website: <www.hermetic.demon.co.uk/index.html>.

Currently, Mr. Brown is working on a double-CD of Icelandic tales, which will serve as his Master-Work of Lore for the Rune-Gild.

P. D. BROWN.
(PHOTO COURTESY OF P. D. BROWN)

How did you discover your vocation as a storyteller? Were you able to develop your craft solely as an individual, or did you have the opportunity to learn from other, more seasoned performers?

I listened to a tape recording of Robin Williamson telling a short version of *Tristan and Isolde* and a story called *Fionn MacCumhail and the Old Man's House*. I was impressed by the emotive power of the stories, and learnt them both by heart. In my early days of storytelling, I listened to tapes of storytellers, and if I liked a story and the way it was told, I would memorize it, including the tones and inflections. Without realizing it I was perhaps learning from more seasoned storytellers. But I wasn't sitting at their feet—I was sitting by my old cassette player!

I went to two storytelling "workshops" given by full-time storytellers, but found neither of them particularly instructive. I began to work on my own versions of the stories I wanted to tell, and found that this came quite naturally to me.

Scholars distinguish between many different types of stories—fairy tales, legends, memorates, fables, tall tales, and humorous anecdotes. How do your own stories fit within these genres, and what can you tell us about the different types of folktales, historically?

All the stories I tell are traditional and so will fit within one genre or another. I do a lot of storytelling in schools, and so have some truck with fairy tales and folktales. I do not tell jokes, anecdotes, or personal stories. I understand that the latter are very popular in the American storytelling world. I do enjoy Garrison Keillor's *Lake Wobegon* tales, more because of the way that he tells them than because of the type of stories that they are. I do not like fables, because of their moralizing tone.

I do like legends. Legends have some element of historical truth to them, which can neither be proved nor disproved. They are nearly always linked to a particular area. When people visit a place with legendary associations, their imaginations give them a sense of connectedness to the past—provided that the place is not too commercialized and overrun with tourists!

Other genres I enjoy and tell are ghost and horror stories. These are also often linked to particular places. Ghost stories have always been enormously popular in oral tradition and made the transition to a literary genre, a genre that peaked in the late nineteenth century and which even the all-too-real horrors of two world wars could not entirely dispel. (Britain is said to have, if every ghost story is to be believed, more ghosts per square mile than any other country in the world.)

The ghost stories, myths, and legends of northwestern Europe exert the strongest compulsion upon me to tell them. I feel a spiritual connection with them. They impart a sense of wonder about the land beneath my feet, rather than some distant "holy land." They tell of peoples, plants, and animals that I know of. It is in these mythologies and heroic epics that the relationship between the natural and supernatural, the realms of the living and the dead, and of the unclear, inconstant boundary that separates us from Otherness, is so strongly depicted. Even in our desacralized, supposedly rational culture, these stories can still hold a fascination for us, especially if we can—literally and metaphorically—turn off the electric lights for a while.

The Grimm brothers' distinguished between *Volksmärchen* (oral folk tales) and *Kunstmärchen* (literary fairy tales). What advantages do oral tales have over written versions? Do you feel that traditional stories can be reinvigorated for modern readers by converting the material back into oral narratives? Why is this important, in your opinion?

I think that an advantage of the oral tale lies in the shared experience of a teller and of those listening, whereas reading is not a performance but rather a solitary activity that throws the mind back on itself. An oral performance encourages both the teller and the audience to identify with the leading characters and to share their anger, grief, and triumphs. Oral tales are participatory.

Traditional stories can certainly be reinvigorated by "liberating them from the page." For me, this is the most important part of my storytelling work. It is important firstly because it affords the stories an opportunity to be heard by an audience who might otherwise never happen upon them. Secondly, it is important because it allows these tales to be presented in something of the manner in which they were originally intended. Thirdly, it is an activity that is not sight-dominant. Most popular culture is based around viewing screens. Even popular music is losing ground to the videos that go with it. People have to imagine their own visual representation of a story, seen by the mind's eye. I often see people listening to stories with their eyes shut.

Can contemporary events be memorialized in oral folk tales in any meaningful way? Some people have tried to treat urban legends in this light, but while many of these episodes are interesting, they would seem to lack the art that went into the traditional storyteller's craft.

I do not think so; storytelling is not part of our modern culture. People tell jokes and, to a much lesser extent, sing songs or are at least culturally conditioned to listen to singers. People understand what is happening when a joke is told, that if they listen to the end they will hear something which will, hopefully, make them laugh. On the other hand, when I tell people that I am a storyteller they often assume that I read from books. Sometimes I have told stories on occasions other than at a storytelling club or event where people, who have not before happened across what is still really a minority-interest revival, are looking around to see how other people are reacting—so they will know how to respond!

Urban myths are a genuine oral tradition. They always begin with a spurious pedigree of transmission such as "My friend told me about her mother's friend's doctor's son who had a terrible experience…," and usually involve an escaped criminally insane person or other modern bogey man. What interests me is that these tales are presented as being true, and are believed to be so by their audience—or at least they were believed, until published collections began to show how similar versions of the same stories appear on several different continents! What to us is a charming folktale of a traveler meeting goblins on the moors was once believed in this same literal fashion.

I do not think people nowadays would memorialize contemporary events in folktales, partly because there is so little commonality of interest and viewpoint. Oral folktales reinforce commonly held beliefs. In the fifteenth century witches existed, witches were evil, and they had supernatural powers. In 2003 people will hold widely divergent opinions about witches; one contemporary person's hero is another's criminal. Either view is more likely to be portrayed in a film or a book than in an oral story.

As a performer, you have worked with both children and adults. Are children, generally, a more receptive audience? Describe a typical performance.

Children are more at ease listening to stories. Stories are still a part of their culture. The age at which some children become too self-consciously "cool" to listen to stories is dropping and some deliberately do not listen—they are at school, after all!

I use a lyre, a bodhrán, and bones during stories, if and where appropriate. I use props, talking about my saex knife and pole-axe to introduce Viking stories. I will always tell some unpleasant and bloodthirsty tales as children are natural gore-hounds, and love to be revolted. They will always want to know if even the most outlandish tales are true. I either reply, "Yes, every word!" or say that the story is so old now, that no one knows. I also make the point that if a headless horseman were to ride through the classroom now, no one we told would believe us.

Modern people are constantly bombarded with manufactured "entertainment." Can a population so desensitized learn to appreciate a medium as nuanced as the oral folktale? Do you think these traditions will ever be accessible to the vast majority of people, again?

To the former question, I would say that it depends on the individual and whether the will-to-ignorance or the will-to-learn predominates. To the latter, I fear that these stories could not be accessible to the spoon-fed without becoming processed food.

Fermenting Moon Musick:
A Conversation with John Balance of Coil

Michael Moynihan and Joshua Buckley

When he was twelve years old, John Balance wrote to Alex Sanders, Britain's self-proclaimed "King of the Witches." Sanders shot back the discouraging rejoinder that Balance would have to wait until he was older before he could join the coven. Within a few years, Balance's enthusiasm for Sanders's brand of smoke-and-mirrors "witchcraft" had faded. But his willingness to pursue the shadowier side of human (and, perhaps, *more-than-human*) existence had not.

By 1980, Balance had begun publishing the early industrial music fanzine *Stabmental*, chronicling the activities of seminal groups like Cabaret Voltaire and SPK. His work as an underground journalist would eventually lead to a chance meeting with Peter "Sleazy" Christopherson, then a member of Throbbing Gristle. Christopherson had also been a part of the legendary design firm Hipgnosis, and would later make a name for himself directing music videos for everyone from Barry Gibb to Rage Against the Machine. But it was Christopherson's and Balance's mutual interests in Crowley, surrealism, avant-garde music, and the deliberate alteration of consciousness which cemented their working relationship. This partnership would form the core of Balance's "musick" group Coil, and a long and by now fabled career has followed.

Describing Coil's music is no easy task; each album can be seen as a sort of self-enclosed statement, and there is little stylistic continuity between one offering and the next. Early releases like *Scatology* and *Horse Rotorvator* alternated between bowel-churning dissonance and crystalline, euphonious clarity. Coil's often brilliantly subversive soundtrack work for European television commercials has been documented on the *Unnatural History* series of discs, while their original score for one-time friend Clive Barker's *Hellraiser* film was rejected by the major studios for not being commercial enough. *Love's Secret Domain*, perhaps the group's most accessible album, attempted to read early-1990s rave culture as something more than just aimlessly indulgent hedonism. Other projects have been decidedly more unusual. Coil have experimented with "sidereal sound," inspired by Austin Osman Spare's sidereal illustrations, and have created whole albums out of found sounds and studio glitches, reinterpreted as transmissions from a disembodied intelligence. Coil designed their *Time Machines* project to facilitate time travel, and calibrated each piece to the sensations brought on by a variety of obscure psychotropics.

But Coil's solstice albums, and their incredible, two-volume *Musick to Play in the Dark*, undoubtedly represent the most mature phase in the group's development. Balance has truly come into his own as a vocalist, while Coil's music seems to have achieved a certain consistency, despite remaining as challenging as ever—if not more so. Much of Coil's history has now been documented in David Keenan's laboriously detailed new book *England's Hidden Reverse: A Secret History of the Esoteric Underground* (London: SAF Publishing, 2003), which traces their career, along with those of occasional collaborators Current 93 and Nurse With Wound. Those new to Coil's intimidatingly varied catalog also have a much needed place to start: the recently issued retrospective, *The Golden Hare With a Voice of Silver*.

You have said that you were born with a "pagan sensibility." You have also spent years exploring the possibilities of magic, psychedelics, and other tools designed to alter consciousness. What is the relationship between these types of pursuits and paganism? One can practice magic, for instance, without being a pagan—and vice versa. But as far as you're concerned, are these things all somehow connected?

Yes, they are connected—most definitely, both in plain sight and also in the most subtle ectoplasmic and tendril-like ways. There are countless definitions of Magick and as many branches and paths that the pagan can travel down. I am a pagan.

I derive my inspiration and my life energy from the observation of, appreciation of, and intercourse with Nature. Natural Magick. Currently I am deep into a year-long encounter with what I describe as "PAN energy." I am closely bound together in this with Ian Johnstone, who I met last year and who has been a central effervescence, guardian, and guide throughout the tur-

"I ONLY HAVE EYES FOR THE BEETROOT."
(PHOTO COURTESY OF JOHN BALANCE)

COIL "MUSICK."

moils and trials that adhering to such a strange, rarely traveled path brings with it. This whole year has been one of new beginnings, dark echoes of previous events, and ghostly encounters. We have lived a raw-nerve procession of seasons. It is as if we are clearing dense, thorny foliage both for ourselves, and therefore in each of our personal lives, and also for others who come swiftly behind in parallel explorations.

As regards psychedelics, narcotics, and vegetable allies, I presently only have eyes for the beetroot.

Shamanism is the root and the branch and the leaf of my particular World Tree. Last year when Coil played live it seemed very much to be an ending of one sort of exploration and mode of expression. I had a particularly lonely and hard winter and was thrown into a bleak place the likes of which I have never encountered before. A dark night of the soul. The worlds of politics and art and spirituality and of almost every belief and inner drive and enthusiasm for life and for living were tested until I nearly broke.

I think I did break, in fact, but was mended again over time with my friends' help and especially with Ian's help, for he never stopped believing in me despite the ugly distortions that I was creating and presenting outwardly, lost in the shamanic tangle. I became a *shame-man*, revolted to the point of acute rejection and illness by what "Man*un*kind" was doing in the world and to the planet at large.

Now I'm out the other side of this crisis and am full of joy and am finalizing my turnaround. Ian and I, along with Simon Norris and others, are planning a printed project, or rather, series of projects, under the overall name of *ONE*. There will be a magazine (Pan-zine?) and printed posters and broadsheets, etc. I feel that to set into word and image the results and conclusions, the catalyzing ideas and images that we have imagined and evolved and worked on, and most importantly *lived* this year, is the way forward. To make a mark and a difference we now have to publish and disseminate the PAN ideas and beliefs. These include organic gardening and food production, growing and working with medicinal fungi, establishing and encouraging private press editions, public poetry readings, performances and events, reducing and making people aware of light pollution, reducing consumption of everything, buying locally, helping establish woodlands with native species of trees, reactivating old ceremonies and traditions. I don't mean that we ourselves will be doing all these things all the time, but we will attempt to inspire via *ONE* a sense of place and purpose. There is an excellent organization doing this kind of work already called Common Ground. They are based in the U.K.

One of Coil's most ambitious projects in recent years has been the *Moon's Milk* cycle of musical works for the solar/astronomical quarter days. Each equinoctial or solstitial piece appears to have been begun in one year and completed at the same time the following year. What led you to conceive this project, and how did you see it through to completion—did you make initial recordings on one equinox and then set them aside, only reapproaching and finishing them a year later?

I was interested in exploring time in *musick*. And musick in time. I coined the phrase "Musick cures you of time." I was interested in the phenomenon of literally being "lost in musick." I wanted Coil to play continuously for a week, eating and sleeping where we played for a whole cycle of time, working in shifts to ensure the chain of events and expression was never broken. One person could play for twelve hours solo and then be joined by the rest for forty minutes. All sorts of combinations become possible. The individual becomes part of a much larger and boundless vehicle of sound. Moving to a larger house by the sea where the tides and their cycles can be seen from many of the windows deepened my sense of ebb and flow, of lunar rhythms and patterns and the whole procession of the seasons. When Sleazy and I lived in Chiswick, London, we used to take our two basenji dogs for walks down to the river Thames. It was a five-minute walk from Threshold House. The Thames has a high tidal volume and there were times when you could literally walk on the exposed riverbed. In these walks and at this time I became very aware of the moon and its power and influences and I decided to begin to call our work with Coil "Moon Musick." This meant that instead of working with preconceived and structured pieces, we would trust to chance and intuition. Nearly all the lyrics and vocal takes from the solstice/equinox series were one-offs. First takes. I didn't have any words or ideas written down in advance (actually I would have a vague notion or theme in mind, but this was deliberately left fresh and unformed until the recording of my vocal). The result is there to hear. Some of the words are sounds and impressions and are unformed, not finished, but that is how they are meant to be. I had to learn to trust to my inner system of images and poetics. The same went for the majority of the actual sounds you hear—the musick was written live. Improvised. Bill Breeze's extraordinary viola parts on *Moon's Milk* were one-take performances. The only thing we did was to edit and select the pieces and sections that worked best for our purpose, and to shape the final songs from the streams and shards that the experiment became.

We did record at the correct astrological time to the best of our admittedly limited knowledge. If mistakes were made they are excused by the fact that we remained faithful to the spirit of the adventure. The bones are all shown there and they are all bare or partially concealed by after-work and tidying up. Yes, we did record passages and then set them aside until the time was again right. They were left to ferment with Moon Juice.

Coil has always had a reputation for confronting the darker aspects of existence—chaos, violence, and deviant sexuality have been recurrent themes throughout most of your career. In recent years, however, you seem to have moved towards a more earth-centered type of spirituality (although not at all in the regrettable, New Age sense). In the end, is this where the "path of excess" has led you?

Personally I found that the path of excess leads to the palace of excess, and to insecurity, neuroses, a profound disillusionment with almost everything, and an insurmountable depression. I have never been one to do things by halves and I have suffered as a consequence of my youthful adventures with the Left-Hand Paths. I ended up on antidepressants and found myself burdened with the ugly common yoke of alcohol abuse and addiction. I am currently free of these ordinary and dismal traps. I wish I had never gone onto antidepressants. They were a nightmare to come off of and my doctor, along with nearly all the medical industry, seems to want people *on* the fucking things. I recommend that everyone read the fantastic Feral House book *Pills-A-Go-Go*.

I was profoundly depressed. I needed a *deep-rest*. To be surrounded by Nature and natural things was the way in which I eventually walked away (well, with more of a lopsided hobble) a free man.

Now I find a time to be silent with myself every day. I exercise my voice and my body by chanting and singing. I am swimming more and most of all I'm going out into the countryside and just being there in it. Finding a deep spiritual drive and energy from immersing myself in the green and in the wood and in the water and the light that plays on the water. I'm in love and of course that helps enormously, but fundamentally being alone in Nature provides all the psychic nutrition my soul needs. Anything else is a joyful and heart-bursting gift. I still carry an intrinsic deviancy with me wherever I go. It's part of my askew take on the universe. I revel in the gnarly, the crippled, the liminal, and the sidereal. Distortions, outcasts, hybrids populate my crepuscular celebrations. Polymorphous perversions. All horned animals!

It would seem, then, that relocating to the British countryside played a significant part in your spiritual development.

Indeed it did. We have a young oak forest right behind our house—in fact, the garden merges with it. We have an Iron Age fort directly above our house, and evidence of a very early goddess-centered temple in the middle of the woods. The local museum has a small white stone statue of what looks to me very much like Astarte that was found up in the woods in the 1890s. The remains of a Roman altar were found in the garden next to ours around the same time. There is a place on the narrow steep peninsula that our house is located on where you can hear the sea on both sides of you, and it mingles with the sound of the dry leaves rustling to create a very special place.

Zinnober : Ästhetische Mobilmachung

Industrial : Apocalyptic Folk
Military Pop : Avantgarde
Psychedelia

Tradition : Blood Mysticism
Apocalypse Culture

At least three issues per year.
Contact us for promotional information,
wholesale prices, etc.

Zinnober
www.zinnober.net
zinnober-magazin@gmx.net

P.O. Box 3166
54221 Trier
Germany

Zinnober # 6 Out Now

Michael Moynihan's Interview with Dr. Stephen Flowers
Pierre Drieu La Rochelle – The Man and His Times
Factrix

76 pages of interviews, articles and reviews.
All text in German.

Regular contributors include Markus Wolff (Waldteufel)
and Gerhard (Allerseelen).

Reviews: Music

Goldfrapp—*Felt Mountain* (Mute)

As pop records go, Goldfrapp's *Black Cherry* is far more imaginative than 99% of what slides off the music industry's assembly lines, even on a good day. Still, *Black Cherry* feels like Alison Goldfrapp's attempt to reinvent herself as an alt-pop diva, along the lines established by Björk (or her fellow Icelander Emiliana Torrini). Even if *Black Cherry* lands her in Top 40 territory (and it very well might), *Felt Mountain* will remain Goldfrapp's masterpiece.

Of course, the Hampshire native was no stranger to pop music when *Felt Mountain* was recorded. During a performance art piece in which she yodeled while milking a cow, Goldfrapp was "discovered" by members of Orbital, who gave her a guest slot on their *Snivilisation* LP. Later, she spent two years touring with trip-hop giant Tricky. There are definitely elements of electronica on *Felt Mountain*, which slinks along with the kind of subtly percussive ambience one might find on a Massive Attack record—albeit without the "urban" edges. Goldfrapp's musical accompaniment is provided by the soundtrack composer Will Gregory, and her live performances have incorporated strings, guitars, and percussion. In keeping with Gregory's craft, the music on *Felt Mountain* is breathtakingly cinematic, while Goldfrapp's singing (not to mention her yodeling and whistling) enfolds the listener in swathes of opulent sensuality.

Perhaps one reason *Felt Mountain* differs so dramatically from *Black Cherry* is the environment in which it was created. For the six-month duration of the project, Goldfrapp and Gregory sequestered themselves in a cabin on a Wiltshire hillside, and much of the album was recorded outdoors, under the stars. It shows. Weirdly alternating between Weimar decadence (comparisons to cabaret revivalist Ute Lemper are unavoidable) and what might only be described as a sort of tweaked-out Alpine mountain music, *Felt Mountain* might be the most unusual big-selling album in recent memory. The beautifully realized packaging (also assembled by Goldfrapp herself) is similarly evocative of the mountain landscapes that helped inspire the music. The back of the CD contains a *Wandervögel*-style photo of the peaks, while the gatefold opens up to reveal a German forest glistening with snow. Goldfrapp's lyrics—mostly "cut-up" fragments that hint at sexual innuendo, murder, and other perversities—will only further confuse the perplexed. "Utopia" may be the first pop song ever written about eugenics (or at least that's what I think it's about), and has subsequently been re-issued as a remastered, "genetically enriched" mini-CD.

Ultimately, it's practically impossible to describe a group that have claimed influences ranging from Carl Orff to Burt Bacharach to Ennio Morricone to vintage Detroit techno. Suffice it to say, Goldfrapp are living proof that modern music can still transcend its own clichés, and that there remain unopened paths for artists—with a little ingenuity—to explore.

Joshua Buckley

Sigur Rós—*Rimur* E.P. (Krunk)

Sveinbjorn Beinteinsson, who died in December of 1993, single-handedly spearheaded the reconstruction of the old religion in Iceland, and served for years as the Allsherjargoði of the Icelandic Ásatrúarfélag. It was thanks to Beinteinsson's tenacity that the Ministry of Justice and Ecclesiastical Affairs officially recognized the organization in 1972. But Beinteinsson was also instrumental in reviving interest in *rimur*—Icelandic sung poetry, which features verses "of varying length and form, often with extremely intricate rhyme schemes." Beinteinsson also used his knowledge of *rimur* to reconstitute the lost art of epic singing, which was once such an integral aspect of pre-Christian Scandinavian culture. Unfortunately, his efforts were for the most part ignored or ridiculed by the Icelandic literati. But among some younger Icelanders, Beinteinsson's work struck a chord. In a seemingly bizarre twist, the "grand old man" of Icelandic Ásatrú found himself appearing on albums by groups like Purkur Pilnikk, Kukl, and Þeyr (all three of which featured future members of the Sugarcubes, Björk's old band). Beinteinsson even contributed a solo performance to the Enigma compilation *Geyser: An Anthology of Icelandic Independent Music of the Eighties*. Later, he would work with Psychic TV, and a meeting with David Tibet would result in a full-length LP of his poetic recitations being re-released by the

SVEINBJORN BEINTEINSSON.
(PHOTO COURTESY OF RON RENIEWICKI)

United Dairies label as *Current 93 Presents: Sveinbjorn Beinteinsson: Edda*.

Nearly ten years after Beinteinsson's death, the *rimur* traditions he championed are getting another boost from the hugely popular Icelandic group Sigur Rós. Unlike the groups who once worked with Beinteinsson, Sigur Rós have garnered the attention of an audience that spans continents. Though sometimes compared to Radiohead, Sigur Rós's music is hardly typical of any mainstream music genre, however "alternative." Although employing electronic instrumentation, the group has striven to recreate the feel of traditional music. One key player in Sigur Rós's development has been the soundtrack composer (and ex-Psychic TV member) Hilmar Örn Hilmarsson, who himself was recently elected head of the Ásatrúarfélag. For Hilmarsson, the attempt to reinvigorate traditional material by wedding it to commercially accessible rock'n'roll is deliberate. "We [Icelanders] lost most of our folk music, our traditional dances," he explains. "They were seen as obscene, so they were outlawed by the Danish in the eighteenth century. It is left to us to rebuild our ancient culture."

On *Rimur*, Sigur Rós (Kjartan Sveinsson, Jón Birgisson, Georg Hólm, and Orri Páll Dyrason) are joined by the 49-year-old fisherman and *kviðamaður* (*rimur* singer) Steindór Andersen. Andersen has worked for some time to bring *rimur* singing to the public's attention, and it stands to reason that this latest collaboration will net him his biggest audience yet. To Sigur Rós's credit, their musical manipulations never overshadow Andersen's performance. Surging and undulating with an understated force, the music adeptly accentuates Andersen's stirring delivery (less gruff, and more listenable to untrained ears, than Beinteinsson's). Unfortunately, the six-song EP contains no liner notes or other texts, so it is difficult to tell when, or under what conditions, the music was actually recorded.

Andersen's work with Sigur Rós, however, continues. In April, 2002 Sigur Rós, Hilmar Örn Hilmarsson, and Steindór Andersen were joined by the London Sinfonietta and a choir known as The Sixteen for a performance of "Odin's Raven Magic" at the Barbican Concert Hall in London. According to the program notes, attendees were told to "expect epic, cinematic, ambient soundscapes ... expect to hear archaic folk music mutated through contemporary analogue studio technology; expect dramatic, beautiful music which taps into thousand-year-old stories." As of this writing, the performance has been nominated for the Nordic Council's 2003 music prize.

Sveinbjorn Beinteinsson, one might imagine, would be pleased.

Joshua Buckley

Ostara—*Kingdom Gone* (Eis & Licht)

Ostara rose out the ashes of Richard Leviathan and Timothy Jenn's previous band Strength Through Joy, and promised to tread a different musical path. And though the advance single *Operation Valkyrie* still featured that familiar acoustic guitar, the rest of their debut album *Secret Homeland* consisted of fairly straight-ahead pop numbers, on which the duo was aided by what seemed like jazz-pop session musicians. The result was equally despised and loved.

Since then they have perhaps realized their stylistic mistakes, and taken new approaches that ennoble their pop stylings in unexpected ways. This was obvious on the *Whispers of the Soul* 10" which featured some of the songs that ended up on this second full-length outing, *Kingdom Gone*. Gone are any of the arguably tasteless touches of the first CD; instead, Ostara deliver taut, rhythmic arrangements that are a perfect vehicle for Jo Richard's dynamic cello playing, especially on "The Trees March North." The strongest of the pop songs are "Never Weep," which is dominated by Jenn's emotive vocals and guest drummer John Murphy's interesting rhythmic groundwork, and the anthemic "Bavaria." Another standout track is "Life's Symmetry," again with vocals by Jenn. Indeed, lyrically, Ostara's material sometimes approaches poetic brilliance and takes the listener into the often dark abysses of the spiritual quest and the yearnings of the soul.

These proper songs are interspersed with more experimental pieces like "March of the Rising Sun," an instrumental, martial collage with loops of Japanese dialogue. The Japanese theme is also found on two pseudo-techno tracks; "Tatenokai," named after the private army, or "Shield Society," of the famous Japanese writer Yukio Mishima, and "Divine Wind," an analog meditation on death. The well-paced album culminates in the title track, a spoken lament obviously written after 9-11, in which Leviathan ponders the "Inferno of History" and the passing of traditional empires and cultures.

In a recent interview in *Zinnober* magazine, Leviathan summed up the attitudes behind the album thusly: "The absence or the passing of something great is as important as its presence and might even be the force that makes the search for this presence possible."

Markus Wolff

Leger des Heils—*Aryana* (Eis & Licht)

Legers des Heils is a relatively new German project which has released a few limited-edition vinyl records that failed to impress this reviewer. The music was characterized by stilted English vocals and martial and neo-classical clichés. However, this CD, presented in handsome packaging with beautiful photographs by Orplid's Uwe Nolte, marks quite a welcome departure from that

LEGER DES HEILS.
(PHOTO COURTESY OF
EIS & LICHT)

predictable course. The synthetic orchestration has improved, with acoustic instruments thrown into the mix as well. But most importantly, the vocals are now delivered in German, and sung very well. And like Belborn before them, they have been influenced by the electronic pop sensibilities of the 1980s German New Wave movement, with interesting results.

The instrumental overture "Erwachen" is followed by "Geistesmahnung," a song dominated by resonant bells and powerful vocals insisting that "the world is yours." In line with its title, "Tanz des Lichtes" is a bright, catchy "dance of light"—a fanfare for a gay science. "Orchestral" Depeche Mode would be an apt description for some of these arrangements; the poppier, later work of the Hungarian group Actus also comes to mind. "Heimat" (Homeland) is the standout track here, a strident march driven along by snares and a watery sample, with vocals that remind the listener "the path to the origins is still open to us." "Ewige Gegenwart" (Eternal Present) is exemplified by brilliant lyrics and strange, fast instrumental parts breaking into a catchy chorus. This CD is definitely only recommended for those with a weak spot for synth-pop or those familiar with the German language, even though the expressed sentiments might appeal to many others as well.

Markus Wolff

Niall and Cillian Vallely—*Callan Bridge* (Compass Records)

When two virtuoso traditional instrumentalists collaborate to record an album, the results are bound to be exciting. When the two are also siblings who grew up playing together, this lends a great potential for further synergy to the whole endeavor. Such expectations will not be disappointed in the case of the Vallely brothers' recent album *Callan Bridge*, named for the place in county Armagh (Ulster) where they are originally from.

Uillean piper and low whistle player Cillian Vallely has made an international name for himself as a member of Lúnasa, the popular band led by flutist Kevin Crawford. Their high-energy live performances are legendary, and Cillian's fast and rhythmically precise piping style provides a driving element that powers some of Lúnasa's most memorable tunes. Niall Vallely plays the concertina with breathtaking agility, no mean feat in itself, and previously was a prime mover in the band Nomos, not to mention performing with his partner, acclaimed singer Karan Casey (formerly of Solas).

CILLIAN AND NIALL VALLELY.
(PHOTO BY JÖRG KÖSTER)

Both musicians have busy touring schedules, which meant that the material on *Callan Bridge* had to be pragmatically recorded over a period of time as opportunity arose, and at different studios on both sides of the Atlantic. Although assembling albums across distances and from disparate sources is made relatively easy by modern technology, the final result will often lack the same cohesion that an album would have if it were recorded all in one concentrated session. But with the Vallely brothers, this was hardly a hindrance. Even with limited rehearsal time, their intuitive and synchronous ability comes instantly to the fore when they perform alongside one another. This is powerfully evident in live concerts, but just as much so on these recordings. Their able accompaniment from friends like Donal Clancy and John Doyle (the latter also a Solas alumnus, and now a brilliant solo artist and concert partner to crack Chicago fiddler Liz Carroll) in the States, and Paul Mehan and younger brother Caoimhín Vallely in Armagh, always enhances the end result.

The Irish (and greater "Celtic") folk music revival has been going on strong for many decades now. Like any popular genre it can at times suffer from a glut of mediocre releases, and there are unfortunate results when bands fall prey to over-producing their recordings or aim for a sentimental, wider audience. But the Vallely brothers make none of these mistakes. They have created an album worthy of repeated listening, with a choice of material that is both varied and exemplary. Some of the tunes on *Callan Bridge* were learned directly from traditional mentors, some were brought to life from old written transcriptions, while others are rollicking original compositions written by Niall. At the hands of these masterful players, the old and the new flow seamlessly together—which is exactly what the best traditional music should do.

Michael Moynihan

Various Artists—*Infernal Proteus: A Musical Herbal* (AJNA)

> "Now these nine herbs against nine super-spirits
> against nine poisons and against nine infections."
> —*The Nine Herbs Charm*, ca. 1000 C.E.

In fact, there are more than nine herbs represented on *Infernal Proteus*—AJNA's incredible "musical herbal" features forty contributions from different musicians, each conceived as a tribute-in-miniature to the healing (and oftentimes mind-altering) properties of a specific plant or tree. Herb charms (*The Nine Herbs Charm* is merely the most famous) abound in medieval literature. Rife with elements of folk wisdom that undoubtedly predate the arrival of Christianity, they are a concrete example of the convergence of magical and early scientific thinking. But even in modern times, herbs have retained their special aura. It is this sense of the mysterious—of a mystical communion with the earth and its fruits—which lies at the heart of the music on this collection. In some instances, the contributors interacted with their chosen plant in wholly unconventional ways. According to the liner notes, one "song" features the sound of a violin bow scraping across the herb's leaves; another was composed on an instrument built entirely from the plant itself. Still other performers allowed the herbs to influence them by more direct routes. It is probably safe to assume that the Lotus Eaters' "Marijuana"—which builds to a droning crescendo of chaotic, funhouse distortion—was produced amongst clouds of thick, potent smoke. So much of late-twentieth-century music has been.

But assembling four compact discs of previously unreleased material was only part of the task AJNA founder Tyler Davis took upon himself in bringing *Infernal Proteus* to fruition. Bound together in a 96-page, hardbound book (which will sit more comfortably in your library than among your other CDs), the album is as visually stunning as it is conceptually interesting. Each contributor was asked to provide a fitting illustration to accompany their music, and *Infernal Proteus's* pages are filled with beautiful paintings, photographs, and drawings. The cover, a striking oil painting commissioned from artist Madeline von Foerster, is as memorable as any of the music you will find inside. California-based illustrator Benjamin Vierling's "Papaver Somniferum" provides the perfect visual complement to The Red King's song of the same name. Not surprisingly, it is an homage delivered with some misgivings. Though it has been an essential tool of traditional healers, and is still perhaps the most important modern anesthetic, the opium poppy's most infamous derivative—heroin—has long been the bane of rock stars and art-house nihilists alike.

Austrian esotericists Allerseelen provide the song "Edelweiss," while Waldteufel's "Eibenlied"—on the yew tree—is an appropriate choice, considering Markus Wolff's fascination with Germanic culture and mythology. The yew is associated with the Norse world-tree Yggdrasil, and has consistently resurfaced as a symbol of death and immortality. As late as the eighteenth century, yew boughs were deposited in coffins and graves in English funerals. Another plant with a sinister reputation is the mandrake. Annabel Lee's group Alraune (so named after the mandrake dolls that were once a popular component of European folklore) has crafted a suitably haunting tune in its honor. Though regarded as a powerful soporific, analgesic, and aphrodisiac, one medieval tradition has it that the mandrake could be seen growing from the ejaculate of hanged men.

In spite of the magnificent packaging, I can't help but voice one minor complaint regarding the way *Infernal Proteus* is organized. A track listing is provided in the book, of course, but no indication is given as to where one disc ends, and another begins. This makes it annoyingly difficult to maneuver from one song to the next. When I mentioned this to a friend, he pointed out that the pages of the book are color-coded in a way that is supposed to remedy the problem. As I never managed to figure this out on my own, however, it doesn't seem like a very effective solution. Next time, number the tracks!

AJNA does seem to have divided up much of the material here in terms of style or genre—disc one seems to consist of more structured material ("songs" in the traditional sense), while the other three discs are primarily ethereal and atmospheric (although there are some exceptions here, as well). As such, most of the real standouts appear during the first hour of listening. Hekate's "Wegewarte" juxtaposes joltingly sensual female vocals with a subtly massing, then violently exploding, white noise attack. Venereum Arvum's "The Heavenly Gates," based on a traditional English May carol, is one of the best attempts at medieval revivalism I've heard. B. Sedayne, who would appear to be the driving force behind the quartet, has described his music elsewhere as "Proximal Indo-European No-Age Ambient Exotica"—don't expect to find this category in the bins at your local record shop any time soon. Sedayne's piece segues nicely into In Gowan Ring's "Dandelion Wine." Endura's use of an old Hogarth print to illustrate their song "Medicine of the Poor" (hops) is appropriate. With its bustling, chaotic tempo, the song is a vivid aural snapshot of the muddy, boozy, eighteenth-century English inner city, where ale- and gin-houses were the only respite for the overworked and underfed. Apoptose's "Eichensiechtum"—on Donar's mighty oak—typifies the sort of surging, undulating noise that fleshes out most of the remainder of *Infernal Proteus's* playing time.

My earlier gripe about the track-listing aside, this is a fantastic achievement, and everyone involved should be proud that they were able to bring such an ambitious project to completion at all. While many compact discs (particularly those in the American, jewel-case format) have a cheap, disposable quality about them, AJNA's meticulous packaging and obsessive attention to detail sets an impressive standard for what this medium could be. Someone suggested to me an excellent idea for a sequel, and in the hopes that AJNA will take them up on it, I'll add my voice to the chorus: now that the herbal is finished, how about a bestiary?

Joshua Buckley

Therion—*Secret of the Runes* (Nuclear Blast)

Northern Tradition–loving heavy metalers might remember Black Sabbath's album *Tyr* some years ago, and the relevant references therein. But this CD is something else, as befitting ten years of progress. Swedish heavy metal band Therion have created a remarkable piece of operatic metal that in eleven songs tells of the coming-into-being of the nine worlds of northern cosmology, and the Way of Odin. With classical musicians and opera singers, the excellent musicians of Therion take us from Ginnungagap through Midgard, Asgard, Jotunheim, Schwarzalbenheim, Ljusalfheim, Muspelheim, Nifelheim and Helheim. The songs, mainly in English, but also Swedish and German, masterfully echo the feel of each world. Occasional invocations, such as "Thursar! Jotunheim! Resar! Jotunheim! Jotnar! Jotunheim!" and "Jormungand! Nidhogg!" combine with a deep understanding of the nature and meaning of the northern gods and goddesses. Here is a piece of totally contemporary Northern Tradition music that needs to make no apologies. "Somewhere behind the border of the known world you may hear the drumming and the heavy steps of the giants."

Nigel Pennick

Ewan MacColl and Peggy Seeger—*Classic Scots Ballads* (Tradition)

I first heard Ewan MacColl on a folk anthology that featured the song "Go Down Ye Murderers" from MacColl's 1960 album, *Songs From the Gallows*. There was something primal about the way MacColl sang that song—it sounded the way a folk song should. You have probably heard MacColl's songs too, although you might not have known it. During his lifetime he composed over 300 original pieces, including "The First Time Ever I Saw Your Face," "Dirty Old Town," and "The Manchester Rambler."

MacColl and his longtime companion Peggy Seeger were also tireless collectors of traditional music from the British Isles. Of particular interest were the Scottish songs and stories MacColl absorbed at the feet of his parents. MacColl even cultivated the myth that he had been born in Scotland, although the general consensus is that he was christened Jimmy Miller in Salford, Lancashire in 1915. But there is no doubt that the whole MacColl (or Miller) family was steeped in an atmosphere of tradition. Until her death in 2000, MacColl's daughter Kirsty was well on her way to an established career of her own. Some might recall her duet with Shane MacGowan on the Pogues' classic "The Ballad of New York." (The Pogues' version of MacColl's "Dirty Old Town" was also one of their more popular renditions.) In addition to his work as a musician and folk-archivist, MacColl was also a successful dramatist. George Bernhard Shaw once opined that he was the best living playwright in Britain besides, of course, Shaw himself. And, like Shaw, MacColl was a life-long socialist.

On the one hand, it is easy to understand the connection between folk music and socialism—folk culture is, by and large, the common currency of the workers and the socially disenfranchised. But it is nonetheless difficult to reconcile an artist like MacColl's insistence on folk music's ethnic and national-cultural component with Marxist internationalism. Both MacColl's and Seeger's Singers Club and its successor, the Critics Group, encouraged their members to perform songs that had been written in the performer's native language, and which had emerged from a culture in which the performer himself had been brought up. The purpose was to preserve the songs in such a way that their original intent and "feel" would not be lost. In most (but not all) instances this was simply not possible when a song was transplanted cross-culturally into an inappropriate idiom. The folksinger—according to Seeger—must act as "a representative of a culture ... interpreting a song that had been created within certain social and artistic parameters."

In the liner notes, MacColl further explains that the purpose of recording *Classic Scots Ballads* was to present Scottish folk poetry in song (the way it was intended), and to perform the songs in their original lowland dialect, rather than in watered-down, modern English versions. Nevertheless, Seeger would later lament that the album had not been more authentic (*Classic Scots Ballads* was recorded before the Critics Group instituted its strict standards as to what did or did not constitute tradition). Seeger's accompaniment, on guitar and banjo, is certainly not historically justifiable. Still, it lends itself considerably to the intimacy of MacColl's style. Even at this early stage, his voice had the rich earthiness and depth that is the hallmark of the seasoned storyteller. And these songs are stories, first and foremost. These include Jacobite "protest songs," romantic ballads, and bothy songs (a "bothy" was the type of shack in which farm laborers lived). The latter were sung by Scottish farmhands, and include tunes like "The Monymusk Lads," about a ploughman's efforts to outsmart his employer. "Glasgow Peggy" and "The Trooper and the Maid" also fit within this genre. MacColl's mother taught him "The Gairdener Child," which recounts its protagonist's thwarted attempts to woo his beloved. All in all, this is a magnificent record, and an important artifact of the early Folk Revival. The reissue was long overdue.

Joshua Buckley

Värttinä—*Live in Helsinki* (NorthSide)

Karelia sits poised between Russia and Finland, and this unfortunate geographical situation has been the chief catalyst driving much of its history. Always a source of contention, parts of Karelia were ceded to the Soviet Union during the Winter War (1939–40), and the Continuation War (1941–44). But culturally, Karelia has been vitally important to Finland. The *Kalevala*, Finland's national epic, consists largely of mythology and folklore culled from northern Karelia. The region has also inspired a number of visual artists and musicians. The composer Jean Sibelius's "Finlandia," as well as the lesser-known tone poem "En Saga" and the four "Lemminkäinen" legends, all draw on Karelian themes. The Karelian people are of primarily Indo-European origins, with a small admixture of Uralic stock.

Värttinä was founded in 1983, having developed out of an informal youth group devoted to the preservation of Karelian folk poetry and music. The group's first incarnation featured fifteen female vocalists, accompanied by six male musicians playing instruments like the guitar, tin whistle, and the *kantele*—or Finno-Ugric "table-harp." As Värttinä evolved, they also began exploring other aspects of the Finno-Ugric tradition. The group would eventually incorporate material from Setuland, Mariland, and Ingria. The 1992 *Seleniko* album was the crystallization of this progression, and featured several original compositions, as well as updated rock/pop arrangements. It debuted to considerable crit-

VÄRTTINÄ. (PHOTO COURTESY OF NORTHSIDE)

ical acclaim, and entered the European World Music charts in the number one slot.

Only three of Värttinä's original members are present on *Live in Helsinki:* Mari Kaasinen, Janne Lappalainen, and Kirsi Kähkönen. Susan Aho joined the group for 1998's *Vihma* album, and is present here on vocals. Aho is also a member of the group Vaeltajat, and—like many of Värttinä's personnel over the years—has been involved with Sibelius Academy's Folk Music Department. Other musicians contribute accordion, bouzouki, saxophone, double bass, violin, drums, and guitars. But Värttinä are a vocal ensemble first and foremost, and beautiful female harmonies have always been the group's biggest appeal.

So much for background. As for the music, it is not at all what you might expect—at least if you haven't heard Värttinä before. These women sing with such force and intensity—often matching the tempo of techno or other electronic dance music—that it's a wonder they are ever able to get in a breath. Imagine Enya played at 45 RPM, and you'll get the idea (although the comparison—I realize—is an unfortunate one). All of Värttinä's music isn't like this, but they seem to have selected some of their most up-tempo pieces for this live engagement—and it must have been quite a show. Despite the frenetic, rollicking pace, however, the singing is always tight and on key (the use of extremely close harmonies gives this a somewhat strange quality, at least initially), and the rapid-fire delivery belies a simmering feminine sensuality. Several of the selections are based on mythological themes. Both "Viikon

Vaivane" and "Hoptsoi" (the album's only instrumental track) are structured around Karelian and Ingrian rune songs (a rune, in this sense, refers to "a Finnish poem, or division of a poem, especially one of the seperate songs of the *Kalevala* "). "Ukko Lumi," another Ingrian piece, is about Ukko—one of the gods of the Finnish pantheon. A traditional Karelian wedding song, a traditional Estonian piece, and a Sámi joik melody are also included.

As an added bonus, the CD itself is enhanced with biographical material, photos, and a live performance video for the uncharacteristically sinister tune "Äijö." The video is well produced and entertaining, and confirms that the women of Värttinä are not only top-drawer performers, but aren't too hard on the eyes, either. If you can read Finnish, Kimmo Nevalainen's definitive Värttinä biography, *Korkeelta ja Kovvoo*, has recently been published.

Joshua Buckley

Rita Eriksen and Dolores Keane—*Tideland* (Alula Records)

Irish performer Dolores Keane is undoubtedly well known to fans of traditional music; Rita Eriksen, a Norwegian, is somewhat less so, at least insofar as Norwegian folk music is less well known generally (although labels like NorthSide are making considerable efforts to change this). Ireland and Norway are "two nations sharing an ocean," but as this album is designed to demonstrate, they share much else besides. For the recording, Keane and Eriksen met at a geographical midpoint: the "Tideland" of Caithness in Northeast Scotland. There, in a medieval castle, they put together an anthology of Irish and Norwegian traditional tunes that illustrates the convergence, and common origins, of these styles.

Tideland also features a host of instrumentalists. Eoin O'Riabhaigh contributes Uilleann pipes and tin whistle, while the Norwegian Einar Mjolsnes plays hardanger fiddle (perhaps the central element in most Norwegian traditional music). But certain unconventional instruments are also to be found here, including the electric guitar, sitar, and Kona Hawaii guitar. A number of Irish standards are showcased, many of which will be familiar ("Moorlough Shore" and "The Low, Low Lands of Holland"). Less familiar are the Norwegian pieces. One of my favorites is

"Kvi Gjeng du sa Einsleg og Stundar." Oddly enough, my own exposure to this particular tune is the result of having heard it played by the Norwegian black metal group Storm. The final track was written by session guitarist John Faulkner. The ocean has always played an important part in the lives of both the Irish and the Norse, and the sound of waves lapping against the shore formed an ever-present backdrop to this recording. Thus, Faulkner's lyrics are an appropriate concluding homage to "the great northern ocean, where the cold and icy winds blow."

Joshua Buckley

In Gowan Ring—*Hazel Steps Through a Weathered Home* (Lune Music)

I came across an interview with In Gowan Ring's "conductor" B'eirth, in which he said, "I regard certain music as a means of survival in an increasingly hostile world." To his credit, B'eirth's own music fits this description quite nicely. This is the stuff of pure reverie, and—listened to in the right spirit—will carry you far beyond the bustle and ugliness of the modern world. It would be highly unfortunate for such a release to slip away into obscurity. As a songwriter and musician, B'eirth is easily the equal of psychedelic folk virtuosos Robin Williamson (The Incredible String Band) or the late Nick Drake. Comparisons to virtually any other musicians exploring similar territory would simply not do this justice.

There are no traditional songs here. However, the spirit infusing *Hazel Steps* is entirely consonant with the feel of traditional music. B'eirth's vocals are delivered in quiet intimacy yet seem to issue from another time. Like the Romantic poets, he has described his inspiration as stemming from a personal engagement with nature—whether wandering in the snowy northern woods, or marveling at the vast open spaces of his one-time home of Utah. In Gowan Ring's music is likewise a largely organic creation. At times it almost sounds as if this might not be the case—there were moments listening to this when I thought I'd detected the presence of a synthesizer. But this is merely a testament to the versatility of the traditional instruments actually present. The sackbut, for instance, was popular in the sixteenth cen-

In Gowan Ring
Hazel Steps through a Weathered Home

Euphonious arrangments of original compositions with acoustic, archaic and homespun instruments
With guests Annabel Lee, Michael Moynihan, Philip & Gayle Neuman and Margie Wienk

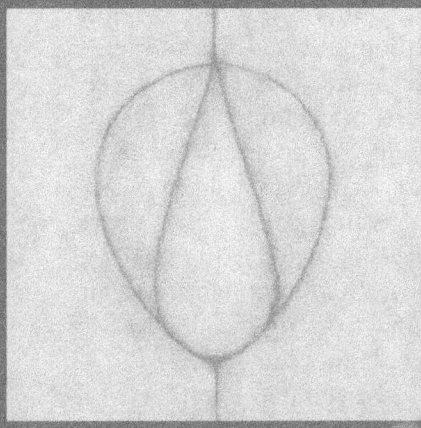

"Poetically, the ideas here reflect upon the material life-world as an oft trodden habitation. The enigmas of nostalgia, impermanence, and existential transcendence are recurrent.
  Musically, the arrangements portray a pensive cyclical polyphony whereby each constituent enfolds within another, evincing an integral geometric symmetry.
  This is at once the most simple and the most involved album of In Gowan Ring." -B'eirth

"This is one of only a few recent releases that might genuinely be called inspired."
                                                                              -Tyr

"A unique synthesis of folk, mediaeval and psychedelia that could only be In Gowan Ring. Listening to this album is like sliding into a warm bath infused with oils and perfumes."   -Flux Europa

"A poetic release of intimate mystic songs, more minimal than earlier releases, sparsely arranged, towards the core of an essential expression."   -Psych Van Het Folk

Other titles by In Gowan Ring:
The Glinting Spade (1999)
The Twin Trees (1997)
Love Charms (1994)

Distribution in North America by CTD, Soleilmoon and Middle Pillar.
Also available at uncommonly discerning record stores worldwide.

Mp3s and complete catalog available online:
InGowanRing.com

tury as an accompaniment to choral music in churches and cathedrals, precisely because it sounded so much like the human voice. Played here by early music exponents Philip and Gayle Neuman (Oregon Renaissance Band), it serves very much the same function. Another amazing aspect of this release is that B'eirth built most of his instruments himself, including his harp, guitar, and cittern. The latter of these also has an interesting history. The modern Celtic cittern and bouzouki both evolved from citterns popular in the Middle Ages, on through to the Renaissance. According to one article, by the seventeenth century it had fallen into disfavor as an instrument played only by "fools and barbers." Although B'eirth plays his cittern with considerable agility, I will give him the benefit of the doubt, and assume that he is neither a barber, nor a fool. Other guest musicians include Annabel Lee (violin and viola), Michael Moynihan (bodhrán), and Margie Wienk on cello. "Two Towers," the final track on the album, also features a piano—and is one of the real highpoints here.

Sadly, this is probably destined to be lumped together with the gothic and ethereal music produced by labels like World Serpent and Projekt, and will attract a similar audience. But In Gowan Ring deserves better. This is one of only a handful of recent releases that might genuinely be called inspired. It is European "soul music" of the highest order. Miss it at your peril.

Joshua Buckley

Sonne Hagal—*Helfahrt* (Eis & Licht)

Since their debut *Sinnreger* 10" on Eis & Licht (the title refers to the sacred Eddic mead of inspiration, while the packaging contains illustrations by Franz Stassen taken from a 1920 edition of the *Edda*), Sonne Hagal have followed a dedicated path of making new heathen music. On *Sinnreger*, this path was exemplified by a spirited cover of Ernte's classic summer solstice anthem "Sonnenwende" and the aggressive "Odin," which displayed a strong Sol Invictus influence. The group sings in both English and German, even using lyrics by the notorious occultist Aleister Crowley on their split-LP with Aurum Nostrum, *Sinister Practices in Bright Sunshine*. This was followed by a highly original 7" named *Starkaðr* which combined strange loops and Old Norse

SONNE HAGAL. (PHOTO COURTESY OF EIS & LICHT)

lyrics for an unsettling effect. Eis & Licht has recently released a split-CD of Sonne Hagal and Nerthus, on which Sonne Hagal's material consists of a collaboration with the ambient project Polarzirkel, with beautiful results. But admittedly, much of their work owes a strong debt to the World Serpent apocalyptic folk scene, a trait that is on ample display on their first full-length CD and LP *Helfahrt* ("Journey to the Realm of Hel," Hel being the goddess of the underworld). It starts off well with two guitar-driven numbers that feature strong yet lyrical violin arrangements. The German lyrics to the second song, "Eismahd," dramatically describe the destructive effects of hail on the harvest crops. With its strong vocal phrasing and martial tone, "Midwinternight" comes along like a lost early Sol Invictus tune. The plaintive "Raidho" features Kim Larsen of Of The Wand And The Moon on vocals and guitar. "Midgard" is the gem of the album, with excellent German lyrics that describe men's "victorious path, like the path of the sun and the eagle's flight" while the stirring chorus reminds us that the "sunwheel is turning above us." "Thrymskviða" recounts Thor's adventures from that Eddic poem.

To their credit, Sonne Hagal are obviously dedicated to runic lore and Nordic heathenism and their work delves deeper into these areas than a lot of other groups who use runes. That said, this record is to be recommended for some well-executed and memorable songs. And in time, this young band could develop into a more original and crucial force on the German "Neofolk" scene.

Markus Wolff

Forseti—*Windzeit* (Goeart/Grunwald)

The new Forseti title is inspired by the ancient poems of the *Edda*, which talk of a cataclysmic twilight of the gods, which also destroys the world of men: "Wind Age, Wolf Age—Light gives way to the darkness. Wind Age, Wolf Age—A storm rages in the sky. Wind Age bursts forth upon the world..." Like Orplid's Uwe Nolte, Ritter works with photography and the results adorn both the booklet and the cover of this exquisitely packaged release. But unlike Nolte, who sees his photographs as paintings and whose work stands in the tradition of Symbolist art, Ritter's works consist of impressions of his native Saxon landscape and are a perfect complement to his nature-mystical lyrics. As on his debut, *Jenzig*, which has been re-released on CD, acoustic guitars and fluid violin predominate, ably supported by drums and Ritter's simple and effective accordion and melodica playing. The result is a timeless and deeply romantic sound, a gorgeous organic puzzle where every piece has an essential role and place. Almost as an afterthought, a famous guest appears as if out of nowhere on the last song. Douglas P.'s contribution, "Black Jena," cryptically referring to Ritter's hometown, is more of a gesture of thanks for the latter's focused accordion playing on Death In June's last outing *All Pigs Must Die*, perhaps a passing of the torch from one generation to the next. Without reading too much into this, one can still safely say that *Windzeit* will go down as an enduring milestone of German lyricism, happily devoid of any pretense or posturing.

Markus Wolff

Terry Earl Taylor—*Another Time* (Dark Holler)

For a number of years now the tiny independent music label Dark Holler has been seeking out and discovering obscure gems of otherwise overlooked traditionally based folk music. This is not the contrived coffeehouse-style folk of the 1960s, influenced by the protest culture of the hippies, but music with deeper roots and darker underpinnings. As any folklorist, musicologist, or astute listener knows, the various strands of American folk can be traced directly across the sea to the European lands which have provided waves of migratory settlers to the New World since the seventeenth century. Often poor, persecuted for their religious or political beliefs, or fleeing famine and misery, these brave, reckless—or just plain restless—souls formed the original backbone of this country. And they brought with them their songs, ballads, and melodies. Handed-down instruments like the fiddle likewise made the seaside journey, being lightweight and easily portable.

Rural folklore and belief, like the music they were intertwined with, rapidly died out over the last few centuries in most of Europe as cosmopolitanism gained precedence, but they were often kept alive in the hinterlands and isolated pockets of the New World. Places such as York County, Pennsylvania (home to the Dark Holler label), with its longstanding German connections (i.e., the "Pennsylvania Dutch"—which in fact means Pennsylvania *Deutsch*), became repositories of copious amounts of folklore and traditional conceptions. Nearby Appalachia, with its difficult, hilly terrain of winding trails and hidden hollers, provided an ideal geography for the preservation of both lore and music. Passed down among an isolated and conservative rural population, the songs of the immigrants remained largely unchanged, whereas in the Old Country, new versions and "improvements" were commonplace. This phenomenon came to the attention of Victorian-era British folksong scholars like Cecil Sharp (1859–1924), who as a result turned their attention for a time to America, even making journeys here to engage in field research (a theme depicted in the recent film *Songcatcher*, despite suffering predictable Hollywood embellishment). They were amazed to discover the archaic versions of English and Scottish ballads still being sung by Appalachian country people, and rushed to document everything they could. Such endeavors accelerated with the advent of modern recording equipment, and the tireless work of trailblazing folk music archivist Alan Lomax. In many ways this kind of documentation is a race against time, though, for the more evolved modern technology becomes, the less likely it is for the old traditions to survive in the first place.

The increasingly widespread availability of inexpensive audio recordings, first on vinyl and now in digital form, has nonetheless encouraged a worldwide interest in all manner of traditional music forms. It is not uncommon for modern-day American traditional musicians to look back to ancestral regions of Europe for the greatest degree of their inspiration and stylistic influences. Less common, however, is for the equation to go in reverse, although this seems to have been the case with the English banjo player and singer Terry Earl Taylor. In the liner notes to his debut CD *Another Time*, Taylor writes that he originally was inspired by blues harp playing and country music, particularly that of Merle Haggard. Essences of both make appearances on these recordings, as do the ghosts of American banjo icons like Dock Boggs and Bascom Lunsford (the "primeval twins" as Taylor calls them; on the album he also includes a stoic tribute to the former titled "Dock Boggs is Dead"). For the most part these songs are just banjo and voice, in a few cases dressed out sparsely with harmonica or electric guitar. Despite the fact that Taylor spent years playing in London rhythm-and-blues bands, he is clever enough not to take the easy way and cut loose or "rock out" (on the songs "Hanging at Picnic Rock" and "November 31st," Taylor's unnamed guest on electric guitar strums with a perceptive sense of restraint), preferring instead the more somber and genteel, rickety front-porch blues of the old American South.

Appearing here alongside various classic British folk ballads is a series of original numbers, all of which resonate well with the rural folk vernacular. Taylor's simple plucking style of short, repetitive runs provides a solid structure to support his unpretentious and expressive vocals, which have a timeless country charm about them. His new arrangements of classic English ballads such as "Long Lankin" (here called "John Lankin," and quite different in inflection from either older traditional versions or Steeleye Span's elaborate and electrified 1970s reworking of the song) and "Sadie Grove" are distinctive, but at the same time sound as if they might have existed for untold generations, passed down through a secret lineage.

In his choice and delivery of slightly ominous—or, in some

cases, bluntly macabre—songs Taylor carves out a well-suited niche for himself. The lyrics to "Go Make Another Grave" sound like they could have been written by Charlie Starkweather, or culled from the padlocked diaries of ornery, belligerent Appalachian hill folk: "I shot that revenue man / Buried him in the sand / Won't be botherin' me anymore…"—and that's before the song makes a chilling psychological detour straight inside the mind of its murderous narrator. The fact that Taylor looks a bit like a dashing lost twin to infamous 1960s "moors murderer" Ian Brady only complements the dark aura that hovers over much of his musical material.

Let us hope that Taylor continues recording in such a starkly inimitable fashion, and keeps himself inoculated from trite or overly smooth contemporary influences. In the meantime this first album can be readily recommended to anyone addicted to the grim and tragic visions of the rustic folk singers from ages past. In his own way, Terry Earl Taylor has conjured up the same sleepless old spirits and become a bona fide conduit for their archaic energies. Hopefully the appearance of *Another Time* will bring some much-deserved attention to an artist whose work spans—or rather transcends—the pond separating Old World and New.

Michael Moynihan

Various Artists—*Songcatcher II: The Tradition That Inspired the Movie* (Vanguard Records)

The hills of Appalachia were settled mainly by Scots-Irish lowlanders, many of whom arrived in the United States before the American Revolution, and considerably in advance of the second wave of Irish immigration that followed the great potato famine. Although these settlers had left their native lands behind, they brought many of their traditions with them. Elements of Anglo-Saxon and Celtic folklore survive to this day in these isolated mountain communities, including customs that faded away long ago in England, Wales, Ireland and Scotland. But most importantly, perhaps, the Scots-Irish brought their music.

Maggie Greenwald's film *Songcatcher* tells the story of Dr. Lilly Penleric (Janet McTeer), an academic musicologist who travels to the mountains of North Carolina, where her sister runs a school. McTeer's character is based loosely on the real-life musicologist Olive Dame Campbell, who made a similar journey to the Blue Ridge Mountains in 1908. Like Campbell, Penleric is shocked to find how many traditional Scots-Irish and English songs have been preserved amongst the locals, passed down virtually intact from one generation to the next. She hauls her recording equipment up the rocky crags, hoping to catch this rare mountain music on wax cylinders before the songs are lost forever. Much of the film concerns the inevitable clash between the anachronistic, closed society of the hillbillies and the alien, outside world. There are also a number of romantic twists and turns, including an unexpected lesbian love affair. For the most part, though, *Songcatcher* is about the music. The characters regularly break into song (in a wholly natural, and not at all contrived, way) and the performances are stellar. Iris DeMent belts out an amazing tune from her front porch, and opera singer Emmy Rossum is captivating in her role as Penleric's chief advocate among the understandably suspicious mountain folk.

Unfortunately, the first *Songcatcher* soundtrack did not contain the songs featured in the movie, but slick, contemporary versions of traditional tunes like "Barbara Allen" and "Wind and Rain" performed by mainstream country stars like Dolly Parton, Emmylou Harris, and Patty Loveless. With *Songcatcher II*, Vanguard Records provides us with the real "old-timey" music that inspired the film. Producer Fred Jaspers assembled most of these recordings from the Newport Folk Festival archives. The performers, almost all of whom have long since passed on, learned their craft from their elders before the wide accessibility of recorded music. Thus, they stand within the direct line of oral transmission, through which these songs passed from the Scottish lowlands to the mountains of the Deep South. Unlike most Celtic music, the harp and the uilleann pipes are conspicuous here by their absence. The Scots-Irish, after all, were never really pipers, and the harp was an aristocratic instrument never favored by the working people who ended up in Appalachia. The fiddle, on the other hand, is a ubiquitous component of mountain music, although many Appalachian fiddles were built from "found" objects like shoeboxes and gourds. But the presence of banjo most distinguishes mountain music from its Celtic and English antecedents. Developed largely by African-American pickers, the banjo lends mountain music its distinctive rhythmic style, a style that would later define much of the country and western music that followed.

Doc Watson contributes four of the seventeen tracks on *Songcatcher II*, including a jaw-dropping version of the traditional standard "Matty Groves." Blind since birth, Watson was discovered in Deep Gap, North Carolina, and made a career out of playing country, blues, gospel, and rockabilly. At 79, he continues to tour. Herbert Smith's "The Coo Coo Bird" will knock you back in your seat like a stiff shot of moonshine. Banjo maestro Moran Lee "Dock" Boggs's famous version of "Oh Death" is here as well. Folk archivist Mike Seeger discovered Boggs in the early 1960s, and Seeger recorded the most famous version of "Oh Death" at the American Folk Festival. Almeda Riddle's croaking "Babes In The Woods" and "Black Jack Davy" are rough and earthy scorchers. Sarah Ogan Gunning's "Girl of Constant Sorrows" veritably oozes pathos. But this is true of almost all the songs here, which demonstrate a heartfelt sincerity and earnest singularity that have all but disappeared from most over-produced, modern music. While rock'n'roll—in some ways the bastard offspring of old-timey country music, by way of Elvis Presley and others—has taken a turn towards whiny introspection, this is music that truly comes from the heart. Compared to hillbilly greats like Watson and Boggs, the self-pitying crooning of most contemporary alt-rockers merely reveals them as the sheltered suburban brats that they are.

Joshua Buckley

Julian Cope—*Discover Odin* (Head Heritage)
Julian Cope—*Odin* (Head Heritage)

Even in the Velvet Underground's darkest moments, Lou Reed's infectious faith in rock'n'roll's transformative potential diverged sharply from the rest of the Warhol set's pose of cynical ennui. The future might not amount to much, the drugs may have lost their bite, but rock'n'roll still had the power to lift you high above the hum-drum realities of parents, teachers, and bosses. Undaunted after a career that now spans decades, Julian Cope is a man who still believes this—with a vengeance. Rock'n'roll might not save the world—it's far too late for that—but it could make

the End come down a whole lot smoother.

Cope first emerged from the Liverpool punk scene as part of the influential group The Teardrop Explodes in the late 1970s. Melding synth-pop and three-chord punk (in a style not unlike that of art-punk legends Wire), The Teardrop Explodes weren't shy about acknowledging their indebtedness to the mind-blowing potential of LSD, either—hardly a stance calculated to win them friends in punk's formative climate of anti-hippie reaction. Nevertheless, the Teardrop's debut album, *Kilimanjaro*, instantly landed on the UK charts, and a follow-up single, "Reward," rocketed to the Top 10. But this wasn't enough to hold the group together. In the midst of recording their third studio album, and hot on the heels of a disastrous American tour, the Teardrops exploded in a clash of psychedelically-inflated egos. And thus began Julian Cope's solo career.

This has been an unbelievably varied, colorful, and prolific affair. From the Krautrock-inspired madness of his recent Brain Donor project, to the commercial viability of 1991's critically acclaimed *Peggy Suicide* CD, Cope has dabbled in everything from psychedelic electronica, to New Wave pop, to funk-laden R & B, folk, blues, noise, and straight, no-holds-barred rock'n'roll. But despite the variations in style, every project that bears the Cope name is shot throughout with his irrepressible spirit and personality. Whether it's a love song, social commentary (Cope is a committed ecologist and anarchist), or quasi-mystical meditation on the sheer mystery of life itself, Cope's sense of humor, vitality, and an almost childlike (in the best sense of the word) enthusiasm are always there, bubbling up to the surface. "Senile Gets," very likely the only power-chord anthem ever composed about an elderly mother-in-law's losing battle with Alzheimer's, rocks harder than anything played on mainstream radio in the last twenty years.

In 1998, Cope authored *The Modern Antiquarian* (Thorssons/Harper Collins), a field guide to over three hundred Neolithic monuments, each of which Cope personally visited, often with his wife and two daughters in tow. In addition to cataloging the sites (as well as the folklore and history surrounding them), the book is filled with Cope's personal observations and commentary, beautiful original photography, and the occasional poetic meditation. Unfortunately, it also recycles much of the suspect revisionist history now the vogue with feminist scholars like Riane Eisler—such as the idea that Neolithic society was an Edenic, pacifistic matriarchy. While this may satisfy the Golden Age fantasies of liberal intellectuals, there is little to substantiate it in the historical (or in this case, *prehistorical*) record.

Cope's interest in the prehistory of the British Isles, and prehistory in general, is based largely on his intuition that the frenzied, Dionysian spirit behind rock music is the very same spirit evident in certain facets of pagan and "shamanic" culture. Of course, this has been capitalized on for years by heavy metal acts, but never with Cope's dogged persistence and panache. In his autobiographical *Repossessed: Shamanic Depressions in Tamworth and London* (Thorssons/Harper Collins, 1999) Cope writes, "male rock'n'roll is a pounding earth rhythm which incorporates the violent alongside the effeminate and the poetic ... Look at the myths before the Vikings and you'll discover Odin at the root of all rock'n'roll, and most of all in glam rock." No doubt such speculations will send shivers up the spines of stodgy traditionalists. But Cope means every word.

Discover Odin features both music and spoken-word performances, mainly written for Cope's two-night engagement at the British Museum in October of 2001. The CD begins with "The 18 Charms of Odin," a rock'n'roll adaptation based on Kevin Crossley-Holland's "The Lord of the Gallows." Delivered with a strong, passionate enunciation, this track alone would be worth the price of the album. "Discover Odin" is a twelve-minute meditation on the historic and mythical nature of the god. Although the text is a fairly elementary introduction, the vocal delivery is again top-notch, and the backdrop of electronic ambiance befits the mysterious nature of the one-eyed wanderer. "Ode to Wan" and "Road to Yggdrasilbury" (which clocks in at nearly eighteen minutes) are typically psychedelicized digressions, while "I Want To Go Wandering" features an excerpt from the American poet Vachel Lindsay's *Runes of the Road*. In the liner notes, Cope describes Lindsay—a self-styled wandering bard—as "the living embodiment of the Odinist priest."

There is less to say about Cope's other *Odin* CD, although it is an equally enticing endeavor. Inspired by the "hill altar" Silbury, in whose shadow the Cope family home is built, the disc consists of a 73-minute "parallel-harmonic" meditation entitled "The Breath of Odin." Composed primarily on a Mellotron 400, this is the sort of record Brian Eno might have made had he first quaffed the mead of inspiration. The album was produced by Thighpaulsandra, who also works with Coil, Spiritualized, and was once a member of the glam rock outfit Nancy Hitler.

Joshua Buckley

Cotton Ferox—*First Time Hurts* (Kooks)

If you harbor more than a passing interest in the contemporary occult "scene," you have probably encountered Carl Abrahamsson's work before. A writer, artist, publisher, photographer, and musician, Abrahamsson has channeled his unusual interests into an extensive resumé of art, music, and writing that seldom fails to impress (or at least to elicit more curiosity). Perhaps the unifying element in these projects is an eagerness to investigate unexplored dimensions of consciousness—whether through magick, sex, drugs, or the serious consideration of marginal and taboo ideas. As such, Abrahamsson's name has been associated with a number of similarly motivated groups and individuals, from the Ordo Templi Orientis and Thee Temple Ov Psychick Youth to Anton LaVey's Church of Satan (Abrahamsson published the first Swedish translation of LaVey's *Satanic Bible*). Other publishing ventures have included a paperback edition of H. M. Chadwick's long out-of-print *Cult of Othin*, and the seminal "occultural" journal *The Fenris Wolf*. In the musical realm, Abrahamsson is probably most recognized for his work with the group White Stains (so christened after Aleister Crowley's erotic novel of the same name—the connotations of which are undoubtedly "seminal" as well).

Cotton Ferox is Abrahamsson's latest experiment as a recording artist and, as you might expect, incorporates elements from most of the other fields in which he has left a mark (or stain, as the case may be). Cotton Ferox's music is almost exclusively trip-hop—at times droning, at times almost shimmering electronic ambience, textured around heavy, deep-bass beats. The tempo and style are both reminiscent of the popular Scottish group Boards of Canada. And, as with that puzzlingly titled duo, the Cotton Ferox sound is crafted throughout with a sinister flourish unexpected in most beat-driven, disco-derivative electronic music.

THOMAS TIBERT AND CARL ABRAHAMSSON OF COTTON FEROX.
(PHOTO BY BRAM ANGSTROM)

Lyrically and thematically, *First Time Hurts* features a genuinely offbeat collection of original and borrowed texts, many of them delivered by guest vocalists. Abrahamsson's own "Cotton Ferox Manifesto" (which might more accurately be described as an *anti*-manifesto) starts off with the explanation that no explanation will be forthcoming, then proceeds to deliver statements like: "Cotton Ferox is the wonderful cloud in the blue sky when you're lying down on the grass, your head spinning on LSD." After that much needed bit of clarification, the album segues into "Red Light Glow," a meditation on the "PerversCity" which plays like a Travis Bickle monologue. A backdrop of police-radio banter and jazz samples evocative of Bernhard Herman's *Taxi Driver* score completes the effect. Genesis P-Orridge appears on two tracks, providing both text and vocals. On a personal note, I must admit to finding P-Orridge's post–Throbbing Gristle output somewhat less than appealing. His recent explorations of transvestitism, for example, seem more repulsive than intriguing. But that's just my opinion. Of more interest to *TYR* readers is the Julius Evola–inspired "Modern World." *TYR* editor Michael Moynihan also lends vocals to "Sanguine Essence," his own translation of Ernst Jünger's long, unrelentingly frank tribute to man as *homo destructivus*. This is followed by "Volatile Eternity," with text by Albrecht Haushofer. Haushofer and his father Karl served as advisors to Rudolf Hess, and Albrecht landed in a German prison after Hess's failed peace mission to Britain. Justifiably or not, Haushofer also figures prominently in the oddly resilient modern myth of "occult Nazism." But he is better known for the sonnets he composed during his incarceration.

Though uneven in spots, *First Time Hurts* is still a welcome example of the kind of music being produced beyond the pale of the mainstream, and the rewards awaiting those with the motivation to seek it out.

Joshua Buckley

Various Artists—*Tempus Arborum* (Ars Auditionis)

This CD was released on the occasion of a German concert featuring some of Europe's finest "Neofolk" projects, and contains unreleased tracks, or at least alternate versions of previously released songs. Argine contributes "Rifrazioni," noteworthy for its unabashed pop instrumentation, but showcasing the same haunting, ethereal qualities that are so prominent on their amazing CD *Luctamina in Rebus*. Next, Sonne Hagal turn in two of their best songs so far, one sung in German and one in English. They could easily have replaced two songs on their CD (also reviewed in this issue) and improved it considerably. Forseti offer an alternate version of a song on their *Windzeit* CD, as well as a cover of the Sonne Hagal song "Eismahd." Both stand as typical examples of the subtle arrangements and atmosphere that Andreas Ritter's project has become known for. Gae Bolg and the Church of Fand revolves around Eric L., a sometimes member of Sol Invictus who has been wandering down some strange paths as of late. At its best, Gae Bolg manages to be martial as well as whimsical, as in their brilliant version of "John Barleycorn." Here they contribute a warped and miasmic piece of psychedelia, appropriately named "Magic and Ecstasy," which starts with a stately organ, trumpet, and choral arrangement, and then goes off the proverbial deep end. The related, usually folksy project Seven Pines finishes the disc with a murky yet hypnotic instrumental.

Overall, *Tempus Arborum* is a fine introduction to some of the more creative European folk and just plain weird projects. It shows the breadth of expression possible in this frequently pigeonholed "scene," and whets the appetite for the further exploration of some of these musical obscurities.

Markus Wolff

Darkwood—*Weltenwende* 10" (Eis & Licht)

Henryk Vogel grew up in a sleepy town in Brandenburg called Finsterwalde. To encapsulate his love of his origins and his hometown, he called his musical project Darkwood, the closest English translation of Finsterwalde. However, the German name exudes a mysterious, forboding quality that the English version completely lacks. The same problem has stayed with Vogel's music. On those few songs that he sings in his mother tongue, a vibrancy is present that is somehow missing from a lot of the others, regardless of the quality of the music. And even though he has visited the United States for long periods, Vogel's usage of English can be a bit awkward.

So far, Darkwood has released a trio of CDs, of which the second, *Heimat & Jugend* (Homeland & Youth), is an industrial instrumental meditation on journeys abroad and returning home. Like his debut, the most recent CD is carried by acoustic guitar-based songs, which are sung in English except for two notable exceptions, "Deutsche Sonnwend" (German Solstice) and "Lied der Kämpfer" (Warrior's Song), both of which use nineteenthth-century poems.

In contrast, the new vinyl-only release on Eis & Licht is a departure for Henryk. His unique vocals, which had always been a strong point, are confidently placed more upfront in the mix. The cello and flute playing is elegant and marked by spartan yet uniquely beautiful arrangements. Interesting and dynamic percussion accentuates the sometimes driving, at other times delicate guitar playing. But most importantly, most of the songs here are sung in German, and represent Darkwood's best effort yet.

It is also the most "heathen." Whether one looks to the inspiring lyrics of "Der Schaffende" (The Creative One), which are based on Nietzsche, or to the Old Norse intonations courtesy of Voxus Imp. on "Tochter des Waldes" (Daughter of the Forest), it becomes readily apparent that Vogel has an avid interest in his homeland's traditions and landscapes which was never expressed as eloquently on previous releases. He also realizes that in today's world, this path is often a lonely quest; such a profound love is most frequently kindled in solitude and reflection, far away from the influence of the common and base motivations of most moderns. This record manages to communicate these subtle themes well, with pure emotion and spirit. It is a noble work, and hopefully will find receptive ears and minds.

Markus Wolff

Turbund Sturmwerk/Inade—*Peryt Shou* LP Box (Loki Foundation)

This concept album is the successor to 2000's excellent double 10" box *Saturn Gnosis*, which concerned itself with the German occult order Fraternitas Saturni, and is hence the second installment of the *Germania Occulta* series. Here the two main projects behind this series concentrate their energies to transform into sound the esoteric theories of an almost forgotten figure in German occultism: Peryt Shou (1873–1953). Because all accompanying texts are in German, some brief notes on their content might be in order.

Peryt Shou's dense writings deal with two main themes: self-initiation and cosmic transformation. As was common practice with the early-twentieth-century heirs of the Theosophical movement, he freely combines influences from various religious and mythological systems, correlating them to arrive at his universal tenets. One of these sources is the Germanic *Edda*, which he frequently compares with biblical passages. His studies also yielded his own teachings on breathing, yoga, and mantra practice. The resulting mix was very influential among esoteric writers of the day, which included Ernst Tristan Kurtzahn, whose writings on the runes in turn influenced Friedrich Marby and Siegfried Kummer. It is Shou's ideas on the transformative powers of sound that form the impetus behind this record.

Inade, the masters of cosmic deep ambient music, chose to compose one side-long piece, entitled "Kwa Non Seh," after a Shou publication on Buddhism. According to the liner notes, "in Tibetan, KWA-NON-SEH describes the 'resounding inner voice.'" Inade's piece is based in Shou's conception of the mantra as a means of awakening higher states of being and starts appropiately with drones. Yet as the piece progresses it reveals itself to be more percussive than most Inade material, as a slowed-down march collides with electrical storms and disembodied German voices.

Turbund Sturmwerk, on the other hand, explore the macro- and microcosmic correspondences between the world tree or column and the human body in a three-part opus entitled "Igg Dra Sil." In the first part, a fanfare-like backward melody rises against a backdrop of slowly ascending tones. Organ motifs invoke an atmosphere of the sacred. Part two comes across like a decadent version of Isao Tomita, with resonant piano and analog drones and vibrations elegiacally rising to a stirring peak. During the last part, aptly titled "Bewußtseinsbresche" (Breach of Consciouness), layered voices of the aether rush in and engulf the listener in a maelstrom of messages, ending with the sound of human breath, the life force itself.

The Peryt Shou essay reproduced inside the gatefold sleeve is a personal account of an initiatory experience that Shou had in a catacomb in Rome in the mid-1920s, where he heard sounds and had a vision of a star, among other things. Entitled "The Secret of the Catacombs: How I Experienced the Return of Christ," it details the relationship of sacred words and sounds in attaining "Christ consciousness" in the original esoteric sense of the early Christians. To Shou, these sounds enable one to approach "the will of the world" and a "new mysterium of the blood."

Music, as practiced by a master like Wagner, is also able to usher in a "state of resonance with the harmony of the cosmos." After some obscure astro-biblical observations regarding Isaiah's rod, Shou makes a typical reference to the *Edda*:

> In conclusion, I don't want to obmit the fact that the Germanic *Edda* also mentions the "rising branch of Jissai" (Jesse), in strange concurrence with Isaiah's messianic vision. In the *Edda*, in the so-called "Raven's Charm" (Hrafna galda), we read of the sign of the new world: "Thus will appear the thorny rod of the giant," of "'Thjassi,' the eagle king of primordial times." The *Edda* also recognizes the same apocalyptic phenomenon of salvation.

These phenonema, so Shou believes, will transform and purify man. His blood will regain its original crystallized state and become a supra-sensual organ enabling man to directly experience and resonate with the "cosmic Eros-Christus."

The accompanying large-format booklet is exquisitely designed and contains an introductory essay, liner notes by both groups, and several reprints of Shou-related material. Especially noteworthy among these is a reprint from Rudolf Gorsleben's *völkisch* esoteric journal *Hag-All=All-Hag* (which later also published articles by Karl Maria Wiligut), entitled "Das Zeichen des wiederkehrenden Menschensohnes in der *Edda*" (The Sign of the Returning Son of Man in the *Edda*). Beautiful artwork by Fidus, Franz Stassen, and Theosophical artist Fritz Haß rounds out this attractive and inspirational work, which will stand as a masterful combination of word, sound, and power.

As part of this "rediscovery" of Shou's work, two recent reprints are worth mentioning: The Turbund and Loki Foundation have collaborated as Edition Schattenhold to issue a new edition of Shou's classic 1920 work *Die Edda als Schlüssel des kommenden Weltzeitalters: Die Runen als Weltsprache der Geister* (The *Edda* as Key of the Coming World Age: The Runes as the Universal Language of the Spirits) which also includes another essay, a thorough biographical introduction, and the most complete Shou bibliography to date (contact <peryt@loki-found.de>). The other is a booklet reissue of *Die Geistes=Waffe des Nordischen Menschen* (The Spiritual Weapon of Nordic Man), a shorter work in which Shou puts forth his views concerning the esoteric significance of Wagner, the Externsteine, and the Irminsul. Like many of his other works, it includes actual directions for mantric and yogic exercises based on his findings. It has been published by the German association Freundeskreis für Brauchtum and Kultur (contact <fbk@sonnenwacht.de>).

Markus Wolff

Spear of Longinus—*The Yoga of National Socialism* (Vinland Winds)

With a title worthy of Dr. Demento, this would seem to be one of the more aberrant manifestations of underground pop culture, a postmodern pastiche that is all the more ironic for its apparent sincerity. But this is merely one example of a whole genre of music—call it "Nazi Occult Metal," or "National Socialist Black Metal." This is how the movement's followers describe the style, and, by all appearances, they seem to take themselves quite seriously. "Grimnir," who runs the Vinland Winds label, is a member of the late William Pierce's extreme racialist National Alliance, which now seems intent on pandering to skinheads and black metalers. This strange marriage of hardcore racist politics (whose elder statesmen are often the last vestiges of Goldwater conservatism and the segregationist Deep South) and alienated, antisocial youth culture is a testament to the bizarre sociological dynamics of modern (and especially modern American) political extremism.

Over the years, a number of Ásatrú and heathen-related publications have chronicled the rise of heavy metal music with distinctly Germanic and pagan overtones. Many of these "heathen metal" (or "Viking metal") acts have cultivated this aspect of their personas to great effect—producing music that can be both inspired and inspiring. Ultimately, however, most extreme metal bands still fall back on the schlock Satanism that has always been the stock and trade of the genre. This is neither the imaginative iconoclasm of Satanic High Priest Anton LaVey, nor the intellectualized self-actualization theology of rival Satanist Michael Aquino. Rather, heavy metal Satanism tends to belie a sort of adolescent antinomianism. It is a desperate lashing out at the whitebread, middle-class world from which it issues, a final cry of defiance before the realities of adulthood set in. In the 1980s, in the wake of the McMartin preschool case and a host of supposedly "Satanic" suicides, the media was quick to cast Satanism as a viable threat to Western civilization, or at least something every Godfearing churchgoer should keep an eye on. But in the 1990s, the Satanic aesthetic fared considerably worse: it was relegated to joke status as youth culture became savvier, or at least more cynical. It was inevitable that kids with a taste for shock value would be forced to look elsewhere for an emblematic totem to express their alienation. And where better to look than Hitler? While virtually every other moral evil in our society has been relativized, Hitler remains the West's sole secular devil, a man virtually everyone feels comfortable condemning as "evil."

Despite their ability to mouth slogans fed to them by their elders in the "movement," this seems to be the real motivation underlying most Nazi rock music. Regardless of its ideological pretensions, skinhead music (for example) has always been characterized more by generalized nihilism and misanthropy than political commitment (most far-right leaders who have attempted to organize the skinheads have quickly realized that their youthful charges are primarily interested in fighting and drinking beer). But *The Yoga of National Socialism* may be the oddest example yet of the percolating strangeness now festering on the margins of youth culture. Unlike most black metalers, who have typically donned white "corpse paint" (reminiscent of Tim Burton's lovable freak *Edward Scissorhands*), Spear of Longinus's lead singer appears in a garish grease-paint mask that makes him look like a cross between a Maori warrior and a member of the Insane Klown Posse. In an unexpected nod to New Age eclecticism, S.O.L.'s "Camazotz" peppers his interviews with allusions to Freemsonry, Buddhism, Taoism, rune magic, yoga, Gnosticism, and Tai Chi—all subjects about which he seems to know very little. Nevertheless, most of these references crop up on *The Yoga of National Socialism*, although the group's incomprehensible brand of Nazi Satanism takes pride of place. After starting things off with a sample from *Conan The Barbarian*, songs like "The Sine of Satan is 56," "Stuka Song," "Rommel," and "Shiva Dancing" (as well as the inexplicably titled "Piano Concerto No. 9") demonstrate the band's competent, but ultimately mediocre, thrash metal abilities. That anti-racist watchdog groups could perceive this sort of thing as a threat to the dominant political and social order (or anything else, for that matter) is simply laughable. If there is anything "frightening" about Spear of Longinus, it is that they and their ilk may be the unexpected byproduct of a rampantly permissive, fragmented society, where anything—and everything—goes.

Joshua Buckley

About the Editors

PHOTO: SHAWN YOUNG

Joshua Buckley was born in 1974 in Sharon, Connecticut. He has been an occasional contributor to several heathen and music-related periodicals, including *Vor Tru* and *Rûna*. Currently he lives and works in Atlanta, Georgia. In addition to publishing *TYR*, he has released several CDs via his Ultra imprint, and will publish an English translation of Alain de Benoist's book *On Being a Pagan* in 2004.
Email: <info@arcanaeuropa.com>

PHOTO: CARL ABRAHAMSSON

Michael Moynihan was born in 1969 in New England. He is an artist, musician, author, editor, and occasional winemaker and bookbinder. He has traveled and performed music throughout Europe, as well as in Japan. The latest release of his and Annabel Lee's music project Blood Axis is *Absinthe: La Folie Verte* (Athanor), a collaboration with the French group Les Joyaux de la Princesse. His record label Storm has recently produced the debut album from the northern Portuguese/Gallæcian traditional band Sangre Cavallum. His book *Lords of Chaos* (revised edition: Feral House, 2003), co-written with Didrik Søderlind, was published in Germany (Prophecy, 2003) to widespread recognition. He is a contributor to *Book of Lies: The Disinformation Guide to Magick and the Occult* (Disinformation, 2003) and to the *Encyclopedia of Religion and Nature* (Continuum, forthcoming 2004). With Annabel Lee he also runs Dominion Press, which will soon issue works by Hans Bellmer and John Michell. In addition to his work for *TYR*, he is a co-editor of *Rûna*.
Email: <himilkraft@comcast.net>

About the Contributors

Peter Bahn, Ph.D., was born on 5 February 1953 in Koblenz am Rhein, Germany. At the University of Mainz he studied folklore, German, bibliology, journalism, and comparative literature. Subsequently he has held positions in teaching and research (at the Universities of Mainz and Oldenburg), adult education, cultural administration, and at various museums. Besides various books, Dr. Bahn has published numerous articles in Germany, Austria, Switzerland, Italy, Belgium, and France on historical topics, particularly cultural, social, technological, and intellectual history, as well as genealogy and heraldry. Recent thinkers who have provided the greatest inspiration to him include Julius Evola and Ernst Jünger, but most of all the German scholar and philosopher Friedrich Hielscher, whose life and work have for a number years been at the forefront of his studies.

Alain de Benoist was born on 11 December 1943. He is married and has two children. He has studied law, philosophy, sociology, and the history of religions in Paris, France. A journalist and a writer, he is the editor of two journals: *Nouvelle Ecole* (since 1968) and *Krisis* (since 1988). His main fields of interest include the history of ideas, political philosophy, classical philosophy, and archaeology. He has published more than fifty books and 3,000 articles. He is also a regular contributor to many French and European publications, journals, and papers (including *Valeurs actuelles, Le Spectacle du monde, Magazine-Hebdo, Le Figaro-Magazine* in France, *Telos* in the United States, and *Junge Freiheit* in Germany). In 1978 he received the Grand Prix de l'Essai from the Académie Française for his book *Vu de droite: Anthologie critique des idées contemporaines* (Paris: Copernic, 1977). He has also been a regular contributor to the radio program *France-Culture* and has appeared in numerous television debates.

Charles Champetier is a young writer and scientist. He was born in 1968 and served for ten years as the editor-in-chief of the journal *Eléments*. He has also published a book entitled *Homo consumans: Archéologie du don et de la dépense* (Paris: Labyrinthe, 1994).

Contributors

Collin Cleary, Ph.D., is an independent scholar living in Sandpoint, Idaho. He is a Fellow in the Rune-Gild and a contributor to *Rûna*.

Stephen Edred Flowers, Ph.D., is the world's leading expert on esoteric, or "radical," runology. He has published over twenty books on this and related subjects. In 1980 he founded the Rune-Gild, the world's largest and most influential initiatory organization dedicated to Rune-Work and the Odian path. His work in runology extends into academic pursuits and in 1984 he received a Ph.D. from the University of Texas at Austin with a dissertation entitled *Runes and Magic*. He is presently working on three books of general cultural interest: *The Northern Dawn: A History of the Reawakening of the Germanic Spirit*; *Wave of the Future: The European New Right and its Meaning for America*; and *The Pagan Right*. Dr. Flowers has recently founded the Woodharrow Institute for general studies in the culture and arts of the Germanic and Indo-European peoples. He and his wife, Crystal, are also the owners of Rûna-Raven Press. His work is devoted to seeking the principle of RUNA—the Mystery—as understood in the mythic idiom of the Germanic peoples.

Joscelyn Godwin, Ph.D., has written books on esotericism that have been translated into French, German, Spanish, Italian, Greek, and Japanese. They include *Robert Fludd*, *Athanasius Kircher*, *Mystery Religions in the Ancient World*, *Harmonies of Heaven and Earth*, *Music and the Occult*, *Arktos*, *The Theosophical Enlightenment*, and many editions and translations, notably of the *Hypnerotomachia Poliphili* of 1499. His latest book, *The Pagan Dream of the Renaissance*, appeared in 2002 from Phanes Press. He was born in England and has taught since 1971 in the Music Department of Colgate University, Hamilton, NY 13346.

Jon Graham is a translator, writer, and editor who was born in 1954. His well-received translations include *Arthur Rimbaud: Presence of an Enigma* by Jean-Luc Steinmetz, *The Immaculate Conception* by André Breton and Paul Eluard, *Immortality and Reincarnation* by Alexandra David-Neel, and numerous works by the French Celticist Jean Markale. Forthcoming translations include works by Philippe d'Iribarne, Hans Bellmer, and

Alain de Benoist.

Elizabeth Griffin is a translator of Romance languages with over twenty years of professional experience. She has worked for Naval intelligence and the Smithsonian, and as an artist has had her work published in national magazines. She has three children and lives in the eastern United States.

Annabel Lee, M.A., M.F.A., is a musician, writer, and amateur mountain climber (the highest peak attained so far is 18,192 ft./ 5,545 m.). Born in Manhattan and raised in the industrial landscape of Germany, she now spends most of her time in the northern woods. Her most recent work includes translating *Witchcraft Medicine: Healing Arts, Shamanic Practices, and Forbidden Plants* by Claudia Müller-Ebeling, Christian Rätsch, and Wolf-Dieter Storl (Inner Traditions, 2003) and *Shamanism and Tantra in the Himalayas* by Claudia Müller-Ebeling, Christian Rätsch, and Surendra Bahadur Shahi (Inner Traditions, 2002). She is the co-director of the independent publishing company Dominion Press. In addition, her violin and compositions can be heard on more than fifteen recordings, including those of Alraune and Blood Axis.

John Matthews is a writer and mythographer living in Oxford. He teaches courses on myth and the Matter of Britain worldwide. He is the author of over fifty books, including *Taliesin: The Last Celtic Shaman* and the forthcoming *King Arthur: From Dark Age Warrior to Mythic Hero*. Visit <www.hallowquest.org.uk> for more information.

Stephen McNallen founded the first organization dedicated to indigenous Germanic religion in the United States in 1971. Since then he has maintained an active role in that movement as head of several organizations and as a trend-setting thinker. A former US Army Ranger, he maintains an active interest in military subjects and the cause of Tibetan freedom ("by any means necessary," he adds). McNallen is a member of the Rune-Gild and a former president of the European American Issues Forum. A Texan by birth, he currently lives in northern California surrounded by family, wildlife, and trees.

Contributors

Nigel Pennick was born in Guildford, Surrey in southern England in 1946. Trained in biology, for fifteen years he was a researcher in algal taxonomy for a government institute. During this time, he published twenty-nine scientific research papers including descriptions of eight new species of marine algae and protozoa before moving on to become a writer and illustrator. He is the author of over forty books on European folk arts, landscape, customs, games, magical alphabets, and spiritual traditions.

Steve Pollington is a freelance researcher and teacher in the field of Old English studies. His recent works include a treatment of military themes in Old English literature and Anglo-Saxon archaeology; fresh translations of three Old English medical texts with detailed examination of their magico-medical background; and a unique *Old English—Modern English Dictionary and Thesaurus*. He is a contributor to the prestigious *Oxford Companion to Military History* and has appeared on radio and television. He is currently researching the social aspects of the warband in pre-Christian Europe.

Christian Rätsch, Ph.D., is a world-renowned anthropologist and ethnopharmocologist. For more than twenty years he has researched the medicinal and ritual use of plants, and in particular the cultural usage of psychoactive plants in shamanism. His work has been published in numerous scholarly publications and recently he provided extensive contributions to the revised edition of Richard Schultes's and Albert Hofmann's classic text *Plants of the Gods* (Inner Traditions). Books by Christian Rätsch that have appeared thus far in English translation include *Plants of Love* (Ten Speed) and *Marijuana Medicine* (Inner Traditions), and he is a coauthor, along with Claudia Müller-Ebeling and others, of *Shamanism and Tantra in the Himalayas* and *Witchcraft Medicine* (both published by Inner Traditions).

Markus Wolff is an artist, musician, and lay historian residing in Portland, Oregon. He was born in Germany and has also lived in Austria and Australia. His current interests include the history of Jugendstil and German Symbolist art. Wolff's articles have appeared in such magazines as *Hagal, Zinnober, Sigill, Irminsul* (Australia), *Esoterra,* and *Vor Tru*. Email: <dagaz@spiritone.com>

About the Cover Artist

Odin Wiesinger is a painter, graphic artist, and sculptor who was born in 1961 in Andorf, Upper Austria. He received his training in the master class for painting and graphic arts at the Hochschule für Gestaltung in Linz, where he also took part in seminars on sculpture. His influences range widely from the archaic creations of prehistory, to Renaissance art, Symbolism, and Expressionism. In a 1998 interview he described art as a "cultic element," and stated: "The time is ripe for myths. Above all, that should be true for the mythology of one's own forefathers … Alongside Greek and Roman mythology, the Celts and ancient Germans have an intense influence on my work and my choices of motifs, since there are very many intersections, or points of overlap, in the European primordial religions and sagas. If one wishes to describe what I make as representative of 'Tradition,' that is only partially the case. Viewed in its entirety, I would personally describe it more as part of a 'Renaissance.'"

Photographs courtesy of the artist.

Contact address:
Atelier, 4770 Andorf, Austria
Tel.: +43-7766-3388 / Fax: +43-7766-2278-4
Email: atelier.odin@utanet.at
Website: www.atelier-odin.at

Some Words Written in Response to the First Volume of TYR

Dr. Kathleen Raine, C.B.E., who was born in 1908 and died in London on 6 July 2003, was an eminent poet, author of a three-volume autobiography, and a scholar of the perennial philosophy with a particular love for William Blake, Thomas Taylor the Platonist, and W. B. Yeats. In later life she founded the journal Temenos: A Review Devoted to the Arts of the Imagination *and the Temenos Academy, which continues under the patronage of HRH Prince Charles.*

On 2 September 2002, after receiving volume one of TYR, *Dr. Raine wrote in a letter to Joscelyn Godwin the following thoughts about Julius Evola:*

Evola seems not to have had compassion or love or wonder and that seems to me comparable to blindness or deafness or some physical disability rather than a moral defect. One does not blame people for being blind or tone-deaf but it is something that should not be so, or that limits their (our?) understanding nevertheless. One should be sorry for such people; have 'compassion,' which is perhaps a higher wisdom than 'love.' [. . .]

One might of course see it quite differently, that this really is a flawed world, that there is no divine creator (how then does anything exist at all? how does anything come into being out of nothing?) and that Evola is simply right in his total pessimism. I still think we could—can—nevertheless "build a heaven in Hell's despite" and create a universe as a shelter over our naked souls. And we have, or are, souls, by whatever chance or mischance. But for me Blake's "innumerable company of the heavenly host" do sing "Holy, Holy, Holy is the Lord God Almighty." Whether they "really" do or not, who can say?

As you see, Evola has stung or touched me very vitally and he certainly stands as a challenge to us all.

Historian James J. Martin was born in 1916 and received his Ph.D. in 1949 from the University of Michigan. He has taught at institutions across the U.S., most memorably at Deep Springs, a California college which Newsweek *once suggested was "the most isolated, obscure, and selective college in the entire U.S." Dr. Martin's numerous books include the seminal history of individualist anarchism in the United States,* Men Against the State *(1953),* American Liberalism and World Politics, 1931–1941 *(2 vols, 1964),* The Saga of Hog Island and Other Essays in Inconvenient History *(1977), and* An American Adventure in Bookburning *(1988). He has also edited and introduced various classics of libertarian thought such as Lysander Spooner's* No Treason *(1966) and Max Stirner's* The Ego and His Own *(1963). He lives in Colorado Springs, Colorado.*

On 15 June 2002 Dr. Martin wrote the following comments to Michael Moynihan in regard to his review of John Zerzan's Running On Emptiness *in volume one of* TYR:

I have read your review three times and all of Mr. Z's book, some essays in the latter several times. I would say your review was quite fair and your criticisms restrained and reasonable. Somehow or other I seem to feel there is a kind of thin haze of Marxism over Mr. Z's whole project which influences the total impact of it, even if mainly unconsciously since he iterates that he no longer is of the persuasion/influence or whatever of this approach. But his enthusiasm for the possible revolutionary overthrow of the existing civilization/system reveals a sort of residual impact of the Manifesto and what happened in Russia in the WWI era. But maybe I err here. Mr. Z's description of the many nightmare aspects of what prevails I cannot quarrel with, but as bad as it all is, I cannot imagine our vast multitudes of bowling-ball-IQ creeps replacing it with scrounging for roots and berries for food and sleeping on the ground in lean-tos.

I wrote about the anarchists for a quarter of a century (my sketches of Emma Goldman and Alexander Berkman are still in the *Dictionary of American Biography*, I think) and I guess I opted for the one-man revolution as personal choice. I withdrew from the labor force thirty-four years ago and have never voted, among other gestures, though I am sure that adopting the lifestyle of a concentration camp rat impressed no one. But I think that leaving the club is an easier way to bring down the club than burning down the clubhouse. My guess would be that the hundreds of billionaires and their trillion-dollar operations globally will be able to head off any revolution I can imagine likely today. But there is plenty of room for the one-man revolution, and that they can't control or suppress.

Mr. Z wrote as though the whole world was in the shape of the U.S., but a look at black Africa reveals a lot of it is about what his revolution would approximate, and I don't know anyone trying to copy that in any particulars, especially the many millions down with AIDS.

And on 29 July 2002:

As I tried feebly to explain in my June letter, I am from an older time and influenced by even older approaches, suggesting that it all began wrong and no kind of "therapy" will get things "on the right track." It all began as a plutocracy and has grown into a bigger one yearly for twenty-one decades. I think I mentioned the "Connecticut Wit," Joel Barlow, publishing a pretty sound analysis of this whole mess in this sense back in 1805. I started school in 1922 and was not ready to cope with the problem for twenty years or so, and when I was, it was the analyzers [from] when I was a school kid and before. Their solution was withdrawal and/or emigration, not hoping to make things right by total destruction. One view I never got over was that of Iowa-born James Norman Hall, writer and famous flyer in WWI in France. He never came back here, and this aroused the curiosity of the editor of the *Atlantic Monthly*, who spent some time locating him, and induced him to write a piece, which was published if I remember right in the April 1926 *Atlantic Monthly*, titled "Why I Live in Tahiti"; in this piece Hall declared, "The United States are not a country and show no signs of ever becoming one." Hall became famous later as co-author in Tahiti of *Mutiny on the Bounty* with Nordhoff. [...]

Well, as I say, my mentors favored withdrawal, going underground, or emigration. But I did enough travel in nine European lands in the '50s to suggest to me that there really is nowhere to run to. It was G. B. Shaw who once remarked that it was obvious that other solar systems were populated, as one of the planets involved was using this one for an insane asylum.

Also Available from Arcana Europa Media:

The Northern Dawn: A History of the Reawakening of the Germanic Spirit

Stephen Edred Flowers

ISBN 978-0-9720292-8-5, 188 pages, paperback, $20.00

Throughout the United States and Europe, a revival of interest in all things Germanic is taking place. But as Stephen Flowers argues in the pages of his far-reaching book, this is only the latest phase in a larger reawakening with a rich, if troubled, history. He defines what constitutes the Germanic Tradition, and explains how this tradition was fragmented and submerged with the coming of Christianity to the Goths, the Franks, the Anglo-Saxons, and the Scandinavians. More importantly, he shows how the northern spirit survived in myriad and sometimes surprising places: from literary works such as *Beowulf* and the *Nibelungenlied*, to the teachings of Christian mystics like Meister Eckhart, and in the religious, political, and legal institutions of medieval England, Iceland, and Scandinavia.

History of the Rune-Gild

Edred Thorsson

ISBN 978-0999724545, 270 pages, paperback, $24.00

In this fascinating and informative volume, Edred Thorsson describes his childhood as a "monster kid" in the late 1950s and early 1960s, and documents the first stirrings of *Rûna*—or "the Mystery"—in his life. He describes his formative (and often humorous) experiences with various occult organizations and the strange and eccentric personalities whom they attract. He chronicles his distinguished academic career and his relationship with scholarly mentors like Prof. Dr. Edgar Polomé and Prof. Dr. Klaus Düwel. He provides the background for his connections to the world of occult publishing and his involvement with neopagan (or heathen) organizations like the Asatru Free Assembly and the Ring of Troth (now known simply as The Troth—the name Thorsson originally gave it). Throughout it all, Thorsson has relied on the hidden hand of the "Old Man" (Odin or Woden) to guide his life's mission of (re-)establishing a traditional Rune-Gild in North America and Europe.

Remnants of a Season:
The Collected Poems of Robert N. Taylor

Robert N. Taylor

ISBN 978-0972029278, 173 pages, hardcover, $25.00

Issued on the occasion of Robert N. Taylor's seventieth birthday, *Remnants of a Season* is the first major retrospective of Taylor's poetry. Published as a handsome clothbound volume featuring a stamped cover, black endsheets, and archival-quality paper, the book also includes a new introduction by *TYR* editor Joshua Buckley, illustrations, a select bibliography of Taylor's published work, and a discography of his music. Now available in a limited edition of 500 hand-numbered copies, *Remnants of a Season* is sure to become a sought-after collector's item, and is a fitting tribute to a fascinating, if little-known, figure on the outer fringes of American culture.

Asatru:
A Native European Spirituality

Stephen A. McNallen

ISBN 978-0972029254, 212 pages, paperback, $20.00

When Steve McNallen pledged his loyalty to the Gods and Goddesses of Northern Europe in the late 1960s, he could have hardly imagined the far-reaching implications of this personal act of devotion. Now, over forty years later, Asatru (an Icelandic word that means "true to the Gods") is one of the fastest growing new religious movements in America. In *Asatru: A Native European Spirituality*, McNallen describes the origins and development of Asatru, its kinship with other tribal and ethnic religions, and the cosmological and philosophical underpinnings of this dynamic and inspiring faith. More importantly, McNallen explains his vision of what Asatru can and must become. Asatru is more than just another empty offering on the spiritual smorgasbord of post-religious America. For men and women of European descent, Asatru is a key to unlocking our vibrant spiritual heritage.

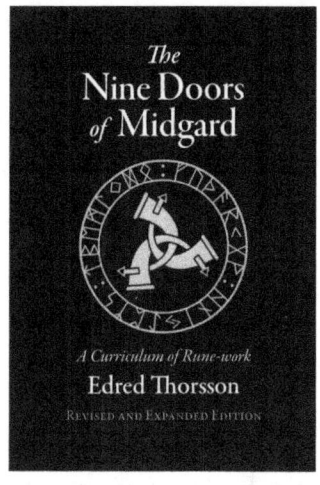

The Nine Doors of Midgard:
A Curriculum of Rune-work

Edred Thorsson

ISBN 978-0971204485, 272 pages, paperback, $24.00

The Nine Doors of Midgard are the gateways to self-transformation and mastery through the Runes. This complete course of study and practice has been used by the initiates of the Rune-Gild since 1980. Long out-of-print to the wider public and difficult to obtain, it is now being made available in a completely revised and updated fifth edition. The Runic Tradition represents a whole school of inner work as ancient as any other and with the added importance that it is the ancestral, or natural, path for folks of Germanic background. Through nine "lessons" the book takes the Rune-worker from a stage in which no previous knowledge of Runes or esoteric work is assumed to a high level of initiation.

A Book of Troth

Edred Thorsson

ISBN 978-0972029261, 149 pages, paperback, $20.00

Originally written in 1988 as the foundational document for the Ring of Troth (now known simply as The Troth), *A Book of Troth* is Edred Thorsson's vision of how Germanic paganism, or Ásatrú, can be practiced in the modern world. While The Troth itself failed to live up to his expectations, today there are thousands of individuals performing the rites and rituals of Ásatrú, and Edred's ideas have been embraced by a whole new generation of readers. *A Book of Troth* contains a complete liturgy of rituals for 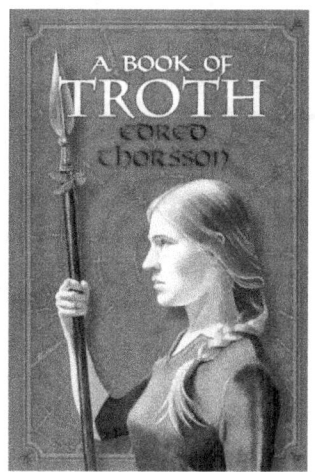 celebrating both personal turning points in the life of the individual and the Great Blessings of the Year. This wholly revised third edition includes a new introduction by Asatru Folk Assembly founder Stephen A. McNallen, and also includes Edred's seminal essay "The Idea of Integral Culture: A Model for a Revolt Against the Modern World."

TYR: Myth, Culture, Tradition 1

Edited by Joshua Buckley and Michael Moynihan

ISBN 978-0999724568, 286 pages, paperback, $20.00

Stephen Edred Flowers on "Integral Culture"; Joscelyn Godwin on the Italian esotericist Julius Evola French philosopher Alain de Benoist's interview with "new comparative mythologist" Georges Dumezil; Nigel Pennick on the "Spiritual Arts and Crafts"; Steve Pollington on the Germanic war god Woden; Michael Moynihan on divine traces in the Nibelungenlied; Collin Cleary on the anti-modern television series The Prisoner; Joshua Buckley's interview with Ian Read of the English heathen music group Fire + Ice, and much more.

TYR: Myth, Culture, Tradition 3

Edited by Joshua Buckley and Michael Moynihan

ISBN 978-0999724552, 538 pages, paperback, $25.00

Thomas Naylor on "Cipherspace," Annie Le Brun on "Catastrophe Pending," Pentti Linkola on "Survival Theory," Michael O'Meara on "The Primordial and the Perennial," Alain de Benoist on "Spiritual Authority and Temporal Power," Nigel Pennick on "The Web of Wyrd," Thierry Jolif on "The Abode of the Gods and the Great Beyond," Stephen Flowers on "The Spear of Destiny," Joscelyn Godwin on Philip Pullman's "Dark Materials" trilogy, Ian Read on "Humour in the Icelandic Sagas," Geza von Neményi on the "Hávamál," Gordon Kennedy on the "Children of the Sonne," Michael Moynihan on "Carl Larsson's Greatest Sacrifice," Christopher McIntosh on "Iceland's Pagan Renaissance," Jónína Berg on Sveinbjörn Beinteinsson, "Selected Poems" by Sveinbjörn Beinteinsson, Vilius Rudra Dundzila on "Baltic Lithuanian Religion," James Reagan on "The End Times," interviews with the stalwart folk singer Andrew King and the modern minnesinger Roland Kroell, Collin Cleary on "Paganism Without Gods," Róbert Hórvath on Mark Sedgwick's "Against the Modern World," and extensive book and music review sections.

TYR: Myth, Culture, Tradition 4

Edited by Joshua Buckley and Michael Moynihan

ISBN 978-0972029247, 430 pages, paperback, $25.00

Alain de Benoist on "What is Religion?", Collin Cleary on "What is Odinism?", Nigel Pennick on "Traditional Time-Telling in Old England," Claude Lecouteux on "Garden Dwarves" and "Geiler von Kaiserberg and the Furious Army," Steve Harris on "Barbarian Suffering," Stephen Pollington on "Germanic Art in the First Millennium," Michael Moynihan on "Rockwell Kent's Northern Compass," and Christian Rätsch on "The Mead of Inspiration," interviews with pioneering psychedelic explorer Ralph Metzner, Sequentia's Benjamin Bagby, and Cult of Youth's Sean Ragon, and much more.

TYR: Myth, Culture, Tradition 5

Edited by Joshua Buckley and Michael Moynihan

ISBN 978-0999724521, 394 pages, paperback, $25.00

Collin Cleary's "On Being and Waking," Jack Donovan on "Starting the Sacred World," Bradley Taylor-Hicks on "Reclaiming Sacred Space," Joscelyn Godwin on "Alain Daniélou in the Age of Conflicts," Steven Posch on "The Last Pagans of the Hindu Kush," Nigel Pennick on "Northern Cosmology: The World Tree and Irminsul," Richard Rudgley on "Pagan Palingenesis," Stephen Edred Flowers on "Germanic and Iranian Culture and Myth," Wolf-Dieter Storl on "Indo-European Healing Lore," Michael Moynihan on the cult film *Koyaanisqatsi*; interviews with traditional bladesmith J. Arthur Loose and avant-garde composer Dylan Sheets; and much more.

On Being a Pagan

Alain de Benoist

ISBN 978-0999724507, 262 pages, paperback, $20.00

What is paganism? In this penetrating and tightly argued manifesto, French philosopher Alain de Benoist seeks to answer this question with passionate intellectual vigor and a tremendous erudition. Arising out of the "monotheism vs. polytheism" debate that reverberated through Parisian intellectual circles in the late 1970s, this is neither a survey of ancient pre-Christian religions, nor is it an argument on behalf of any modern neopagan sect. *On Being a Pagan* draws on Nietzsche, Heidegger, ancient philosophy and mythology, and biblical hermeneutics to articulate a pagan theology based on a common Indo-European foundation.

In keeping with the critical tradition which hearkens back to the Greek philosopher Celsus, Benoist contrasts the heroic pagan worldview with Christianity's attempts to hobble everything that is beautiful and strong. He compares the cyclical pagan conception of time to the de-mythologizing, linear understanding of history favored by the prophets. Most disturbingly, he traces the roots of modern totalitarianism and intolerance—of both the left and the right—to the leveling ideology of ancient Judeo-Christian monotheism, with its underlying rejection of diversity and *différence*.

Originally published to wide critical acclaim in 1981, Benoist's text is as relevant today as it was when it first appeared—and perhaps even more so for the English-speaking world. This newly revised translation now features a new Foreword, an extensive interview with the author, and includes his reflections (both positive and negative) on the various groups and individuals that have attempted to resurrect the pagan spirit. Rather than simply dissecting the 2,000-year Christian interregnum, Benoist's greater purpose is to point the way forward to a world that *could have been*, and which may only now be in the first stages of being reborn.

Alain de Benoist was born on December 11, 1943 and studied Law, Philosophy, Sociology, and the History of Religions in Paris. The author of more than 100 books, 2,000 articles, and 700 interviews published over the last half-century, his work has also been translated into fifteen languages. He is the editor of three journals: *Nouvelle École* (since 1968), *Éléments* (since 1973), and *Krisis* (since 1988). In 1978, he received the Grand Prix de l'Essai from the Académie Française for his book *Vu de droite: Anthologie critique des idées contemporaines* (Copernic, 1977). His two most recent books, both published in 2017, are *Le moment populiste: Droite-gauche, c'est fini!* (Pierre-Guillaume de Roux) and *Ce que penser veut dire* (Le Rocher).

Coming Soon from Arcana Europa Media:

The Eldritch World

Nigel Pennick

Deluxe Hardcover Edition

"We shall follow the footsteps of Orpheus, Thomas the Rhymer, Tannhäuser, Flannery, MacCrimmon, and the Pied Piper of Hamelin. We shall visit the Weïrd Lady of the Woods, hide with King Charles in the Royal Oak, and frequent the forest crossroads under the raven wings of night on a mission with the Freischütz. *Do you dare take the first step on a journey from which there can be no return?*"

For most of us, life is a largely monotonous affair—an endless round of school, work, and social and family commitments, punctuated by idle chatter. But beyond this drab and uninspiring reality, there is another world altogether, a world where the contours are sharper and the colors are brighter. This is the domain described by mystics and Surrealists, esoteric poets and psychedelic voyagers. For Nigel Pennick, who has spent much of his life mapping out this hidden terrain, there is a name for it: the Eldritch World.

The way that we experience the eldritch is invariably tied to the circumstances of our birth, or to what philosophers might call our *being-in-the-world*. The eldritch has a history and its roots run deep in the land. In Nigel Pennick's case, it manifests through the myths, folklore, and customs of his native Britain. A gentleman scholar in the Victorian style, Pennick has made a career out of documenting these fast-disappearing traditions and of working toward their revival. He is a mummer and a magician, a Pagan, and a practitioner of the traditional arts and crafts.

Yet unlike many of Pennick's other writings, *The Eldritch World* is not about runes, or geomancy, or the ancient customs of pre-Christian Europe. *The Eldritch World* is a meditation on what these things mean and why Pennick has devoted his life to them. It is also a manifesto: against the soulless mediocrity of the modern world, and for a reinvigorated Spirit of Place.

Nigel Pennick is the author of over fifty books, and his work has been translated into ten languages. He is an artist and a musician and is a member of the Traditional Music of Cambridgeshire Collective. His recent titles include: *The Toad Man* (2012) and *The Ideal Tower* (2018), both published by the Society of Esoteric Endeavour; and *Runic Lore & Legend: Wyrdstaves of Old Northumbria* and *Witchcraft & Secret Societies of Rural England: The Magic of Toadmen, Plough Witches, Mummers, and Bonesmen*, both forthcoming from Inner Traditions in 2019.

www.arcanaeuropamedia.com